RESEARCH METHODS AND SOCIETY

RESEARCH METHODS AND SOCIETY
FOUNDATIONS OF SOCIAL INQUIRY

Linda Eberst Dorsten
SUNY—Fredonia

Lawrence Hotchkiss
University of Delaware

PEARSON
Prentice Hall

Upper Saddle River, New Jersey 07458

Library of Congress Cataloging-in-Publication Data

Dorsten, Linda Eberst.
  Research methods and society : foundations of social inquiry /
Linda Eberst Dorsten and Lawrence Hotchkiss.
    p. cm.
  Includes bibliographical references and index.
  ISBN 0-13-092654-X
  1. Sociology—Research—Methodology. 2. Social sciences—Research—
Methodology. I. Hotchkiss, Lawrence. II. Title.

HM511.D67 2004
301'.072—dc22   2004053439

Publisher: Nancy Roberts
Editorial Assistant: Lee Peterson
Full Service Production Liaison: Joanne Hakim
Senior Marketing Manager: Marissa Feliberty
Assistant Manufacturing Manager: Mary Ann Gloriande
Cover Art Director: Jayne Conte
Cover Design: Bruce Kenselaar
Manager, Cover Visual Research & Permissions: Karen Sanatar
Cover Photo/Illustration: Lou Wall/Corbis
Director, Image Resource Center: Melinda Reo
Manager, Rights and Permissions: Zina Arabia
Manager, Visual Research: Beth Brenzel
Photo Coordinator: Vickie Menanteaux
Composition/Full-Service Project Management: GGS Book Services, Atlantic Highlands

Credits and acknowledgments borrowed from other sources and reproduced, with permission, in this textbook appear on appropriate page within text.

Pearson Education LTD., London
Pearson Education Singapore, Pte. Ltd
Pearson Education, Canada, Ltd
Pearson Education–Japan
Pearson Education Australia PTY, Limited

Pearson Education North Asia Ltd
Pearson Educación de Mexico, S.A. de C.V.
Pearson Education Malaysia, Pte. Ltd
Pearson Education, Upper Saddle River,
    New Jersey

14 15 16 CRW 14 13 12

ISBN 0-13-092654-X

Contents

Chapter 3 Foundations of Social Research 43

Chapter 4 Variables and Measurement 67

Chapter 5 Designing and Social Research 89

Chapter 6 Observation and Ethnography   122

Chapter 7 Indirect Methods   152

Chapter 8 Surveys 174

Chapter 9 Population, Samples, and Sampling 210

Preface

This book is designed to help undergraduate students acquire basic skills in the methods of social science research. These skills provide a foundation for understanding research findings in the social sciences and for conducting social research. An increasing number of employers and graduate and professional schools expect at least a basic knowledge of research methods. Perhaps just as important for undergraduates, principles of inquiry for social research may be applied to situations in general. We believe they are essential for making sense of the endless stream of claims and counterclaims confronted daily in magazines and newspapers, on television, and elsewhere.

This book uses three learning steps:

- *Read the outline of each chapter*, and then *read the chapter*. Important terms and concepts are in **bold type** and are defined in the text and at the end of each chapter. Each chapter contains several examples and excerpts from published research. These examples provide a variety of concrete instances of the abstract ideas associated with research methods.

- *Read the chapter summary* and *write answers to the questions contained in the section titled, "Your Review Sheet."* Students may have to reread portions of the chapter before answering some of the questions.

- *Complete the exercises at the end of each chapter*. Although instructors may assign specific exercises, we recommend that students complete all exercises.

STRENGTHS OF THIS BOOK

The special strengths of this book include:

- Straightforward prose, including key concepts, tools, and their applications.
- Concrete and everyday examples and "hands-on" practice activities that reinforce concepts and help students retain the fundamental ideas. The examples and activities are designed to be interesting and useful to students in preparation for future careers and in everyday life.
- Organization to accommodate term-length research projects such as secondary data analysis or mini-projects.
- Assignments to meet specific learning goals such as:
  - Evaluation of excerpts from research reports that have been published in professional journal articles and popular press.
  - Analysis of secondary data (e.g., from the General Social Survey).
  - Analysis of primary data from mini–research projects.
  - Combination of more than one activity (e.g., evaluating published reports and completing secondary data analysis or mini-projects).

CHAPTER OUTLINE

Each chapter begins with an outline of the major subheadings for the chapter and an introduction intended to capture student interest in the topic.

Chapter 1. Introducing Social Research

Chapter 1 introduces the fundamental issues in social research by considering several examples. The first three examples come from everyday experience. Then three examples from published research are presented. Despite the apparent diversity in the content of the examples, most, but not all, share a unifying theme: *comparisons*. Most examples also imply or illustrate an implicit search for cause-and-effect relationships. Exercises ask students to think actively about and to evaluate the major issues in research methodology.

Chapter 2. Doing Social Research: An Overview of this Textbook

Chapter 2 summarizes each subsequent chapter in the book. The chapter is designed to provide an introduction to the detailed discussions in later chapters. It contains an overview of the scientific approach to inquiry, measurement, experimental design, qualitative methods, indirect methods, sampling, data preparation and analysis, report writing, and application of the principles of inquiry to everyday questions. The chapter also summarizes ethical questions associated with conducting research on human subjects. These summaries are targeted particularly to students who conduct term-length research projects as part of their course work.

Chapter 3. Foundations of Social Research

Chapter 3 begins by looking at how people generally go about drawing conclusions from everyday learning experiences, and it identifies some common difficulties we face in this process. The ability to discover predictability develops from experience, and science imposes a systematic process for identifying predictability. Subsequent sections sketch out scientific approaches to learning. The chapter describes how theory directs research, which in turn generates modifications in the theory.

Chapter 4. Variables and Measurement

Chapter 4 outlines the process of turning abstract concepts into measurable quantities or categories. Measurement concepts are complex to present and difficult for budding researchers to grasp, yet they are indispensable to high-quality research. Although measurement is introduced in this early chapter, issues related to the accuracy of measurement arise repeatedly in later chapters.

Chapter 5. Designing Social Research

Although social scientists use experiments relatively infrequently, the logic of experimental design with random assignment provides a pivotal benchmark for understanding and critiquing nonexperimental research. Chapter 5 reviews the compelling logic of random assignment and summarizes the substantial ethical and practical barriers to its use in the social arena.

Chapter 6. Observation and Ethnography

Chapter 6 reviews key issues in obtaining accurate and complete information from observations and observational/ethnographic data. The chapter shows by example how direct observation and ethnography provide opportunities to learn about the complexity and subtleties of human social interactions that would be difficult, and often impossible, to learn otherwise.

Chapter 7. Indirect Methods

Indirect methods do not involve contact between the researcher and subjects; this feature distinguishes them from all other methods of data collection. Otherwise, indirect methods are highly varied in the types of information collected and the processes by which it is obtained. Chapter 7 examines several indirect methods of data collection and sources of data, including content analysis, unobtrusive observation, gravestone markers, archival data, and physical trace data.

Chapter 8. Surveys

Chapter 8 begins with excerpts of three types of surveys, which present "real-world" research using survey methods. The chapter summarizes the strengths and weaknesses of personal interviews, telephone interviews, mail surveys, and Internet surveys. It reviews in some detail principles of question writing and questionnaire layout. It emphasizes the importance of tending to details such as proofreading and conducting a pilot test.

Chapter 9. Population, Samples, and Sampling

Chapter 9 summarizes the main ideas underlying the use of probability samples to draw inferences from a sample to apply to its population. However, few samples, in fact, meet the criterion of a probability sample, because of factors such as nearly universal nonresponse to surveys and difficulty of identifying all elements in a population. The chapter summarizes several types of nonprobability samples and points out the many cautions that must be applied in evaluating them while, at the same time, noting the valuable information they contain—information that we probably would not have if we insisted on a probability sample.

Chapter 10. Data Preparation and Basic Analysis

Chapter 10 begins with a specific example using a real-world finding on an important social issue. It provides a step-by-step approach to carrying out basic data-analysis procedures: Data preparation, univariate frequencies and summary measures, and bivariate cross-tabulation.

Chapter 11. Data Analysis 2: Describing, Explaining, and Evaluating

Chapter 11 extends the concept of cross-tabulation to three-variable tables. It emphasizes how the critical concept of control is approximated in the analysis of nonexperimental data. The inherent limitations of multivariate tables are noted, and some comparatively advanced methods are sketched out to suggest how these limitations can be addressed. All or part of this chapter can be skipped for classes in which advanced methods of data analysis are not required. But the chapter does give concrete meaning to the abstract idea of control emphasized in earlier chapters.

Chapter 12: Preparing the Report

The previous chapters introduced the logic and processes of social research. A critical feature of science is that the findings are public and subject to formal peer review. Chapter 12 summarizes the final step in the research process—the report of findings and the associated peer-review process. The ideal of peer review stipulates that the review be done by knowledgeable experts with no vested interest in the conclusions. This ideal stands in sharp contrast to standards applied to many of our most accessible sources of information.

Chapter 13. Applying Principles of "Science Learning" to Everyday Learning

Chapter 13 presents several illustrations of how principles of inquiry extend well beyond the comparatively narrow scope of formal research. How accurate is a story in a popular sports magazine claiming that professional baseball players routinely take anabolic steroids banned in most other sports? How accurate are published evaluations of the repair records of automobiles? Why did the Women's Health Initiative halt a major study of the potential benefits of hormone supplements for postmenopausal women? Accurate answers to questions like these are not easy to obtain. Methodological principles of social research extend to each of these questions. This chapter explains how.

PEDAGOGY

Highlighted Concepts and Terms for Each Chapter

Fundamental concepts and key terms are highlighted in **bold type**. A list of key terms appears at the end of each chapter.

Chapter Summary

Each chapter summary reviews the major themes presented in the chapter.

Review Questions

Immediately after each chapter summary is a section titled: "Your Review Sheet: Questions Discussed in This Chapter." The purpose of these review questions is to encourage students to reflect about key points presented in the chapter. Also, instructors can use these questions during class discussions and as preparation for exercises or exams. The text of the chapter contains answers to the factual questions, typically one or more examples. Discussion questions ask students to offer interpretations and draw implications from factual information presented in the text.

Exercises

Some exercises are designed as real-world activities, such as conducting a field observation, doing content analysis, and drawing samples. Other exercises are based on excerpts from professional journal articles. Most exercises include questions for discussion. These questions generally have no fixed "correct" answer.

The exercises can be completed as homework or as in-class individual or group assignments.

Excerpts from Research Literature and Popular Media

Excerpts from published scholarly research and the popular press illustrate specific issues related to social-research methodology. The text refers repeatedly to the excerpts to explain methodological principles. Full bibliographic information allows access to the original source.

Only material from the excerpts immediately relevant to the content of the chapter is presented. Ellipses (. . .) indicate deleted text. Therefore, **the excerpts should not be used for other projects in lieu of reading the full text of the source**. Most sources are available from college and university libraries. Increasingly, the full text of professional journals is available electronically through college and university libraries. It's a lot faster than going to the library stacks and photocopying articles from printed volumes. Typically, the journals are available in "pdf" (portable document format) and therefore can be printed at high resolution, which appears nearly identical to the copy in the print version of the journal.

APPENDICES

A. CODE OF ETHICS

Appendix A contains extended excerpts from the code of ethics of the American Sociological Association and the American Anthropological Association.

B. RANDOM NUMBERS TABLE

Appendix B contains 2112 pseudorandom digits for limited use in sampling exercises.

C. INTRODUCTION TO GENERAL SOCIAL SURVEY (GSS) DATASET

Appendix C contains an overview of the use of computers to manipulate data and perform basic calculations with the GSS data.

ACKNOWLEDGMENTS

We would like to thank the following reviewers for their helpful comments and suggestions: John Mitrano, Central Connecticut State University; William T. Clute, University of Nebraska at Omaha; Luis Posas, Minnesota State University, Mankato; Christine L. Himes, Syracuse University; Ann R. Tickamyer, Ohio University; and Theodoric Manley, Jr., DePaul University.

Linda Eberst Dorsten
Lawrence Hotchkiss

INTRODUCING SOCIAL RESEARCH

INTRODUCTION: LOOKING AT HOW THE SOCIAL WORLD WORKS

"If I can talk my parents into buying a new SUV, then. . . ."

"If I call my parents before they hear about this from someone else, then. . . ."

"If I work out with weights every day, then. . . ."

The people at your local automobile dealership would love to persuade you that buying their newest sport utility vehicle will do all sorts of wonders for you, particularly "improving" your love life. If you believe that a new car would help your love life, and you could afford it, would you be tempted to buy one?

What do the above snippets of conversation have to do with social research? Each one contains an *if . . . then* question. The goal is to predict what will happen next, based on current conditions—*if A occurs, then will B follow?* This abstract question defines the fundamental goal of social research, and of all of science. In highly simplified terms, it captures the notion of **cause and effect**, but there is more to causal relationships than just comparisons. The point is, we all engage continually in our own informal social science!

Goals of This Chapter

This chapter introduces fundamental goals and issues in social research by considering several examples. The first three examples come from everyday experience; the next three come from published research. Despite the apparent diversity of the examples, most, but not all, share a unifying theme: *comparisons*. For example, compare people who work out with weights every day to those who don't work out with weights to see which group has a more active social life.

As you read each of the examples below, make a list of whether or not it implies a comparison. If so, *what is compared to what?* What cause-and-effect question might the comparison suggest?

SUCCESS IN EVERYDAY LEARNING: THREE EXAMPLES

How does "trial-and-error" success in everyday learning determine the conclusions we draw about how our world works?

Fixing a Meal

The first example of an everyday learning activity is "fixing a meal." Suppose you've never done it. How long would it take you to fix a meal that would satisfy your hunger—given that you have food items in your kitchen and you aren't too picky about what constitutes a "meal"?

The motivation is there (hunger) and you probably have or can readily locate some information about how to prepare the food. If you decide to have macaroni and cheese, for example, instructions probably are printed on the package. And, if you cook it too long or not long enough, you'll probably make a mental note about what to do differently next time. In this type of everyday learning, you are likely to have a high level of success in one or two tries, if success is measured as "not hungry."

How Late Is "Late for Work"?

A second example is a little more complicated. Suppose your job requires you to be at work from 8 A.M. to 5 P.M. During the first week on the job, you are 10 minutes late one day, and no one seems to notice. A week or so later you are 20 minutes late, and no comments come up. You might begin to wonder, *How late is "too late" to come to work on this job?* How many trials of being late do you think it will take before you learn the answer?

Of course, a specific answer depends on your boss and other job characteristics, such as how visible your absence is and how much it affects the work setting. Although it probably requires a few more trials than fixing a meal, success in finding out "how late is too late" will come with relatively few trials, but you might be looking for another job when you find out!

"Why Can't Some People *Understand*?"

Have you ever been pursued by another person to be close friends when that is not what *you'd* like? Suppose you've dropped what you believe are clear hints about your preferences. You next confront the person and gently explain that you're not interested, but the person still attempts a relationship with you. You tell a friend, "I'm not interested in (him/her)! Why can't some people *understand*?"

It might take several tries before you "get rid of" this person. The number of needed trials is harder to determine than in the other two examples. Why?

Perhaps the other person didn't understand your comments and behaviors because you've been unclear (too indirect). Maybe you are secretly flattered—ever so little—by the attention and are not really sure you want the person to go away. Or the person and you have different expectations about relationships because you've been socialized under different cultural or subcultural norms about how many times to keep trying. Perhaps the hints and direct statement are ignored by the other person, who hopes that you'll change your mind, or even are misinterpreted as a challenge—you're playing hard to get!

THREE PUBLISHED EXAMPLES—AND ONE MORE

Excerpt: *Drugs on Campus*

Next, let's look at a report in a university newspaper about drug use on campus. Recall from the Preface that ellipses (. . .) in the excerpts indicate where text from the original article was deleted.

> An informal survey conducted by *The Review* of drug usage and attitudes among university students found that while hard-core drugs are rare, marijuana and tobacco use is common on campus.
>
> The poll of 100 students, conducted in-person in the *Scrounge* [an on-campus, fast-food place], found almost all students felt they could easily obtain marijuana.
>
> Nearly half of the students surveyed believe they could get cocaine and more than 25 percent think they could get heroin. All students surveyed said they felt cocaine and heroin usage is dangerous if done more than once a month.
>
> Marijuana used more than once a week was also considered harmful, according to 52 percent of those surveyed. Of those surveyed, 94 percent felt they could easily obtain marijuana. . . . "I know lots of people who use marijuana and a few who use cocaine," [a sophomore male student] said. "They seem to have no problems getting it." "If you want something bad enough," [a sophomore female student] said, "you can always find it."
>
> Although 88 percent felt smoking cigarettes is harmful, even in small dosages, 38 percent of the surveyed students were smokers. Almost two-thirds of the surveyed smokers go through two or more packs a week. . . . Illicit use of hard-core drugs (cocaine and heroin) is not as widespread. Eight percent of students surveyed said they have used cocaine and 2 percent admitted to previous heroin use. All those surveyed said they no longer use the drugs.
>
> However, 66 percent of those questioned said they have used marijuana at least once in their life. Thirty-six percent of surveyed marijuana users smoke once a week or more. Those who use marijuana between once a week and once a month account for 21 percent of the marijuana users. The remaining 43 percent said they use marijuana less than once a month. (Weaver, 1994)

The goal of this study was to describe student use of and their beliefs and attitudes about illegal drugs on the campus. This is a **descriptive study** and therefore doesn't attempt to identify any causes of drug use on campus.

How well do you think the goal was accomplished? For example, is 25 percent a good estimate of the percentage of students on the campus who know where to get heroin? Can you tell whether or not 25 percent is a good estimate for that campus, based on information from 100 students found in the Scrounge?

Excerpt: *Prostitutes in Jail?*

A recent study about the treatment of prostitutes offers an interesting conclusion: Putting prostitutes in jail is not a good policy.

> ". . . get tough" policies are often counter-productive. For example, arresting prostitutes increases the level of violence both against these women and by them. Rehabilitation programs based on the lives and experiences of street prostitutes that will provide a path into legal employment need to be developed. (Norton-Hawk, 2001, p. 403)

Norton-Hawk conducted extensive interviews with 50 prostitutes while they were serving time in the county jail. Some of the questions were short, asking for basic information like age and when they got started in prostitution. Other questions were open-ended and complex, intended to reveal how the women got started practicing prostitution and why they continued in it.

What do you think the reaction would be if Norton-Hawk's conclusion were brought up as a bill in the U.S. Congress or in the state legislature of Massachusetts, the site of the study? Probably it would be met with much skepticism! Yet, the author offers several arguments for her proposal. Here are three.

- *Argument 1:* For 200 years, the city has used incarceration to discourage prostitution. It hasn't worked. Prostitution continues unabated. Why hasn't incarceration worked? The women in Norton-Hawk's sample had no job skills that would permit them to make more than the minimum wage, except for working in the "sex trade." Therefore, most of them returned to prostitution soon after release from jail, considering the risk of "doing time" a cost of business.

Also, the women grew up in a poor environment. Many had limited formal education and few job skills. Nearly 50% had left home by age 16, and 25% first ran away from home before age 10. Why did they leave home at such young ages and without completing their educations? Reasons include drug- and/or alcohol-abusing parents, severe verbal abuse, and physical abuse. Forty-two percent reported sexual abuse, and 26% had been raped (p. 406).

- *Argument 2:* Fear of arrest forces the women to work alone, because many prostitutes in one place draws the attention of police. Yet, working alone increases the danger of physical and psychological abuse. Moreover, reporting abuse is likely to end up with the victim in jail and no punishment for the perpetrator.

Fear of arrest and the fact of doing time in jail puts the women in an environment that draws them into drug addiction, subjects them to danger, and often results in their working for pimps. The women did not originally work in prostitution to support a drug habit. Although most respondents had tried drugs at an early age, they didn't become addicted until after they first were paid for sex.

■ *Argument 3:* Alternatives to incarceration would cost less than the cost of policing and maintaining the women in jail. The author cites several statistics about the cost of incarceration—for example, the average cost of law enforcement alone per year per city is $7.5 million, as reported in one 16-city study.

Excerpt: *Proximity of Schools and Use of Contraceptives*

Is there a connection between contraceptive use and living close to school? A study conducted in the Himalayan nation of Nepal reports a surprising finding.

> A woman's proximity to a school during childhood dramatically increases permanent contraceptive use in adulthood. This finding is largely independent of whether the woman subsequently attended school, whether her husband attended school, whether she lived near a school in adulthood, and whether she sent her children to school. (Axinn and Barber, 2001, p. 481)

What does the finding mean? The first sentence implies that living close to a school as a child influences a woman to use contraceptives after she grows up. The authors also imply that living close to a school as an adult reduces the fertility of women. A sketch of this connection is:

proximity to school → contraceptive use

read as "proximity to school leads to contraceptive use."

Axinn and Barber base their conclusions on a survey of 1395 married women in Nepal. The authors argue that girls living in a neighborhood with a school encounter many more family, friends, and neighbors who support the idea of small families. The girls—and boys—tend to adopt the ideas of people around them.

Are you thinking—*Aren't there likely to be many differences between neighborhoods with and without schools that might lead to differences in attitudes about contraceptive use?* The answer is—Yes! Before reading further, write down one characteristic of neighborhoods that might influence attitudes toward contraception.

Parents of girls living close to a school likely are more highly educated than parents in neighborhoods without a school, and highly educated parents influence their children to use contraceptives when they grow up. Therefore, parental education should be "controlled" before we can confidently conclude that living close to a school as a youth actually does influence adult contraceptive practices. As the contraception study suggests, the idea of control in social research is very important.

The notion of **control** is basic in science. It means to "hold constant" one or more factors that might affect both the supposed cause and the effect. The point is to *avoid misinterpreting an incidental relationship as a cause-and-effect relationship*. This mistake is very easy to make when studying the social world, as we'll see throughout this book.

In the Nepal study, for example, living close to a school as a child is one presumed cause of contraceptive use as an adult; parental education is one factor that might need to be controlled, because it probably affects both residence near a school and contraceptive use.

Unlike the descriptive research of the campus drug survey, study of cause and effect—such as in the research about residence and contraception use—is called **explanatory research**. Two types of control are used in explanatory social research: *physical control* and *statistical control*.

Using **physical controls**, the researcher determines the *values of all causes thought to affect the outcome*. In the contraception study, the researcher would need to exercise physical control over (a) where each subject lived and (b) how much education her parents achieved. As this example illustrates, researchers typically have limited ability to use physical controls in studies of social life. Therefore, most social research is based on *statistical control*.

In social and biological sciences, a very good approximation to physical control is done by **random assignment**. The researcher controls dosage level of a drug, for example, by assigning subjects at random to different dosage levels. How does random assignment "control" unwanted influences? Under random assignment, the expectation is that *the average of all potential influences on the outcome other than the dosage is the same for all subjects*, regardless of the dosage they received.

Statistical control is an approximation of physical control. The researcher has no control over any of the factors that affect the outcome. Instead, the relationship between a presumed cause and presumed effect is *examined separately under constant levels of other factors thought to influence the outcome*.

For example, using statistical controls in the contraception study, the researcher would observe the relationship between residence near a school and contraceptive use *only* for women whose parents had less than 6th-grade education, then *only* for women whose parents had between 6th- and 10th-grade educations, and so forth. In each comparison, parental education is held *constant* statistically (approximately), even though the researcher *had no physical control over it*. The discussion of statistical control is taken up in more detail in Chapters 10 and 11.

One More Example: "Sticky Theory"

Quentin is a strong supporter of the death penalty. He participated in a psychology experiment. For the experiment, he read an article containing compelling evidence that the death penalty has almost no deterrent effect. At the conclusion of the experiment, *his support of the death penalty increased*.

Jared is a strong opponent of the death penalty. He participated in the same experiment and read an article containing compelling evidence that the death penalty deters crime. At the conclusion of the experiment, his *opposition to the death penalty increased*.

What's going on here? These two cases illustrate the findings of an interesting experiment in which two versions of "compelling" evidence were included. Half the subjects were assigned *at random* to read an article supporting the effectiveness of capital punishment, and the other half read an article undermining it. Ross and Anderson (1982) summarize the findings.

> At strategic points in the reading of these two studies, the two groups completed ratings dealing both with their evaluations of the two studies and with their own changes in attitudes and beliefs. These ratings dramatically revealed the capacity of theory-holders to interpret new evidence in a manner that strengthens and sustains their theories. First, both proponents and opponents of capital punishment consistently rated the study that supported their beliefs as "more convincing" and "better conducted" than the study that opposed those beliefs. Second, and in contrast to any normative strategy imaginable for incorporating new evidence relevant to one's beliefs, the net effect of reading the two studies was to polarize further the beliefs of the death penalty opponents and proponents. (p. 145)

What does it take to discredit existing beliefs? Are humans always so seemingly irrational in the face of evidence? Not always, but often enough that we are going to give it a name: **sticky theory**—sticky because some ideas stick so tightly that no amount of contrary evidence dissuades people from them!

Do you know anyone whose beliefs appear to fit the idea of "sticky theory"? No one is immune—although some ideas seem to stick better to some people than do other ideas. We'll ask you to think about the idea of "sticky theory" throughout this book.

SIZING UP EVERYDAY LEARNING AND SCIENCE LEARNING

Except for the campus drug study, all of the examples, including the one you just read on capital punishment and "sticky theory," make comparisons designed to test an *if . . . then* statement. The *if . . . then* comparison generally implies some idea about a causal influence, or a **cause-and-effect relationship**. *If* prostitutes are put in jail, *then* they are more likely to develop a drug habit. *If* girls are reared close to a school, *then* they are more likely to use contraception as adults. *If* one reads an article about capital punishment, *then* it is likely to reinforce one's preexisting view, no matter what the content of the article.

An important thread running through the above examples—and throughout this book—is the continuity between everyday learning and science learning. The common thread arises because both the layperson and the scientist *look to experiences to identify rules*, such as, "If I do A, then B is the result." *If* the rules are cause-and-effect rules, *then* they provide reliable ways of making decisions. This is true, almost by definition, of the notion of causation.

So, how does the scientific approach to learning *differ* from the everyday approach? Not surprisingly, they blend into each other, as you probably noticed in the above examples. Not all everyday learning is useless—and not all science finds "the truth." But science does extend everyday learning in very important ways.

- In scientific research, extensive attention is given to *producing reliable and valid measurements*—much more than is attainable by any one individual.

- Scientific research pays close attention to *how to get a fair sample and how to avoid* **overgeneralization** *of sample observations beyond the sample*. Overgeneralization from just a few, often unrepresentative, observations is a typical error made in everyday experience.

- Science pays close attention to *control of competing explanations for what seem to be cause-and-effect relationships*. Scientific research can afford to be much more deliberate and systematic than can any individual.

- Science expands the natural reasoning power of people by relying on formal reasoning—particularly mathematics and, to a lesser extent, formal logic.

- *Science subjects its conclusions to formal and public review*, called "peer review." Given the avalanche of claims and counterclaims we encounter in our everyday lives, the importance of peer review in science learning would be difficult to overstate!

- Science *keeps much better records about its findings* than individuals are able or inclined to do. Typically, findings are written down and published in scholarly journals and books. Consequently, scientific findings are more cumulative than common sense.

The remainder of this textbook clarifies and extends discussion on these aspects of science learning—what is more formally called "the scientific approach." We'll examine the topics of measurement, inference from samples to populations, control, public scrutiny and review, and record keeping in social research, among others.

But it is good to keep in mind that the line between a scientific approach to learning and common sense is not always clearly delineated. An interesting way to view science is as an institution that over many centuries systematized and institutionalized the way people learn naturally.

Here's an example of everyday learning that has several characteristics of scientific knowledge. What is your favorite holiday food? Do you have a recipe for it? Usually we don't classify recipes as scientific. But they do exhibit some of the characteristics we associate with science. Look back at the six ways science extends everyday learning. Before reading further, write down at least one way that recipes could be classified as scientific and one way in which recipes are an example of everyday learning.

Recipes usually are written down. They are passed from generation to generation. They often are explicit and relatively precise, even containing some basic mathematics. And they have been subjected to many tests. But, of course, the tests are mostly informal and their results are not recorded. And, no one pays any attention to how to measure the outcome. We just want to know—*Does it taste good*? Except in large food-producing firms, there is no explicit "measurement" of the taste. But some measure of taste is possible if we construct repeatable rules for doing so—a rating scale, for example.

Recipes also illustrate how much we can learn without doing formal science. In fact, it's probably the case that most recipes would never have been invented if we had imposed rigid experimental rules on their development! Yet, we still believe in a scientific approach—at least most of us probably do. This leaves an intriguing question: *What is the appropriate role for science in everyday life?* Think about this question. See if your opinion is the same when you read the last chapter of this book as it is now.

SUMMARY

This chapter presents several examples, some from everyday experience and some from published social science research. Except for the campus drug survey, all of the examples contain *if . . . then* comparisons. Except for the campus survey, all imply a search for cause-and-effect relationships. The capital-punishment study also illustrates the idea of "sticky theory," which applies to all of us at least sometimes.

Sticky theory is a phrase we invented to try to capture the widespread observation that people sometimes hold ideas so strongly they refuse to acknowledge evidence that contradicts them. In science, however, skepticism is a strong norm. Still, science is conducted by humans; sticky theory creeps in.

If . . . then rules propose uniform expectations, so that we can use past observations as a guide to the future. Consequently, there is no way to "prove" a cause-and-effect rule—we have to wait to see whether it keeps on working. Our willingness to bet on it increases as it passes more and more of the observational tests it could have failed.

In this chapter, why did we include experiences from everyday life and published research? The main intent is to point out the similarities and the differences between everyday approaches to learning and social science. The same types of questions arise in both instances, but there are important distinctions between scientific investigation and everyday learning. The social sciences obviously have more resources and more refined methods for answering questions than does any individual, but social science still encounters many obstacles to achieving definitive answers. These themes will be developed throughout the rest of this book.

YOUR REVIEW SHEET: QUESTIONS DISCUSSED IN THIS CHAPTER

1. The goal of the campus drug study was to describe students' beliefs and attitudes about illegal drugs on their campus. How well do you think the goal was accomplished? Do you believe 25 percent is a good estimate of the percentage of students on the campus who know where to get heroin? How can you tell?

2. There are likely to be many differences between neighborhoods with and without schools that might lead to differences in attitudes about contraceptive use. One example presented in the chapter is that parents of girls living close to a school may be more highly educated than parents in neighborhoods without a school, and highly educated parents influence their children to use contraceptives when they grow up. Offer one other explanation for why living in neighborhoods with and without schools could lead to differences in contraceptive use.

3. What is a "control" variable? Briefly explain in your own words the purpose of control in discovering cause-and-effect relationships, both in everyday learning and social research.

4. How does a scientific approach to learning differ from an everyday approach to learning? How is it similar?

5. What is the role of science in human affairs?

STUDY TERMS

cause-and-effect relationship Manipulation of the cause is followed by a change in the effect, "everything else being equal," as illustrated by *if . . . then* statements. The study of cause and effect is called explanatory research.

control To "hold constant" one or more influences that might be related to both the presumed cause and the effect. The purpose of using controls is to avoid mistaking an incidental or chance "relationship" for a causal relationship (see physical controls and statistical controls).

descriptive research Research intended to present a profile of subjects' characteristics, one at a time, such as in the campus drug study. This drug study does not present comparisons designed to identify causes of drug use.

explanatory research Research with the goal of identifying cause-and-effect relationships (e.g., residence affects contraceptive use). Compare to descriptive research, which does not attempt to discover cause-and-effect relationships.

overgeneralization Concluding that a pattern observed in too small a number of instances is typical of other situations not observed. For example, you observe in 100 lottery drawings that the number 22 turns up more often than any other number, and conclude that future drawings are more apt to turn up 22 than any other number.

physical control Control in which the researcher determines the values of all causes thought to affect the outcome. To use physical controls in the study of contraceptive use and residence, the researcher would need to determine (a) where each subject lived and (b) how much education her parents achieved. As this example illustrates, social researchers have limited ability to use physical controls and must rely on statistical control instead.

random assignment Assigning subjects at random to one value of a causal factor, such as different drug dosage levels. Because of random assignment, all causes other than the treatment thought to affect the outcome are "controlled," because the expectation is that the average of *all* other potential influences on the outcome is the same for all subjects, regardless of the treatment (dosage) they received.

statistical control An approximation of physical control based on the idea of observing relationships between a presumed cause and an outcome within constant levels of the control factor. For example, the relationship between residence near a school and contraceptive use would be examined separately for women with parents of differing levels of education (e.g., less than sixth grade, between sixth and eighth grade, more than eighth grade). The researcher does not determine the values of the causes in a study.

"sticky theory" A phrase we invented to try to capture the widespread observation that people sometimes hold ideas so strongly they refuse to acknowledge evidence that contradicts them. In science, no norm is stronger than the norm of skepticism, which should overcome sticky-theory thinking. Still, science is conducted by humans; sticky theory creeps in.

EXERCISES

Exercise 1.1. Examining Everyday Learning: Observation in a Crowded Room

Directions: Locate a room that is fairly crowded with people and items, and that you can easily enter and leave. Choose a room in a setting that you seldom visit. Examples of settings include an exercise or workout room at a busy time, a produce market, and a dining area during mealtime.

    a. Enter this room and look around for about 2 minutes.

    b. Now leave the room. Make a list of the items that you can recall.

    c. Answer the questions below.

    d. Be prepared to hand in your lists.

Questions

1. Briefly describe your setting.
2. Rewrite items you recall from your first list into categories that have a common theme. What do you conclude about your initial observation?
3. The assignment did not provide a specific goal for your observations. For example, if you worked in a frame gallery, your focus might have been primarily on wall decorations.

   When conducting scientific study the first step is to establish a research goal, often written in the form of a question. Write one question that you could use to focus your observations in the room that you selected. (*Example:* What types of clothing items does this campus bookstore sell?)
4. Return to the same room. Keeping your research question in mind, again look around for about 2 minutes. After leaving the room, make a list of the items that you can recall. If needed, rewrite the list into categories. Compare your two lists. What do you conclude about the differences between the two lists?

5. Did your research question help you to focus on specific items to answer your research question? Briefly explain the importance of having a research goal.

6. Why is comparison important in social research?

Exercise 1.2. Examining Everyday Learning: Using a Control

This exercise helps you to see the importance of considering alternative explanations for relationships. You are asked to "physically control" potential age differences by limiting the second set of observations to one age group: people 25 years old or younger.

Directions: Select a busy entrance to a building. Hold the door open for one person who is following you, then walk through the doorway. Record the characteristics (e.g., age, gender, race) of the person, and whether or not they said "thank you" (or "thanks"). Repeat this procedure 15 times. Then, answer the questions below. Be prepared to hand in your notes.

Questions

1. What *personal characteristics* differentiate those who said "thank you" from those who did not? For example, did more males than females say "thank you"?

2. Suppose you found that a higher percentage of males than females thanked you. However, you also noticed that most of the males were older than the females. You might wonder: Did gender or age make the difference in how they responded?

    Repeat the procedure, but this time hold the door open *only for people who appear to be 25 or younger*. Again record each person's gender and whether or not he or she said "thank you." What can you say now about whether gender or age makes the difference in responses?

3. Describe a control other than age from your list of personal characteristics that you could use to conduct another door-opening procedure. Briefly explain how your control would help you to see a relationship between saying "thanks" and gender.

4. Look again at the information for the first procedure. In everyday life we typically don't record people's behaviors and characteristics. Suppose that you held the door for the same 15 people, without recording, or even noticing, their characteristics and whether they said "thanks." What do you think you might recall in a week or two? How would your recollections affect your conclusions?

5. How confident are you with results based on 15 people? Explain briefly.

Exercise 1.3. Evaluation of Research: Overgeneralization

Directions: First, read the following excerpt. Then, answer the questions that follow.

Bossiness in Firstborn Girls *by Beverly Capofiglia**

A total of 40 girls and 40 boys, ages 4 to 5 years, participated in this research; all of them were firstborn and had at least one younger sibling. . . . Protagonists were 3- and 4-year-old younger siblings of the study participants. . . . Each firstborn child was paired with another younger and unrelated child. The two were introduced to each other and were instructed to play while their mothers were "right outside talking to the teacher." Half ($n = 20$) of the firstborn girls were paired with other girls, and half ($n = 20$) were paired with boys. Half of the firstborn boys ($n = 20$) were paired with boys, and half ($n = 20$) were paired with girls. [Play] Sessions lasted 20 min.

Ratings of bossiness were made from the videotapes. A Checklist of Bossy Behaviors was constructed for this research. . . . When contrasted to firstborn boys. . . . the data clearly show that firstborn girls are significantly more bossy than firstborn boys. The bossiness ratings of the girls were higher when they were interacting with other girls than they were when interacting with boys. . . . Not only does birth order make a difference in the trait under inquiry, but it has a differential effect on boys and girls. (Meltzoff 1998, pp. 207–209)

*"Capofiglia" is Italian for "boss-girl." Excerpted from a fictional article developed for research education.

Questions

1. What are the two comparison groups in this excerpt?
2. Why do you think subjects were paired with younger children, rather than with older children?
3. Do you agree with the conclusion presented? For example, could differences in "bossiness" be explained by some characteristic of children other than gender? Briefly explain.

A Follow-up Exercise

Find an example of overgeneralization in your newspaper. Explain the conclusion, then add your critique. Be prepared to hand in a clipping of the article.

DOING SOCIAL RESEARCH: AN OVERVIEW OF THIS TEXTBOOK

INTRODUCTION: LOOKING AT HOW THE SOCIAL WORLD WORKS

Did you know that societies around the world with the highest levels of maternal education have the greatest rates of infant survival? In their extensive review of research on illness behavior in the developing world, Christakis, Ware, and Kleinman (2001, p. 148) report that many mothers in the less-developed nations have between 1 and 6 years of primary schooling. Before reading further, take a minute to jot down how schooling for women might reduce the risk of death for their children and generally improve child health.

Perhaps you wrote that students, as future mothers, might learn basic health practices, such as hand washing, keeping away from sick people, and getting immunizations. You might also have said they learn the value of nutrition and to avoid health behaviors such as smoking and drinking alcohol during pregnancy. Past research has associated many of these behaviors with favorable outcomes for children.

Research also suggests spacing births farther apart increases child survival. Why? One reason is that infants can be breastfed longer and there is less competition from a subsequent child for the mother's resources. Christakis et al. also point out other circumstances that improve child survival, including postponing marriage and childbearing, using schooling to obtain greater economic resources, and learning assertiveness to seek health care for oneself and one's dependents (pp. 148–151). In addition, more schooling is associated with later marriage, fewer children, developing skills to seek health care, and learning basic health practices.

These are intriguing explanations. But the positive association between maternal education and child health is not certain evidence that mother's education actually *affects* the health of her children. Women who achieve high levels of schooling also tend to live in locations where sanitation standards, diet, and medical care are above average. Maybe these factors are the primary determinants of both child health *and* women's education.

What does it take to produce *believable* explanations? A finding is not true automatically because it's in print. A study reported by Desai and Alva (1998), summarized in the next section, confronts the question head on: *Does maternal education actually affect child health, or is the association between the two just incidental?* See how they address this question.

Goals of This Chapter

This chapter introduces the major topics in social research methods: (1) the strategies of social research, (2) the role of theory and a scientific approach; (3) types of research designs, methods of data collection, sampling, and methods of data analysis; and (4) the increasingly important need for careful attention to ethics in research.

The aim of this chapter is to provide a brief introduction to the detailed discussions in later chapters. If you're assigned a research project as part of your methods course, this chapter can help you get an early start by providing an overview of the major issues that researchers confront—and how they address them—before you begin to develop your project.

STRATEGIES OF SOCIAL RESEARCH

How might one begin to study a topic like the effect of maternal education on child survival, or, more generally, on child health? A researcher can choose one of two fundamental research strategies: conduct *basic research*, or perform *applied or evaluative research*. These strategies can be distinguished by (a) the goals of the research and (b) the intended audience for the results.

Basic Research

Basic research is research undertaken with no immediate practical application as the goal. Sometimes this type of research informally is described as, "asking the question for the question's sake." In the social sciences, most basic research is undertaken by faculty and staff at colleges and universities or in research institutions, sometimes supported by research grants from government, foundations, or corporations. All types of data collection are used in basic research—surveys, direct observations, indirect observation, and experiments.

For example, Desai and Alva (1998) report research designed to identify the reasons that maternal schooling is associated with positive health outcomes of children. The authors point out that although there is a strong association in past research between a mother's education and indicators of her child's health, unanswered questions remain. Specifically, they argue that maternal education could be a substitute for (a) socioeconomic status of the household and (b) characteristics of community of residence—like sanitation standards, access to health care, and diet. They include *statistical controls* for these alternative possible influences on child health. Using these controls, three measures of child health are examined—likelihood of death before 1 year of age, height-for-age, and number of vaccinations for children at least 1 year of age.

Excerpt: *Maternal Education and Child Health: A Strong Causal Relationship?*

> Introducing controls for husband's education and access to piped water and toilet attenuate [reduce] the impact of maternal education on infant mortality and children's height-for-age. This effect is further reduced by controlling for area of residence. . . .
>
> [M]aternal education has a statistically significant impact on infant mortality and height-for-age in only a handful of countries. In contrast, maternal education remains statistically significant for children's immunization status in about one-half of the countries even after individual-level and community-level controls are introduced. (Desai & Alva 1998, p. 71)

The goal of this study is defined by a theory that predicts a positive effect of maternal education on the well-being of children. There is no immediate practical application offered as a goal of the study. The data only partially confirm the theory. In the excerpt, Desai and Alva report few or weak relationships between a mother's education and the outcomes of infant mortality and height-for-age after statistically controlling for alternative possible causes of mortality and height, such as father's education, access to piped water, and community of residence. However, mother's education does have a direct effect on immunization in about half of the countries in the sample. The study (a) reaffirms the importance of mother's education in the well-being of her children, and (b) clarifies the pathways by which education might improve child health, such as through immunizations.

Even though this is basic research, the findings might be combined with other research to produce practical applications for policy, such as increasing access to primary health care and clean water. However, the goal of this study is basic research—to clarify unanswered questions about the importance of maternal education on the well-being of children.

Applied Research

A second research strategy is to assess the outcomes of projects, programs and policies associated with social interventions. A *social intervention* is an activity undertaken to produce an intended practical outcome. The investigation of a social intervention is called **applied** or **evaluation research**.

Evaluation research is not a method of data collection or analysis. Experiments, surveys, personal interviews, and other methods of data collection are used in evaluation research, just as they are in basic research. And any method of data analysis that is used to test theory might also be used in applied research.

To evaluate a social intervention, the researcher must know the intended outcome. However, individuals involved with a social intervention ("stakeholders") do not necessarily agree on an outcome, its definition and measurement, or the time period required to achieve it. For example, teachers, administrators and parents might not agree about how to measure improvement in "student learning," or how long an innovative teaching technique takes to achieve desired learning gains. A semester? A school year? Several years? A researcher undertaking the evaluation must consider the different viewpoints of many "stakeholders."

Excerpt: *Evaluation of a Pregnancy-Prevention Program for Teenagers*

Zabin et al. (1986) evaluated a school-based program for the prevention of pregnancy among inner-city adolescents in Baltimore, Maryland. For nearly three school years, the program offered education and counseling about sexuality and contraception, and medical and contraceptive services to students attending one of two schools—a junior high school and a senior high school. Students in two other schools (one junior high and one senior high) received no such services; they were included to provide *comparison data.*

The evaluation was designed to compare changes in the knowledge, attitudes, and behaviors between students offered and those not offered pregnancy-prevention services. Data were collected from the students through self-administered questionnaires. The researchers conclude that:

> [o]ne of the most striking findings from the project is the demonstration that boys in the junior high school used the clinic as freely as girls of the same age. . . . Increased and prompt clinic attendance and the resulting increased use of effective methods of contraception appear to have had a significant impact on pregnancy levels. . . .
>
> One of its [the project's] major effects . . . is that it appears to have encouraged the younger sexually active teenagers to develop levels of knowledge and patterns of behavior usually associated only with older adolescents. This accelerated protective behavior, coupled with evidence that first coitus was not encouraged but, in fact, postponed, should provide solid support to the current movement toward the introduction of school-based clinics. (Zabin et al., 1986, pp. 124–125)

This evaluation excerpt suggests the two school-based clinics did influence students' behaviors and attitudes, as anticipated.[1] Although the researchers imply that other schools might benefit from similar programs, the primary goal of evaluation is to assess the contributions from the specific program studied.

In contrast, a goal in basic research might be toward clearer understanding of the role of school clinics in pregnancy prevention. Basic research might attempt to learn, for example, the cause-and-effect relationship between components of the program, such as whether individual counseling or the availability of nursing staff in school-based clinics reduces the risk of pregnancy.

Despite their differences, there is a common theme in both basic and applied research. Both types of research nearly always focus on *comparisons*, as illustrated in the examples presented so far in this chapter—

1. *Study of child well-being:* compared infant mortality, height-for-age measures, and immunization among mothers with differing education levels.

2. *Evaluation of pregnancy-prevention program:* compared various outcomes such as age at first coitus between students in the experimental program and students not in the program.

In basic research, however, the comparisons derive from theory. In evaluation research, comparisons come from the goals of the program being evaluated—that is, assessing program effectiveness substitutes for theory. Nonetheless, social interventions nearly always are based on some theory about what affects the outcome. In the pregnancy-prevention study, the selection of the services offered to students surely was based on some theoretical notion about influences on the sexual behaviors of students, such as knowledge of risks associated with sexual activity and contraceptive practices.

OVERVIEW OF CHAPTER 3: FOUNDATIONS OF SOCIAL RESEARCH

Common Sense, Theory, and Science

As Chapter 1 points out, each of us assesses relationships on an ongoing basis throughout our lives. A preschooler might wonder, *Will mom and dad let me stay up later when grandma visits?* In middle school, a concern might be, *If I don't get my science project done, will the teacher help me or get mad?* As a college student, you might think, *If I go to the freshman mixer, will I meet someone interesting?* And if you do "meet someone," a subsequent question might be: *What is the relationship between getting good grades and going out every night?*

Discovering predictability in everyday life is a process of learning from experience. We see what happens and use it as a guide to the future; that is, we make rough predictions of "what will happen if. . . ." Usually we have a realistic understanding of what might happen in simple scenarios. However, mistakes often are made about complicated questions. The Chapter 1 example titled, "Why can't some people *understand*?" illustrates how one might end up repeatedly trying to discourage an unwanted friendship despite what seem to you to be clear signals to the other person.

In science learning, the ultimate determinant of what is and is not true is **observation** (i.e., looking to see what happens), a near synonym for experience in everyday life. Testing an idea by observing what happens is called an **empirical test**. Both the study of maternal education effects on child survival and the study of pregnancy-prevention program in schools reviewed earlier in this chapter conducted empirical tests in real-world projects.

As an everyday example of observation, suppose you have two plants, perhaps philodendrons. In the winter, you put one in a south window and one in the far corner of your north bedroom. You leave them there for a month. At the end of the month, the one in the dark corner seems droopy and doesn't seem to have grown as much as the one in the south window. But, all in all, differences between the two plants appear slight. You conclude that philodendrons probably are tolerant of low light. But you probably didn't draw this conclusion just on the basis of this one experiment. You likely already had an impression that philodendrons don't need a lot of light. You may have observed this, or you may have heard it from others.

Taking the same question, the scientific approach would use exactly the same general strategy: expose plants to different conditions and observe how they differ with respect to some interesting outcome, like growth and "droopiness." The details of the scientific approach are quite different from your informal experiment, however.

First, science worries about *control*. Suppose the plant in the south window were a cactus and the plant in the north room were a fern. They both thrive. You conclude plants don't care how much light they get. *No! No!* That's not right! The plants must be the same species. (But you knew that.) You can find the effect of light only if other influences on the outcome are *controlled*, that is, unvarying. What else must be constant? Quantity of water, quantity and mix of plant nutrients, quality of soil, amount of soil in the pot, and room temperature are among the influences that should be controlled if you want to know how light affects the plants. But there may be other influences you can't identify or control, even if you know what they are. One possibility is the hardiness of the individual plants to withstand low light. Like people, individual plants naturally vary in many ways that can't be known or controlled.

What can be done to avoid confusing the effect of another, perhaps unknown, influence with the effect of light? The standard procedure is to randomly assign plants to one of the two light conditions. Whatever effect the uncontrolled influences have will *not* be confused with the effect of light, as we'll briefly review later in this chapter and in detail in Chapter 5 ("Designing Social Research").

Is one plant in each location sufficient? Not likely, but how many plants are needed? The answer depends on how much the individual plants differ in their response to light. If all the plants responded exactly the same way, one plant in each location is sufficient, at least in theory. But the plants aren't the same, so at least several in each location are needed, depending on how much plants vary.

A scientific approach makes careful measurements of the outcomes. The conclusion doesn't depend on a vague notion of "droopy" or a subjective assessment of growth ("looks taller than last week"). It's necessary to specify *how to measure* "droopy" and *how to measure* plant growth. "Before and after" measurements also probably would be taken, but this feature is not always necessary, as we'll see in Chapter 5.

After the research is complete, the findings are written down and published in a scientific journal. Before publication, they are reviewed by other scientists to reduce the chance of methodological errors.

Obviously, no one would get anything done by using the scientific approach instead of common sense! Generally, science is worthwhile only as a collective enterprise.

Generalization means to extend what *has* been observed to situations not yet observed. The study of the reaction of plants to varying light conditions is not done because anyone cares much about the specific plants in the study. The point is to generalize to other plants, in fact, to all plants. The question is, in *general*, how does light affect plant growth? Generalization is a fundamental feature of both science and common-sense learning. Learn from the past and present to project into the future.

Whether you are thinking about everyday questions or scientific research, no amount of observation can guarantee what will happen in the future. Yet, the more often we see that an *if . . . then* statement makes a correct prediction, the more willing we are to bet that it will make the correct prediction the next time we use it.

Theory is a guide telling us where to look for useful relationships. Theory often contains models, analogies, and images. For example, to test the statement that

maternal education → child health

Desai and Alva (1998) included mother's education plus several other factors likely to be related to child health, such as child's age, urban residence, father's/stepfather's education, whether the mother ever had a partner, and whether the household had access to piped water and had a toilet in the household (p. 80). Using statistical procedures to "hold constant" these factors, the researchers were trying to rule out noncausal explanations for the relationship between maternal schooling and child well-being. Note that there is an underlying reason why these alternative explanations were considered. Each factor, such as piped water, likely is associated with *both* mother's education *and* child health.

Many scientific investigations are intended to construct descriptive profiles. Their immediate goal is not to find a **cause-and-effect relationship**. In general, **descriptive research** is indicated when the subject matter is complicated. Scientists conducting descriptive studies record what happens and describe the structure of what they see, such as an emotional reaction to events or circumstances. An everyday example of one type of descriptive study is your work for Exercise 1.1, in which you listed all items you could recall in a crowded room and then sorted them into groups with a common theme. The result is a profile of the room you selected.

OVERVIEW OF CHAPTER 4: VARIABLES AND MEASUREMENT

A **variable** is a set of categories or numbers defined so that each category is *mutually exclusive* and *exhaustive*—each observation (e.g., person or object) fits into exactly one category, and all needed categories are included. Familiar examples of variables include race, gender, age, and self-esteem. Variables also can describe elements other than people, such as colleges. College campuses can vary in number of residence halls, size of student population, ratio of males to females, number of faculty, upkeep of buildings, prestige, size of endowment, and geographic location. Each of these items is an example of a variable.

A variable requires at least two categories, otherwise the factor is a **constant**. For example, "gender" has two categories: male and female. However, if information is obtained from students at an all-girls school, gender could not influence an outcome (e.g., opinions about the quality of dormitory food) because gender is constant (there are no opinions from males). This idea is captured in the refrain: "*a constant can't cause a variable.*"

The categories defining a variable must be **mutually exclusive** and they must be exhaustive. These terms used together mean that *each observation must be classified into one, and only one, category*; that is, no observation may be left unclassified, and no observation may be placed into more than one category. Again, the variable "gender" is a useful instance; each person can be classified as either female or male, and these categories are exhaustive; everyone in the general population fits into one category. There are exceptions, of course, but they are so rare that they seldom, if ever, are a consideration in defining the variable of gender.

The term **independent variable** refers to a cause. An independent variable generates or "causes" change in the value of another variable. The **dependent variable** is the "outcome," or the effect; *its variation is dependent on change in the independent variable(s).*

Note that *the terms "dependent variable" and "independent variable" suggest their meaning.* Keeping this idea in mind, you'll find it easier to remember the meaning of the terms independent and dependent variable.

Reliability refers to consistency of a measurement procedure. It is the extent to which a measurement yields the same answer each time it is used, in the absence of change in the variable that is measured. The doctor's scales (and our home scales) should indicate the same weight each time we weigh a baby, but only if the baby's weight has not changed. Any changes in weight should reflect changes in the baby's weight as growth occurs, not inconsistency (unreliability) of the scales.

Validity refers to the accuracy with which a measurement procedure indicates the construct it is designed to measure. For example, we expect the doctor's scales to provide the weight of the person, not height, age, gender, or how many pets the person has at home.

OVERVIEW OF CHAPTER 5: DESIGNING SOCIAL RESEARCH

Have you ever conducted an informal "experiment"? For example, can a cat be trained to come home when you whistle? If you smile at strangers as you pass them on the street, will they smile back? Did you ever smooch a pooch to find out whether there *is* such as a thing as "doggy breath"? (Maybe you should skip the last experiment!)

An **experiment** is a process in which a researcher manipulates or changes the values of at least one variable and observes what happens to the values of another variable. In research on people, the objects of the manipulation are called **subjects**. In the simplest experiment, one variable is manipulated, called the **treatment variable**. The term *treatment variable* is a near synonym for *independent variable*, but *treatment variable* usually is used in experimental research and *independent variable* in most other settings. Both terms designate a presumed cause in a relationship.

Experiments are conducted infrequently in the social sciences, particularly **controlled experiments** in which the experimenter determines what is changed, by how much and what is not changed (or is kept constant). The questions social scientists typically ask seldom are adaptable to experiments. Nonetheless, the logic underlying a randomized experiment is so powerful that it provides a benchmark for assessing cause-and-effect conclusions from all types of research.

The Logic of Experiments

The *if . . . then* statement captures an essential part of the conception of causality. For example: "If a person gets a pet, *then* s/he will feel less lonely than before." But before accepting an *if . . . then* statement as a cause-and-effect relationship, it must meet three requirements: (1) There must be an observed relationship between two variables, (2) the cause must not occur *after* the effect in time, and (3) the relationship must not be due to the effect of another variable that *precedes* both cause and effect in time.

The **classical experimental design** includes (a) random assignment to treatment and control groups (the treatment group receives the *treatment*), and (b) a **pretest** and a **posttest** of both/all groups (Campbell & Stanley 1963). The pretest and posttest must consist of the same or equivalent measures of the outcome (dependent variable) taken before and after the treatments are administered. Pretest and posttest data can be obtained by questionnaire, observations, interviews, and other data-collection procedures. The pretest is not essential, though a design without it is not called the classical experimental design.

For an example, suppose you wish to know whether mothers given a picture chart showing changes in the weight of their babies develop more favorable attitudes toward well-baby checkups than new mothers who don't receive a chart (see Figure 2.1). Mothers are randomly assigned to either experimental (receive chart) or control group (no chart), for example, by a coin toss. Attitudes toward well-baby checkups are measured by a questionnaire for both pretest and posttest. Each mother receives information about the weight changes of her baby, but mothers in the experimental group also receive the chart depicting the baby's weight gain.

Only the experimental group gets a picture chart, but experimental *and* control groups are pretested and posttested. Of course, there are likely to be many influences on mothers' attitudes toward well-baby care, but on average these influences

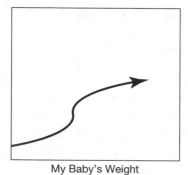

My Baby's Weight

FIGURE 2.1.   Hypothetical Baby-Weight Chart.

should be the same in both the treatment and control groups, within the margin of random error (which can be estimated). Statistical analysis is used to decide whether the observed change in the treatment group is "enough larger" than any observed change in the control group to justify concluding that the charts do foster favorable attitudes toward well-baby care.

In addition to the classical experiment, Campbell and Stanley present 16 types of experiments, some of which will be reviewed in Chapter 5.

OVERVIEW OF CHAPTERS 6–8: METHODS OF DATA COLLECTION

Observation and Ethnography

Using the word in a general sense, "observation" includes any information we get that describes the world—from questionnaires, interviews, and directly seeing what people do. A second meaning of "observation" is to describe a profile summary of variables for one individual or other unit such as a college campus. For example, in a survey, a list of the values of variables such as age, race, and gender for each respondent comprise an observation.

A third sense of the word "observation" (**observational analysis**) means to go out and talk to people, see what they do, stay for a while, and see what develops. This latter type of observation provides opportunities to obtain detailed information about the complexity and subtleties of human interactions that could not be collected in any other way (for example, by a survey).

It is the third sense of "observation" that describes ethnographic research. **Ethnographic research** examines the purposes and meanings of human actions using verbal descriptions and explanations for a small number of **cases** (e.g., persons, couples, social groups, etc.). For example, ethnographic researchers gather data using in-depth interviews with open-ended responses. A familiar example of open-ended response questions is an essay exam, in which the test-taker must supply the response. However, multiple-choice and true–false questions are closed-ended, because response options are provided.

The strength of observation and ethnography is the potential to make sense of phenomena by examining the meanings that people themselves bring to them. Social theory often arises from insights gained from this type of data. However, an important design issue is which type of role to take during data collection.

A **participant observer** is a researcher who is completely immersed in the regular activities of the subjects. **Nonparticipant observation**, sometimes called **complete observation**, usually is undertaken in public settings, where the researcher is unlikely to know the subjects. Complete observation allows observations to be made without the subjects being aware they are being observed. The nonparticipant observer is less likely to influence the behavior of subjects, since the subjects are unaware they are being observed. An example of nonparticipant observation is sitting unobtrusively in a busy mall observing people as they pass by.

The researcher must quickly adapt to the social setting, so that those being observed are less likely to avoid behaviors that might not be acceptable to "outsiders." Also, information must be verified and cross-checked constantly, by reviewing notes and other data collected.

Indirect Methods

In contrast to other methods of data collection, **indirect methods** do not involve direct contacts between the researcher and subjects. Indirect *sources* of data include contemporary records (e.g., books, newspapers, magazines, music, TV), archival and historical records, and physical traces. *Types* of indirect methods include content analysis, historical and archival studies, and unobtrusive observation.

Content analysis is the study of recorded communication. Recorded communication is found in books, magazines and journals, newspapers, and other print media; audio, video, and audiovisual recordings; and electronic images such as those at commercial Web sites and Web "bulletin boards."

For example, suppose a research goal is to determine whether children's books make sex-stereotyped references to jobs. All children's books (or a sample of them) for a specific time period (e.g., last 5 years) must be examined for passages referring to jobs. Each passage (or portion of a passage) might be coded by description of the job and gender depicted or implied. The passages then would be analyzed to determine whether there is sex-typing of work roles.

As you might anticipate, a strength of content analysis is that it is unobtrusive, meaning no subject is aware of being observed by the researcher. In addition, the sources can be reexamined as needed during the study to assess reliability of the codes assigned for job and gender. The major limitation of content analysis is that much important information is never recorded.

Historical researchers use historical sources, usually to examine changes over time. Similar to content analysis, sources of data include newspapers, magazines, hospital and physician records, legal proceedings, political campaign information, letters, and church documents.

As with content analysis, advantages of historical research are access to information without affecting the subject being studied, and the ability to reexamine the original sources as needed. However, historical data represent longer time periods than content analysis of contemporary sources. Consequently, data needed for many analyses simply are not available.

Unobtrusive observation relies on "trace" data left behind as a residue of subjects' *previous activity*, usually over a relatively short period. Examples include discarded items, such as liquor bottles in trash cans, debris left after a rock concert, and fingerprints left at the scene of a crime. Unobtrusive study of everyday life can provide unique insights and essential supplemental information about social experiences and problems that might not be obtained in other ways.

Surveys

A **survey** consists of questions posed directly to a large sample of respondents. One type of survey is the **personal interview**. Data are obtained from **respondents** in face-to-face communication with the researcher or an interviewer hired by the researcher.

What are some advantages of personal interviews? "Being there" encourages completion of the interview, and the researcher can clarify questions that are unclear to the respondent. In addition, information can be recorded about the respondent and the social context that might be difficult to obtain otherwise, such as body language of individuals or characteristics of the social environment. Some data can be recorded without asking any questions, for instance gender, race, and residence.

On the other hand, respondents might not wish to provide certain types of private information during face-to-face interviews, such as deviant or socially questionable behavior (e.g., number of arrests). Also, the interviewer must quickly adapt to the respondent and social setting, so that the respondent feels comfortable during the interview and doesn't give answers primarily designed to impress (or deceive) the interviewer.

The **telephone interview** is an efficient alternative to personal interviews. Compared with personal interviews, telephone surveys require fewer scarce resources—time and money. A number of phone calls can be conducted during the time it takes to drive to one respondent's location. Also, a telephone survey can easily cover a much larger geographic area than a survey conducted by personal interviews, and telephone calls do not require the interviewer to travel into unsafe environments.

But it is easier to decline a telephone survey than to turn down a personal interview—hanging up the phone ends the interview. And it's easy to do. Newer technologies such as answering machines and caller ID are changing the process of telephone interviewing.

A **mail survey** collects information by mailing a questionnaire to respondents. An advantage of self-administered mail surveys over personal or telephone interviews is that they permit inclusion of a greater number of respondents scattered over a wider geographic area with lower time and money costs.

A second advantage of mail surveys is confidentiality. **Confidentiality** means the researcher knows respondents' identity, but does not reveal information in any way that can be linked to individual respondents. Confidentiality often is important. Suppose someone you know earned money for college selling stolen merchandise. How likely is your acquaintance to reveal this in a face-to-face interview, or even in a telephone interview?

Anonymity, a term sometimes confused with confidentiality, means the researcher keeps no records that can link respondents with their answers to the questionnaire. Therefore, the researcher is not able to reveal any answers given by individual respondents. Anonymity is an important consideration for the study of highly personal experiences, illegal activities, and other sensitive topics. Because of no face-to-face interactions, mail surveys encourage respondents to reveal information of a personal or sensitive nature.

An important limitation associated with complete anonymity is that respondents cannot be followed up in a second survey to see how they changed. Often observing individual change over time is critical. For example, if you observe that marijuana users get lower grades in school in a one-shot survey at only one point in time, how do you know what is the cause and what is the effect? Did low grades lead to marijuana use, or did marijuana use lead to low grades or both?

A major problem with mailed questionnaires is low return rate. Unreturned questionnaires reduce the sample size, but the more important problem of non-completion is **nonresponse error**—generated by potential differences between individuals who complete and return a questionnaire and those who do not. Those who fail to return a completed questionnaire might be different from respondents in ways that influence the results of the study. Chapter 8 ("Surveys") describes some ways to reduce the risk of nonresponse error.

With self-administered questionnaires, the researcher cannot probe for additional details, nor can respondents ask for further information about a confusing question or response options. But extensive and careful pretesting can substantially reduce the potential for respondent confusion.

Multiple Methods

Each method of data collection has advantages and limitations. For example, participant observers are likely to influence the social processes being studied, and the sample size necessarily is small. Mail questionnaires can produce a large sample but a low response rate, suggesting nonresponse bias in the results. Telephone respondents can hang up the phone, or refuse to answer it, particularly if they have caller ID and don't recognize the caller.

Therefore researchers sometimes use several methods in combination to reduce the shortcomings of data collected by a single method. For example, a frequently used **multiple-method** approach is to combine a type of survey with observation. Or, one might choose to do a content analysis, followed by personal interviews. The primary advantage of using multiple methods is that they permit comparison of the results from each method to see whether different methods yield consistent results.

The following excerpt creatively employs several methods of data collection to answer the question: *Do boys and girls have similar or different play behaviors?*

Excerpt: *Sex Differences in Complexity of Children's Play*

Using multiple methods to collect the data, Lever (1978) studied the complexity of play activities of boys and girls ages 10–11.

> Each morning, under the direction of the researcher, the children filled out a short form [diary] on which they described (1) what they had done the previous day after school, (2) who they did it with, (3) where the activity took place, and (4) how long it had lasted. . . .
>
> The questionnaire, designed to elicit how children spend their time away from school, also was administered by me inside the classroom. I conducted semistructured interviews with one-third of the sample. Some were done in order to help design the questionnaire and diary; others were done later to help interpret the results. I gathered observational data while watching children's play activity during recess, physical education classes, and after school. . . .
>
> Observations of children at play during recess, gym classes, and after school . . . indicate very distinct play patterns for boys and girls. As in the diary data, boys' activities were found to be more complex. The largest category of girls' public activity was the same as their private activity, namely single-role play. . . . The great majority of observed games [for boys] were team sports with their multiple roles. (Lever, 1978, p. 64, 68–69)

Lever found that boys are more likely to be involved in team sports, and that boys' games have an extensive set of rules. When girls play interdependently, they are more likely to be involved in activities with turn-taking and few formal rules— action typically is among members of a single group. The Lever study appeared in 1978. It would be interesting to compare these gender differences in play behaviors to contemporary differences.

Why did Lever use a research design that combined multiple methods? One likely reason is that she was able to draw comparisons among the findings from each method, thereby giving additional credibility to her conclusions. Her outcome, or dependent variable, is "complexity of play." Complexity of play is a multidimensional variable—the accuracy or validity of its measurement may be questionable. Multiple methods improve credibility about the accuracy of the measurements.

OVERVIEW OF CHAPTER 9: POPULATION AND SAMPLES

A **population** is a defined collection of all individuals or other units (e.g., families, corporations, textbooks, videos) from which data could be collected. A population should be defined to include individuals we want a study to describe (for example, all registered voters), not just people who return a questionnaire. A **sample** is a subset of a population—the part of the population from which data are collected.

Probability and Nonprobability Samples

Although researchers usually rely on data from a sample, the goal is to draw conclusions about the entire population. For this, we need a representative sample—but there is no way to guarantee one. However, a **probability sample** gives each member of the population an equal (or known) chance of being included in the sample. *A probability sample does not ensure a representative sample, but it does support generalizing results to the population based on probability calculations.* Probability samples are drawn with the idea of calculating a **sample statistic** as a way of estimating the corresponding population value. Examples of sample statistics include the sample mean (average) and sample percentage. The most basic probability sample is called a **simple random sample (SRS)**. An SRS is a sample for which each element *and* each combination of elements in the population has an equal chance of selection. Chapter 9 ("Population, Samples, and Sampling") reviews a few other types of probability samples.

Suppose it isn't possible to compile a comprehensive listing of a population—for example, of homeless persons or drug dealers. How is a sample obtained? A probability sample is impossible without a defined population, so the sample has to be a **nonprobability sample**—the idea is that some information is better than no information. For example, you may have conducted an informal research project for a course by asking some of your friends or dorm mates a few questions. Or, you might have asked several students about a course or professor you were considering.

Since the probability of selection into a study is not known for a nonprobability sample, conclusions cannot be generalized rigorously to any larger population. But the results from a nonprobability sample often provide invaluable information—and some information often is a lot better than none. For example, who would discard data about dinosaurs because it doesn't come from a probability sample? But, it's very important to be careful about potential biases in nonprobability samples. Chapter 9 reviews several types of nonprobability samples.

TABLE 2.1.   Relationship between Smoking Status and Smoking Status of Best Friend (Hypothetical Data).

Smoking Status of Respondent	Smoking Status of Best Friend	
	Smoker	**Nonsmoker**
Smoker	62.2	15.0
Nonsmoker	37.8	85.0
Total	100.0%	100.0%

OVERVIEW OF CHAPTERS 10 AND 11: DATA ANALYSIS

Suppose you are interested in the social causes of smoking tobacco. One theory predicts that the tendency to smoke is affected by "significant others"—for instance, by whether your best friend, parents, or siblings smoke. Table 2.1 shows one instance of a relationship implied by this theory. This is a **bivariate table**, because it contains two variables: "friend smokes" and "I smoke."

The main purpose of a bivariate table is to *compare responses for the dependent variable between (or among) categories of the independent-variable categories*. Table 2.1, for example, shows whether there is a greater chance of smoking if one's best friend smokes than if the friend doesn't. The original (raw) numbers in the table are converted to percentages. Percentages "standardize" the raw numbers so you can easily tell how many per 100—regardless of the actual count in each comparison group.

Table 2.1 shows that if your best friend smokes, you are much more likely to smoke than if your best friend does not smoke—62.2% vs. 15.0%. But, isn't it possible that smokers choose friends who also smoke, and nonsmokers choose friends who don't? How do we decide which is the *independent* variable? Theory and past research are important guidelines—but it's a difficult question. In this example, we'd need repeated observations for the same people. (Be sure to note that the data in Table 2.1 are hypothetical.)

The data-analysis chapters (Chapters 10 and 11) review in detail how to construct and interpret percentage tables and other data-analysis procedures.

OVERVIEW OF CHAPTER 12: PREPARING THE REPORT

Chapter 12 presents an overview of writing a scientific report. It is an important chapter. As we have emphasized, a critical part of science is careful record keeping and the public nature of findings.

Scientific reports exhibit a lot of variety. The format and content depend on the type of research and type of report. Chapter 12 focuses on four of the more common types of reports:

- Empirical journal article
- Evaluation report
- Monograph
- Government document

The empirical *journal article* probably is the most prestigious type of report. Each paper submitted to a peer-reviewed journal must pass rigorous tests before it is accepted to become an article in the journal. Few papers are accepted without substantial revisions, as specified by reviewers. The content of an empirical journal article generally follows a broad outline consisting of an introduction, a review of the theory that motivates the data analysis, a summary of the statistical methods, a report of the findings, and a discussion. The theory section nearly always includes a review of the scientific literature related to the theory. It must present a convincing argument that the theory is sensible, is related to past research and is pertinent to the data analysis.

An *evaluation report* often follows a format similar to a journal article. A description of the intervention generally substitutes for the theory section in the journal article. Often the intervention must be described in more detail than is devoted to theory in an article, because readers are unlikely to be familiar with the intervention. Presented earlier in this chapter, the example revisited in Chapter 12 is the program conducted in Baltimore schools to inform students about safe sexual practices. The goals of the program included improved knowledge of safe-sex practices, reduced pregnancies, and delayed age of first coitus.

A *monograph* is a special type of book. But it is not a book in the conventional sense. It focuses on a narrow technical topic and is much more technical than other types of books. Monographs may be entirely composed of theory, report details of extended ethnographic observations or focus on statistical analysis of quantitative data. The content of a monograph, of course, depends heavily on the topic and the research methodology. The example in Chapter 12 is a report of an ethnographic study. The narrative describes details of the life of street people as seen by the author during extended observation. Part of the monograph discusses the ethical concerns related to revealing the identity of the people the author observed. Part of it describes methods people used for coping with street life.

Government reports vary a great deal, again depending on the content. Chapter 12 uses as an example the "classic" 1964 report of the Surgeon General of the United States on the hazards of smoking. This report is book length. But it was written by a committee consisting of many people who served on a commission to evaluate evidence related to health risks of tobacco smoking. The first section of the report contains an extended summary of the findings. The second part contains several technical chapters, each focusing on an evaluation of a specific aspect of smoking and health, such as mortality and cancer. Part of the report presents an insightful discussion of the criteria for establishing a causal connection between smoking and health. Since it is not permissible to assign people at random to be life-long smokers or not, no experimental data were available.

A second part of Chapter 12 contains a short *guide to report writing*. It presents advice about how to get started writing and detailed recommendations for developing the content, reviewing the literature, constructing the list of references and how to organize topic headings. It also advises you about the dangers of plagiarism. Separate subsections summarize report writing for qualitative and quantitative studies.

OVERVIEW OF CHAPTER 13: APPLYING PRINCIPLES OF "SCIENCE LEARNING" TO EVERYDAY LEARNING

The final chapter in the book illustrates how the principles of evidence for social science apply to everyday life. The chapter develops several examples:

- Steroids in baseball
- GBL (Gamma-Butyrolactone) in dietary supplements
- Hormone therapy for women (Is it the "Fountain of Youth"?)
- Games of chance and probability rules
- Automobile reliability

The first section evaluates recent reports claiming that steroid use among major-league baseball players is widespread and very dangerous. The second section evaluates potential dangers of GBL contained in various dietary supplements. Much evidence suggests it is dangerous, but it is difficult or impossible to tell from supplement labels how much, if any, GBL is contained in a supplement.

The section on hormone therapy for women summarizes the history of excessive claims indicating that hormone supplements taken by women after menopause pretty much guarantee a long and happy life. Recent experimental evidence indicates the contrary, however.

Many people apparently carry erroneous beliefs about the chances of winning in games of chance such as lotteries. In particular, it is fairly common to keep records of winning numbers and bet on numbers observed with high frequency in past winning sequences. The section on games of chance reviews how natural variation in completely random sequences of numbers does, in fact, generate uneven distributions. But, the unevenness of any history has no predictive value for future betting whatsoever. Play the games if you enjoy them, but don't expect anything you can do will affect your chance of winning.

The section on automobile reliability summarizes the quality of available evidence for predicting the durability of different makes of automobile. Available evidence is useful but contains many shortcomings. Predicting the reliability of a car is a very imperfect "science." And your purchasing decision is a good example of the very general necessity of making judgments without complete information.

ETHICAL ISSUES IN RESEARCH

Most social research is comparatively benign, but not all of it is. The infamous Milgram (1974) experiments, for example, had subjects administer fake electric shocks to "confederate" learners (persons who knew that the shocks were fake but were told to pretend otherwise). The idea was to see how far subjects would go to obey authority. Many subjects administered what they believed were dangerous levels of electrical shocks to the confederates. The experiments were developed to try to learn what prompted Nazi subordinates to engage in the horrors of concentration camps. As this example makes clear, the question of ethics is important in research with human populations.

The Belmont Report

Attention to the treatment of human subjects has intensified in recent years. The National Commission for the Protection of Human Subjects of Biomedical and Behavioral Research was created in 1974 by the National Research Act. The commission was charged with codifying protections that must be afforded to human subjects in research.

Basic Ethical Principles. The Belmont report summarizes the principles formulated by the Commission. The Report identifies three ethical principles: "respect for persons," "beneficence," and "justice."

1. *Respect for Persons.* The principle of respect stipulates that each person must be considered an independent person, capable of looking out for his/her own welfare. Persons with handicaps limiting their capacity have the right to protection.
2. *Beneficence.* The principle of beneficence (compassionate behavior) imposes two obligations on researchers who use human subjects: (a) do no harm to the subjects, and (b) strive for maximum benefit for the subjects.
3. *Justice.* The principle of justice identified by the Commission is difficult to summarize. The basic idea is to strive for equitable distribution of benefits and burdens of research. But, in practice, determining what is equitable is very difficult. Equitable is not necessarily the same as equal. Factors such as age, experience, deprivation,

competence, and merit enter into equity judgments. The Commission lists five considerations: (1) to each person an equal share, (2) to each person according to individual need, (3) to each person according to individual effort, (4) to each person according to societal contribution, and (5) to each person according to merit. These principles are not necessarily consistent and often must be balanced against each other.

Applications. The Commission identified three types of activities designed to ensure protection of human subjects: informed consent, risk and benefits assessment, and equitable selection of subjects.

1. *Informed Consent.* Informed consent is designed to implement the first ethical principle: respect for persons. It requires that each subject be given a fair summary of the research, its potential risks and benefits, and that each subject sign a formal consent document. Few dispute this requirement in the abstract, but, as you might imagine, many disputes arise in its specific application.

2. *Assessment of Risks and Benefits.* Risk assessment is intended to help ensure the second ethical principle, beneficence. It requires careful consideration of whether the potential benefits of research offset the risks to subjects. This consideration often may stipulate comparison of alternative methodologies for achieving the same knowledge. Review boards are expected to discuss explicitly these issues before approving a proposed research study.

3. *Selection of Subjects.* Selection of subjects must be designed to satisfy the principle of justice. That is, procedures must be adopted that do not put some individuals or groups at unfair risk of being subjected to dangerous research procedures. The implementation must be free of personal favoritism and generalized prejudice against classes or groups of people such as racial minorities or one gender.

The Belmont Report can be viewed online at: *http://ohsr.od.nih.gov/mpa/belmont*.

It is very important to understand the expectations for research with human subjects, such as "do no harm," *before* planning a research project. Researchers are likely to need permission from an **institutional review board (IRB)**. On college campuses, this group often is called the **human subjects review board** (or **human subjects committee**). IRBs review research proposals for potentially harmful impacts on research participants (social, psychological, emotional, physical) and advise researchers about required changes in procedures before research may begin. IRBs pay special attention to subjects such as children, prisoners, pregnant women, mentally disabled persons, and the economically or educationally disadvantaged, who might be unduly coerced or influenced to participate.

A copy of the *Code of Ethics of the American Sociological Association* and the American Anthropological Association are reproduced in Appendix A. These codes of ethics require **informed consent** from research subjects. Subjects have the right to know about the risks and benefits of their participation. Informed consent is obtained and documented from each prospective subject or the subject's legally authorized representative (e.g., parent).

Practical Dilemmas

In practice, the principles of the Belmont report are not easy to implement. They generate a lot of controversy and a lot of bureaucracy. For example, is it harmful to ask people about respondent's age, level of education, weight, or how many alcoholic drinks they consumed last week? As you likely have anticipated, "harm" can depend on a variety of considerations, such as who is being asked the question, who is asking the question, and how the question is asked. At the same time, the requirement to "do no harm" is of increasing concern to universities, to sponsors of research such as federal agencies, and to the public.

Disaster research, which Chapter 6 ("Observation and Ethnography") reviews in some detail, illustrates many of the conflicts arising from the requirement of informed consent. Disaster researchers are interested in how a community responds during natural disasters, such as an earthquake, hurricane, flood or fire, and human-generated disasters like the destruction of the World Trade Center buildings in New York City. In the past, disaster researchers typically explained the purposes of their research, promised confidentiality, asked for permission to tape interviews, and answered questions from prospective interviewees (Tierney, 1998, pp. 5–6). Today, workers at a disaster site usually are required to present written documentation that explains the research in detail and to obtain written consent from research participants. People living in disaster-stricken communities during a disaster and also the disaster workers are likely to be considered "disaster victims," who require special protection. Yet, highly formalized approaches to obtain informed consent are inconsistent with the informal data collection approaches used in postdisaster studies (Tierney, 1998, pp. 6–7). Moreover, time-consuming procedures for ensuring informed consent often conflict with the need to move quickly to keep up with unfolding events.

The requirement of informed consent also poses particularly knotty problems for observational research. For example, should an on-site researcher inform potential participants they will be research subjects? This question is of special concern for participant-observers who need to blend into a group appearing as a bona fide group member. Being known as a researcher during data collection can influence responses. Subjects might choose behaviors and comments to please or displease the researcher.

Researchers have made important contributions from studies in which they were not known as researchers, such as accounts of how the American nursing home industry is producing great profits at the expense of the well-being of residents. Yet, to *not* disclose one's role as a researcher violates the norm of informed consent. As Punch (1986, p. 36) points out, there are no easy answers to many situational ethics in ethnographic and observational work. He suggests seeing research subjects as "collaborators" in the research, and behaving toward them as we are expected to behave toward friends and acquaintances in our everyday lives (p. 83).

SUMMARY

This chapter introduces the major topics in social research. It is designed to provide a brief introduction to the detailed discussions in later chapters, and to the increasingly important issue of ethics in social research.

Two research modes are presented: basic research and applied or evaluation research. When conducting basic research, typically there is no formal intent to evaluate a specific social policy. Applied or evaluation research assesses the outcomes of social interventions. A social intervention is an activity undertaken with the explicit goal of producing a specified outcome. In practice, however, the dividing line between basic and applied research often is blurred.

Most social-science research is not conducted by experiments. But, the logic behind an experiment with random assignment nonetheless provides an important benchmark for evaluating all types of research. The key feature of a randomized experiment that makes it such a good standard is the clever way it controls *all* variables except the treatment that might affect the outcome of the experiment. Consequently, the researcher can be confident that observed differences in the outcome among treatments are due to the effects of the treatment and not to the effects of other variables.

Direct observation and ethnographic research, indirect methods and surveys comprise the major types of methods used to collect data. Direct observation provides opportunities to obtain detailed information about the complexity and subtleties of human interactions that cannot be assessed adequately by an interview or questionnaire. Ethnographic research examines the purposes and meanings of human actions using verbal descriptions and explanations with a small number of cases.

Indirect methods include content analysis of recorded communication, historical studies, and unobtrusive observations, such as studies of discarded items and traces indicating previous activity (e.g., wine bottles in a trash can, fingerprints at a crime scene).

A survey is a data-gathering tool conducted by asking questions of a large sample of respondents. The three major types of survey research are the personal interview, telephone interview, and mailed questionnaire.

Researchers sometimes use several methods in combination to improve confidence in their findings. For example, one might combine a survey with direct observation.

Data nearly always come from a sample rather than from the entire population. A probability sample is one for which each member of the population has a known chance, greater than zero, of being included in the sample. Probability sampling does not ensure a representative sample, but it does provide the basis for rigorous estimates of the magnitude of sampling variability. A simple random sample (SRS) is the most elementary type of probability sample. In an SRS, each element and each combination of elements in the population have the same chance of selection into the sample. Nonprobability sampling is necessary when a population cannot be defined and/or no complete listing of population elements is feasible. Precise estimates of the accuracy of these generalizations cannot be made, but often some information is better than the alternative—no information.

Ethical issues must be weighed carefully in social research. Researchers generally need permission from an institutional review board (IRB) before initiating a study involving human subjects. IRBs examine research proposals for potentially harmful influences on research participants and advise researchers about needed changes before research may begin.

YOUR REVIEW SHEET: QUESTIONS ASKED IN THIS CHAPTER

1. Is evaluation research a method of data collection? Why or why not?

2. Use the example of exposing plants to high and low light to summarize similarities and differences between everyday learning and science learning.

3. If information is obtained at an all-boys school, does gender vary among these students? Briefly explain in your own words the difference between a variable and a constant.

4. What is a dependent variable? How does it differ from an independent variable? Provide an example of each.

5. An experiment can "control" *all* variables that might account for an observed relationship between the treatment and the outcome. How?

6. A fundamental benchmark of social-science research is based on experiments and what can be learned about cause-and-effect relationships. Yet, experiments are conducted infrequently in the social sciences. Why does a randomized experiment provide an important standard of evaluation? Why is it seldom used?

7. What is nonparticipant observation? How does it differ from participant observation?

8. What is one advantage and one disadvantage of content analysis? Briefly explain in your own words.

9. Provide a short definition and two examples of unobtrusive observation, one of which is your own.

10. List some advantages and disadvantages of a personal interview compared with a mail survey and a telephone interview.

11. What are some advantages and disadvantages of a telephone interview compared with a personal interview and a mail survey?

12. What are some strengths and limitations of mail surveys, compared with the other two major methods of collecting survey data?

13. Why did the researcher Janet Lever use a research design that combined multiple methods?

14. Thinking about children's play and games, list one play behavior that could be studied by more than one method. Describe the methods appropriate for that play behavior. What is one reason researchers might *not* choose multiple methods?

15. Suppose members of a population can't be listed, for example, homeless persons or all drug dealers in a city. How is a sample of the population obtained? What type of sample is this? What are its strengths and weaknesses?

16. Look at the row for "Nonsmoker" in Table 2.1. Write a concise sentence describing in your own words the difference between respondents whose best friend smokes and respondents whose best friend does not smoke.

17. Should a researcher inform potential participants that they will be research subjects? Provide one reason why and one circumstance under which one might not inform participants.

18. What is an IRB? Summarize their activities.

END NOTES

1. A limitation of this study, common in evaluation research, is "clustering" of students in the two groups, which increases sampling error. It's not a fatal flaw, but one that must be considered. Chapter 5 discusses the issue from a research-design perspective.

STUDY TERMS

anonymity The researcher does not know the identity of respondents, and the researcher therefore cannot link data to specific individuals (compare with confidentiality).

applied (evaluation) research Investigation of a social intervention designed to find out whether it works. Evaluation is a goal or objective, rather than a method of data collection (compare with basic research).

basic research Investigation for which the goal is to expand the level of knowledge rather than to change or evaluate a social intervention or social policy. The study of the possible effects of maternal schooling on child health is an example (compare with applied research).

bivariate relationship Association between two variables; for example, a bivariate table displays the relationship between just two variables.

case One instance of the unit being studied, such as persons, couples, social groups, and organizations like schools. In this use of the term, for example, each respondent in a survey is a case, and so is each subject in an experiment.

cause-and-effect relationship Association in which manipulation of the cause is followed by a change in the effect, "everything else being equal."

classical experimental design Research based on random assignment to treatment and control groups, with a pretest of both groups, and a posttest of both groups.

confidentiality The researcher knows respondents' identities, but does not reveal information in any way that can be linked to individual respondents (keeps their information confidential) (compare with anonymity).

constant A measure with only one category; all cases fit into one category (compare with variable).

content analysis Study of recorded communication.

controlled experiment The experimenter determines what is changed, by how much and what is not changed (kept constant).

dependent variable "Outcome" variable or effect; it *depends* on the independent variable(s).

descriptive research Investigation that records what happens and describes the structure of what is recorded but does not attempt analysis of cause and effect. For example, Exercise 1.1 asked you to list all items you could recall in a crowded room and then sort them into groups with a common theme.

empirical test Testing an idea by observing what happens in the tangible world.

ethnographic research Investigation based on a broad perspective that emphasizes looking for the meaning attached to social settings by the participants. Ethnographic research is not confined to any method of data collection. But it typically is based on a small number of cases and depends on intensive open-ended interactions with them. The goal is to reveal the meanings and functions of human actions and interactions.

experiment Investigation in which a researcher manipulates or changes at least one variable and observes what happens to at least one other variable. The objects of the manipulation in experimental research with people are called subjects.

generalization To extend what has been observed to situations or persons not observed.

historical research Study based on data in historical records, typically focusing on changes over lengthy periods of time.

human subjects review board See institutional review board.

independent variable Variable assumed to generate or "cause" variation in another variable.

indirect methods Type of observation that does not involve direct contacts between the researcher and the subjects. Examples include content analysis, historical research and unobtrusive observation.

informed consent Formal statement obtained from research subjects prior to starting the research. The statement affirms that the subject agrees to participate with full understanding of the risks and benefits of participation.

institutional review board (IRB) A formal committee that examines research proposals for potentially harmful impacts on research participants (social, psychological, emotional, physical). The IRB advises researchers about needed changes before research may begin. On college campuses, this group might be called the human subjects review board (or human subjects committee).

mail survey A survey that collects information by mailing a questionnaire to respondents.

multiple methods More than one method of data collection used in combination to measure one variable. The objective is to reduce or eliminate many of the shortcomings associated with each individual method.

mutually exclusive Each observation is classified into one, and only one, category.

nonparticipant observer (complete observer) A researcher who makes observations, usually in public settings, without the subjects being aware they are being studied.

nonprobability sample A sample in which the probability of selecting each element is *not* known, usually due to lack of a comprehensive list of elements.

nonresponse error Errors in sample statistics due to differences between individuals who complete and return a questionnaire and those who do not. Those who fail to return a completed questionnaire (nonrespondents) might be different from respondents in ways that influence the results of the study.

observation The term observation is used in three ways: (1) to indicate a process for getting information by looking to see what happens, (2) to indicate a profile summary of variables for one individual or other unit (case) such as a college, and, (3) to indicate observational analysis, which means, roughly, to go out and talk to people, see what they do, stay for a while, and see what develops. This latter sense of observation is associated with ethnographic and other qualitative approaches to research.

participant observer A researcher who is completely immersed in the regular activities of the group under study.

personal interview A method of data collection in which information is obtained from each respondent in a face-to-face meeting with the interviewer.

population Defined collection of all individuals or other units from which data could be collected.

posttest Measurement of the outcome in an experiment taken *after* the treatment is administered. The posttest must use the same, or equivalent, data-collection procedures as used for the pretest.

pretest Measurement of the outcome in an experiment taken *before* the treatment is administered. In a randomized experiment, a pretest provides baseline average scores for both experimental and control groups.

probability sample A sample for which the probability of selection is known and greater than zero for each element in the population.

random assignment A procedure in which each subject is placed in the treatment group or control group using a "pure chance" method.

reliability (of a measure) Consistency; a consistent measure yields the same answer each time it is used, in the absence of change in the "true score."

respondent An individual who answers the questions on a survey; analogous to case in ethnographic/observational research and subject in experiments.

sample Some part of a population.

sample statistic A numerical calculation, such as an average using data from a sample, to estimate the corresponding population value.

simple random sample (SRS) A sample for which each element *and* each combination of elements in the population has an equal chance of selection.

statistic A number such as an average calculated from sample data, usually intended to estimate the corresponding population number, like the population average. Examples of sample statistics include the sample mean (average), sample percentage (proportion), and the difference between sample means or percentages (proportions) for two groups.

subjects Objects of the manipulation in an experiment, usually people in social research; analogous to **case** in ethnographic/observational research and respondent in surveys.

survey A method of data collection in which questions are posed directly to a large sample of respondents.

telephone interview An episode in which a respondent is surveyed by telephone.

theory A guide usually consisting of several interrelated *if . . . then* statements telling researchers where to look for useful relationships; theory often contains models, analogies, and images.

treatment variable (independent variable) In an experiment, the variable that is manipulated (the "treatment"). Analogous to independent variable in nonexperimental research.

unobtrusive observation Data collection that relies on "trace" data left behind as a residue of subjects' *previous activity*, usually over a relatively short period. Examples include examination of discarded items, footprints in the snow, and wear patterns on stairs.

validity (of a measure) Accuracy with which measurement procedures indicate the construct they are designed to measure.

variable A set of categories or numbers defined so that the categories are mutually exclusive and exhaustive. Each observation (e.g., person, object) fits into exactly one category. Familiar examples of variables in social research include race, gender, and age.

EXERCISES

Exercise 2.1. Writing Research Questions for Quantitative Research*

The goal of this exercise is to develop skills in writing research questions, so you might need to rewrite a question several times. For example, "What are children's problems?" is too broad. Better questions are, "What types of behavior problems do children display between the ages of 3 and 5 years?" (descriptive research*), or "Does mother's job type influence child's behavior between the ages of 3 and 5 years ?" (explanatory research). Of course, there may be causes of child's behavior problems other than the mother's job, such as family problems and health of the child, for example. Chapter 11 presents ways to test multiple causes.

*Note: Qualitative research doesn't require nearly as much focus at the beginning of a study.

Directions: Choose a social science topic. You may use one of the topics discussed in this chapter (exclude topics from an excerpt), or select one of your own.

1. Write your topic here (e.g., *children's behavior problems, ages 3–5*).

2. Write a one-sentence research question for a *descriptive study*.

3. List the information needed to study the topic for a *descriptive study* and how it might be obtained (e.g., *types of behavior problems for children, ages 3–5. Data from observations of children, or from questionnaires completed by children's preschool teacher*).

4. Write a one-sentence research question for an *explanatory study*. Use the *if . . . then* format.

5. List the information needed to study the topic for an *explanatory study* and how it might be obtained (e.g., *types of behaviors for each child ages 3–5 in the study, obtained from parent or teacher reports; and job type for each child's mother from telephone interviews of mothers*).

(*Hint:* Recall that you need *two pieces of information* for an explanatory (causal) study: the "cause" and the "effect." In the example, "job type of mother" is considered to be the cause of "child's behavior problems," which is the effect. The idea is to study whether the mother's type of job has an effect on her children's behavior.

Exercise 2.2. Evaluation of Research: Multiple Methods

Directions: Reread the excerpt on "sex differences in children's play" in this chapter and answer the following questions.

Factual Questions

1. Did the researchers conduct basic or evaluation research? Briefly explain your answer.

2. What is the research question?

3. Did the researcher use a population or a sample? Who are the cases (subjects/respondents) of the study?

4. What method(s) were used to collect data?

Questions for Discussion

1. State one advantage and one limitation of observations as a method of data collection in this study.

2. State one advantage and one limitation of questionnaires as a method of data collection in this study.

3. State one advantage and one limitation of using multiple methods of data collection in this study.

Exercise 2.3. Advanced Evaluation

Evaluation of Research Article: Content Analysis

Directions: Read the journal article, Schultz, Martin. (1992). "Occupational pursuits of free American women: An analysis of newspaper ads 1800–1849." *Sociological Forum*, 7(4), 587–607. New York: Plenum.

Your instructor will provide instructions for obtaining the article.

Factual Questions

1. What is the research question? What are the comparison groups?

2. What are the primary findings?

3. What type of indirect method was used by the researchers? What is the unit of observation?

4. Are the data from a population or a sample? What is their source, and how were they obtained?

5. Is the study descriptive or explanatory, evaluation or basic research? Briefly justify your answers.

Questions for Discussion

1. Briefly describe two limitations of the method of data collection (see question 3).

3

FOUNDATIONS OF SOCIAL RESEARCH

INTRODUCTION: LOOKING AT HOW THE SOCIAL WORLD WORKS

> Joan says she is going to stop smoking. Skip says he is going to lose 15 pounds. The sign says: "Speed checked by radar." The government says it is safe to bury nuclear waste in Utah salt mines. A total eclipse of the Sun will be visible in the continental U.S. on August 21, 2017.

Which of the above statements do you consider the most likely to be correct? Why? Assuming astronomers have predicted a total eclipse of the sun for the U.S. on August 21, 2017 (which they have), most people probably judge this statement to be the most likely. As far as we know, astronomers have never been wrong about a predicted date and location for an eclipse. On the other hand, lots of people say they will stop smoking and fail to do so. Many cars exceed the speed limit on a section of road posted as "monitored by radar" without being issued a ticket. Many people intend to lose weight but don't. And we know the government hasn't tested the integrity of the salt mines over the many hundreds of thousands of years that nuclear waste will remain dangerous.

Your judgment about each statement depends on predicting what will happen, given what you know currently. And each judgment or "rule" is based on experience—the more regular the pattern in the past, the more confidence you have that the pattern will continue. Astronomers' predictions of eclipses also are based on experience. Of course, the way astronomers learned how to predict eclipses is a lot more elaborate than the way we learn common-sense rules.

Goals of This Chapter

A prominent theme of this chapter continues an idea introduced in Chapter 1: *Science learning is an extension of what all of us do continually: look for predictability.* In science, the idea of predictability is expressed in the concept of "causal law." The definition of causal law isn't a settled issue, but highly technical scientists generally don't worry about how to define a causal law. They look for *patterns in data that can be used as rules for prediction.*

A second important theme of this chapter is: *The best strategy for "finding out" is to search continually for new information and to update current understanding continually as new information is produced.* Continually searching for new information and ongoing updates of current understanding are in clear contrast with "sticky theory" beliefs—that people sometimes hold ideas so strongly they refuse to acknowledge evidence that contradicts their ideas. Of course, many questions are so complex we are incapable of identifying definitive causal laws about them. The complexity of the world is one important reason for a skeptical attitude and for developing the habit of continually updating our understanding of it.

EVERYDAY KNOWLEDGE AND RELATIONSHIPS (STATISTICAL, NOT LOVE)

What is the relationship between studying hard to get good grades and going out several times a week with friends? A simple schematic for representing a relationship is the 2×2 table, as shown in Table 3.1. This table illustrates a strong relationship. It implies that studying hard is detrimental to your social life! Specifically, "go out frequently" is much less likely (10%) among those who "study hard" than it is among those who "neglect studies" (85%). (The data are hypothetical.) How can you tell from the table whether there is a relationship between studying and going out? In this example, a relationship occurs to the extent that the percentage who go out frequently is different for those who "study hard" than it is for those who "neglect studies." The larger the difference, the stronger the relationship.[1]

Are people capable of interpreting a table like this? Some intriguing research suggests that they are not.

> One important line of prior research has dealt with people's ability to recognize . . . relationships presented in simple 2×2 contingency tables. . . . With bivariate data so neatly assembled and 'packaged,' the subjects' task seemingly was an unusually simple and straightforward one. Nevertheless, the evidence . . . shows that laypeople generally have fared quite poorly at such tasks. (Jennings, Amabile, & Ross, 1982, p. 212)

Does inability to read a contingency table indicate inability to assess relationships in everyday life? Jennings and colleagues (1982) cite informal evidence for this assertion, arguing that reading a table is easier than evaluating real-life situations because most of the work is complete by the time a table is constructed. Also, many questions already have been answered, such as: *What is worth observing and what is not? How should the variables be defined and measured? And What*

TABLE 3.1.   Sketch of the Relationship between Studying and Going Out.*

	Study Hard	Neglect Studies
Go Out Frequently	10%	85%
Go Out Infrequently	90%	15%
Total	100%	100%

*Data are fictitious, constructed to show a strong relationship.

TABLE 3.2.   Sketch of the Relationship between
Smiling at Friend and Friend Smiling.

	Smiled at Friend	Did Not Smile
Friend Smiled at Me		
Friend Did Not Smile		

type of sample is needed? These often are difficult questions, and few people answer them well in all circumstances.

Are people *really* so inept? Most people do identify a relationship between gender and hair length, for example. Many people also see an association between the price of a car and its age, mileage, and make. On reflection, it seems that there are many obvious relationships that most people learn without any formal training or even any tutoring on the topic! Consider another relationship, shown in Table 3.2. Most of us probably know from experience that there is a positive relationship between the two variables smiling at a friend and friend smiles at you. And we didn't need a table to learn it.

On the other hand, brand loyalty probably is a good example of *erroneous* assessments of relationships. Some people are convinced brand "X" works, and it's difficult to tell them otherwise. Some people are "Ford" people, some are "Chevy" people, others are loyal to Chrysler, and so forth; is brand loyalty an example of "sticky theory"?

Look at one more case of personal assessment of relationships—the health benefits of wearing magnets, summarized in Table 3.3. You might guess that you can evaluate this type of relationship, but you might be wrong. Probably there is a lot of error in making this type of assessment.

A recent review of the evidence showed no benefit to wearing the magnets, yet enough people believe there is a benefit to sustain commercial sales of the magnets. If these consumers didn't believe that there is a relationship between wearing the magnets and the reduction of various ailments, such as carpal-tunnel pain and arthritis, they surely wouldn't spend money on the magnets.

Jennings and his associates offer a dismal assessment of human mental abilities that lead to such decisions.

There is thus a wealth of empirical and anecdotal evidence that . . . *the intuitive scientist's preconceptions about empirical relationships are apt to determine what he*

TABLE 3.3.   Sketch of the Relationship between Wearing a Magnet and
Experiencing Pain.

	Wore Magnet on Wrist	Did Not Wear Magnet
Carpal-Tunnel Pain		
No Carpal-Tunnel Pain		

> *detects, what he fails to detect, and what he sees that is not really there to be seen.* (emphasis added; Jennings et al., 1982, pp. 215–216)

But if the human species is so dumb, how did it survive so long? The same authors whom we have just quoted offer the following perspective:

> Sometimes, of course, everyday circumstances *are* optimal for learning. Thus, in our everyday experience we learn what countless switches, levers, buttons, and other manipulanda do, and what a bewildering variety of signs, symbols, and signals mean, because the relevant covariations are so close to perfect. Equally important, perhaps, is the fact that the layperson, like the formal scientist, often can "test" new hypotheses that he has come to entertain. (Jennings et al., 1982, pp. 229–230)

Perhaps people aren't so dumb after all. But they do have limitations. Moreover, our world is so incredibly complex that we don't have a prayer of fully understanding it. The above examples point out some of the limitations we all face. We conclude: *People are very good at assessing relationships—sometimes.* Other times they're not very good, and may even be very bad at it on occasion. What is the difference? When are we good at it, and when are we not so good? *Do you think that "sticky theory" might help to answer this question?*

BASIC CONCEPTS: VARIABLES, OBSERVATIONS, AND RELATIONSHIPS

So far we have looked informally at several examples of relationships but haven't defined explicitly what a relationship means. The concept of *relationship* depends on understanding the term *variable* and is closely connected to the concept of an *observation*. So we start with these three terms, then use them to define relationship.

Variables

A **variable** is a way of describing people or objects by assigning a category or a number to each person or object. For example, the word "color" can describe houses, flowers, animals, automobiles, and numerous other items. To create the variable "color" to describe houses, we can assign a color category to each house (e.g., white, blue, gray, brown) or a number (e.g., a blue house is a "1," a gray house "2," and so forth). In the social sciences gender probably is the most frequently cited example of a variable, and it is easy to define. There are two gender categories: female and male. Each person fits into exactly one. With *very* few exceptions, there is little ambiguity about gender classification, and nearly all social research can proceed on the assumption that gender classification is unambiguous.

The people or objects being described are "elements." Elements include individual people, couples, families, cities, and countries. Every variable is defined by at least two categories, and *every* element fits into *exactly one* of the categories. The categories must be exhaustive and mutually exclusive of each other. **Exhaustive** means that all possible categories for elements are included as part of the definition of the variable. **Mutually exclusive** means that each element fits into only one category. Numbers (e.g., . . . 18, 19, 20, . . .) naturally are exhaustive and mutually exclusive, and when numbers are used to represent a variable, *each* element is assigned *exactly one* number per variable.

Another frequently cited example of a variable is race. Defining the categories of race is subject to a lot more controversy than is defining the categories of gender. A commonly used collection of categories is: Asian, Black, White, Native American/Pacific Islander, Other. However, operational rules must be established to ensure that each person fits into exactly one racial category. Inclusion of the "Other" category is necessary to ensure that the categories are exhaustive—that is, accommodate everybody.[2]

The **value** of a variable is the category or number assigned to it for one element. For example, the monetary value of your 1982 "heap of junk" is $300. In 2004, the year of this writing, the value representing its age was 2004 − 1982 = 22 years (or 23, depending on the exact current date and the date of manufacture).

Defining and Constructing Variables. It's not entirely clear just exactly how scientists go about defining a variable, but it *is* clear that the definitions are critical to the success of the research. In many instances the definitions are long-standing in a discipline, so the individual scientist may take them as given. Newer scientists—including student researchers—can look in published research to learn long-standing definitions. In other instances, new variables must be constructed and their definitions developed, or old definitions revised.

Variables that are not directly measurable often are called **concepts** or **constructs**. Variables such as prejudice, self-esteem, occupational status, and intelligence are examples of constructs. To assign numbers or codes to abstract concepts like prejudice or self-esteem, explicit, detailed rules must be devised.

Codes are numbers or letters representing values of a **categorical variable**, such as the categories of male and female for the variable gender. For example, you may decide to assign the letter "F" to represent female, and the letter "M" to represent male. More commonly, *numeric* codes are used, for example, "1" for female and "2" for male. The rules for obtaining observations and assigning the numbers or codes is the **operational definition** of a variable.

Of course, when numbers are used as codes for categories, they lose their meaning as numbers (e.g., as codes, "1" is not ranked lower than "2"). But numeric codes can be used in calculations, if they are selected carefully. For example, if you assign 0 = male and 1 = female, then the average is the proportion who are female in the sample, for example, 0.53 female (or 53%). This type of coding is very convenient and used so frequently that this type of variable is given a special name: **dummy variable**. Chapter 4 ("Measurement") extends the discussion of constructing and defining variables.

Observations and Relationships

In the English language, the word *observation* is used in many contexts. In this section, we give it one specific meaning—an **observation** is the collection of values for all the variables in a study for one element. In short, it is a profile. For example, here are two hypothetical observations:

| female | 63 inches tall | 23 years old | black hair | white race | $12.50 per hour |
| male | 68 inches tall | 21 years old | black hair | black race | $12.75 per hour |

Usually number codes are assigned to represent the values of each variable and the profile is condensed into a sequence of numbers and stored in a computer file—

1 63 23 1 2 1250
2 68 21 1 1 1275

Here, female = 1, male = 2; black hair = 1, black race = 1, white race = 2. The decimal points are omitted from the wage variable; they are inserted when the computer reads the data.

A **relationship** (association) is defined for two or more variables. By definition, *two variables are related if knowing the value of one of them reduces uncertainty about the value of the other one.* For example, knowing the gender of a person reduces uncertainty about the length of the person's hair. Knowing the age of an automobile reduces uncertainty about its monetary value. A relationship may involve more than two variables. For example, to reduce uncertainty about a car's monetary value, you might combine information about age, mileage, and make of the car. (Here, both numeric and categorical variables appear in the same relationship.)

When knowledge of one variable reduces uncertainty about the other variable to zero, there is a **perfect relationship**. For example, there is a perfect relationship between your age and your mother's age. Knowing both your current age and your mother's age when you were born predicts exactly your mother's current age.

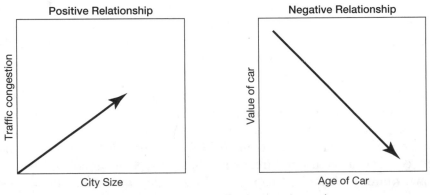

FIGURE 3.1.   Examples of Positive and Negative Relationships.

Relationships may be positive or negative. A **positive relationship** is one in which the two variables are related so their linkage "travels" in the same direction. As one goes up the other goes up, and vice versa. For example, as city size increases, traffic congestion increases. A **negative relationship** is one for which the direction of change of the two variables is opposite. As a car gets older, its monetary value declines. Figure 3.1 illustrates positive and negative associations.

THE CONCEPT OF CAUSAL LAW

We've loosely defined a causal law as a "rule for prediction." The rule is a *relationship*, based on what has already been observed. But the concept of causal law is more subtle and complex than you might expect. In fact, it has generated much debate among philosophers, beginning with the ancient Greeks and continuing today.

In everyday conversation, the word *cause* generally carries some connotation of *produces*, and the idea of *produces* is present in many philosophical debates about causation as well. For example, the microwave heats the popcorn which *produces* enough pressure to cause the corn kernels to explode. But careful analysis reveals that the idea of *produce* is not necessary. All that's required is a *relationship permitting one to predict what happens next*, given current conditions. *If* popcorn kernels are heated, *then* they pop.

More generally, a **cause-and-effect relationship** (**causal relationship**, "causal," *not* "casual") occurs where current knowledge of the cause reduces uncertainty about the effect in the future. If I smile at a friend, the chance of my friend smiling at me goes up.

The connection between cause and effect must be more than incidental. At least in principle, *changing the value of a causal variable must be followed by a change in the effect variable, everything else constant*. Why? The relationship between two variables might occur because both are affected by a third variable, not because one of the two affects the other. But a relationship cannot be due to anything that is fixed, so any variable held constant cannot account for a relationship (change between two other variables).

Of course, it's impossible to hold "all else constant," but this ideal is, nonetheless, a very useful benchmark. It lies behind the insistence on use of control, described below.

In science, the ultimate determinant of what is and is not a causal relationship is *observation*, as in the philodendron example in the previous chapter. Testing an idea by observing what happens in the physical world is called an **empirical test**.

The concept of "explanation" in science usually is connected to discovering causal relationships. But it's a lot easier to invent explanations that *seem* to reflect understanding than it is to *verify* that the explanation works. You don't "understand" unless your explanation "works." For example, if you claim rattlesnakes don't strike unless they shake a rattle at you first, no matter how reasonable the explanation sounds, the ultimate test is an empirical test—go out and check what happens. (Would you like to volunteer for this study?)

Universal Rules and Specific Instances

Causal terminology is used in many ways. What feature do all of these statements share?

1. Tom is tall because his father is tall (Tversky & Kahneman, 1982, p. 120).
2. The average hourly wage of women is less than the average for men.
3. The more people associate with each other, the more they like each other (Homans, 1950).
4. The fire was caused by a 3-year-old playing with matches.
5. With constant volume, pressure of a gas increases as it is heated and decreases as it is chilled.

Each statement implies some kind of *causal relationship between two or more variables*. The first one relies on expecting a positive relationship between the heights of fathers and sons, and the "cause" of the son's height is the father's height. In example 4, the 3-year-old plays with matches, which "causes" the fire.

Although each statement expresses a causal relationship, there are three important distinctions among them.

1. *Some are universal rules, and others are specific applications of these rules.* Example 4 is a *specific application* of universal rules. The fire was caused by a 3-year-old playing with matches. The reasoning to get from universal rules to this specific instance is rather long. The universal rules have to do with heat, oxygen, and fuel. The particular situation has to do with specific sources of heat and fuel. Oxygen is nearly everywhere, so it does not need to be mentioned. In this context, it is a constant. In this example, heat from a match was a catalyst that set in motion a chain of causes and effects.

In contrast, number 3 (association with others leads to liking them) illustrates a *universal rule* about human behavior: Science focuses on finding universal rules. Applications such as forensic science, police work, and weather forecasting rely on identifying specific instances of the universal rules.

2. *Many of these relationships are between two numeric variables, like height and weight. But some of them refer to categorical variables, like gender.* The distinction between type of variable does not change the essential idea of "relationship"— *knowing the value of one variable (the cause), reduces uncertainty about the value of another variable (the effect).*

3. *Some of these relationships refer to change over time.* For example, "the more people associate with each other, the more they like each other" implies a dynamic process that unfolds over time.

On the other hand, most examples of relationships in social science are observed in **cross-sectional data**, meaning the variables in the relationship were measured at the same time. Generally, the assumption, when analyzing cross-sectional data, is that the relationship is the end result of a completed process—that is, a process that is no longer changing, for example, the relationship between years of schooling and number of children for women 50 years old and older.

Sometimes, the process generating a cross-sectional relationship is clear from informal observation or prior research. The relationship between hair length and gender is due to social norms that encourage women and men to grow their hair to different lengths. Even when observing hair length and gender at the same time, it is obvious which variable is the cause and which is the effect; length of hair doesn't determine one's gender.

In other cross-sectional relationships, the direction of the effect is not clear. A woman's education likely affects the number of children born to her. But might the number of children also affect her years of schooling? So, the correct causal interpretation of a cross-sectional relationship between number of children and education of women is ambiguous. This problem requires knowledge of the time order for women's education and their childbirths.

The notion of "law" or universal rule carries some idea of a "perfect relationship"—meaning, it applies without exception. But there are multiple influences on most variables in the social world, and most of the influences are never observed, or at least never observed accurately enough to reveal a perfect relationship between variables.

Nonetheless, social science does identify relationships that are thought to contain a causal component. Think of several factors that influenced whether you and your high school friends went to college. Social theory and research have found that parental status and income, parental expectations for their children, test scores, high-school grades, and one's own career goals influence college attendance. But, all of these variables together do not fully *determine* whether one attends college. They do reduce uncertainty about it, though.

Do cause and effect ever occur simultaneously? It is tempting to think they don't, that cause precedes effect. What appears to be simultaneous, however, can be characterized by an ever-so-small lag time between cause and effect. Philosophers analyzing the concept of causal law often cite the connection between heat and gas pressure to illustrate simultaneous occurrence of cause and effect (example 5), so we leave this issue to the philosophers to resolve.

SCIENTIFIC APPROACH

Science proposes rules about how the world works and checks to see if they are correct by observing whether they describe what happens. The proposed rules are formulated as relationships called **hypotheses**. An example of an hypothesis is: *rattlesnakes strike only after they warn you with their rattles*. In an empirical test of a relationship, the presumed cause is called the **independent variable**, and the effect is called the **dependent variable**. The determination of independent variable (e.g., rattlesnake shakes its rattles) and dependent variable (e.g., rattlesnake strikes) has meaning only when we think there is a causal connection between two variables—warning followed by strike.

Skepticism and "Sticky Theory"

In science, even the most extensively tested ideas are not final. Some theories and their associated hypotheses have passed so many tests that we are willing to bet they'll pass the next one, but the next test necessarily will happen in the future. There's nothing in logic that guarantees test results will be duplicated in future observations. Because of this indirect way of doing empirical tests of scientific theories, hypotheses associated with a theory must be **falsifiable**. That is, they must be stated so that observations could invalidate the theory. If a hypothesis can't be falsified at least in principle, it isn't a scientific hypothesis (Popper, 1968), underscoring the critical role of skepticism in science. The philosopher Karl Popper considers skepticism to be a defining feature of scientific investigation:

> I generally have a lot of respect for common sense. I even think that, if we are just a little critical, common sense is the most valuable and reliable counsellor in every possible problem situation. But it is *not always reliable*. And in matters of scientific or epistemological theory, it is extremely important to have a really critical attitude to it. (Popper, 1999, p. 6)

> My main thesis, then, is that the novelty of science and scientific method, which distinguishes it from the prescientific approach, is its consciously critical attitude to attempted solutions; it takes an active part in attempts at elimination, in attempts to criticize and falsify. (Popper, 1999, p. 11)

Popper argues that although a critical attitude is important in common-sense decisions, science *requires* a consciously critical mind, the word "critical" here meaning careful and ongoing evaluation of all relevant evidence. A classic work on science and logic makes the same point:

> What is called *scientific method* differs radically from these [common-sense methods] by encouraging and developing the utmost possible doubt, so that what is left after such doubt is always supported by the best available evidence. As new evidence or new doubts arise it is the essence of scientific method to incorporate them—to make them an integral part of the body of knowledge so far attained. Its method, then, makes science progressive because it is never too certain about its results. (Cohen & Nagel, 1934, p. 195)

Skepticism is one contribution of science to everyday learning—the mind-set to reserve judgment, minimizing "sticky theory." However, people have to act, often before compelling evidence is in. So a part of "good judgment" is knowing when to act—and still reserve judgment.

Spurious Relationships and Their Control

Just observing a relationship between two variables isn't convincing evidence for a causal connection between them. Why not, if you've *observed* it?

The term **control variable** designates a variable that is held constant (a constant measure has one category and all cases fit into one category). The purpose of holding the values of a control variable constant is that the control variable might affect both the dependent variable *and* the independent variable, invalidating the hypothesis of a causal relationship between them.

For example, there is a negative relationship between wearing a dress and wearing a beard because both are affected by gender, as shown in Figure 3.2. At least three variables must be considered together for one of them to be called a control variable. In the case of wearing a beard and wearing a dress, the control variable is gender. In this example, gender is a **confounding variable**—a variable producing a **spurious** (noncausal) **association** between wearing a dress and wearing a beard.

How does one *hold constant* the value of at least one variable while observing the relationship between two other variables? Control can be implemented by (1) physical manipulation, (2) statistical control, or (3) random assignment to categories of the independent variable.

An example of *physical manipulation* is chilling several sodas to a specific temperature before conducting a taste test. The idea is to keep the temperature of all drinks the same (constant) so it can't affect judgments of taste. In this instance, control means literally "to control" the temperature of the sodas.

Statistical control may be used when physical control is impossible. Social scientists can't physically control the gender of a person, but they can examine the relationship between wearing a dress and wearing a beard separately for each gender category: for women and for men. This is one type of statistical control.

Control also may be approximated by *random assignment* to levels of the causal (independent) variable. The random-assignment method isn't exactly the

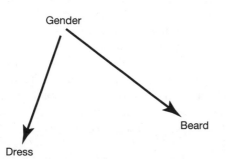

FIGURE 3.2. Gender as a Confounding Variable, Producing a Spurious Relationship Between Beard and Dress.

same thing as control, because nothing is actually held constant. But random assignment does ensure that the expected average of *all* potentially confounding variables is the same for every value of the independent variable. For instance, people may be assigned at random to drink one of several brands of soda, where the outcome is a taste rating. The average of *all* variables affecting taste preferences (other than the independent variable, brand of soda) is nearly the same no matter which brand of soda is drunk. (How many variables can you think of that might affect a taste test of two brands of soda?)

In most social-science investigations physical control isn't feasible, and neither is random assignment. It is not possible to control physically the gender of a person, as we might introduce a control in a taste test by chilling sodas. Neither can people be assigned at random to different genders. Statistical control is the only option.

As with most independent and dependent variables in social research, the selection of a control variable is specific to the situation. Chapter 11 shows how the same analysis permits easy interchange of the role of a variable as a control variable and as an independent variable.

Scientific Theory

The term *theory*, as used in science, doesn't mean exactly what it means in everyday conversation, such as "I have a theory about why people ride motorcycles." But the two meanings of theory are similar. Scientific theory isn't easy to define. The philosopher of science, Salvator Cannavo, says:

> The term, 'scientific theory' brings to mind a swarm of unsettled topics like hypotheses, laws, models, analogies, abstract entities, and more. But throughout the diversification of topics and views one can make out a significant convergence of opinion regarding the basic features of that part of scientific discourse which goes under the name of *theory*. Theory serves science in primarily two ways. In the first place, it provides very general accounts of various chunks and layers of the world. . . . In the second place, theories serve to systemize various matters of fact about the world. (Cannavo, 1974, p. 234)
>
> The terminology or, as one might also put it, the conceptual content of what generally counts as scientific theory differs in very important respects from that of statements reporting observed regularities in nature. The appropriate distinction here seems to be not between law and theory but rather between two kinds of laws: *theoretic* laws (which constitute theories) and *observational* laws. The latter's vocabulary makes direct reference to what we are inclined to call *observables*, that is, things which are sometimes said to be directly perceivable, with or without the help of instruments. . . . Theoretical vocabulary, on the other hand, though it occurs as descriptive terminology as, for example, 'electron', 'molecular velocity' . . . does not make direct reference to so-called observables. (Cannavo, 1974, p. 235–236)

One way to think about **theory** is as a collection of hypotheses about a coherent topic. A set of hypotheses about the cause-and-effect relationships among parental status, mental ability, and educational degrees on occupational status and earnings, for example, has collectively been called a "theory of status attainment." A random collection of hypotheses isn't a theory, however. The hypotheses must "belong together." For example, hypotheses about the behavior of the planets and the behavior of children with a learning disability do not belong in the same theory. Yet, as the excerpt from Cannavo makes clear, theory is more than a collection of hypotheses. Often, but not always, theory includes models, both physical and mathematical; analogies; and unmeasurable constructs. A **model** is a simplification of reality—designed to promote understanding by summarizing essential elements and reducing complexity.

You've probably experienced living with a "thin wallet"—a limited budget in which money spent on CDs, for example, can't be spent on food, and vice versa. In the social sciences, a good example of a theoretical construct is "utility." Utility is an economic concept referring to the self-perceived benefits people get from economic goods and services. Put simply, you are engaged in an ongoing process of making choices to maximize the benefit you get from the income you have; what you spend on CDs can't be spent on food. The question in this example and more generally is: Do observations fit predictions of the theory? The observations don't have to match exactly, just be close enough to be "useful." The judgment about "useful" is very much an intuitive one, however.

The Importance of Hypotheses—The Case of the Naked Scalp. Cohen and Nagel (1934) present a "hairy" example of why hypotheses about relationships are essential:

> Now baldness in men is a phenomenon for which the cause is not known. If the canon [method of agreement] is an effective instrument of discovery, no student of logic need suffer long from a naked scalp. In accordance with the canon, we find two or more bald men and search for a single common circumstance. But immediately we run into great difficulties. The method requires that the men should differ in all respects except one. We will have rare luck indeed (or we are perhaps rather unimaginative in noting common circumstances) if we succeed in obtaining a collection of men who satisfy this condition. . . .
>
> How shall we go about identifying the common circumstance or circumstances? If one specimen has blue eyes, must we examine all the others for color of eyes? If one of the bald men confesses to having been brought up on cod liver oil, must we discover whether the others were brought up the same way? But the number of such circumstances to which we might be directed is without limit. Date of birth, books read, food eaten, character of ancestry, character of friends, nature of employment, are some examples of circumstances to which we might pay attention. If, therefore, the *common* circumstance can be found only by examining all the instances for *every* circumstance which some one or other of the bald group may possess, we can never find *all* the common factors in this way. We can carry on the search for a common factor only if we disregard most of the circumstances which we may find as not *relevant* to the

phenomenon of baldness. We must, in other words, start the investigation with some hypothesis about the possible cause of baldness. (Cohen & Nagel, 1934, p. 252)

Clearly, the formation of hypotheses is a necessary early step in quantitative science, and a cause-and-effect relationship can be identified only by examining the most relevant factors.

Parsimony. Suppose you have two theories that make the same predictions. Which one do you choose? In science, the simpler theory is preferred. This principle is called **parsimony**. The principle of parsimony often is associated with William of Ockham (1285–1347/49) and sometimes is called "Ockham's razor," because he used it so frequently to dispense with what he viewed to be redundancy. But the principle predates even William Ockham and has been used often in subsequent scientific debate, by Galileo for example, to defend his view that the sun is the center of the solar system (*Encyclopædia Britannica* online [*www.eb.com*]).

Probably the most famous example of the idea of parsimony is connected to the Sun-centered theory of the solar system. For centuries the accepted theory was based on the "obvious" fact: The Earth is the center of the universe. The heavenly bodies were modeled as residing on crystal-clear spheres that rotated about the center of the Earth. This system describes the motion of stars quite simply and accurately, but requires an exceedingly awkward and elaborate system of what were called "epicycles" to account for the motion of the Moon and planets. Also, it did not explain why the planets Mercury and Venus exhibit phases, like the phases of the moon. (The phases could be seen only after the invention of the telescope.)

Copernicus is credited with bringing the sun-centered (heliocentric) theory to prominence, but his system was based on circular orbits and therefore still required complex epicycles. Kepler modified the Copernican system by postulating that orbits fit the equation of an ellipse. The orbits of the Moon and all the planets could be fit simply to an elliptical path; the complicated epicycles no longer were necessary.

Circles are special cases of ellipses, so Kepler's system can be viewed as a generalization of the idea of circular orbits. Figure 3.3 shows three overlaid ellipses, one of which is a circle. The figure illustrates how ellipses blend into a circle as the degree of eccentricity diminishes. Switching from one ellipse to another is simply a matter of changing the constants in a single unifying formula. No epicycles are needed.

Ironically, the definition of simplicity is complex. There is no simple rule for differentiating degrees of simplicity. Why is the theory that the Sun is the center of the solar system simpler than the theory that the Earth is the center of the solar system? The Sun-centered theory, after all, defies common sense.

The answer has to do with the number of questions that can be answered with a few underlying principles. Newton's theory of gravity combined with the Sun-centered view of the solar system answers numerous questions that otherwise

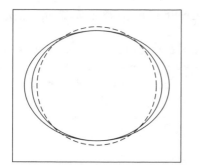

FIGURE 3.3.   Three Ellipses Overlaid.
One ellipse is a special case: a circle (dashed line).

seem unrelated. These questions include predictions of the motion of the stars, planets, and the Moon; predictions of eclipses; an explanation and prediction of the phases of the planets Mercury and Venus; the progressions of the seasons on Earth; and many more. The Earth-centered theory, on the other hand, requires special ad hoc explanations for each of these questions. The simplicity with which the revised system describes a seemingly disparate collection of observations is quite stunning (*Encyclopædia Britannica* online [*www.eb.com*]).

The impulse for parsimonious theory can be seen in many aspects of social science. For instance, stratification theory is aimed at developing a comprehensive explanation of inequality encompassing class, race, gender, ethnicity, and many other factors that give rise to inequality among people. The intention is to identify the common processes among these apparently distinctive threads.

Philosophers of science have connected the idea of simplicity, or parsimony, with *testability*. A theory that creates a new hypothesis for each new observation it can't predict otherwise is difficult or impossible to falsify (Cohen & Nagel, 1934; Popper, 1999).

Serendipity and Scientific Discovery

An important component of scientific development might ironically be called "finding the unexpected"—an irony (contradiction) because most scientific discoveries come after long, arduous, and tedious work. But an element of surprise, often called **serendipity**, also is thought to figure prominently in the history of scientific discovery.

The discovery of penicillin is a well-known example of serendipity. Alexander Fleming discovered penicillin by noticing that a particular bacterium would not grow on mold which had infested cultures of the bacterium. Edison also "found the unexpected." He was engaged in an experiment to transfer the human voice so it could be sent by telegraph when he noticed that impressions on paper of sound vibrations from speaking could be "played back" when a stylus was drawn over the impressions. He stopped work immediately on the telegraph project and turned his attention to inventing the phonograph (*Encyclopædia Britannica* online [*www.eb.com*]).

Notice that in both of these examples, the investigator was immersed in the research. There was an element of serendipity in their discoveries, but it's hard to imagine these discoveries would have been made "out of the clear blue" by someone not engaged in the research. Hard work and expertise definitely were essential.

Science as Public Knowledge

Recently, *The New York Times* published a summary of a study about the benefits of support groups for breast cancer patients—with findings opposite to the conventional wisdom of the time:

> Contrary to popular opinion, support groups do not extend the lives of women with advanced breast cancer, according to a large study being published today. The study disputes a belief that has been stated so often it is almost considered a truism—that the mind influences the course of advanced cancer so powerfully that patients can hold off death by getting emotional support in a group. (Kolata, *New York Times*, December 13, 2001, p. A36)

Given the belief of the general population about the benefits of "social support," why was this study undertaken? The investigators began their study because they were concerned that many patients felt obligated to join support groups to fight their cancer, whether they wanted to or not. Many were convinced of the benefits of support groups by a small and inconclusive study published more than a decade ago indicating that support groups could substantially prolong patients' lives. The *New York Times* article quotes leading medical researchers praising the new findings, because they are based on a much larger sample and use better methods than the original study.

The debate about the benefits of support groups to cancer patients illustrates a basic aspect of science. *Scientific research is open to public scrutiny, particularly by other scientists with the same or related specialties as those who conducted the research.* Findings are published in scientific journals. Each paper must be reviewed critically by peers before it is published. Frequently there is debate about a published paper. The debate also is published in the journal.

In contrast, as "lay scientists," we often keep our "findings" private. At most, we may try them out on a few family members, friends, and acquaintances. Many informal insights are passed along to others and become part of the informal culture. The process of accumulating findings in science is much more systematic, however. In science, written records are kept, and the whole process is very deliberate. Because of these steps, erroneous ideas are much less likely in science than in the general culture. Of course, individual scientists often do hold tenaciously to their theories; their theories can become "sticky." And whole periods in scientific history sometimes are dominated by erroneous ideas, as in the example of the Earth-centered theory of astronomy.

The basis of science embodies a *built-in mechanism* designed to be *self-correcting* in the long run, because of the open competition in the "marketplace" of ideas.

Qualitative Science and Causal Laws

Not all scientific investigations look for causal laws, at least not directly, and not all science is **quantitative** (numbers-based) **research** that is highly quantitative and mathematical. **Qualitative** (meaning-based) **research** is relatively unstructured, with an interpretive, naturalistic approach to its subject matter. Often the goal is to make sense of, or interpret, observations in terms of the meanings people bring to them. Qualitative science generates invaluable information about topics as varied as the natural history of life, and of *Homo sapiens* in particular; experiences of patients in nursing homes; humans coping with disasters; and the mentality of street gangs.

Many qualitative studies are conducted in the social and behavioral sciences. As in biology, many aspects of human behavior are difficult or impossible to study with quantitative methods. The Disaster Research Center (DRC) located at the University of Delaware maintains an ongoing research program that depends heavily on qualitative methods. For instance, a quick-response team was dispatched to the site of the disaster at the World Trade Center on September 11, 2001. Shortly after 9/11, the DRC Web site summarized the agency's activities:

> On September 13th, a quick-response field team from the Disaster Research Center traveled to New York City to observe the efforts underway in response to the tragic attack on the World Trade Center. Since that time, faculty and staff from DRC have been returning to New York City to systematically observe emergency management activities, conduct informal interviews, attend planning meetings, collect documents, and employ other unobtrusive field work strategies in the impacted area. Among the settings in which fieldwork has been conducted include the City's Emergency Operations Center, incident command posts in the Ground Zero area, the FEMA Disaster Field Office, supply and food staging areas, bereavement centers, and hospitals.
>
> Additionally, DRC has been systematically collecting news reports on the relevant information on the management of the WTC disasters and is developing an electronic archive. The objective of these efforts is to collect perishable data on organizational mobilization, interorganizational coordination, decision-making, and other social and organizational aspects of the response. In the coming weeks, DRC will be exploring other areas of research related to the WTC attack. Faculty and staff at DRC have been interviewed about their ongoing research by news sources such as *The New York Times, The Chicago Tribune*, Paterson, NJ *Herald News, Fortune Magazine, The Wilmington News Journal*, the *University of Delaware Review*, the *University of Delaware Update*, CBC Radio, and *The Winnipeg Free Press*. (*http://www.udel.edu/DRC/wtcupdate.html*, January 5, 2002)

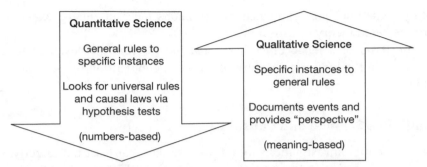

FIGURE 3.4.   Comparison of Quantitative and Qualitative Science.

The potential importance of documenting the kinds of activities mentioned in this statement is clear. Yet, quantitative methods often associated with science do not apply. Neither are causal laws likely to be an immediate outcome of such activities. The descriptions are done with the expectation others will find them useful—probably not in developing explicit causal laws, but to help determine effective policy related to disasters. "Useful policy" has to do with reducing uncertainty about the future based on what we know today.

Qualitative science provides at least two important functions.

■ Qualitative science documents what has happened, either in human affairs or in other matters.

■ Qualitative science provides important perspective for current decisions and strategies. The documentation provides the "input" for the perspective. Without information, there is no perspective—that is, where to focus our attention, a narrowing of possibilities. Figure 3.4 provides a comparative summary of the distinctions between qualitative and quantitative science.

SUMMARY

This chapter opens with several illustrations of how each of us looks for relationships in everyday learning. For example, what is the relationship between studying hard to get good grades and going out every night with friends? The idea is to use experience to develop rules for reducing uncertainty in everyday life and in scientific research. The second section reviews several basic concepts that are needed in the remainder of the chapter, throughout this textbook, and in the social sciences generally. This material includes definitions of the fundamental concepts of variables, observations, and relationships. A variable is a way of describing differences among people or objects; examples include gender and age. An observation is a profile showing the value of one or more variables for a single person or object. Two variables are related if knowing the value of one of them reduces uncertainty about the value of the other.

Much science has to do with identifying cause-and-effect relationships. A causal relationship is a rule for expectations about the future based on current knowledge. But discovering causal relationships isn't easy. One of the primary reasons for the difficulty is that an observed relationship between two variables might be due to another variable. Wearing a dress and growing a beard *are* related, but only because both of them are dependent on gender.

In a cause-and-effect relationship between two variables, the cause is called the independent variable and the effect is called the dependent variable. A causal relationship must persist when other variables are held constant (controlled). Also, the effect can't precede the cause in time in a causal relationship and changing the cause is *followed* by a change in the effect (or, at least the effect does not precede the cause).

Scientific investigation doesn't proceed by observing every detail in the world but depends on hypotheses. A hypothesis is a proposed causal relationship. Hypotheses must be formulated so that they can be falsified by observation. One way to view scientific theory is as a collection of hypotheses about a topic. Theory is an essential guide indicating where to look for useful relationships. Often theories contain unmeasurable variables, like the economic concept of utility, which are used in models to predict relationships among measured variables. Theory ties together (provides a unifying framework for) broad classes of behavior.

Parsimony refers to the preference for simplicity. Given that two theories make the same prediction, the simpler theory is preferred. Serendipity is a fancy name for the role of luck in research: finding unexpected relationships. But, most discoveries probably arise from long arduous investigations with much trial and error.

Generally, qualitative investigation is used when the subject matter is too complicated to be quantified. Qualitative research documents what happens and describes the structure of what is seen, such as human emotional reactions and the meanings people attach to events or circumstances. Qualitative research also provides many insights into cause-and-effect relationships that we likely would overlook otherwise.

What can you learn from the scientific approach? In short, be flexible, learn from experience, be skeptical, and avoid the fallacy of "sticky theory." Be aware that a limited sample of observations might not be typical of the rest of the world. Always be on the lookout for possible alternative explanations of relationships that you do observe.

YOUR REVIEW SHEET: QUESTIONS DISCUSSED IN THIS CHAPTER

1. In 2×2 tables, how can you tell whether there is an association between two variables? Use the relationship between studying and going out as an example.

2. What is "theory," and what role does it play in science?

3. Suppose you have two theories that make the same predictions. Which one do you choose? Why?

4. How does science differ from how people learn informally—that is, from common sense? How are they similar?

5. If your 8-year-old cousin asked you, "What is science?" how would you answer the question?

6. In your own words, what are the contributions of qualitative science?

7. In social science, perfect relationships almost never are observed. Why not?

8. Are even the most extensively tested scientific ideas ever considered to be final? Why or why not?

9. What is a hypothesis? Why can we *reject* a hypothesis but never prove a hypothesis?

10. Observing a relationship between two variables is not convincing evidence for a causal connection between the two variables. Why not, if you've observed it? Offer an example to illustrate. (*Hint:* Think about control.)

11. In a summary sentence, how does social science differ from other sciences?

END NOTES

1. The relationship also could be checked by comparing the percentages of those who go out *in*frequently across the two columns of the table: "study hard" versus "neglect studies." To make both comparisons is redundant, because the percentages add up to 100 in each column. Chapter 10 shows how to read and construct tables.

  Also, the variables in the table are loosely defined. What do "study hard" and "neglect studies" mean in concrete terms? Is there an omitted middle category? Similarly, what do "go out frequently" and "go out infrequently" mean? The main point of the table is to show how to display and interpret a relationship between two variables. But it is important to recognize that defining the variables is a critical and often difficult task. (See Chapter 4, "Variables and Measurement.")

2. The 2000 U.S. Census permitted people to select more than one racial category. This means that the collection of answers to the race question do not form a single variable. A sequence of variables, each with two categories, must be constructed. Each racial category (e.g., White) may be assigned a yes or no. In this case, for example, one may be both Black and White, but there are two variables to handle this possibility.

  The phrase "African American" gradually is replacing the term "Black" in popular U.S. culture. However, this phrase doesn't capture what usually is meant by Black (a race category) in social research. African-American mixes the concept of nationality with the concept of race. "American" in this context stands for "U.S. citizen." So "African American" suggests one cell in a table comparing race and citizenship. The term works in everyday use but is not a useful term in social research.

STUDY TERMS

categorical variable A variable with a finite number of categories. The categories are different, but one category is not greater or less than any other category (e.g., gender contains two categories).

causal relationship A relationship that occurs where current knowledge of the cause reduces uncertainty about the effect some time in the future.

cause-and-effect relationship Manipulation of the cause is followed by a change in the effect, "everything else being equal."

concepts (constructs) Variables that are not directly measurable; examples include prejudice, self-esteem, occupational status, and intelligence.

confounding variable A variable producing a spurious (noncausal) association between two variables.

control Observing a relationship between two variables, while holding constant at least one other variable that might threaten a cause-and-effect interpretation of the relationship.

control variable A variable that is held constant; a constant is a measure with one category, and all cases fit into one category (e.g., female gender).

cross-sectional data A collection of variables measured at the same time for each case.

dependent variable The effect or outcome variable in a relationship. *contraception*

dummy variable A categorical variable with two categories represented by the numbers 0 and 1.

empirical test Testing an idea by observing what happens in the physical world.

exhaustive categories Set of categories that accommodate every person or object; no person or object is left unclassified.

falsifiable Hypothesis formulated so that observations might show it is wrong.

hypothesis Speculation about how the world works. In science it's usually a proposed causal relationship that, at least in principle, can be checked by observation.

independent variable The variable that is understood to be a cause in a relationship between two variables. *school*

model A simplification of reality designed to promote understanding by summarizing essential elements and reducing complexity.

mutually exclusive categories Set of nonoverlapping categories defined so no person or object fits into more than one category.

negative relationship Direction of change of two variables is opposite. As one goes up the other goes down, and vice versa.

observation The collection of values for all the variables in a study for one case (subject, respondent); a profile.

operational definition Collection of rules for obtaining observations that will become a variable.

parsimony Simplicity; in science, the simpler theory is preferred when two theories make the same predictions.

perfect relationship Relationship for which knowledge of one variable reduces uncertainty about the other variable to zero.

positive relationship Direction of change of two variables is the same, as one goes up the other goes up, and vice versa.

— **qualitative research** ("meaning-based" research) A relatively unstructured approach to social science, involving an interpretive, naturalistic method, attempting to make sense of, or interpret, phenomena in terms of the meanings people bring to them.

— **quantitative research** ("numbers-based" research) Comparatively structured research that emphasizes causal relationships among variables, using data represented by numbers.

relationship (or association) A relationship exists between two variables when knowing the value of one variable reduces uncertainty about the value of the other variable. Knowledge of gender, for example, reduces uncertainty about hair length.

serendipity Finding the unexpected, thought to figure prominently in the history of scientific discovery.

spurious association A noncausal relationship between two variables, generated by their common dependence on another variable.

theory In brief, a collection of hypotheses about a coherent topic.

value (of a variable) Category or number assigned to a specific observation.

variable Way of describing people or objects by assigning a category or a number to each person or object. There must be at least two categories, and every person or object must fit into exactly one of the categories. We say the categories must be exhaustive and mutually exclusive of each other.

EXERCISES

Exercise 3.1. Operationalizing Concepts

Directions: This exercise gives you chances to practice converting abstract concepts into measurable variables, the process called "operationalization."

> **Example:** Hypothesis: Black males who assault white women are more likely to be sent to prison than are white males who assault white women.
>
> Concept 1: racial background (of males)
>
> Concept 2: sent to prison (for assaulting white women)
>
> Independent Variable: race Categories: black and white*
>
> Dependent Variable: sent to prison (yes, no) or Categories: years (in 5-year time periods)*
>
> *Other categories could be proposed, depending on the study design.

Topic 1: Are males or females more likely to be admitted to medical school?

> What is the independent variable?
>
> List its categories. _____

What is the dependent variable?

List its categories (consider as a dummy variable).

Topic 2: Do younger or older teens spend more time on household chores?

What is the independent variable? _____

List its categories. _____

What is the dependent variable?

List its categories (collapse it into three categories and explain why the three you chose are sensible).

Exercise 3.2. Evaluating Hypotheses

Directions: For each of the following hypotheses:

1. Identify the variables.
2. Define operational definitions for each variable.
3. Determine whether or not each hypothesis could be tested as written, and briefly explain your answer.
4. Identify at least one variable that should be "controlled" before accepting a causal connection between the variables.

    a. High school students with good grades are more likely to attend college than students with low grades.

    b. Opinionated people live shorter lives than open-minded people.

    c. Men who participate in organized sports are cocky.

Exercise 3.3. Evaluation of Research: Testing the Relationship between Variables

Directions: Read the following excerpt to answer the questions below.

Excerpt: *Husband and Wife Differences in Undesirable Life Events*

. . . [W]e hypothesize that men in the present sample of husbands and wives would be more likely than women to demonstrate symptoms of distress indicative of overt antisocial behavior, operationalized in these analyses as hostile behaviors or feelings. Women, on the other hand, were expected to report higher levels of depression, anxiety, or somatic [physical] complaints. . . . [W]e also hypothesized that husbands would report more undesirable events related to financial circumstances, and women would report more crises regarding interpersonal relationships. . . .

A total of 451 White, married couples were recruited for the study. On average, they had been married 18 years when interviewed in 1989. . . . The sample includes families that had a child in the seventh grade in a public or private school in one of these eight rural counties during the 1988–89 academic year. . . . In addition to the 7th grader, at least one sibling was within four years of age in each household. . . . Of those families eligible for participation, 78 percent agreed to be interviewed. To be included, all four family members (husband, wife, 7th grader, sibling) had to agree to participate.

. . . [E]ach family was visited twice at home. During the first visit, the project interviewer explained the purpose of the study, and obtained informed consent and demographic information (e.g., ages of all family members, number of people living in the home, etc.). Then each of the four family members separately completed a set of questionnaires that asked about topics such as recent life changes, family economic circumstances, the quality of family relationships, styles of family interaction, psychological distress, and other issues relevant to the study.

. . . [T]he results demonstrated that men are more likely than women to report exposure to and to be distressed by work and financial events. Women, on the other hand, are more strongly influenced by exposure to negative events within the family but not within their network of friends. Outcomes vary according to the type of emotional distress. Financial stress . . . increases hostility among men more than among women, but wives are more likely than husbands to report somatic complaints in response to the same stressor. (Conger et al., 1993, pp. 71, 74–76)

Factual Questions

1. In your own words, state the general hypothesis(es) tested in the study. In each hypothesis, underline the dependent variable and circle the independent variable (or its categories).

2. Is this study an example of qualitative or quantitative research? Explain your answer.

3. Summarize in your own words the findings of the study.

Question for Discussion

1. How well do you think the results from this sample generalize to all married couples? Why?

4 VARIABLES AND MEASUREMENT

INTRODUCTION: LOOKING AT HOW THE SOCIAL WORLD WORKS

"The Eagles have 'Big Mo' on their side—momentum, that is. The Chiefs have team chemistry."

"Hey! Go after it, man! Work hard, and you'll get rich!"

"You've got to believe in yourself."

"Study hard and you'll make it. America is the land of opportunity!"

What do these claims have in common? They all imply we have in ourselves the capacity to succeed against impossible odds, in the greatest *Star Trek* tradition. But to succeed, we have to believe in ourselves and work hard! The notion of "controlling your destiny" by hard work and ability is more apparent in most of these statements than in the one about team chemistry. What is "team chemistry"? It's not an easy term to define, but it seems to include several components:

- team members like each other
- team members anticipate what their teammates will do next
- the team exhibits high team spirit—there is an atmosphere of joking and confidence
- each team member "goes at 110 percent, 110 percent of the time."

A key idea implied in the phrase *team chemistry* seems to be that good team chemistry fosters team success, and that team chemistry is something that coaches and "team leaders" can nourish to improve the fortunes of their team. It does appear that winning teams tend to have better team chemistry than losing teams. Even supposing this appearance is correct, it's not clear whether teams win because they have good team chemistry, or teams have good team chemistry because they win, or a little of both.

The notion of team chemistry is an everyday example of what social scientists call a **construct**—a **variable** that is abstract and not directly measurable. But the construct "team chemistry" probably is too complex and poorly defined to be used in research.

Goals of This Chapter

What does it mean that "a construct is abstract and not directly observable"? What is measurement error, how do we try to avoid it, and what role do concepts such as "reliability" and "validity" play in assessing measurement error? What does "correlation" mean? What are items, indicators, and indexes? To answer these questions, this chapter extends the brief introduction to the idea of a construct in Chapter 3 by showing how to turn abstract constructs into variables or **measures**. The process of converting abstract concepts into measurable variables is called **operationalization**.

The next section summarizes a study that illustrates how constructs are used in research.

EXAMPLE: ATTITUDES TOWARD SELF AND SUCCESS IN SCHOOL

A recent study examines the cause-and-effect relationships among the abstract concepts of "self-esteem" and "personal control." Look at how the authors operationalized these concepts.

Excerpt: *A Study of Self-Esteem and Grades*

Most previous research on adolescent self-concept has included self-esteem or, less commonly, the sense of personal control, but not both. Using three waves of panel data from the National Educational Longitudinal Study, the authors examined the effects of academic achievement in the 8th grade on the sense of personal control and self-esteem in the 10th grade and the subsequent effects of control and esteem in the 10th grade on academic achievement in the 12th grade.

They present evidence that the sense of personal control affects subsequent academic achievement, but that self-esteem does not. Earlier academic achievement and parental support increase self-esteem and the sense of personal control. (Ross & Broh, 2000, p. 270)[1]

In this study, "personal control" refers to one's generalized belief about how much influence the person has over successes and failures in life. Unlike grades, personal control and self-esteem aren't directly *observable*. That is, no one can directly see, hear, feel or touch either personal control or self-esteem. Yet there is pretty good indirect evidence that people differ on tendencies thought of as personal control and self-esteem. In everyday life, people tend to classify each other along such dimensions, often based on subtle cues about the individuals.

In place of subtle cues, Ross and Broh depended on answers to questionnaire items. For "personal control" the questions asked whether respondents believed (1) they had no control over life, (2) luck is important, (3) others stop their personal progress, and (4) their plans rarely (or always) work out. Questions for

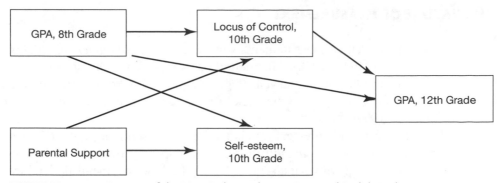

FIGURE 4.1. Diagram of the Main Relationships in Ross and Broh (2000).

"self-esteem" were respondents' beliefs about whether they (1) are a person of worth, (2) do as well as others, (3) are satisfied with self, (4) feel useless at times, (5) feel no good, and (6) are not proud. Higher values for the personal control and self-esteem variables represent higher sense of personal control and self-esteem, respectively.

The authors posed the question: *Do students with high self-esteem make good grades because they have high self-esteem, or do they have high self-esteem because they've made good grades in the past?* (Ross and Broh also are interested in the influence of parental support on attitudes and achievement.) Figure 4.1 summarizes the main ideas.

In general terms, what are Ross and Broh trying to accomplish? They're trying to unravel the old question of how achievement affects one's attitudes toward oneself, and how one's attitudes affect achievement. This is another version of the theme in the first paragraph about success and sports: the way people think of themselves affects whether they succeed, rather than success breeding confidence. They conclude that it is the latter—success leads to higher self-esteem.

self-esteem → *success (grades)*

versus

success (grades) → *self-esteem*

The theory tested by Ross and Broh depends on complex constructs such as self-esteem, personal control and parental support. Of course, not all social-science variables are complex constructs. For example, age is pretty straightforward to operationalize—it is just the number of years between your date of birth and your most recent birthday. However, age isn't automatically easy to measure; people do refuse to answer a question about their age, and some lie about it. But a concrete variable like age poses fewer measurement difficulties than complex, abstract constructs like self-esteem. Consequently, most of the discussion in this chapter focuses on measurement of constructs—variables that are abstract and not readily observable. Much social research depends on complex constructs.

THE NATURE OF MEASUREMENT

S.S. Stevens defines measurement as *the assignment of numbers to objects according to rules* (1946, 1958). This definition is repeated often, sometimes with and sometimes without citing Stevens (e.g., Maxim, 1999). For the most part, Stevens's formulation is accepted in the social sciences, but its acceptance is not universal (Michell, 1999).

Ultimately, measurements are judged by how useful they are—*Do they support prediction or serve as diagnostic tools?* A paper by Ferraro and Farmer (1999) shows an example of what appear to be "useful" measurements derived from complex constructs.

Excerpt: *Physician Assessments or Patient Self-Report of Patient's Health?*

Kenneth Ferraro and Melissa Farmer (1999) compared physician evaluations to patients' own answers about their health. They pose the question: "Does self-reported morbidity better predict a patient's health status than physician-evaluated morbidity?" (Morbidity is the tendency toward, or presence of, ill health or sickness.)

They use two measures of "health status": (1) *mortality*, and (2) *self-assessed health*. Mortality is defined by whether the patient survived until the follow-up survey, or, if not, what was the date of death? Self-assessed health was based on the answer to a single survey question: "Would you say that your health in general is excellent, very good, good, fair, or poor?"

The research used two constructs to create the independent variables.

- Construct 1: Physician-evaluated morbidity. Two physician evaluations of morbidity were conducted containing extensive measurements.

  The first physician instrument was a general medical exam consisting of eight components: Examinations of (1) head, eyes, ears, nose, and throat; (2) thyroid; (3) chest; (4) cardiovascular function; (5) abdomen; (6) musculoskeletal systems; (7) neurological function; and (8) skin.

  The second physician instrument consisted of physician evaluations using the *International Classification of Diseases* (ICD). The ICD contains 15 categories, such as infectious and parasitic diseases, cancers and neoplasms, and diseases of the respiratory system.

- Construct 2: Patient self-report morbidity. Self-report morbidity was measured by 36 items contained in an interview administered to patients by the survey staff. For example, "Has a doctor ever told you that you have . . . hypertension or high blood pressure?" (p. 307)

The findings seem unexpected. The authors summarize as follows:

It is not surprising that self-reported morbidity is the stronger predictor of self-assessed health, given that the outcome was a subjective appraisal of health. Yet even when mortality [death] is the outcome, physician-evaluated morbidity was not the superior predictor. Self-reported serious illness and morbidity from the general medical examination predicted mortality among white respondents, but neither type of physician-evaluated morbidity was predictive of mortality among black respondents. In summary, the evidence shows that self-reported morbidity is equal or superior to physician-evaluated morbidity in a prognostic sense. (Ferraro & Farmer, 1999, p. 313)

For white (but not black) patients, a patient's self-estimate of health predicts risk of death at least as accurately as do physician assessments. This result illustrates what we mean by "useful" measures. It's impossible to know exactly how accurately the self-report survey items measure morbidity, but it is possible to know whether the result predicts something concrete, such as mortality. Does the study invalidate medical checkups? No! In the case of health, no single measure exists and there is no unambiguous criterion for it. Mortality may seem like a good criterion for assessing the validity of morbidity measures, but it's far from perfect. A person in "perfect health" can be fatally injured in a car crash, or even struck by lightning and killed.

The next sections examine how to create concrete measures, and how to assess and improve their validity.

Indicators, Items, and Indexes

The first step in creating a measurement is to define the variable you want to measure. This is easy for concrete variables like age and gender; definitions already exist. But it is more complicated for constructs like morbidity, personal control or team chemistry, none of which can be observed directly.

Because constructs can't be observed, their measurement depends on **indicators**. Indicators are observable variables used as *indirect measures* of a construct. An example is a single question on a survey. Several indicators often are combined to measure the construct. The assumption is that the unobservable construct "causes" or influences the answers that people give to observed indicators. For example, the state of patients' health influenced how they responded to the interview questions of self-assessed health and morbidity.

Generally, constructs are developed from everyday ideas, with specific rules about how they'll be turned into variables. In general, an **index**, or **scale**, is defined by combining two or more variables, usually by adding or averaging the values of the component variables.[2] The individual components are called **items**. In the Ross and Broh paper, self-esteem and personal control were defined as indexes, comprised of six items (questions) and four items, respectively.

Classification of Variables

In the social sciences, why are variables classified into types according to the math operations that sensibly can be used with them? One reason is that the type of data analysis for a study depends heavily on the types of measures. For example, calculation of a *correlation coefficient*, a measure of association between two variables (discussed in the next section) requires variables that permit addition, subtraction, multiplication, and division.

Stevens (1946) introduced a classification scheme consisting of four types of variables: nominal, ordinal, interval, and ratio.

A **nominal variable** classifies persons/objects into different categories. The categories are not "greater than" or "less than" each other. Examples include gender, color, and make of an automobile. No math operations are sensible. That is, you can't add, subtract, multiply, or divide, with nominal variables such as gender. Two values of a nominal variable are either equal to each other or they are not. If two automobiles both are Fords, make of car 1 = make of car 2. If one is a Chevy and the other a Dodge, make of car 1 is not equal to make of car 2. Nominal variables often also are called **categorical variables**.

Ordinal variables rank persons/objects in one category as "greater than" or "less than" persons/objects in other categories, but they don't support math operations like addition or multiplication. The place (1st, 2nd, etc.) in which a person finishes a marathon is an example of an ordinal variable. It isn't sensible to subtract 2nd place from 1st place, for example. The difference doesn't indicate how much time separates first-place finisher from second-place finisher. All that can be said is that one individual is faster or slower than another.

In social research, ordinal variables include responses to attitudinal scales that have response options like "strongly agree" to "strongly disagree." The categories clearly imply order, but they do not support statements like: Ashley agrees twice as strongly with statement A as Matt does, because Ashley's score is a 2, and Matt's score is a 1.[3]

Numeric variables without a natural zero point are called **interval variables**. The most frequently cited example of an interval variable is temperature measured on the Fahrenheit or Centigrade scale. The zeros on these scales are arbitrary points—they don't indicate the complete absence of heat. With interval variables, it makes sense to add and subtract the numbers however. For example, the "high temperature today is 10 degrees warmer than it was yesterday." But multiplication and division don't make sense. It isn't sensible to say: "The high temperature yesterday was 20 degrees, today it is 40 degrees; it's twice as hot today as it was yesterday."

"Pure" examples of interval scales in the social sciences are rare or nonexistent. Most researchers probably would say that the indexes of self-esteem, personal control, and morbidity are not interval scales. In this case, addition and subtraction do indicate how much the averages differ between two respondents. And the process generating the numbers is well defined. Borgatta and Bohrnstedt (1980) argue strongly that numbers like these can be treated as if they are interval scales in statistical calculations.

Numeric variables containing a natural zero are called **ratio variables**. The zero stands for complete absence of some real-world quantity. For example, wage = 0 means you earn nothing, so wage is a good example of a ratio variable. Adding and

Type of Variable	Characteristics
Nominal	Unordered categories: The only mathematical operation supported is equal or not equal.
Ordinal	Ordered categories: Each category is either greater than or less than each of the other categories.
Interval	Numeric variable with no natural zero: Addition and subtraction are supported.
Ratio	Numeric variable with a natural zero: All mathematical operations (addition, subtraction, multiplication, division, and all others) are supported.

FIGURE 4.2. A Classification of Variables.

subtracting are sensible. Ten dollars per hour is a dollar less than 11 dollars per hour. Multiplication and division also are meaningful. Twenty dollars per hour is twice as much as 10 dollars.

Figure 4.2 shows a summary of the classification of nominal, ordinal, interval and ratio variables.

Variables also may be classified by whether their categories are *finite* (limited) or *infinite*. A **discrete variable** is one that either has a finite number of categories, or an infinite number whose values correspond to whole numbers (. . ., -2, -1, 0, 1, 2, . . .). Examples of discrete variables include gender, race, number of arrests, population size of counties, and number of household pets. A **continuous variable** is one whose values correspond to numbers, both whole numbers and parts of numbers. For example, many, many values lie between the integer numbers 1 and 2, like 1.32, 1.5, 1.71. . . . The values of a continuous variable correspond to *any* point along a continuous line. Measures of height and weight are good examples. Given precise enough measuring devices, your height and weight could take any one of an infinite number of distinct values, that is, any value along a continuous line.

As noted in the previous section, many statistical procedures depend on calculating an average score (requiring addition and division) or other math operations, and not all variables support all math calculations. Consequently, the type of data analysis for a study depends on the types of measures, a topic further examined in Chapter 11.

MEASUREMENT ERROR

Suppose you are the interviewer, and a 69-year-old man reports he is 39. You might be a little skeptical, but must report the information as given. This is an extreme case of measurement error. **Measurement error** (ME) is the difference between an observed value of a variable and its "true score": ME = **observed score** $-$ **true score**. In this example, the man's reported age minus his actual age

$(39 - 69 = -30$ years) is the measurement error. Hopefully, errors of this magnitude don't occur often.

Measurement error makes it difficult to detect a relationship that might actually exist. For example, Ross and Broh (2000) were surprised to find that self-esteem does not predict later grade-point average. Perhaps a better measure would show that self-esteem does predict academic achievement. If it did, we might be inclined to accept the new measure as an improvement. But—and this is an important point—we don't want to accept a measure *just* because it supports our favorite hypothesis.

How can one ever know whether an unobservable construct like self-esteem is measured accurately? There's no way to know for sure, but there are several methods for evaluating measures. However, none of them, taken singly or together, provide a definitive answer to questions like: Is self-esteem measured without error? Do we have an accurate measurement of health? or Have we measured "team chemistry"? Ultimately, measures like these are evaluated by whether they predict more concrete variables, like academic achievement or longevity.

The Correlation Coefficient

Consistency and accuracy of measures depend on the concept of correlation. **Correlation** is a generic term standing for "relationship" or indicating some measure of the strength of a relationship. Usually, when the term *correlation* is used to refer to a specific measure of relationship, it's understood that the **Pearson product-moment correlation coefficient** is the specific measure. The remainder of this book uses the term *correlation* or *Pearson correlation* as shorthand for the Pearson product-moment correlation.

The Pearson correlation measures prediction accuracy in linear relationships. What is a linear relationship? The idea is easy to grasp from an example: "One gallon of gasoline costs $2.10, two gallons cost $2 \times \$2.10 = \$4.20$, three gallons cost $3 \times \$2.10 = \$6.30$, and so forth. Total cost and quantity are related on a straight line because price is constant.

The relationship between total cost and quantity of gasoline purchased is an example of a **positive** relationship. Here, positive relationship means the more you buy, the higher the cost. Figure 4.3 shows an example of a perfect positive linear relationship, where "perfect" means if you know the value of one variable, you know exactly the value of another variable. Price is a constant in this example. The two variables are gallons and total cost of the purchase. Recall from Chapter 3 that a **negative** relationship is one in which two variables move in opposite directions; as one goes up the other goes down. For example, the more you spend the less you save; this is a perfect negative relationship, by definition. Most relationships aren't perfect however. For example, the quantity of gas left in your gas tank declines as the distance you've driven since the last fill-up increases. But you can't predict exactly how much gasoline is left just by knowing the distance you've driven.

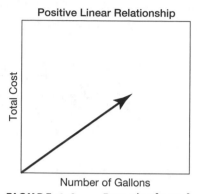

Positive Linear Relationship

Total Cost (vertical axis)

Number of Gallons

FIGURE 4.3. Example of a Perfect Positive Linear Relationship.

The Pearson correlation measures how accurately one variable predicts another variable using a straight-line approximation. It ranges from -1.0 (perfect negative correlation) to 1.0 (perfect positive correlation). A correlation of zero indicates there is no straight-line relationship between two variables: $r = 0$, where r stands for "correlation coefficient calculated from a sample." The closer a correlation is to $r = -1.0$ or $r = 1.0$, the stronger the linear association between two variables. (A perfect *nonlinear* relationship can produce a correlation coefficient of 0, but this is unusual.)

Figure 4.4 shows examples of imperfect linear relationships. It illustrates a scatterplot for four correlations, including one where the correlation is near zero ($r = 0$, no linear relationship), two with a positive correlation ($r = 0.49$ and $r = 0.82$), and one with a negative correlation ($r = -0.50$). The diagonal line running through the points on each plot is the predicted straight-line relationship. The more closely the points cluster around the line, the higher the absolute value of the correlation.

What relationships might these correlations represent? The positive correlations might represent the association between height and weight. Height and weight are positively correlated, but it's not a perfect relationship. The statement: The more you smoke tobacco, the poorer your health, is an example of a negative relationship. As tobacco consumption goes up, health goes down. Another example of an imperfect negative relationship is the one we just mentioned: the more miles you have driven since your last fill-up, the less gasoline left in your gas tank. There probably is near-zero correlation, however, between height and musical talent!

Suppose two variables are not measured accurately. What happens to the correlation coefficient? If the measurement error is *random* (occurs unpredictably), the correlation is reduced, and therefore the relationship is hard to detect. The error adds a random component to each variable, and the random components are not related to each other, lowering the association between the two observed variables. But if the error is *systematic* (not random), all bets are off! The correlation coefficient could even be inflated. For example, suppose respondents who have completed many years of schooling but earn a low wage exaggerate their reported hourly wage. The

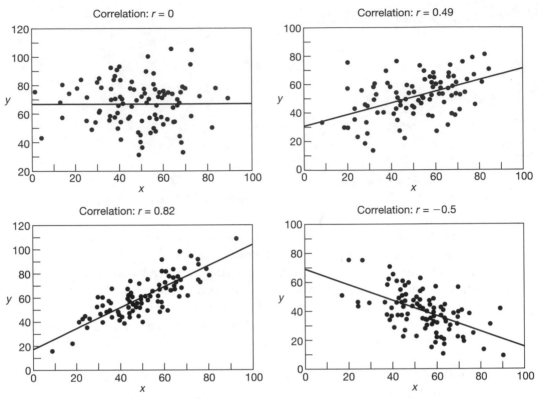

FIGURE 4.4. Four Sample Correlations.

correlation between education and wage is inflated, because the error is positively related to education.

EVALUATING VALIDITY

Validity is the accuracy with which an observed variable measures the construct it is designed to measure. The correlation between the true score and the observed score is called the **validity coefficient** (Lord and Novick, 1968, p. 261). In the health study discussed earlier in this chapter, the researchers were trying to determine whether patient or physician information had greater validity. Of course, if one knew the "true" score (e.g., that 69 is the true age of the man described above), there would be no need to worry about measurement error. Because there's no way to know for sure how accurate a measurement is, validity must be evaluated indirectly. Three forms for evaluating validity indirectly are identified: content validity, criterion validity, and construct validity (see Figure 4.5).

Content validity is a method of evaluating validity based on the judgment of researchers. If they judge that measurement procedures accurately measure the

Content validity	Validity assessment based on researcher's judgment.
Face validity	Type of content validity: Assessment of whether a specific indicator measures some part of the construct. Is the measure valid "on the face of it"?
Domain coverage	Type of content validity: Assessment of whether a collection of indicators measure all the content of the construct.
Criterion validity	Validity assessment based on prediction of a criterion or standard.
Construct validity	Validity assessment determined by whether a measure behaves as predicted by a theory.

FIGURE 4.5.   Types of Validity Assessment.

construct intended, then the procedures exhibit content validity. In the health study, the researchers decided that a general exam by a physician provides one way to measure the construct called "health." They also judged individual self-report health information measures health (or the opposite of health, morbidity).

Content validity includes two components: (1) face validity and (2) domain coverage. A single item (e.g., a survey question) has **face validity** when there is general agreement that the measure represents the underlying idea. For example, does a question like "How old were you on your last birthday?" have good face validity for measuring age? Yes, it appears to contain the definition of the concept. But a question such as, "How old is your mother?" doesn't provide information about the respondent. It is clear "on the face of it" that the second question doesn't measure the respondent's age. Usually face validity isn't easy to determine, however. Consider the definition of self-esteem (e.g., your beliefs about whether you are a person of worth, you do as well as others, etc.)

Domain coverage refers to how well the measurement procedures reflect the entire range (domain or dimensions) of content of the construct. A concept like "age" is unidimensional—it has one dimension or "size." In contrast, "math achievement" is multi-dimensional. It contains several specific skills. For third-graders, math skills probably include addition, subtraction, multiplication, and division. Therefore, addition questions on a third-grade math test exhibit face validity as addition is one third-grade math skill. But if the entire test contained only addition questions, it wouldn't be a valid measure of third-grade math achievement. The test wouldn't cover the full *domain* of content of what is meant by third-grade math achievement.

A concept like "health" is even more complex than third-grade math achievement. Each of the components of the physician exam and the ICD (*International Classification of Diseases*) have good face validity for the health researchers. But what if one of the components, for example, "cardiovascular disease," were omitted? The other measures would still have good face validity, but the collective measure of health would be missing an important component. That is, the measure wouldn't include the full range of what is meant by the concept called "health." Domain coverage of "health" is incomplete.

Content validity is the first line of defense against inaccurate measurement. Content validity generally is necessary, but not sufficient, to convince other scientists that you have a valid measure. For example, it is possible that respondents don't give accurate answers. When asked their age, adults tend to underreport it—perhaps until they reach their 100th birthday!

Criterion validity is a method for assessing validity based on whether a variable predicts a criterion (or standard). Again, age is an easy example. The criterion validity of a survey item asking respondents' age is the correlation between (1) their answers to the question and (2) the number of years between their last birthday and their birth date as given on birth certificates, for example.

If the variable used to assess criterion validity is measured at the same time as the variable being evaluated, the criterion validity is called "concurrent validity." Suppose you ask respondents how much they earn on their current or most recent job and then check employer records. The correlation between these two measures of earnings is an example of concurrent validity. If the criterion is measured at a later point in time than the variable being evaluated, the validity assessment is called "predictive validity." The health-study measures, for example, were evaluated by checking how accurately they predict mortality and self-reported morbidity at a later date than the time of the initial measurements.

Construct validity assesses the validity of a measure by checking to see whether it operates as predicted by theory. In the Ross–Broh (2000) study of personal control and self-esteem, these measures illustrate construct validity, though the researchers don't mention the term. Their measures do show relationships with other variables, as predicted by their theory. For example, personal control does predict academic achievement, but self-esteem does not. However, the strength of these relationships is modest, at best, so construct validity is not compelling in this instance.

Assessing Reliability

Reliability refers to consistency. A measure is reliable to the extent it yields the same answer each time it is used, in the absence of change in the true score. A measure can't be valid unless it is reliable, but a reliable measure is not necessarily valid. Usually it's easier to check reliability than validity. Reliability is measured by the test–retest method and by internal consistency.[4]

Test–retest reliability is evaluated by the correlation between the same measure observed at two time points, in the absence of change in the "true score" and the "absence of memory." This correlation is called the **reliability coefficient**. Suppose you measure the heights of students in Mr. Sponge's third-grade class at 9:00 A.M. and 2:30 P.M. on the same day. The correlation between the two measures should be nearly perfect (a "true score" for height, depending on precision of the measurements). It's pretty certain that the children's heights haven't changed in a few hours, and memory doesn't affect height. In contrast, suppose you ask

Mr. Sponge's students at 9:00 A.M. and 2:30 P.M. on the same day about the grade they think they'll get in math for the current 6 weeks. It would be hard to argue that the second measurement was done in the "absence of memory." And students' "true-score estimate" of their math grade might have changed, particularly if they took a math test between the two times they were asked to estimate their grades.

Internal consistency is the second way to measure reliability. Internal consistency means to compare more than one measurement of a construct when all the measurements were taken at the same time. The agreement of thermometer readings illustrates the idea of internal consistency. Not all thermometers give the same reading when placed together. In fact, they often vary by a degree or two, quite noticeable if you look at several cheap models on display in a store. If you really wanted to know the best estimate of the room temperature in the store, you could calculate the average of all the readings. We expect that this average reading would be more reliable, and its reliability coefficient higher, than the reading on a single thermometer.

Suppose there are several indicators of reliability (e.g., several correlations) among items used to measure a construct. In the Ross and Broh paper, for example, there are 21 correlations among the 7 items used to measure self-esteem. Each correlation is an indicator of reliability. Is there a single measure of internal consistency? Yes. **Cronbach's alpha** is based on all correlations among the items, and provides a minimum (lower-bound) estimate of the test–retest correlation, in the absence of change in the construct. Figure 4.6 summarizes the methods for evaluating reliability.[5]

Did you ever take an exam and think, "I might have had a higher score if the exam had included more questions?" You might be surprised to know you are more likely to be lucky on a ten-item quiz than on a 75-item exam. Of course, you might be unlucky as well. A quiz containing few questions is not as reliable as a test containing many. Reliability increases with the length of the test (number of items), everything else being equal.

Be sure to note the difference between validity and reliability: Validity = accuracy of measurement of the construct. Reliability = consistency. It's impossible to have highly valid measurements unless they are reliable. But it's easy to imagine highly reliable measurements that are not valid. A ruler used to measure the length of one's index finger is very reliable, and probably would be positively correlated with height, but it's obviously not a perfectly valid measure of height.

Test–Retest method:	Based on the correlation between the same variable measured at two (or more) different times.
Internal consistency:	Based on the correlations among two or more measures of the same construct taken at the same time.

FIGURE 4.6.   Methods for Evaluating Reliability.

THEORY, DATA ANALYSIS, AND MEASUREMENT

A study reported by Parcel and Menaghan (1994) illustrates some of the close connections between types of variables and theory. The study also provides intriguing findings about how the type of work a mother does influences her choice of child care.

Excerpt: Linking Theory and Measurement— *Mothers' Jobs and Child Care Arrangements*

As maternal employment has increased, so has research on the consequences for children of time spent in supplemental care arrangements. . . . It is likely that families with differing resources have children in differing types and quality of care, but few child care studies explore *whose* children are apt to experience better or worse arrangements. . . .

As Kohn's (1977) [theoretical] framework would suggest, mothers with more prestigious occupations . . . placed a lower value on conformity. . . . Parents in such occupational settings are also more likely to earn adequate incomes, which permits them to purchase higher-quality care. These findings suggest that higher-quality parental employment predicts higher-quality child care arrangements, at least among those who use formal care.

We argue that characteristics of employment such as wages and hours . . . and parental characteristics such as education, positive self-concept, and cognitive skills influence the quality and continuity of the supplemental care arrangements mothers make. . . . [W]e developed measures of type of care and location of care, as well as indicators of quality (child/adult ratio). . . . [W]e distinguished four types of care: formal group care in centers or schools, informal arrangements with relative caregivers, informal arrangements with nonrelative caregivers, and other arrangements. . . .

. . . [T]he children's care arrangements clearly vary with their mothers' cognitive and psychosocial resources and the characteristics of her employment. Mothers who have higher cognitive skills, higher educational attainment, and higher-paying work are more likely to make arrangements for care out of the home, both in the child's first 3 years and later. They are also more likely to have a nonrelative caregiver. Mothers with more positive self-concept are also more apt to use out-of-home care in the child's early years. . . . Associations with fathers' occupation and complexity are weak. . . . Rather than compensating for initial differences and disadvantages, nonmaternal care arrangements are apt to *reflect* other existing inequalities among families. (Parcel & Menaghan, 1994, pp. 179–191)

The primary hypothesis proposed by Parcel and Menaghan is that maternal job characteristics influence type of child care:

maternal job characteristics → *type of child-care arrangement*

Here, one of the independent variables, *maternal wage*, is a ratio scale; the dependent variable *type of child care arrangement* is a nominal scale. Maternal wage was measured by the mother's hourly wage at several predetermined time points, for example, when type of care was assessed at child's ages 1 and 3 years.[6]

Parcel and Menaghan cite research evidence presented by Kohn and others. Kohn and colleagues theorize that parental values about the importance of conformity versus creativity for their children is determined in part by how much autonomy the parents have on their jobs. Working-class jobs tend to be repetitive, with little room for variation. In contrast, middle-class jobs tend to require individual decision making and provide higher job autonomy. The theory is that repetitive jobs influence parents to emphasize conformity in their children, and job autonomy influences parents to value creativity over conformity. These ideas have received extensive development and testing by Kohn and his associates (Kohn, 1977; Kohn & Slomczynski, 1990).

After having read this chapter, you can appreciate that this line of research depends crucially on the definition and measurement of complex constructs like "job autonomy" and "child-rearing values"!

SUMMARY

This chapter outlines the process of turning abstract concepts such as self-esteem, health, and job autonomy into measurable variables. The first section includes an excerpt from a research study about self-esteem, personal control, and school grades. This study is used to illustrate many of the basic terms having to do with measurement, such as validity and reliability.

The type of variable determines the types of mathematical and statistical operations that are appropriate, and shapes how one formulates theory about the variables. Four types of measures generally are identified: nominal, ordinal, interval, and ratio variables. Nominal variables are defined by unordered categories like gender (male, female) or type of cheese (Colby, Swiss, cheddar, . . .). Ordinal variables are defined by categories, each of which is either greater than or less than each of the others, but ordinal variables contain no indication of how much their categories differ, for instance, first place, second place, third place in a race. An interval variable measures quantity, but has no natural zero, for example, the temperature scale. A ratio variable measures quantity, and the zero means the absence of some physical quantity, for example, annual earnings. Discrete and continuous variables are defined by whether their values can be represented by any point along a line. If the answer is no, the variable is discrete; if the answer is yes, it is continuous.

Validity refers to the accuracy with which a variable measures the construct it is intended to measure. Three forms of assessing validity are discussed: Content validity, criterion validity, and construct validity. Content validity depends on a judgment of whether a variable measures what it is designed to measure. Criterion validity is an assessment of validity based on how accurately a variable predicts a criterion. For example, how closely does self-reported wage match employer wage records? Construct validity is an assessment based on how closely a measure matches theoretical predictions about its relationship with other variables. For instance, does the measure of self-esteem predict grades in school, as theory indicates it should?

Reliability refers to consistency. An observed measure is reliable to the extent that it gives the same answer on repeated measurements, in the absence of change in the "true score" and in the absence of memory. Reliability is measured by the test–retest method and by internal consistency. Test–retest reliability is determined by the correlation between the same measurement taken at two different times, in the absence of change in the true score and in the absence of memory. Internal consistency is measured by the correlation between/among two or more variables designed to measure the same construct when all the variables are measured at the same time. Remember also: A valid measure necessarily is reliable, but a reliable measure is not necessarily valid.

The last section includes an excerpt from research about the relationship between mother's job type and child-care arrangements. The excerpt illustrates the close interdependence among measurement, theory, and analysis in social research.

YOUR REVIEW SHEET: QUESTIONS DISCUSSED IN THIS CHAPTER

1. In a few sentences of your own words, explain the term *team chemistry* to a 10-year-old. What do you conclude about our understanding of complex, yet familiar, terms?

2. Some often-used independent variables in social research include gender, age, race, and ethnicity (ethnic background). Identify the type, nominal—ordinal, interval, or ratio—for each of these variables.

3. A statement made in the chapter is: "We don't know whether we really measure self-esteem or personal control. However, the real question is: "Are the measurements useful?" How can usefulness of measures be determined?

4. What might one learn about room temperature in a store by looking at several thermometers? How is your answer related to the topic of measurement?

5. What is split-half reliability? Does *how* one splits the items in split-half reliability measurement affect the estimate of reliability? With what consequence? How does Cronbach's alpha improve on split-half estimates of reliability?

6. Write a short essay answer to the question: Why is it important to know the types of measures to be used in a research project?

7. Give an example of a variable that is a latent construct and one that is not.

8. "Even if we have assigned codes for race such as 1 = Asian, 2 = Black, 3 = Other, and 4 = White, we would not calculate a correlation between race and wage" using these numbers. In your own words and considering the meaning of these codes, explain why not.

9. Why should you be a little skeptical about procedures that claim to "measure" a complex idea such as self-esteem even if the researchers combine the answers to seven questions on a survey?

10. What happens to the correlation between two observed variables if they are measured with random error?

11. What are the numbers that are the minimum value and the maximum value of the product-moment correlation? What does a positive correlation indicate about the relationship between two variables? A negative correlation? Does a correlation of 0.60 indicate a stronger relationship than a correlation of -0.60? Explain your answer.

12. Illustrate each of the aspects of validation: content validity, face validity, domain coverage, criterion validity, and construct validity.

13. Does a question such as "How old were you on your last birthday?" have good face validity for measuring a respondent's age? Provide one question other than those discussed in the chapter that does not have good face validity, and briefly explain why not. Try to think of a realistic example.

14. Would using a 1-foot ruler to measure a 4-foot bookcase yield the same answer each time? What problems are likely to arise with the test–retest method in social research?

15. List two examples each of a nominal and an ordinal variable, other than examples mentioned in this chapter.

16. What is a "natural zero"? List at least one social or behavioral variable that has a natural zero and one that does not. Why is the distinction between a natural zero and no natural zero useful?

17. What is a continuous variable? Provide one example. Are all ratio scales continuous variables? Explain.

18. How are measures related to theory? How are types of measures related to type of data analysis? What is Borgatta and Bohrnstedt's argument on this issue?

STUDY TERMS

categories (of a variable) Classes of a variable; values of a nominal variable, for example, state of residence, with categories: Alabama, Alaska, . . . , Wisconsin, Wyoming.

concepts (or **constructs**) Variables not directly measurable; examples include prejudice, self-esteem, occupational status, and intelligence.

construct validity Method of evaluating validity by observing whether measurements of constructs exhibit relationships with other variables as predicted by theory.

content validity Method of evaluating validity that relies on researchers' judgments about whether procedures reflect the construct they are designed to measure.

continuous variable Variable whose values correspond to numbers that lie at any point along a straight line.

correlation (Pearson product-moment correlation) Number ranging from −1 to 1, which measures the degree of linear relationship between two variables. A correlation of 1.0 indicates a perfect positive linear relationship. A correlation of −1 indicates a perfect negative linear relationship; a negative relationship means that values of the variables change in opposite directions (one increases as the other decreases). A correlation of 0.0 indicates no linear relationship.

criterion validity Method for assessing validity by testing whether a variable predicts a criterion or standard. For example, does self-reported age predict the age calculated from one's birth certificate?

Cronbach's alpha Most general single measure of reliability based on internal consistency. It is calculated by using all of the two-variable correlations between scale items.

discrete variable Variable with a finite number of categories or whose categories correspond to whole numbers (compare with continuous variable).

domain coverage Degree to which a set of variables measures the entire range of content (domain) of a construct. A math test for third-graders should cover all the math operations they have learned, not just addition, for example.

face validity Judgment of researchers about whether a specific item measures at least part of the construct it is intended to measure. An addition test for third-graders measures skills in addition but not multiplication.

index (or **scale**) Variable defined by combining two or more other variables, usually by adding or averaging the values of the components (for each person or observation).

indicators Observable variables such as a survey question that partially measure complex, abstract concepts (constructs) such as "self-esteem" or "parental support."

internal consistency Comparing more than one measurement of a construct when all the measurements were taken at the same time.

interval variable A continuous variable whose values are numbers but which does not include a natural zero, such as the Fahrenheit temperature scale.

items Term used to refer to the individual components of an index.

measure (or **variable**) Operational version of a concept; an indicator (e.g., a survey question) with each response assigned a *unique* category or value.

measurement error Difference between an observed value and the "true" value of a variable.

negative relationship Relationship in which values of two variables move in opposite directions. As the value of one variable increases, the value of the other variable decreases, and vice versa.

nominal variable (categorical variable) Variable that classifies objects or elements into one and only one class or category; the classes simply are different (e.g., color).

observed score Value of a variable obtained through procedures such as personal interview or observed behaviors (compare with true score).

operationalization Process of converting abstract concepts (e.g., academic achievement, self-esteem) into measurable variables.

ordinal variable One type of categorical variable defined by a set of categories, each of which is either greater than or less than each of the other categories, but with no indication of the magnitude of the differences among the categories (e.g., agree–disagree questionnaire item).

positive relationship Relationship in which values of two variables move in the same direction. As the value of one variable increases, the value of the other variable also increases.

ratio variable Variable defined by values that are natural numbers *and* zero indicates the absence of some real-world quantity (e.g., wage).

reliability (consistency) The degree to which a measurement gives the same result each time it is used, in the absence of change in the true score and in the absence of memory.

test–retest reliability Correlation between the same measure observed at two time points, in the absence of change in the true score and the "absence of memory."

true score Correct value of a variable, for example, age = date of last birthday − date of birth on a birth certificate (compare with observed score).

validity Accuracy with which an observed variable measures the concept or construct it is designed to measure.

validity coefficient Correlation between the observed score and the true score.

variable Set of categories or numbers defined so that the categories are mutually exclusive (unique) and exhaustive. Each observation (e.g., person, object) fits into exactly one category, and all needed categories are included. An example is gender (two unique categories); other variables include race, age, and self-esteem.

END NOTES

1. In this excerpt, the authors do not indicate whether academic achievement has a positive or negative effect on self-esteem or personal control. Neither do they indicate the direction of any of the other effects. But it is fairly clear from the context that all are positive relationships (e.g., as academic achievement goes up, so does self-esteem). It's a good practice to state the direction of effects when summarizing relationships, even when it is fairly evident from the context.

2. If none of the components of the index are missing, the difference between a summed index and an averaged index is trivial. But if a respondent skipped some of the items comprising the index, then the difference isn't trivial. Adding together the nonmissing components is equivalent to setting the missing values to zero, but averaging the nonmissing components is equivalent to setting the missing items to the *mean of the nonmissing items*. Clearly, the average is more sensible in most instances of missing items. If you prefer the metric of a sum, you can multiply the average by the number of items comprising the index.

3. In practice, numbers (e.g., 1 through 4) usually are assigned to agree–disagree responses, and the results treated as if they were numbers, as in the study of self-esteem, personal control, and high-school grades by Ross and Broh (2000). Purists often object strenuously to this practice, but Borgatta and Bohrnstedt (1980) defend it. Perhaps what's important is whether something useful emerges from assigning numbers to ordinal variable categories. One useful outcome might be a stimulus to develop better measurements.

4. Measurement theory first developed in areas of intelligence and knowledge testing, so a combined score was called a "test." This terminology sometimes carries over into attitude measurement, so that the term *test* sometimes includes both knowledge tests and attitude assessments.

5. Initially, the *split-half method* was used to assess the internal consistency of a scale. The split-half procedure divides the items into two parts, calculates an index from each half, and then calculates the correlation between the two indexes. But this correlation is too small, since each half of the test is only half as long as the total test. Also, how one splits the items affects the split-half estimate of reliability. This is why the split-half method seldom is used today. Cronbach's alpha is a much better measure of reliability, since it is based on all the correlations between items in each pair of variables, and is equivalent to combining all the split halves.

The correlation between the two halves is used as a basis for estimating the reliability of the complete scale, using a formula called the "Spearman–Brown prophecy formula." This is an estimate of the reliability of an index composed of all the items. The formula is:

$$\text{reliability} = 2r_{12}/(1 + r_{12}),$$

where r_{12} designates the correlation between the two halves of the test, labeled 1 and 2.

6. Parcel and Menaghan wanted a statistical analysis that would assess how increasing maternal wage affects the *probability* of each of the types of child care. This is a different type of analysis than an analysis to check whether a variable affects the *actual value* of the outcome, such as race affecting wages, and it requires a different type of statistical method.

EXERCISES

Exercise 4.1. Specifying Variables

Directions: Choose three variables that are not discussed in this chapter, one nominal, one ordinal, and one interval or ratio. Provide the following information for each: (1) a variable name; (2) categories or values for the variable; (3) level of measurement, with a brief explanation; (4) a short explanation why the variable satisfies the definition of a variable; and (5) a way to operationalize the variable (an indicator and its values).

> **Example:**
>
> | | |
> |---|---|
> | Variable name: | gender |
> | Categories: | male, female. |
> | Level of measurement: | nominal scale, because females and males are different. No operation is sensible except a test for equality—Are two people the same gender or different? |
> | Explanation: | Each observation can be classified into only one category, and there is a category for everyone to be studied. |
> | Indicator: | Are you male or female? (Survey question, categories 0–1) |

Exercise 4.2. Developing Hypotheses

Directions: In your own words, provide the requested information. Review relevant chapter sections first.

1. List as many categories as you think are needed for a variable called "type of religion" (religious denomination). Be sure to meet the two criteria for a properly defined variable (mutually exclusive and exhaustive categories).

2. Construct a hypothesis stating a relationship between "type of religion" (e.g., Roman Catholic, Jewish) and one other variable. Religion can be either the independent or dependent variable. Circle your independent variable and underline your dependent variable. Then, select a population to which your hypothesis applies.

3. Construct a second hypothesis of a relationship in which the categories of "type of religion" might have to be different from those for your original hypothesis. Again, identify your independent and dependent variables, and a population to which your hypothesis applies.

4. Define an ordinal, interval, or ratio variable about some aspect of religion. Propose a hypothesis, identify the dependent and independent variables, and specify a population.

Exercise 4.3. Evaluation of Research: Linking Theory and Measurement

Directions: Refer to the discussion on "child care arrangements" in this chapter to answer the following questions.

Factual Questions

1. State the research hypothesis.

2. Identify the dependent variable. What is the level of measurement (nominal, ordinal, interval, ratio)? In your own words, explain the justification for this level of measurement, referring to the researchers' specific use of this variable.

3. Identify the independent variable(s). How is each measured?

Questions for Discussion

1. Based on the findings, briefly suggest one topic for future research (if needed, modify the theoretical framework). Offer a research hypothesis for your topic.

5

DESIGNING SOCIAL RESEARCH

INTRODUCTION: LOOKING AT HOW THE SOCIAL WORLD WORKS

"He lives with only one parent. That's why he keeps getting in trouble with the law."

"She's pregnant? No surprise—her parents got a divorce and both immediately remarried."

"The twins' stepfather mercilessly picks on them. Both the boy and the girl have threatened to run away from home more than once."

Do nonintact homes "cause" these disadvantages, or are these disadvantages coincidental? Painter and Levine (2000) report:

[O]n average, youths living with a single mother are roughly twice as likely as other youths to drop out of high school, become pregnant, and be arrested. Moreover, most studies find that youth living with a biological mother and a stepfather are almost as disadvantaged. (Painter & Levine, 2000, p. 524)

However, Painter and Levine also quote Charles Manski and his coauthors on this subject:

It may be, as the [cross-sectional] empirical evidence suggests, living in a nonintact family has adverse consequences for children. On the other hand, it may be that some unobserved process jointly determines family structure and children's outcomes. For example, parents who are less committed to their family may be more likely to divorce and may also provide less support for their children. Behavioral and/or medical problems such as alcoholism, depression, or drug addiction may make a person more likely to divorce and less effective as a parent. (Manski et al., 1992, p. 25. Quoted in Painter & Levine, 2000, pp. 524–525).[1]

The Manski quotation is a good example of why control of alternative explanations is necessary when attempting to establish a cause-and-effect relationship. Determining the effect of family structure on children is not a simple matter—there are many possible explanations for the observation that children from "broken homes" fare poorly.

Controlled experiments (using physical controls) generally are thought to set the standard for **causal inference**. Causal inference is a conclusion that an observed relationship is due to the effect of the independent variable on the dependent variable. Using **physical controls** in an experiment, the researcher determines what is changed, by how much, and what is not changed (kept constant). An **experiment** is a process whereby a person changes at least one variable and watches to see what happens to one or more of the other variables. For example, substitute a low-calorie sweetener for sugar in a recipe for peanut-butter cookies, and compare that taste with the taste of cookies made with sugar. In the cookie baking experiment, what is controlled? All the ingredients, the temperature of the oven, and the length of time the cookies bake.

In sharp contrast to the process of baking cookies, however, no one knows the "complete recipe" for determining the outcome of nearly all social experiments. Consequently, it is impossible to control all causes. How, then, can one identify a cause-and-effect relationship in social research if many alternative explanations are possible?

The short answer is: use random assignment to different treatments. In an experiment, the independent variable is called a **treatment** variable, and the dependent variable is the outcome of the experiment. **Random assignment** means that each subject is assigned at random to levels (categories) of the treatment variable.

In the simplest experiment, there are just two levels—an experimental treatment and a control; the treatment variable is *defined* by these two levels. Subjects are assigned to one of two alternatives: an **experimental group** or the **control group** using a "pure chance" method. The experimental group receives some type of "treatment," like a drug, and the control group gets no treatment; the control group (absent of treatment effects) is included simply for comparison.

Random assignment is an ingenious device, but as we'll see, it's definitely not a cure-all for finding cause-and-effect relationships. Nonetheless, it does set a very useful standard.

Goals of This Chapter

A major goal of this chapter is to examine the reasoning underlying experiments and to evaluate many threats to drawing valid conclusions about cause and effect.

Several "contrived" and real-world examples are considered first. The chapter then gives a systematic summary of the standards of experimental design, including some of the basic types of experimental and related nonexperimental designs. The review emphasizes both the power of randomized experiments and their very substantial limitations.

THREE EXAMPLES: ONE CONTRIVED, TWO REAL

A Contrived Little Experiment

Suppose you decided to conduct an informal cookie experiment with a handful of people to find a low-calorie cookie people actually will buy. How likely are you to be successful? Probably not very likely, partly because you (like everyone else) don't understand all the factors that influence people's personal tastes. You just know that different people have different taste preferences. Consequently, it isn't possible to control every variable that might influence people's preferences for the cookies.

Suppose, however, that the cookie experiment is laid out as shown in Figure 5.1. What does the experimenter physically control in this example? The only difference between the two recipes is whether they contain sugar or (nonsugar) sweetener, and that is what the experimenter controls. "Sugar" and "other sweetener" are the two categories of the **treatment variable** for this experiment. Neither category is called "control" in this instance.

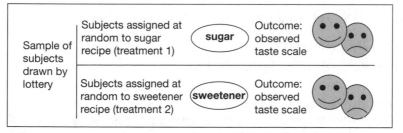

FIGURE 5.1.   Cookie Experiment.

Since you can't control subjects' preferences for the cookies, random assignment to sugar and sweetener groups is critical. To consider how critical, suppose you allow the subjects to decide for themselves which type of cookie to eat. What do you think might happen? One possibility is that a high percentage of "cookie lovers" choose sugar-baked cookies, thereby skewing the results against the sweetener-baked cookies.

The remarkable aspect of random assignment is that no systematic process puts people who are extra fond of cookies into one group or the other. Therefore, within the limits of sampling variation, random assignment eliminates all competing explanations for average differences among the treatments, *except* for the explanation that the treatment does affect the outcome.

Stop for a moment to absorb this point. It's really quite remarkable that random assignment can eliminate the effects of all other independent variables except the treatment.

The taste-scale response is the dependent variable (outcome). Suppose the outcome is a 10-point rating scale, such as in the following question, which is asked of all subjects:

On a scale from 1 to 10 please rate how much you liked the cookies. (Circle 1)

Don't like   *Like*

1   2   3   4   5   6   7   8   9   10

Further, imagine the average of the ratings for people who ate the cookies with sugar is 8.1, and the average of the ratings of people who ate the cookies with sweetener is 7.7. Statistical tests based on probability can be used to decide whether the difference of 0.4 (8.1 − 7.7) is due to the difference between the sugar recipe and the sweetener recipe (the treatment variable), or just due to random variation in individual tastes.

Why use statistical tests when you used random assignment, if the random procedure eliminates the effects of all other independent variables but the treatment? Because "the luck of the draw" might have assigned "sweetener-haters" to the sweetener group, or to the sugar group. Increasing the sample size can reduce this random error to nearly zero, but in most experiments there is a practical limit to the sample size. Chapter 11 introduces you to statistical tests.[2]

A Field Experiment: Does Having a Job Reduce Crime?

Christopher Uggen (2000) reports an intriguing field experiment about the influence of employment on criminal behavior.

> Sociologists have increasingly emphasized "turning points" in explaining behavioral change over the life course. Is work a turning point in the life course of criminal offenders? If criminals are provided with jobs, are they likely to stop committing crimes? (Uggen, 2000, p. 529)

Many studies of criminal behavior show people with jobs commit fewer crimes. But the interpretation of this relationship is far from settled.

> Taken together, existing theory and research point to a complex and perhaps conditional relation between work and criminal behavior. Whether this relation is causal remains unresolved, as does the direction of causality. (Uggen, 2000, p. 530)

Uggen, citing Rubin (1974) and Winship and Mare (1992) concludes:

> Experiments on the effect of employment on crime convert uncontrolled variation in personal criminal propensities into random variation. . . . (Rubin 1974) Therefore, designs that randomly assign people to work and nonwork statuses are preferred over nonexperimental designs, especially when a convincing model of selection into employment is unavailable. (Winship and Mare 1992, as quoted in Uggen, 2000, p. 531)

What are they saying? They are saying that maybe a lifetime of experiences determines both whether a man is inclined to be a criminal *and* whether he is inclined to get a job, thus generating a *spurious* negative relationship between working and crime. What's one possible alternative explanation (confounding variable), one that might determine *both* having a job *and* not committing a crime? Religious upbringing might be one. Being reared in a high-crime neighborhood might be another.

Uggen analyzes data from a nationally funded field experiment called "The National Supported Work Demonstration Project." This project was conducted on a sample of more than 3000 men whose work and arrest history was traced during the period from March 1975 until July 1977. The sample was selected from men with an official arrest history.

Each member of the sample was assigned at random to either (1) a <u>treatment group</u>, with subsidized employment, or (2) a <u>control group</u>, with no jobs (no subsidized employment). As noted in the cookie experiment, the terms *treatment group* and *control group* are used generally to distinguish between subjects who are given a special treatment of some sort (the treatment group) from the control group—those who are given no special treatment or sometimes a **placebo** (a nonreactive agent such as the sugar pill given in medical research).

During the study Uggen compared the arrest history of men in the treatment group with the arrest history of men in the control group. He split the sample into two age groups: those 26 years old or younger, and those over 26. He found that older men who hold a job are less likely to be re-arrested than older men who don't hold a job. *But* this association is absent for younger men. In this example, the variable *age* specifies for whom the job–crime relationship operates—only for older men, as shown in Figure 5.2.

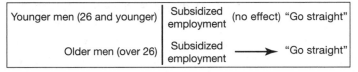

FIGURE 5.2.   Field Experiment Showing the Importance of Controlling for Age.

Had Uggen not split the sample by age, what would he probably have concluded? Differences between arrest rates of those in the treatment and control groups would be averages of "no effect" in the younger group and the "fairly strong effect" in the older group. As a result, the effect estimated from the combined age groups may or may not have been detected, but even if detected probably would have been judged relatively unimportant.

Uggen includes statistical controls for three other possible causes of committing a crime that could not be controlled by random assignment—dropping out of the program, participation in unsubsidized work, and currently attending school.

Uggen's findings illustrate a noteworthy point: Experiments are not automatic finders of cause and effect. Even if it isn't necessary to know every cause of an outcome, such as when using random assignment, the experimenter must know a great deal about a topic before an effective experiment is conducted. In Uggen's study, much previous theory and research suggested that he divide the sample by age.

In a long-running experiment like this one, events that affect the outcome may occur after the beginning of the experiment. In Uggen's case, dropping out of the treatment, getting a job outside the supported work, and attending school all are uncontrolled by random assignment, because some subjects made these choices *after* the experiment began, *and* all three activities likely affect whether subjects commit another crime.

A Nonexperimental Study: Do Schools Determine Sexual Norms?

An intriguing study reported by Teitler and Weiss (2000) attempts to determine whether school and community affect the sexual practices of high-school students. The findings show once again why the concept of control is so important:

> Despite the general trend toward a declining age of onset of sexual intercourse, there are still wide variations in the timing of sexual initiation by race and gender. . . . These variations suggest that there is no single, uniform youth culture regulating youths' sexual transitions; rather, youths are being influenced by norms of behavior specific to subgroups. Youths interact with peers and adults in a number of contexts that influence how long they postpone sexual relationships.
>
> One social context that has received considerable attention recently . . . is the neighborhood. . . . [S]chools may also be expected to exert an influence on youths' behavior. (Teitler & Weiss, 2000, pp. 112–113)

The authors wanted to find out whether community and school norms influence the age of first sexual intercourse. They used census tracts to define the boundaries of the neighborhood. The initial questions were whether there are any differences in the age of first coitus among communities and among schools, due to differing normative climates among the schools and communities or to other factors.

The authors do find substantial differences among census tracts and among schools in youths' answers to the question:

"Have you ever had intercourse with someone of the opposite sex?"

The differences among the schools are much larger than the differences among the census tracts, however. And when the variables representing school and census tract (community) for each person are evaluated simultaneously, only the school differences remain—school attended seems to influence age of sexual initiation.

These are interesting findings, but do they support the conclusion that school sexual norms *affect* the timing of first coitus? Without more information, this conclusion is problematic. Before reading further, write down at least one variable other than school norms that might account for school differences in age of first sexual intercourse.

Maybe school differences are due to age, gender, or race of students, because these variables directly affect sexual conduct. Since the sample consists of about 1200 youths attending 70 schools, the percentage of students in the sample who are female (or male) and the age composition of the sample may differ among the schools. For example, would a higher percentage of younger or older students suggest the potential for a higher level of sexual activity?

The authors applied statistical controls for age, gender, and race. They found that school differences persist when age and gender are controlled, but nearly vanish when race is controlled. This result suggests that school differences in the timing of sexual initiation primarily are due to race; school norms may not be important after all. It's also possible that racial differences among schools generate normative differences that account for school differences in the timing of first sexual intercourse. Teitler and Weiss check for this possibility, but don't find supporting evidence for it.

"What If . . .?": A Controlled Experiment of Schools and First Coitus

What if the study of schools and first coitus were a controlled experiment—one with random assignment to schools, rather than (or in addition to) the statistical controls used by Teitler and Weiss?

First, suppose students were assigned to schools by a fair lottery. In this case, it wouldn't be necessary to include statistical controls for age, gender, or race or any variables. This is because with random assignment to schools for all students, gender, race, and age composition would be nearly the same in all the schools at the beginning of the study. Consequently, differences among schools in age at first coitus is unlikely to be due to any of these variables.

Equally important, even unknown factors (e.g., home environment, religious beliefs, etc.) that might account for differences in the age of first intercourse are "controlled" by the lottery; therefore, the only variable influencing school assignment is a random one: the lottery. Each student in the experiment is assigned to a school by "pure chance" strategy, not by the parents/guardians, the students, the school staff, or even the researcher. In this example, the "treatment" variable is schools, used here as an indicator of school norms.

Again, random assignment doesn't guarantee that the sample averages and percentages are exactly the same in each school. Rather, random assignment ensures that differences among schools on all variables—both known and unknown—are due to a purely random mechanism. This feature permits statistical tests based on probabilities, and statistical tests are powerful checks. In natural settings, it's impossible to know all the ways subjects differ in different settings, such as schools. There are always many possible explanations for observed relationships between school and variables like age at first coitus.

Yet, random assignment is not a very effective way to study the effect of school norms on sexual activity. In fact, in everyday life it wouldn't work at all. Why not? Probably the most important reason is that the study could never be conducted. Political and ethical pressures obviously would prevent random assignment to schools, particularly if the goal is to study sexual behavior. Still, we can learn quite a bit by suspending political and ethical concerns for a moment.

Even if random assignment were possible, however, it wouldn't yield credible evidence about the effect of school norms on student sexual behavior. Why not? If all students were assigned to schools by lottery, and the survey of sexual practices is conducted soon after the school assignments are made, finding "no differences in sexual behavior" is practically assured. However, the longer the elapsed time between the school assignments and the survey, the more likely it is differences *will* be observed. School norms likely would shift over an extended time, but changes in variables other than school norms also are nearly certain, and some of these variables might affect sexual practices. For example, drug use might develop in some of the schools. This might generate school differences in sexual behavior that are related to drug use, not school norms about sex per se. It might also generate changes in *both* norms and behavior, so that the observed relationship between school sexual norms and individual sexual behavior might be spurious—both school sexual norms and individual sexual behavior are due to drug use.

Some of these difficulties could be avoided if only a small sample of youths were assigned at random to existing schools. But the problems of uncontrolled changes during the period of observation remain, no matter how the assignments are done.

What, then, is to be learned about experiments from this fictitious experiment? One point is that there are serious real-world limitations on the use of experiments for social research. That school norms likely change throughout the study illustrates that it might not always be possible to design a convincing experiment, even with no ethical or political barriers to conducting it. Observational analysis, a qualitative data collection method discussed in Chapter 6, might be a better approach to studying school norms and sexual behavior than an experiment or a statistical study. Combining a qualitative approach with nonexperimental statistical analysis might be the best approach of all.

RESEARCH DESIGNS AND THREATS TO VALID INFERENCE

Basic Concepts

As the studies presented above illustrate, experimental design uses a special vocabulary. But sometimes the interchange of terms such as *treatment, control, treatment variable, independent variable, outcome, outcome variable*, and *dependent variable* can be confusing. So let's review the definitions of these terms.

First, recall that the phrase *treatment variable* often is a synonym for *independent variable*. In experiments, the treatment variable is manipulated by the researcher and is the presumed cause. *Outcome* or *outcome variable* often is a synonym for *dependent variable* in an experiment.

The simplest treatment variable has two values or categories, frequently called "treatment" and "control." Subjects assigned to receive the treatment often are designated the "treatment group" or "experimental group," and those assigned to the control are designated the "control group."

Uses of term "treatment"	Uses of term "control"

• as the independent (treatment) variable
• as a category of independent variable
  (*treatment* and control)
• a group of subjects
  (treatment group)
	• as a category of independent variable
	  (treatment and *control*)
	• a group of subjects
	  (control group)

FIGURE 5.3.   Uses of *Treatment* and *Control* in Experimental Research.

So, the word *treatment* is used in multiple ways: (1) as part of a phrase meaning "independent variable" (treatment *variable*), (2) as a label for one category of the independent variable ("treatment"), and (3) to identify subjects assigned to the treatment category (treatment *group*). Similarly, the word *control* is used to (1) designate one category of the treatment variable ("control"), and to (2) identify subjects assigned to the control category (control group) (see Figure 5.3).

When the treatment variable consists of just a treatment and a control, it's a *dichotomous variable*—a variable with just two values or categories. (The terms *value, level*, or *category* often are used interchangeably; all three refer to one category of a variable.) The treatment variable often contains more than two categories. These categories may be labeled treatment 1, treatment 2, and so on. Also, there may be two or more treatments, plus a control—for example, aspirin, buffered aspirin, ibuprofen, and a sugar pill.

The cookie experiment makes a good springboard for summarizing the basic strengths of experiments with random assignment, but notice that there are two uses of a random process.

The first random process is **random** *selection*. Subjects were selected from the population using a lottery, but any random process could be used. The second random process is **random** *assignment*. *After subjects are selected*, they are assigned at random to one of the two experimental groups—sugar or sweetener cookies. Since cookies baked with sugar are standard, the sweetener group might be designated the treatment group and the sugar group the control group.

Random selection eliminates bias in generalizing results obtained from the subjects in the experiment to the population from which the subjects were drawn. Random selection does not eliminate all differences between a sample and the corresponding population. Using random selection just means there is no tendency to overestimate or underestimate the results for the population from which the sample was taken. That is what is meant by the term *unbiased*. For example, a study of sugar–sweetener preferences using a sample of sixth-graders is not a random sample of the adult population, and it might produce biased estimates of how adults react.

Random assignment eliminates bias in estimating the difference between the two treatments. That is, observed differences are due to differences between sugar and sweetener and random variation, nothing else.

The difference between random selection and random assignment is closely related to two important concepts: **external validity** and **internal validity**. In a classic work about experiments, Campbell and Stanley (1963) define external validity as follows:

> External validity asks the question of generalizability: To what populations, settings, treatment variables, and measurement variables can this effect be generalized? (p. 5)

They define internal validity using these words:

> Internal validity is the basic minimum without which any experiment is uninterpretable: Did in fact the experimental treatments make a difference in this specific experimental instance? (p. 5)

Random selection is for external validity, and random assignment is for internal validity. Figure 5.4 summarizes the differences between these two random processes.

Random Selection
- Eliminates bias generalizing from sample to population
- Support **external validity**

Random Assignment
- Eliminates bias estimating differences among treatments
- Supports **internal validity**

FIGURE 5.4.   Comparison of Random Selection with Random Assignment.

Five Basic Designs

Campbell and Stanley (1963) define their preferred design to be an experiment that includes (1) a pretest to measure the dependent variable (outcome) before the treatment is administered, (2) random assignment to treatment and control groups and (3) a posttest, a second measurement of the dependent variable. They present a handy diagram for what they call the **classical experimental design**, which is sketched in Figure 5.5. The symbols in Figure 5.5 are:

	Pretest	Treatment	Posttest
Classical experiment: Pretest-posttest control-group design	R $\quad O_1$	X	O_2
	R $\quad O_3$		O_4

FIGURE 5.5.   Classical Experimental Design.

R denotes random assignment

X denotes treatment; its absence stands for no treatment (control)

O denotes observation, meaning some type of measurement of the outcome variable (e.g., the cookie-rating scale)

O_1 denotes "pretest measurement for the experimental group"

O_2 denotes "posttest measurement for the experimental group"

O_3 denotes "pretest measurement for the control group"

O_4 denotes "posttest measurement for the control group."

What is the goal of this experimental design? Look again at Figure 5.5 before reading further.

The goal is to compare pretest–posttest changes in the outcome for the treatment group $(O_2 - O_1)$ to changes for the control group $(O_4 - O_3)$. In the cookie experiment, the classical design requires feeding everyone cookies twice. Both the control group and the treatment group get sugar-baked cookies for the pretest (time 1), then the initial taste-rating measurements (O_1 and O_3) are taken for both groups. Between the pretest and the posttest, the treatment group gets sweetener-baked cookies, and the control group again gets the standard sugar-baked cookies. Then the taste ratings are done again—O_2 and O_4 (posttest) are taken.

Generally, comparisons are done with averages (or percentages) calculated for each of the groups. In the usual notation, a sample average is indicated by an "overbar." So the change in the average for the experimental group is

$$\overline{O}_2 - \overline{O}_1,$$

and the change in average for the control group is

$$\overline{O}_4 - \overline{O}_3.$$

The experimental research question is

Did the treatment-group mean (average) change more than the control-group mean?[3]

Note: At the pretest, the average ratings for the experimental group should about equal the average rating for the control group:

$$\overline{O}_1 - \overline{O}_3 . \cong 0.$$

"How close to equal" the two pretest averages are at the beginning of an experiment depends on random (natural) variation in the subjects, and random variation is reduced as the number of subjects in the study increases.

The expectation that the pretest (time 1) averages are the same leads to a very interesting conclusion:

> *With random assignment, the difference between the posttest means is a good estimate of the difference in change from pretest to posttest.*

Have you noticed that the original cookie experiment differs from the classical experimental design? Look back to the "contrived little experiment" section to see how it differs before reading further.

No pretest was mentioned in the original statement. In the language of Campbell and Stanley, the original cookie example is the **posttest-only control-group design**. Figure 5.6 illustrates this design.

			Posttest
Posttest-only control-group design:	R	X	O_1
	R		O_2

FIGURE 5.6. Posttest-Only Control-Group Design.

For the cookie experiment, the posttest-only design may be quite a bit better than the classical experiment. Considering that the subjects are eating cookies, can you think of one reason why?

Here are two reasons. First, subjects sample cookies for the pretest and rate them. This experience could alter their posttest ratings. For example, completing the ratings may sensitize subjects to pay closer attention to the taste of the cookies at the posttest than they otherwise would. Second, tasting cookies twice may affect the sensitivity of the subjects' tastes.

Since the pretest average ratings should be about the same for treatment and control groups, the posttest-only design is nearly as good as the classical design. In many circumstances, as in the cookie experiment, it may be better.

In all, Campbell and Stanley describe 16 experimental designs. In addition to the two already discussed, three are important in social research: the **static-group comparison**, the **one-group pretest–posttest**, and the **one-shot case study** designs.

Probably the most often-used design is not really an experiment at all. It's a comparison between naturally occurring groups, as indicated in the sketch in Figure 5.7.

			Posttest
Static group comparison:	—	X	O_1
	—		O_2

FIGURE 5.7. Static Group Comparison Design.

Notice that this design looks like the posttest-only design—but what's missing?

R is absent; the dashed line "—" indicates no random assignment. Here, the idea is to compare natural groups that are present in everyday life. For example, you might compare the highway speed of farmers to the speed of other drivers; the "natural groups" are farmers and nonfarmers. Other natural groups might be males and females, blondes and nonblondes, and so forth. The natural groups take the place of treatment group and control group.

The one-group pretest–posttest comparison is laid out in Figure 5.8. What is different in the design of Figure 5.8 from the previous designs?

	Pretest		Posttest
One-group pretest-posttest design:	O_1	X	O_2

FIGURE 5.8.   One-group Pretest-Posttest Design.

The one-group pretest–posttest design has no control group *and* no comparison group. Therefore, random assignment can't be used—random assignment to what? In this design, the researcher observes change after an event occurs. The event may be a treatment administered by the researcher as in the cookie experiment, or a naturally occurring event. For example, one could compare the speed of automobiles one mile before a speed trap and one mile after the speed trap. In this case, the speed trap is the treatment, or *X*.

The third and most basic experimental design consists of a single measurement made after an event has occurred or a treatment administered. Campbell and Stanley call it a "one-shot case study." Figure 5.9 illustrates the one-shot case study.

	Posttest
One-shot case study:	X O

FIGURE 5.9.   One-shot Case Study Design.

They judge this design to be more or less useless. For example, measure the speed of drivers one mile after the speed trap. The average obtained is 55 MPH, exactly the speed limit. Did the speed trap slow drivers down? There's no way to know for sure. No measure of speed was taken *before* the speed trap. But most of us might suspect it did, because we think most drivers exceed the speed limit most of the time. So the value of the one-shot case study experimental design in this example depends on what we know informally about the topic. However, in the case of the speed trap, without knowing more about weather, road conditions, and other factors affecting speed, it would be risky to draw any more than very cautious conclusions.

Remember that in Chapter 1 we emphasized the importance of comparison. The one-shot case study design helps to bring out this point again: A critical aspect of nearly all research—whether it is an experimental survey or observational study—is that some implicit comparison nearly always is involved. Even when the comparison is not formally laid out, comparisons nonetheless are implicit. In the "speed trap" example, what can be compared? Informal comparisons can be made between the observations of driving behavior in the study and knowledge about driving behavior from other sources.

Consider another example, discussed in more detail in Chapter 6.

> Paradoxically, Hurricane Andrew also brought new opportunities to some women. . . . We learned, for example, of women earning equitable construction wages, developing new employment skills, and using relief monies to leave violent relationships. . . . (Morrow and Enarson 1996).

What comparison groups are implied here? There's no explicit reference to any comparison group, but the implied comparisons are between ordinary circumstances and disaster circumstances brought on by a hurricane. The "treatment" is the hurricane, and the "control" is the absence of a hurricane. Three outcomes are mentioned: (1) wage, (2) job skills, and (3) escape from violent relationships. So there are three outcomes measured instead of just one, as shown in the Campbell–Stanley design sketches.

Comparing "ordinary" and "disaster" circumstances, the implications are that some women earn higher wages, learn different job skills, and more readily escape from abusive situations in the wake of a natural disaster than they otherwise would. Abundant research exists about women's wages, job skills, and ability to escape abuse in ordinary circumstances, and findings from this body of research serve as an informal base of comparisons.

Of course, a second comparison also is implied—between men and women and how they differ in ordinary times versus how they differ in disaster times. From the excerpt, however, it is not possible to determine women's frequency of success in disaster times on the three outcomes. Therefore, the end result is some interesting hypotheses that likely never would have surfaced except by qualitative methods and implicit comparisons.

As with the differences between "everyday learning" and "science learning," experimental and nonexperimental designs should not be put into separate mental compartments. Both are subject to the same rules about (1) internal validity (cause-and-effect inference), and (2) external validity, or generalizing the results from a sample to a population.

THREATS TO VALID CAUSAL INFERENCE

Campbell and Stanley (1963) identify 12 much-cited threats to valid **causal inference**—drawing sound conclusions from research results. These threats are divided into the two types of validity: (1) eight threats are to internal validity and (2) four threats are to external validity.

Be sure to notice the term *validity* doesn't mean the same thing here as it does when applied to measurement. Chapter 4 refers to valid *measurement*—meaning "accurate measurement of the variable one intends to measure." This chapter is about valid inference—drawing correct conclusions from research.

Threats to Internal Validity

Many factors threaten the internal validity of research when random assignment is absent. Table 5.1 summarizes the threats to internal validity identified by Campbell and Stanley. The table classifies the many ways we can be fooled into thinking a treatment had an effect on the outcome when, in fact, it didn't. Each threat is discussed in the paragraphs that follow.

TABLE 5.1.   Threats to Internal Validity (Valid Cause-and-Effect Conclusions).

1. Selection	Subjects choose to be in the treatment or control group. Measured differences between the treatment and control-group outcomes due to subject preferences are mistaken for a difference due to the treatment.
2. Mortality	Some subjects do not complete the study. Therefore, there is no posttest measure for them. Measured differences between the treatment and control group due to differential dropout are mistaken for a treatment effect.
3. History	A natural event occurs between pretest and posttest. Its effect on the outcome is mistaken for the effect of the treatment.
4. Maturation	Subjects change due to natural growth/decline. The natural change is mistaken for an effect of the treatment.
5. Testing	The pretest affects measurements at the posttest. The difference between pretest and posttest generated by testing is mistaken for an effect of the treatment.
6. Instrumentation	Calibration of the measuring device (instrument) changes between pretest and posttest. The resulting difference between pretest and posttest observations is mistaken for an effect of the treatment.
7. Regression	Subjects selected from one or the other extremes of the distribution of scores for the outcome variable gravitate naturally toward the middle. This natural result of selecting from one extreme is mistaken for an effect of the treatment.
8. Interaction of selection and history, maturation, testing, or instrumentation	Treatment and control groups react differently to history, maturation, testing, or instrumentation. The difference in the posttest measure due to differential reaction is mistaken for a treatment effect.

Selection. Most social research is done using the static-group-comparison design. Recall that the static-group design uses comparisons among naturally occurring groups—with no random assignment.

The most frequent source of a false or spurious relationship is a mechanism called "selection." **Selection** occurs when subjects select (choose) to be in the "treatment" or "control group," or otherwise are selected by a nonrandom process. Consequently, outcome differences between the treatment and control groups due to selection are likely to be mistaken for a difference due to the treatment. Again, recall the spurious relationship between wearing a beard and wearing a dress, which is due to a common influence of gender on both beards and dresses. The idea generalizes as shown in Figure 5.10.

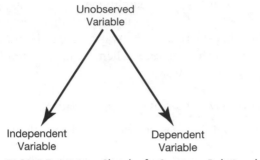

FIGURE 5.10. Sketch of a Spurious Relationship.

The Uggen study about the effect of employment on re-arrest, cited earlier in this chapter, shows how selection might work. Without random assignment, the men might choose to work (select themselves into jobs) and decide not to be criminals for reasons unrelated to the research question of whether employment influences committing crimes. This possible confusion of the effect of selection with the effect of working is part of Uggen's argument for the strength of his data, because respondents were *assigned at random* to a supported work program or to the control group.

Selection doesn't always refer to deliberate choices made by subjects—it just means some selection process other than a random one is occurring. For example, a person who is hostile at work might be more likely to commit a crime and get fired than a mild-mannered person; in this example, hostile behavior is related to both crime and unemployment. When random assignment isn't possible, as in most research, statistical controls are essential. Chapter 11 introduces basic ideas in statistical control.

Note still other uses of the word "control": (1) as one category of the treatment variable (e.g., a sugar pill in drug research); and (2) in statistical analysis, controlling for (holding constant) one variable while examining the relationship between two other variables, for example, controlling for gender by looking at the relationship between height and hair length separately for women and men.

Mortality. Mortality (not necessarily from physical death) means that the rate of dropping out of a study differs among the treatments; the differential dropout rate is mistaken for a treatment effect.

Suppose you offer students in a low reading group a chance to take a remedial reading course. At the end of the course, you compare the average score of those who completed the course to the average of those who did not. Those who completed the course did better on the reading test than those who didn't. Success!

Parents, teachers, and students are pleased! But there's a problem. Participation is voluntary—students were offered a chance to take the course. Who might be more likely to leave the study before the posttest? Probably students who have the most difficulty with reading and who became frustrated. Since poor readers leave before the posttest, their scores are omitted from the average for those who have completed the course. As a result, the average reading score for completers is "too high," suggesting that taking the class had a stronger effect than it did.

Similar results occur in "weight-loss" programs, aerobics classes, and so forth, many of which are promoted during a blitz of television commercials just after the December holidays—with lavish praise from the testimonials of "happy clients." Furthermore, "sticky theory" suggests that once established, beliefs fueled by such commercials are likely to persist. For example, enrolling in a "weight-loss" program might be a good predictor primarily of future enrollment—regardless of whether or not weight loss occurred! The belief that "weight-loss" programs work "sticks" in the minds of the hopeful—despite research indicating they don't work.

Mortality due to dropout is a special concern in long-running experiments, like the supported-work study reported by Uggen. Many subjects in the Uggen study left the supported-employment job before the end of the experiment. Some may have left to take up a life of crime again, some to go to school, and some to take other jobs. These possibilities illustrate the complexity of unraveling program effects in evaluation research, even with random assignment.

If subjects are assigned to treatment groups and control groups using a random process, the chance is reduced that reasons for dropping out differ among the treatments and the control group, but they are not eliminated. Again, we emphasize: the expected equivalence of the treatment groups is ensured only at the beginning of the experiment.

History, Maturation, Instrumentation, and Regression (to the Mean). These four threats to internal validity apply primarily to the one-group pretest–posttest design with no control or comparison group. This design is not seen in published research as often as the static-group comparison. But evaluation research and informal assessments of program effects and social policies often make use of before–after comparisons. And in everyday learning, individuals continually draw on before-and-after comparisons to evaluate their own *if . . . then* hypotheses.

Recall that in the one-group pretest–posttest design, the same group of subjects is compared at different points in time, once before the treatment and once afterward. Therefore, threats to valid conclusions involve some change or event, other than the treatment, that happens between the pretest and posttest. Campbell and Stanley classify these threats into four types: history, maturation, instrumentation, and regression.

History is a shorthand term for the idea that events or circumstances other than the treatment occurring between a pretest and posttest might account for observed changes in the outcome.

For example, your high school does a drug-use survey on students aged 13 and older, and finds an "alarming" rate of marijuana use. The school district quickly implements an elaborate campaign to reduce marijuana use, and repeats the survey at the end of the school year. The reported rate of marijuana use declines by 10 percent, implying that the campaign was effective. But, unbeknownst to school officials, a rumor spread a month or so before the follow-up survey—that undercover police agents are looking for peddlers of illegal drugs. The rumor was influential enough that many suppliers decided to "lie low" for a while. Consequently, the percentage of students reporting they used marijuana during the last month is noticeably lower on the posttest than it was on the pretest, due to the effect of the rumor, *not* the anti-marijuana campaign.

For a second example, consider a recent headline: "Surveys Show Teens, Children Smoke Less: Anti-Tobacco Campaigns Credited" (Douglass, 2002, pp. B1–B2). The treatment in this case consists of the anti-tobacco campaigns. But the time period for evaluating the anti-tobacco campaigns is lengthy, and many events occurred between early and late measurements. It's difficult to know how much influence the treatment actually had.

With no control or comparison group, as in the two examples just presented, history effects threaten the cause-and-effect conclusions of the pretest–posttest comparison. As you can begin to see, history is a major threat to correct evaluation of social, political, and economic policies. There are so many factors that affect the economy, such as the growth rate, unemployment rate, and so forth, that it's nearly impossible to attribute an economic boom or bust to any policies or to any political party or politician, although "sticky theory" beliefs seem to prevail in matters like these.

Maturation is the idea that observed changes in subjects between a pretest and posttest would have occurred with or without the treatment, or any other external event(s). Individuals get older, wiser, return to health, and so forth, without treatment. For example, feed massive vitamin C supplements to a group of children with bad colds, then see if the cold symptoms subside after 2 weeks. Most colds in healthy people will subside within this time period without vitamins.

As with history, maturation effects primarily threaten the internal validity of the pretest–posttest comparison with no control or comparison group. Maturation also is a major barrier to correct evaluation of political and economic policies. For example, the economy appears to have its own built-in complex cycles of growth and stagnation. Since *maturation* as used here refers to "natural change," economic cycles can be considered an example of "maturation."

Testing is the idea that the experience of a pretest might influence results on a posttest. The cookie experiment is one example of potential effects of testing. And examples abound in educational research. The experience of taking a test usually improves performance on a second test, even without any information about which questions you missed.

Another example of potential testing effects is shown in Table 5.2. Are "plots hatched in secret places?" Perhaps, but our point here is that without careful consideration, questions on attitudinal surveys might reveal the "hidden" intent of the research and thereby skew the responses. Can you tell what the question in Table 5.2 is trying to find out?

TABLE 5.2.   Example of Attitude Survey Question with "Hidden" Intent.

Most people don't realize how much our lives are controlled by plots hatched in secret places. (*http://www.anesi.com/fscale.htm*).

Disagree Strongly	Disagree Mostly	Disagree Somewhat	Agree Somewhat	Agree Mostly	Agree Strongly
[ ]	[ ]	[ ]	[ ]	[ ]	[ ]

Many respondents also probably would recognize what the survey is getting at, and might adjust their answers on a second test. Testing effects threaten primarily the pretest–posttest-only design because of the absence of a control or comparison group.

Instrumentation is a term meaning change in the measuring instrument between pretest and posttest. It primarily threatens the pretest–posttest design.

An everyday example of instrumentation effect: after the winter holidays you weigh yourself at the fitness center; come back a week later and weigh yourself again—you've lost weight. But oops! The fitness center bought a new scale the day after your first visit, and it's calibrated too low.

Using the same questions at two exam sittings is likely to show artificial "learning," because you remember questions from the first administration. Exams, tests, or surveys administered to the same subjects at more than one time often use "alternative forms" to avoid effects of memory. Therefore, to avoid the effects of instrumentation when using alternative forms, calibration must be done carefully so that multiple forms have the same mean score and variation.

Regression (to the mean). To understand this threat to internal validity, let us first consider a whimsical example, because it's kind of fun and instructive.

Suppose you choose five cities with the coldest daily high temperature on January 25, 1999, from a sample of 155 U.S. cities. These cities were Bismarck, Helena, Fargo, Minneapolis, and Sioux Falls. Just for fun, you decide to check whether the daily high temperatures for these five cities were just as cold 1 and 2 years later as they were on January 25, 1999. This means comparing temperatures for January 25, 1999, 2000, and 2001. Temperatures for these five cities and three dates are shown in Table 5.3.

Notice something interesting about the temperature changes in these five cities? The five cities with the lowest temperatures on January 25, 1999 had quite a bit higher average temperatures 1 and 2 years later. And most of the temperatures for individual cities were higher in 2000 and 2001 than in 1999. After looking at these data, do you conclude that global warming is occurring? No—a similar but opposite effect occurs for the five cities with the highest average temperatures on January 25, 1999. They have a *lower average* temperature than they did initially! What's going on here?

TABLE 5.3. Temperature Measurements for U.S. Cities with the Five Lowest Temperatures on January 25, 1999.

	January 25, 1999	January 25, 2000	January 25, 2001
Bismarck, ND	−1.6	14.1	13.5
Helena, MT	0.6	21.6	20.7
Fargo, ND	1.5	13.1	7.7
Minneapolis, MN	10.1	16.5	9.3
Sioux Falls, SD	10.3	17.1	4.2
Average	4.18	16.48	11.08

Regression to the mean is a very interesting phenomenon. It occurs whenever a variable is imperfectly correlated with itself over time. Think of 100 contestants in two heats of shooting with a bow and arrow. Each heat consists of 10 shots. The variable is the average distance from the exact center of the target. Contestants who do well on the first heat, for the most part, do well on the second heat, and vice versa. But scores on the two heats are not correlated perfectly. Separate out, say, the top 10 and the lowest 10 contestants in heat 1. These are the extreme scores. Calculate separate average distances for these two groups on both heats. In both instances, their averages on the second heat are closer to the mean of all contestants than they were on the first heat.

Regression to the mean does not imply that every subject with an extreme pretest score is closer to the mean on the posttest. It just means that the average score of subjects in either extreme is closer to the mean score on the posttest than it was on the pretest.

In general, regression to the mean doesn't threaten internal validity, but with a one-group pretest–posttest design, results due to regression to the mean can easily be misinterpreted for an effect of a treatment. For example, choosing five cities with the coldest (or warmest) "pretest" temperatures leads to "natural drift" back to the mean temperature at the "posttest," which easily can be mistaken for a treatment effect.

Suppose you select Bismarck, Helena, Fargo, Minneapolis, and Sioux Falls for a "weather cure," and send a cadre of oracles to each city on December 31, 2000, to do a "warm-weather dance." A posttest reveals that the average temperature increases compared with the original readings taken before the dance, and the effect persists for 2 years. The dance worked! Would people pay for your "weather cure?" Probably not, because no one expects the dance to work. Our theory about weather change is better than that.

The weather example is not credible (at least to most of us). But here's a "cure" some might believe. Suppose you administer a reading test to all 150 third graders at Einstein Elementary School. You then pick the 25 students with the lowest scores for special remedial classes. At the end of the school year, you administer the same (or equivalent) reading test again. Sure enough, the average scores of the treatment group increased. The remedial class worked! Or did it?

Do you think people would be more inclined to believe the remedial reading result than the oracle weather dance? Probably, because it seems sensible in advance that the remedial class might work. But look at the parallel with the temperature experiment. These 25 students—chosen for their low scores—would have had a higher average score on the posttest than on their pretest due to regression to the mean, just like the example with the five coldest cities. In actions such as remedial education, in which subjects are selected because of their extreme initial scores on the outcome, regression to the mean is almost certain to be mistaken for a treatment effect unless you (a) know to look for it and (b) design the experiment to avoid it.

How can you design an experiment to avoid confusing regression to the mean with a treatment effect? The suggested design is to pick 50 of the lowest-scoring students and assign them at random—25 to special remedial classes and 25 to regular classes. This is a much better design than the design without a control group. And, it would work reasonably well with the temperature experiment—that is, pick 10 extreme cities and do dances in only 5 of them, selected at random, and compare the results with the control group made up of the other 5 cities. (Five cases, of course, are too few for stable statistical comparisons. And you might need more than 50 students for the reading experiment.)

But experiments with people are more complicated than comparing the temperature data for cities. For example, the selected children likely would figure out they were doing something different than other children, and this knowledge might affect the outcome. Also, teachers undoubtedly know the difference. Campbell and Stanley label this threat to valid conclusions "reactive arrangements" (see further discussion below).

Here's an everyday example of regression to the mean score. Coaches often seem to yell at their players; does yelling get a better performance? Coaches find that if they praise players for a good performance the players do worse the next game, but if they yell at players for doing poorly, the players do better the next game. So, is the formula for a winning team to withhold praise and yell at the players when they make mistakes? The coaches' observations likely are correct, but the implied cause-and-effect relationship probably is not. Quality of play waxes and wanes because it is not perfectly correlated over time. Therefore, regression to the mean occurs when both exceptionally good and exceptionally poor play is followed by mediocre play.

Grouping. Grouping is not one of the threats to internal validity explicitly named by Campbell and Stanley. But many experiments are conducted in group settings, and the consequence of grouping is not appreciated widely, so we are going to introduce you to the idea.

Grouping effects occur when observations are not independent of each other. What does "not independent of each other" mean? The phrase means that scores are more similar within groups of observations (e.g., cities, classrooms) than across all observations.

In the case of the cold-weather cities, all are fairly homogeneous in terms of weather because they are located in northern Midwestern states and influenced by the same weather systems. Consequently, the temperatures of Bismarck, Helena, Fargo, Minneapolis, and Sioux Falls are not independent observations. Similarly, in the remedial-reading experiment, the reading scores at the end of the year are not independent of each other if the remedial reading is done in a classroom with all 25 students at once. Grouping effects occur because the students in the remedial course have the same teacher and they interact with each other socially. Consequently, their test scores are more similar to each other than they would be otherwise—just as temperature data from cities in close geographic proximity are more homogeneous than those from a random selection of cities.

When observations are not independent, special statistical procedures are needed. Describing these procedures is well beyond the scope of this book, but you should be aware of the grouping phenomenon; standard statistical analysis is based on the assumption of independent observations.

Selection × (Maturation, History, Testing, and/or Instrumentation). Interaction refers to the possibility that selection into the treatment and control groups occurs in such a way that subjects in the treatment group react differently to one of the factors listed in the parentheses than do those in the control group. For short, call this threat to internal validity "selection interactions."[4]

Even if you're not an exercise devotee, you've probably read about the expected benefits of exercise to cardiovascular health. Suppose a vigorous jogging program improves the cardiovascular function of people with healthy cardiovascular systems, but reduces cardiovascular function of those with clogged arteries. However, healthy people are more likely to select a vigorous jogging program than people with cardiovascular problems and thereby distort estimates of the general effect of a jogging program.

Note: Threats to internal validity from selection interactions are different from threats due to the "main effects" of maturation, history, testing, and/or instrumentation in Table 5.1. The main effects threaten valid conclusions when there is no control group, such as the one-group pretest–posttest design. The selection interactions mainly threaten valid conclusions from designs with a comparison group *but no random assignment.*

Threats to External Validity

Recall the distinction between internal and external validity. Jot down these definitions before reading further.

Internal validity addresses the question, Does the treatment have any effect in the particular experiment? External validity addresses the issue, Can the results of the experiment be generalized to people other than those in the experiment?

Table 5.4 summarizes the four threats to external validity (generalizability) given by Campbell and Stanley.

TABLE 5.4.   Threats to External Validity.

Interaction of Testing and *X*	The effect of the treatment is different in the absence of testing or measurements than it is when the testing/measurement is done—a "sensitizing effect."
Interaction of Selection and *X*	The effect of the treatment is different for those who participate in the research than it is for those who do not—the "susceptibility effect."
Reactive Arrangements	The artificial nature of an experiment and subjects' knowledge of being a "guinea pig" prevent generalization to settings outside the experiment—a "guinea pig effect."
Multiple-*X* Interference	More than one treatment is given to each subject. Effects of early treatments last longer than the elapsed time between treatments. Effects of early treatments are confounded with effects of later treatments—an "overlapping-treatment effect."

First, look at an example. Suppose Professor Garb in communication conducts a study of the effects of marketing on buying habits. Half of the students in Professor G's "Marketing 101" class are assigned at random to a "treatment"—view a specially made TV commercial depicting the social acceptability of wearing Gap clothing. The teaching assistants for Professor G are trained to recognize Gap clothing. One week before and one week after showing the commercial, the assistants keep a record of which students in the study wear Gap clothing.

Professor G's data show that members of the treatment group were more likely to wear Gap clothing after viewing the ad, but people in the control group didn't change their propensity to wear (and presumably, buy) Gap clothing over the same period. Does the result look like a real effect of the ad? Yes—students were assigned at random to view it, so internal validity is high. But would the effect of the ad on college students in a marketing class generalize to the rest of the population? This is what the makers of Gap clothing presumably would want to know. The question illustrates the issue of external validity.

External validity in this experiment is more problematic than internal validity, because the sample is a special sample—students in a college marketing class. Of course, the Gap marketers may not care whether the results generalize to 50-year-olds, if their clientele includes very few 50-year-olds. But they very well might be interested in how well the results generalize if they are considering a marketing campaign to broaden their customer base to include middle-aged customers. The general question for external validity is: Do effects that are observed for the sample generalize to the target population?

The Gap marketing example illustrates this point. All threats to external validity involve some type of interaction effect, interaction meaning that the relationship between two variables depends on a third variable. In the Gap study, the question is whether the same ads shown to college students have a different or even opposite effect on an audience of 50-year-olds. If the answer is yes, then the relationship between seeing the ads and buying Gap merchandise depends on age.

Testing × Treatment Interaction. This threat refers to the situation in which the pretest sensitizes subjects to the treatment. In the study of the Gap marketing campaign, for example, suppose a questionnaire is administered before and after the treatment group views the TV commercial. The questionnaire contains pointed questions about the misleading nature of commercial advertising, such as the agree–disagree item illustrated in Table 5.5. What might occur if the subjects read an item like this shortly before seeing the Gap commercial?

TABLE 5.5.   A Pretest Item Likely to Influence Responses to Ads as Treatment.

Do you agree or disagree with this claim? Most TV commercials intend to deceive viewers by flagrant use of social acceptability instead of information about the product.[5]

| [ ] Strongly disagree | [ ] Disagree | [ ] Agree | [ ] Strongly agree |

This pretest question might very well influence subjects to agree more strongly after seeing the commercial than they would if they had not seen the item in the pretest. Or, they might "see through" the experiment and be more prone to disagree at the posttest than they otherwise would. Either case is an example of **testing × treatment interaction**—the pretest generates stronger/weaker reactions to the treatment than would otherwise be the case.

The testing × treatment interaction may appear to threaten internal validity. But a real effect may occur, or may be suppressed. The effect, or lack of it, is unique to the experimental setting because pretesting, such as in the Gap example, is absent in everyday life.

Selection × Treatment Interaction. This threat to external validity refers to a situation in which people who are most (or least) susceptible to the treatment recruit themselves into the pool of potential subjects.

Suppose in the Gap experiment the students select themselves for participation. A flyer is handed out, asking for volunteers to evaluate the commercial for pay. As you might suspect, the students who volunteer are those who are the most fond of watching commercials and perhaps most susceptible to commercial appeal, or who want the money, or both. This selection process increases the likelihood of finding an influence of the commercial—the volunteers are qualitatively different from others who didn't volunteer.

Reactive Arrangements. This threat is an umbrella term covering a variety of experimental manipulations that might not mirror real-world settings.

The idea of reactive arrangements is easier to illustrate than to define. Recall the example earlier in this chapter of selecting only low-scoring students for a remedial-reading program. The selected children likely would figure out that they were doing something different than other children, and this knowledge might affect the outcome. Also, teachers undoubtedly know the difference.

Here's another example to show that lab settings can produce results that might not translate into knowledge about everyday settings. Suppose we wish to know: How does power in a personal relationship affect the relationship? Lawler and Yoon (1996) propose that total power and division of power between two people in a relationship influence several outcomes, including (a) emotional feelings between the two and (b) duration of the relationship.

To test their proposal, Lawler and Yoon used 480 paid undergraduate student volunteers. Each volunteer was assigned at random to conditions of high and low total power, and to high and low difference of power between the subject and partner in the experiment. The experimental setting consisted of a contrived situation in which each subject and partner bargained over the price of iron ore, the goal being to reach agreement on a price so a "sale" would occur. There are two treatment variables in this example: "power" (high and low) of each subject in the pair. Power was "manipulated" by assigning profits to the possible outcomes of the bargaining. "High total power" was measured by adding together the profit assigned to the two subjects. "Power discrepancy" was measured by taking the difference.

Lawler and Yoon found that high total power and equal distribution of power generate positive emotional feelings and long-lasting relationships between the two persons. Because of random assignment, there is little doubt that the effects are real in the laboratory setting. However, the question is: How well does the laboratory setting generalize to real-world settings—like marriage, for example? Are marriages with high total power (e.g., high income) and equal distribution of power between spouses (e.g., husband and wife earn the same income) characterized by a high degree of love between the partners? And do these marriages last longer than other marriages?

As you can see, complex topics like power in marriage relations are difficult to study in a lab setting, and random assignment is not feasible in a complex real-world situation like marriage. The findings here certainly are thought-provoking, however, even if it's not clear how well they apply in diverse real-world settings.

Multiple-Treatment Interference. This threat occurs when multiple treatments are administered to the same subjects, and the effects of early treatments persist longer than the time between treatments.

Commercials, commercials, and more commercials! Does it sometimes seem like the TV station never will return to the program you were watching? A good example of multiple "treatments" in nonexperimental settings is the stream of commercial TV ads many people are exposed to every day. This situation makes it difficult to design marketing research that mirrors real-world settings. Multiple-treatment interference outside the lab likely occurs in ways that are difficult or impossible to duplicate in the lab.

Here's another example. Do you know someone who takes several medications? Suppose several pain-killers are administered to a sample of subjects with chronic pain. A "pain questionnaire" is administered to each subject at several time points after administering each drug. If the effects of drug A have not worn off completely by the time drug B is administered, the effects of drug B will be confounded with the effects of drug A. Perhaps this example also illustrates how a "sticky theory" idea is generalized by misinformation. A person forgets about taking drug A but "sees" the benefits of drug B because "I took it and it helped me," and passes the personal testimony to others.

In summary, there are many threats to valid causal inference, whether the observations come from an experiment, from nonexperimental research, or from everyday life. Clearly, many important issues cannot be verified beyond a reasonable doubt, and not just any experiment offers convincing evidence for a valid cause-and-effect conclusion. The trick is to know when to reserve judgment, to always look for new evidence, and to know how to evaluate evidence.

SUMMARY

This chapter is about experiments and what can be learned from them about standards supporting valid cause-and-effect conclusions. Social experiments using random assignment with people usually are not feasible, due to ethical reasons and other reasons, as illustrated in this chapter. Therefore, most interesting social science questions are not amenable to experiments. However, the study of experiments provides important insights about how to evaluate non-experimental research, as well as how to evaluate information from everyday life.

An experiment is a process in which a researcher manipulates or changes the value of at least one variable (the treatment variable) and watches to see what happens to another variable (the outcome). For example, the treatment might be to show a commercial ad to people, and the outcome might be whether subjects purchase the product shown in the ad.

A relationship between the treatment variable and the outcome might be due to effects of the treatment on the outcome, or it might be due to the dependence of both treatment and outcome on one or more other variables. In the latter case, the observed association is false or spurious. Usually it's impossible to identify and measure all the variables that might affect both the treatment and the outcome, but valid causal inference nonetheless depends on it.

How can an experiment control for *all* variables that might account for an observed relationship between the treatment variable and the outcome? The short answer is: by random assignment. Half the subjects get the treatment and half of them don't, and assignment is done at random. Random assignment means the expected average score before the treatment—on all variables, known and unknown—is the same for treatment- and control-groups. After the treatment, the difference between the treatment and control group average for the dependent variable can't be due to anything other than treatment effects and random variation.

Random assignment is for internal validity of the experiment. It doesn't guarantee exact equivalence at the outset between the treatment and control groups. But it does guarantee that the *expected* differences between treatment- and control-group means are zero. Random assignment also doesn't guarantee equivalence among the treatments over the duration of an experiment. In long-lasting evaluation research, like the field experiment about the impact of jobs on criminal activity, there may be systematic drift away from the initial expected equivalence. Larger samples can reduce initial differences between the groups, at least in principle. Statistical methods can be used to assess the effect of random variation, and statistical controls can help to compensate for differential drift over time between treatment and control groups.

Random selection means that subjects were chosen from the larger population by an "equal chance" process. Random selection is for external validity of the experiment: Does the observed effect generalize to populations other than the one from which subjects were chosen? Does an experiment with college students generalize to the entire adult population, for example?

Generally, a useful experiment is possible only after much is known about a topic. Then a well-designed experiment may answer a perplexing question. However, it is possible to study many complicated issues, even if the barriers to valid conclusions seem to be hopelessly high. The discussion in this and other chapters is intended to help you become a better judge—in your everyday learning and in reading social science reports—of what is and is not likely to be true.

YOUR REVIEW SHEET: QUESTIONS DISCUSSED IN THIS CHAPTER

1. What is an experiment? Provide an everyday example not discussed in this chapter.

2. "Most interesting questions involve imperfect relationships." Using the text example of the cookie experiment as a guideline, what is an example of an "imperfect relationship" on a topic of your interest? Use an *if . . . then* format.

3. Random assignment is not a very persuasive way to study social science topics such as the effect of school norms on sexual activity. Why not?

4. Other than the ways mentioned in this chapter, briefly describe one way in which schools might change, in ways unknown to the researcher, that could affect sexual practices.

5. In the cookie example, what does the experimenter physically control? Why are these controls important?

6. Explain the difference between random selection and random assignment to your 13-year-old cousin. What form of validity is increased by each type?

7. Explain how random assignment "controls" for all possible confounding variables, both known and unknown.

8. What is an important limitation of random assignment for long-running experiments?

9. Summarize the classical experimental design. What is the basic comparison of this design?

10. Why is the posttest-only random-assignment design nearly as good as the classical design?

11. Compared with the "posttest-only control group" design, what's missing in the "static group" design? Why is this missing element important?

12. The "one-shot" design has only one group and no pretest. What could be compared when using this design?

13. When studying extreme-score subjects, such as low-scoring students, what has to be done to avoid mistaking regression to the mean for a treatment effect?

14. Suppose students voluntarily take a remedial reading course. Who might be likely to leave the study before the posttest? What effect is this likely to have on the data analysis?

END NOTES

1. Reprinted with permission from the *Journal of the American Statistical Association*. Copyright 1992 by the American Statistical Association. All rights reserved.

2. Often one or more variables is controlled statistically even with a random-assignment experiment. The controls improve the precision of the experiment by reducing the size of the random variation due to random assignment.

3. The terms *average* and *mean* are synonyms.

4. The term *interaction* is a technical term, meaning that an effect operates differently in some categories of a control variable than in others. Recall the findings of the Uggen field experiment—the supported work program reduced arrests for men over 26 years of age,

but not for those 26 and younger. In this case, statistically controlling for age revealed the differential effects of the work program for the younger and older groups. (This is an example of interaction, not of selection effects.)

5. This item is not a good one because it contains more than one idea and uses inflammatory language. It is used here to illustrate a point.

STUDY TERMS

causal inference Conclusion that an observed relationship is due to the effect of the independent variable on the dependent variable (see also internal validity).

classical experimental design (pretest-posttest control group design) Experimental design in which pretest–posttest changes for the experimental group $\overline{O}_2 - \overline{O}_1$ are compared with changes for the control group $\overline{O}_4 - \overline{O}_3$, and subjects are assigned at random to the treatment or control group.

control group In an experiment, the group that receives no treatment; it is included simply for comparison.

experiment In its simplest form, an experiment is a process whereby a person changes one variable and watches to see what happens to another variable.

experimental group In an experiment, the group that receives some type of "treatment."

external validity Degree to which findings are generalizable beyond the experimental or research setting. Random selection is done to improve external validity.

grouping effects Increased sampling variability when experiments are run with intact groups of subjects, due to dependence among subjects in the same group.

history Events or circumstances occurring between a pretest and posttest other than the treatment that might account for observed changes in the outcome, a threat to internal validity in the absence of a comparison group.

instrumentation Change in the measuring instrument between pretest and posttest that is mistaken for a treatment effect; a threat to internal validity.

interaction The possibility that selection into the treatment and control groups occurs in such a way that subjects in the treatment group react differently to some factor than do those in the control group.

internal validity Degree to which the treatment did, in fact, have the effect attributed to it in the experimental setting; random assignment is undertaken to protect internal validity.

maturation Observed changes in subjects between a pretest and posttest that would have occurred with or without the treatment or any other external event(s); maturation may be mistaken for treatment effects and therefore is a threat to internal validity.

multiple-treatment interference Situation that occurs when multiple treatments are administered to the same subjects, and the effects of early treatments persist longer than the time between treatments. A threat to external validity.

one-group pretest–posttest design Design with no control group or comparison group; the researcher observes change between a measurement taken before an event occurs and a second measurement taken after it.

one-shot case study Most basic design, consisting of one observation after an event has occurred or a treatment administered; usually, informal or implicit comparisons are made between the observations in the study and other information not gathered as part of the formal study.

physical controls The researcher determines what is changed, by how much, and what is not changed (i.e., kept constant). Contrast physical control to "control" by random assignment, for which only the expected differences among means of variables are controlled.

placebo Nonreactive agent, such as the sugar pill given in medical research, to provide a "baseline" comparison group in experiments.

posttest-only control-group design Random assignment design comparing differences between the experimental group and the control group after the treatment is administered to the treatment group. Subjects are assigned at random to treatment and control groups.

random assignment Use of a "pure chance" procedure to determine which subjects are in the treatment group and which subjects are in the control group. The purpose is to improve internal validity.

random selection A "pure-chance" procedure for including subjects in a study. The purpose is to improve external validity.

reactive arrangements Umbrella term covering a variety of experimental manipulations that may not mirror real-world settings; a threat to external validity.

regression (to the mean) Average for extreme scores at the pretest (either very high or very low) moves closer to the middle score at the posttest, because of imperfect but positive correlation between pretest and posttest scores. Regression to the mean threatens internal validity when subjects are selected for their extreme score, often for remedial treatment, and subjects are not assigned at random to the treatment.

selection The result when subjects choose their independent-variable assignment (treatment group or control group) or are selected by a nonrandom process; the most frequent source of a spurious (false) relationship.

selection × treatment interaction Situation in which people who are most (or least) sensitive to the treatment recruit themselves into the pool of potential subjects, a threat to external validity.

static-group comparison A design with no random assignment; comparison is between naturally occurring groups, such as hourly wage between college graduates and non–college graduates.

testing The experience of a pretest might influence results on a posttest. For example, the experience of taking a test usually improves performance on a second test. Effects of testing might be mistaken for effects of a treatment (e.g., tutoring), a threat to internal validity.

testing × treatment interaction Situation in which the pretest sensitizes subjects to the treatment, either increasing or decreasing treatment effects. A threat to external validity.

treatment In experiments, one category of the independent or treatment variable.

treatment variable Alternative name for *independent variable*, terminology generally used in experiments.

EXERCISES

Exercise 5.1. Developing a Nonrandomized Study

Directions: Read each of the following hypotheses and answer the subsequent questions.

1. Roman Catholics are less likely than Protestants to approve of capital punishment.
2. Residents in a nursing home who receive regular visits from relatives report greater satisfaction with the nursing home than other residents report.
3. A college policy of mandatory class attendance leads to higher student achievement.

Questions

1. What are the two variables in the hypothesis? What are their categories?
2. Could the hypothesis be tested in a randomized experiment? Briefly explain.
3. Propose a study of your own that is not a randomized experiment. Identify the independent (treatment) variable and the dependent variable (outcome). Referring to the schematic layout used by Campbell and Stanley, draw a sketch of the design, replacing the X, O, and the blank in the "treatment column" with specific categories of the variable you chose. For example, replace

	Pretest	Treatment	Posttest
Static group comparison:	—	X	O_1
	—		O_2

with

	Pretest	"Treatment"	Posttest
Static-group comparison:	—	Catholic	Approve capital punishment, (measured for Catholics)
	—	Protestant	Approve capital punishment, (measured for Protestants)

4. Describe how you plan to get a sample of subjects for your study.
5. Referring to Table 5.1, why did you choose this design?
6. Looking at Table 5.4, is this design externally valid? Why or why not? *Hint:* On what does external validity depend?

Exercise 5.2. Developing a Randomized Experiment: Posttest-Only Control-Group Design

Do you prefer Pepsi or Coke? Could you tell the difference, if you didn't know which one you were drinking? Do you think most people could, or might this be an example of "sticky theory"?

Directions: For this assignment, use the posttest-only control-group design with random assignment. Pepsi and Coke define the two categories of the treatment variable (or independent variable) for the experiment. The colas are poured into two identical pitchers, with no identifying information other than an "A" on the pitcher containing Pepsi and a "B" on the pitcher containing Coke. (Subjects don't know what "A" and "B" stand for, only that the test includes the two colas.)

Suppose you use a fair lottery to select 100 subjects from the student population at your college and another random method to assign each of these 100 students to taste either Coke or Pepsi. Assume that this puts 50 students into each group.

The hypothesis is: *People can't tell the difference between Pepsi and Coke.* Use the following "taste-identification" indicator.

Please tell me which cola you drank. (Circle 1)
Pepsi   Coke

Questions

1. How many groups define the treatment variable? What are they?

2. What type of "pure-chance" strategy will you use to assign subjects to the two groups? Describe it. What type of invalidity does your strategy avoid?

3. What is "*R*"? How is "*R*" obtained in your study? What type of invalidity does it avoid?

4. What is your "*X*"?

5. Describe your "*O*"s.

6. Suppose 56% of Pepsi drinkers said it is Pepsi, and 40% of Coke drinkers claimed they drank Pepsi—a difference of 16 percent. Based on this difference, can you safely conclude that people can differentiate between the two colas? Why or why not? What method is used by researchers to decide whether observed differences like these are large enough to safely attribute them to an effect, rather than to random variation of your chosen random assignment procedure?

Exercise 5.3. Developing and Conducting a Field Experiment

Directions: You have been hired by Decision Research, Inc., to evaluate the effectiveness of an anti–cigarette smoking campaign in Marlboro School District. The target population consists of all students in the school system who are 11 years old or older.

1. Identify the outcome variable. How will you measure it?

2. Describe the treatment. (Unless your instructor indicates otherwise, limit your answer to one approach of an antismoking campaign.)

3. Sketch a one-group pretest–posttest design. Briefly describe how you will use this design to check the effect of the antismoking campaign.

4. Is random assignment possible? Explain your answer.

5. Using the one-group pretest–posttest design, identify at least three variables whose effects on smoking might be mistaken for effects of the antismoking campaign. Briefly

describe why the effects of these variables might be confounded with effects of the "treatment" (the antismoking campaign).

6. Suppose you pick *schools* in the Marlboro School District at random to be either experimental or control schools. Is this design as powerful as one in which individual students are exposed at random to the treatment? Why or why not? How does the idea of grouping apply here?

7. Describe one "intervention" designed to reduce smoking that might be assigned at random to individual students.

OBSERVATION AND ETHNOGRAPHY

INTRODUCTION: LOOKING AT HOW THE SOCIAL WORLD WORKS

Home! What did you notice about your home the last time you entered it? Any fragrances or aromas that you didn't expect? Could you hear music or voices as you entered the door? Or, was everything still?

What was the first thing you saw as you opened the door? If you opened the door and someone was standing there whom you didn't expect, what would you do? Immediately you would begin trying to interpret their presence: Do you know the person or not? If you do, does the person seem happy to see you? How could you tell? Of course, you might use several of your senses—vision, hearing, and perhaps touch. Smell or taste might be helpful to interpret social life in other situations. For example, what is your favorite food? Can you tell if someone has prepared it before you see it on the table?

We continuously make observations of our everyday world, whether or not we are actively aware of it. Regularities often are so commonplace that we scarcely notice many actions and reactions—unless something unexpected occurs or we are required to recount the actions. For example, did you ever drive down a street or road so often that you couldn't tell another person whether a sign indicating its name is present or not?

Disciplines such as anthropology and sociology have evolved in part to understand the "other" as well as the "self," requiring observation and communication of the results to others (Vidich & Lyman, 1994, p. 24). Ethnography and observation, particularly participant observation, have emerged as two important forms of social research. Each has a strong emphasis on description, rather than on formal testing of hypotheses (Atkinson & Hammersley, 1994, p. 248).

Observational study is a method of data collection in which the researcher obtains information by directly watching social interactions and behaviors. Frequently, the observations are done for an extended time and include direct involvement in the lives of subjects.

Ethnographic research has been described as ". . . the direct observation of social realities by the individual observer" (Vidich & Lyman, 1994, p. 25). It is research often using "unstructured" data, "that is, data that have not been coded at the point of data collection in terms of a closed set of analytic categories" (Atkinson & Hammersley, 1994, p. 248). Ethnographic researchers typically investigate a small number of cases (e.g., individuals, couples, groups, and so forth) for an extended period of time, sometimes years. They look for the meanings and functions of human actions using verbal descriptions and explanations (p. 248). The goal is to understand as fully as possible every aspect of a culture or subculture.

The methods used in observation and ethnography often are called **qualitative methods** and stand in contrast to **quantitative methods**. Qualitative methods do not rely heavily on mathematical and statistical analysis; whereas, quantitative methods rely primarily on these methods. Just as importantly, field workers in qualitative research decide moment to moment exactly what questions to ask, what to observe, and what to record. Only broad guidelines are set before the field work begins. In contrast, data collected in quantitative research is specified precisely and fully, in advance of the field work.

The fundamental strength of observation and ethnography is their ability to see things that almost certainly cannot be observed using surveys or experiments. Direct contact with subjects brings to light much richer detail about people and their interactions than could possibly be obtained from quantitative methods. Just as important, observational and ethnographic research often target unusual populations like homeless persons, drug suppliers, victims of disasters, prostitutes, and economic elites. These populations nearly always are entirely excluded from other methods of data collection such as surveys. Some lines of observational research emphasize the importance of comprehending the personal viewpoints of subjects. A central goal is to understand the meanings attached to life events by the actors themselves.

Many supporters of an observational approach to data collection argue that the most productive way to build social theory is to formulate it as a part of the process of observing—that is, theory arises from insights gained during the field work. This viewpoint contrasts sharply with the formalized approach embedded in quantitative research. In quantitative work, the ideal is to state theory and hypotheses before data are collected, and carry out tests by checking to see whether the data are consistent with the hypotheses. But these are ideal types. Quantitative work sometimes generates hypotheses *after* looking at the data, and qualitative work often begins with some theoretical ideas in mind.

Despite the contrasts, qualitative and quantitative methods share a common goal of understanding social realities. Each is appropriate in some situations, and often it is useful to use both approaches in the same research.

Goals of This Chapter

This chapter shows by example some of the rich detail and insights into human behavior that arise from a qualitative approach to research. Qualitative methods bring to light the constraints faced by people in their daily lives, and their emotional reactions to these constraints. They help us understand the continuity of people's dreams and feelings in highly varied circumstances. Exercises at the end of this chapter offer an opportunity to discover details about your social life, details you might not have noticed previously.

At the same time, qualitative methods are difficult to verify. Samples are small and studies difficult or impossible to replicate. The goals of this chapter are to help you gain a sense of the value and the limitations of observational and ethnographic research approaches and to show how qualitative and quantitative approaches complement each other.

AN OVERVIEW OF QUALITATIVE/DESCRIPTIVE RESEARCH

Denzin and Lincoln (1994) point out that the definition of qualitative research has taken different meanings during the past one hundred years, and emphasize the historical context of qualitative approaches to research. They offer the following broad description. *Qualitative research* is

> . . . multimethod in focus, involving an interpretive, naturalistic approach to its subject matter. This means that qualitative researchers study things in their natural settings, attempting to make sense of, or interpret, phenomena in terms of the meanings people bring to them. Qualitative research involves the studied use and collection of a variety of empirical materials—case study, personal experience, introspective, life story, interview, observational, historical, interactional, and visual texts—that describe routine and problematic moments and meanings in individuals' lives. (p. 2).

In comparison with quantitative research, which emphasizes theories and cause-and-effect relationships, qualitative research

> . . . has no theory, or paradigm, that is distinctly its own. . . . [It has no] distinct set of methods that are entirely its own. (Denzin & Lincoln 1994, p. 3) . . . Qualitative researchers stress the socially constructed nature of reality, the intimate relationship between the researcher and what is studied, and the situational constraints that shape inquiry. Such researchers emphasize the value-laden nature of inquiry. They seek answers to questions that stress how social experience is created and given meaning. (p. 4).

Qualitative researchers target all aspects of the social settings they choose to study and attempt to describe how the varied parts fit together. For instance, if the topic is school curriculum, qualitative researchers might investigate questions about

■ the quality of a selected curriculum, innovation or program.
■ the meaning or interpretation of some component of the curriculum.
■ the political, economic, or sociopsychological aspects of schooling.
■ teachers' implicit theories about teaching and curriculum.
■ the social context of schooling. (Janesick, 1994, p. 210)

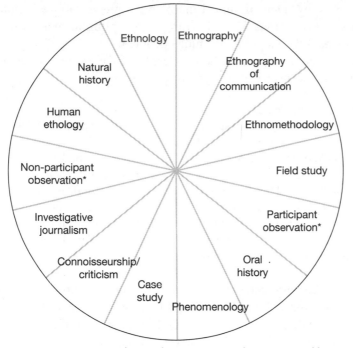

FIGURE 6.1. Qualitative/Descriptive Studies Organized by Research Approach (Wolcott, 1990, p. 65).

*Approaches discussed in this chapter.

Over the years, numerous qualitative designs have emerged. For example, Denzin and Lincoln identify 10 qualitative designs. Janesick (1994, p. 212) lists 18, and notes that the list isn't inclusive of all possibilities. Strauss and Corbin (1990, p. 21) mention five approaches as some of the different types: ethnography, grounded theory, phenomenology, life histories, and conversational analysis. Creswell (1998, pp. 47–64) identifies "five traditions": ethnography, grounded theory, phenomenology, biography, and case study.

Figure 6.1 shows a pie chart comprised of 14 qualitative/descriptive studies; the chart suggests "an interrelatedness among qualitative approaches without implying a hierarchy" (Wolcott, 2001, p. 131). The figure also offers a visual summary of the variety of approaches for ethnographic and observational research. This chapter reviews three frequently used approaches identified in Figure 6.1: ethnography, participant observation, and nonparticipant observation.

An Example: Observation in Disaster Research

Suppose you are interested in how communities respond during natural disasters, such as earthquakes, hurricanes, floods, or fires. One of the important research questions might be: How do community emergency-services groups such as the Red Cross coordinate search and rescue efforts and communicate with hospitals and social service agencies? This research question is an example of the description of qualitative research by Denzin and Lincoln, as quoted above, "qualitative researchers study things in their natural settings, attempting to make sense of, or interpret, phenomena in terms of the meanings people bring to them" (p. 2).

The Disaster Research Center at the University of Delaware applies this type of "holistic" approach to nearly every type of disaster:

> The Disaster Research Center (DRC), the first social science research center in the world devoted to the study of disasters, was established at Ohio State University in 1963 and moved to the University of Delaware in 1985.
>
> DRC researchers have carried out systematic studies on a broad range of disaster types, including hurricanes, floods, earthquakes, tornadoes, hazardous chemical incidents, and plane crashes. DRC has also done research on civil disturbances and riots, including the 1992 Los Angeles unrest. Staff have conducted nearly 600 field studies since the Center's inception, traveling to communities throughout the United States and to a number of foreign countries, including Mexico, Canada, Japan, Italy and Turkey (Disaster Research Center, 2000).

The DRC staff includes graduate students, undergraduates, and research support personnel, who travel throughout the United States and to many other countries. An important part of DRC research is extended investigation of the World Trade Center attack on September 11, 2001, as noted in Chapter 3.

Some other hazards-research institutions are: Hazards Reduction and Recovery Center at Texas A&M University, the Social Research Group at Millersville University (PA), Institute of Emergency Administration and Management at the University of North Texas, and the International Hurricane Center at Florida International University (Phillips, 1997, pp. 184–85).

The first considerations in investigating a disaster are (1) access to key people and organizations and (2) provisions for recording data. As Quarantelli (1997) points out, early arrival at the scene provides a high degree of access to and cooperation from high-ranking officials and key organizations. Also, victims interviewed shortly after an event typically provide candid information that is far more difficult to get later.

The **field** is the location of an observational or ethnographic study. To be the "early birds" at a disaster scene, DRC field researchers have luggage ready for travel at all times, and office staff have been trained in special routines for expediting travel arrangements. All DRC researchers carry the following minimum items in their field kits, which are in their personal possession at all times:

✓ tape recorder (tested by recording and playing back before leaving), charger and cord

✓ blank cassettes and boxes with identifying cards

✓ interview guides

✓ pens, pencils, note-taking tablets

✓ data inventory forms, data analysis forms

✓ DRC leaflets and fact sheets, other special handouts, self-addressed stamped envelopes

✓ personal DRC business cards and personal identification letter
✓ sheet with office, home address and telephone numbers
✓ various other items, such as auto rental credit cards, travelers' checks, receipt forms and forms for reporting expenses (Quarantelli, 1997, pp. 56–57).

Immediately after arrival at a disaster site, field workers must quickly find living quarters, then head to the emergency operations center (EOC). At the EOC, they lay the critically important groundwork for later access, obtain an overview of the situation, identify key officials and organizations, learn about activities of key players, and introduce themselves to people who can assist with the research (Quarantelli, 1997). Disaster researchers collect data in a variety of sites and settings, including search-and-rescue sites where people are trapped, shelters, hospitals, and other places where essential emergency-related activities are taking place (Tierney, 2001). The informal contacts and interviews conducted after the 1994 Northridge, CA, earthquake led to structured interviews later (Tierney, 1998, p. 5).

Participant observation is one of several essential data-collection strategies used in disaster research. A **participant observer** is a researcher who is completely immersed in the regular activities of the group under study. Almost all projects seek multiple perspectives of those involved—a complete picture of the event is of greatest importance, so individual and group interviews aim to collect information from people with every possible vantage point and every conceivable perspective on the event (Quarantelli, 1997). For example, if field observations are conducted at an organization such as the Red Cross, information is obtained from administrative heads, operational heads, clerical staff, and communication personnel. Similar persons are sought when studying emergent or informal groups, such as at protest rallies or riots (Tierney, 2001).

In disaster situations, information is lost forever if the behavior isn't observed and recorded in short order (Tierney, 2001). For example, after the October 1989, Loma Prieta, CA, earthquake, Phillips (1996, p. 94) was watching city workers erecting fence barricades around the stricken downtown area. She noticed a police officer escorting a woman away from the area, during which a spectator pointed out to the officer that the woman was homeless, living downtown, with nowhere else to go. Phillips watched the police officer place the woman outside the barricade and return to the stricken area. The homeless woman wandered away. It's unlikely such scenarios would be recorded by anyone other than the disaster field researcher. Nor would there be records on what Quarantelli (1997) calls "immediate data," such as how emergency tasks initially are carried out and how individuals respond.

Tierney (2001) shares the following insight about the distinctive contribution of observations in disaster research:

Because in disaster situations so much is done under severe time pressure, people who are interviewed later are often unable to reconstruct exactly what they did and when. In some interview situations with key decision makers, for example, I found that I had

> much more accurate information on when certain decisions were made than the decision makers themselves had, because they had been under such pressure and had been making so many decisions during the emergency period. I knew when certain things happened because I was there when they happened—and I was taking notes.

She points out that on-the-scene field work immediately following a disaster can yield data that might become "privileged" later, or that cannot be reconstructed. Moreover, written reports of disaster operations primarily reveal the "official version" of what happened, information can be lost or distorted, and minutes of meetings seldom accurately portray the events that actually took place.

One important finding of the DRC research program is that emergency disaster plans frequently are not followed very closely (Quarantelli, 1997). For example, victims are likely to be transported by private vehicles to the most familiar hospital, regardless of disaster plans, resulting in an uneven distribution of patients among hospitals. At the hospitals, the less seriously injured usually arrive first and therefore tend to be treated first. Also, new groups providing emergency medical services often emerge during disasters, and established groups such as hospitals often are underutilized.

Excerpt: *Hurricane Andrew Through Women's Eyes.* The following excerpt from a study by Morrow and Enarson (1996), sociologists from Florida International University, describes women's increased responsibilities and opportunities after a hurricane.

> The unique experiences of female disaster victims, survivors, and rebuilders tend to be overlooked in disaster studies. Our work analyzes a major natural disaster through the eyes of women. . . . With . . . notable exceptions . . . gender rarely appears even as a variable of analysis in disaster studies and a gendered perspective is almost totally absent from the literature.
>
> To help address these concerns we conducted a qualitative sociological analysis of women's experiences in the aftermath of Hurricane Andrew in the southern part of Florida. We focused on the implications of gender and the roles of women in preparation, relief, and recovery efforts at both the household and community levels. Data were collected through . . . observations in the tent cities used for temporary housing, service centers, provider organizations, and at meetings of emergent community groups. . . . We [also] interviewed immigrant and migrant women from Haiti, Cuba, Mexico and Central America, African-American single mothers and grandmothers, women construction workers, business owners, farmworkers, teachers, social workers, battered and homeless women. . . .
>
> The family caregiving roles of women expanded dramatically at all stages of disaster response. Most of the women we interviewed prepared their family for the approaching hurricane, including stocking supplies and getting the household ready. . . . Women who reached beyond the boundaries of their own homes were crucial to response efforts. They often helped elderly neighbors and friends, either directly or by connecting them with community services. . . .

Households headed by poor, minority women have tended to be the last to recover. . . . According to personnel from the public and private agencies working to help victims find housing, the families who are left in the trailers tend to be the poorest of the poor, most of whom are minority women. . . .

Paradoxically, Hurricane Andrew also brought new opportunities to some women. . . . We learned, for example, of women earning equitable construction wages, developing new employment skills, and using relief monies to leave violent relationships. . . . Women have forged new friendships and found common ground as they struggled to rebuild their homes, neighborhoods, and communities. (Morrow & Enarson, 1996).

The study of women and disaster is based on "observations in the tent cities, service centers, provider organizations, and at meetings of emergent community groups." Data from interviews, documents and newspaper articles also were incorporated in the report. In qualitative research, direct observation is integrated as a part of a variety of data-gathering methods (Adler & Adler, 1994).

SELECTING THE SITE AND THE SUBJECTS

Usually, decisions about the site or setting and selection of subjects for observational study are made when designing a research project. However, sometimes researchers rely on chance encounters in the field (Creswell, 1998).

After a major disaster, where do victims find shelter? How would researchers begin the study of such a topic? Careful thought is needed before choosing the **target population**—the subjects or the specific site(s) in an area struck by disaster. Several sites are possible: (a) in all neighborhoods where damage occurred, (b) only in the hardest-hit neighborhoods, (c) in the shelters or areas to which residents were evacuated, or (d) some combination of these locations.

The primary guide to selecting a site is determined by the research question. For example, if the researcher wants to know whether women or men are more likely to lack access to shelter and housing aid after a disaster, a sample can be selected of adult males and females living in one or more neighborhoods with the most property damage. On the other hand, if the research question is about differences between people who obtain shelter and others who don't, then one might observe two samples—one sample of victims who found shelter and one sample of victims who did not. In general, the selected field site should be a location where:

- the appropriate people to study are likely to be available and accessible,
- the programs, interactions and focuses that are part of the research question are likely to be available and accessible, and
- the appropriate individuals are available to collect the data (Berg, 2001, p. 29).

For example, Phillips (1996) used observational methods to study the processes by which the homeless participated in "place-making" and "place-sustaining" strategies after the Loma Prieta, CA, earthquake in 1989. Examples of her observational sites and subjects include "Salvation Army food operations, public relief and recovery meetings, homeless advocacy efforts, and general public reactions to the homeless" (p. 95). Phillips also examined documents such as organizational memos, flyers from advocacy agencies, and newspapers. She says that "Ideas on the role of places and how they are socially constructed, maintained and defined emerged from these data" (p. 95). She concludes that the homeless are the last to receive aid, and are given it reluctantly.

After choosing the field site and subjects, a second issue is **access**. Lofland and Lofland (1995) say ". . . in the literature of qualitative methodology, *access* is probably one of the most written-about topics—understandably so, for it remains problematic throughout the entire period of research" (p. 22, emphasis in the original). Gaining access depends on a number of complicated questions. Lofland and Lofland identify four important considerations.

1. Do you, the investigator, want to be close to your subjects or a remote "objective" observer? There are advantages and disadvantages to both stances, and the issue of access depends on what kind of observer you want to be.

2. Contrasting ascriptive statuses between you and the people you study often presents substantial barriers. Lofland and Lofland give some interesting examples. A young male may have difficulty studying the subculture of a beauty parlor employing only middle-aged women; a black person probably will find it impossible to study white supremacists.

3. Access for a team of observers requires large-scale coordination, as in disaster research.

4. Many settings are difficult to study. Examples include the economic elite, warring sides in a civil war, and secret societies. Sometimes it's impossible to gain access to settings like these, but Lofland and Lofland urge researchers not to give up easily.

METHODS OF DATA COLLECTION

How do the daily embarrassments, cultural clashes and racism experienced by ghetto residents working in legal jobs in the white upper-class world lead them to seek employment in a local crack house? How does an ethnographer obtain answers to such questions, and at what personal and professional risks?

Researcher as Ethnographer: *In Search of Respect: Selling Crack in El Barrio*

Bourgois (1995), an anthropologist, decided to study crack houses, focusing on one house he called "Game Room." "Game Room" is located in a "bogus video arcade" in El Barrio, an East Harlem neighborhood. Bourgois was particularly interested in studying the "underground economy" of drug sales and what he calls the "inner-city street culture of resistance" of socially marginalized populations. The culture Bourgois studied is

> . . . a complex and conflictual web of beliefs, symbols, modes of interaction, values, and ideologies that have emerged in opposition to exclusion from mainstream society. Street culture offers an alternative forum for autonomous personal dignity. . . . This "street culture of resistance" is not a coherent, conscious universe of political opposition but, rather, a spontaneous set of rebellious practices that in the long term have emerged as an oppositional style. . . . Purveying [supplying] for substance use and abuse provides the material base for contemporary street culture, rendering it even more powerfully appealing than it has been in previous generations. (Bourgois, 1995, pp. 8–9).

Bourgois used participant-observation ethnography to learn about the street culture, establishing long-term relationships that permitted him to ". . . ask provocative personal questions, and expect thoughtful, serious answers" (p. 13).

> I spent hundreds of nights on the street and in crackhouses observing dealers and addicts. I regularly tape-recorded their conversations and life histories. Perhaps more important, I also visited their families, attending parties and intimate reunions—from Thanksgiving dinners to New Year's Eve celebrations. I interviewed, and in many cases befriended, the spouses, lovers, siblings, mothers, grandmothers, and—when possible—the fathers and stepfathers. . . . I also spent time in the larger community interviewing local politicians and attending institutional meetings (p. 13).

Bourgois struggled with a variety of intellectual and methodological issues. For example, he decided to tackle what he calls "historically taboo subjects in anthropology," such as self-destruction, personal violence, alienation, and addiction, which he argues are taboo in part because

> . . . the methodological logistics of participant-observation requires researchers to be physically present and personally involved. This encourages them [ethnographic researchers] to overlook negative dynamics because they need to be empathetically engaged with the people they study and must also have their permission to live with them. . . . [O]n a more personal level, extreme settings full of human tragedy, such as the streets of East Harlem, are psychologically overwhelming and can be physically dangerous (p. 14).

Yet, Bourgois also reveals his conflicts, both professional and personal, about sharing his results with others who did not witness the entire spectrum of inner-city street culture.

> I feel it imperative from a personal and ethical perspective, as well as from an analytic and theoretical one, to expose the horrors I witnessed among the people I befriended, without censoring even the goriest details. . . . [Yet] I continue to worry about the

political implications of exposing the minute details of the lives of the poor and powerless to the general public. Under an ethnographic microscope everyone has warts and anyone can be made to look like a monster (p. 18).

Avoiding personal danger is another issue for ethnographers, what Bourgois calls "learning street smarts," and it is a continual risk in some settings. For example, after more than two and a half years of crackhouse experience, he had secured a "close and privileged relationship with the 'main man' of 'Game Room.' " Bourgois wanted to impress him and his followers, raising his credibility as a "real professor," rather than a "stuck-up professor," a closet-drug addict, pervert, or long-term undercover drug dealer. So, while surrounded by the man's followers and employees, he showed him a newspaper photo of himself and then talk-show host Phil Donahue, taken after a prime-time debate on violent crime in East Harlem. But, the man didn't know how to read and therefore was "disrespected" by Bourgois. However, the "main man" recovered his dignity the next time the two met by using the event to give Bourgois a warning about the risks to security from media attention:

> Felipe (Bourgois), let me tell you something, people who get people busted—even if it's by mistake—sometimes get found in the garbage with their heart ripped out and their bodies chopped up into little pieces . . . or else maybe they just get their fingers stuck in electrical sockets. You understand what I'm saying? (p. 22).

Was Bourgois able to present his findings about the poor and powerless without offering a sensationalized account of violence and racism? Bourgois's answer is ". . . ultimately the problem and the responsibility [of interpreting the findings] is also in the eyes of the beholder" (p. 18).

Researcher as Participant Observer: Everyday Life in Nursing Homes

Recall that a *participant observer* is a researcher who becomes part of and is completely immersed in the regular activities of the group under study. Prior to developing a study, the participant observer might be a member of the group to be observed. Suppose, for example, for research purposes you observe some aspect of life in your campus residence hall—you would be a participant observer. What topic might *you* choose if you were assigned to do such a study? Often, however, the participant researcher joins the group only for the purpose of conducting a study.

Other types of observation are done by **complete observers** (field workers' roles as researchers are unknown to subjects), and **partial observers** (field worker's role as a researcher is known by subjects, but the field worker is not a member of the group). Sometimes these roles run together, for example, when the researcher becomes known only to some group members (Atkinson & Hammersley, 1994, pp. 248–249).

A participant observer whose role as a researcher is known to subjects could affect the events being studied. When a participant observer does not reveal his/her role as a researcher to subjects, it's possible to obtain information about the group that otherwise might not be revealed. Diamond (1986, 1992) describes his observations in nursing homes:

> Initially, I indicated on my job applications that I was a researcher interested in studying nursing homes . . . not once was I offered a job. . . . Eventually, I began to emphasize my training as a nursing assistant rather than as a researcher. Using this strategy, I was soon employed . . . yet . . . my presence was never without suspicion. It was one of the administrators who . . . asked, "Why would a white guy want to work for these kind of wages?"
>
> I worked in both private and state-subsidized homes. . . . Given present economic arrangements for long-term care, a patient moves along a path: the more time in long term care, the poorer one becomes. . . . Many patients told me of their fears as those last weeks of Medicare drew near and, for example, that "damn hip wouldn't heal". . . .
>
> The women and men I met at the expensive home started out in the posh two lower floors. When their money had run out they were moved to the public aid wings, there to receive noticeably inferior care. . . . The management had made it clear that they preferred more short-term Medicare patients, since these patients were worth more. One could feel a murmur of fear among the public aid patients that many would be asked to leave or go to another home. No doubt this would happen to some. I know because I met women and men in the poor homes who had started as private pay residents in other homes and had been forced to leave them. Meeting them made me understand that there is a distinct economic progression in nursing home life—the longer one stays the more impoverished one becomes, and the more unstable one's environment becomes. . . .
>
> I came to change my image of nursing home life as a static enterprise. It is not sitting in a chair "doing nothing." Rather than being passive, it is always a process. The policies that shape this environment inform every moment of nursing home life. Each person is situated somewhere on an overall turbulent path. Each person sits in a chair, or lies on a bed, often appearing motionless, but is moving and being moved, however silently, through the society. . . . Their [nursing assistants' and patients'] standpoint, I conclude, is often opposed to the organizational logic of business that increasingly encases nursing home life (Diamond, 1986, pp. 1287–1289).

The interaction between a participant observer and members of the group being studied might influence the social events in the group. However, a researcher could study an event without becoming a part of it, as the next excerpt shows.

Researcher as Nonparticipant Observer: An Unobtrusive Study of Arousal–Attraction

Nonparticipant observation, sometimes called *complete observation*, is done without informing the subjects they are being studied—the research is not **announced**. It usually is undertaken in public settings, where the researcher is unlikely to know most other people, and the subjects might not even know they are part of a research project.

Have you ever sat in a shopping mall people-watching? Or, ever observed people leaving a movie to get clues about whether you might like the movie you're about to see? Sitting in a mall to observe patterns of communication between children and parents, for example, isn't likely to influence subjects, particularly if the researcher unobtrusively records information about them as they go about their regular activities.

The following excerpt from a journal article reports a study that uses nonparticipant observation to investigate whether the public behavior of couples is affected by the level of emotional drama in a movie they have just viewed.

> The present study attempted to generalize previous findings [that emotional states are a function of physiological arousal and one's perception of the precipitating event] beyond the laboratory by observing the impact of arousal on interpersonal attraction among people attending a movie. . . .
>
> It was hypothesized that couples leaving the high-arousal (suspense) movie (*52 Pickup*) would engage in significantly more affiliative behaviors than couples leaving the neutral movie (*True Stories*, a mock documentary on middle-class life in America that includes no violence or nudity). It was further predicted that couples watching the high-arousal movie would engage more in affiliative behaviors (i.e., talking, touching) when exiting the theater than when entering the theater but that couples watching the neutral movie would not exhibit increased affiliative behavior when exiting the theater. . . .
>
> Seventy-nine mixed-sex dyads were unobtrusively observed entering, and 70 mixed-sex dyads were observed leaving the two movies. The dependent variable, level of affiliation, was measured by the number of couples who were either talking or touching, both talking and touching, and neither talking nor touching. In order to record patron behavior unobtrusively, three observers kept a mental count of the number of couples fitting each of the four categories. The totals were recorded as soon as all the patrons were seated or had left the theater. . . .
>
> These results indicate that couples leaving the high-arousal movie were more affiliative than couples leaving the low-arousal movie. The results from the pre-arousal measure of affiliation reduce the possibility that behavior while leaving the movies was due to preexisting differences in affiliative tendencies between the two groups. (Cohen, Waugh, & Place, 1989 pp. 692–693).

Notice that this study, although illustrating "qualitative" methodology, shares important features with "quantitative" methods. It combines an observational method of data collection with quantitative analysis. The study design is similar to the classical experiment (pretest–posttest control-group design), *except* that couples decided for themselves which movie to watch. They weren't assigned at random to view one movie or the other. Maybe couples who were more affiliative before watching the movie chose to see *52 Pickup* and the lesser affiliative couples decided to watch *True Stories*. If this were the case, couples viewing *52 Pickup* would be more affiliative after the movie than couples seeing *True Stories*, even if the movies had no effect on affiliative behaviors. How does the before-and-after measurement help to reduce this threat to internal validity? Look back at the classical experiment in Chapter 5 if you've forgotten which group comparisons might be made.

The concept "affiliative behavior" raises many issues reviewed in Chapter 4 about measuring a complex concept and assessing validity and reliability of the measures selected. How well do you think the procedures in this study measure the concept that the researchers call "affiliative behaviors"?

One final point about nonparticipant observation—some settings require more detailed information about the social circumstances or subjects than detached observation might provide. In a hospital emergency waiting room, for example, it might be hard to tell without asking whether the person sitting next to you in the waiting room is a neighbor, friend, or relative of a patient, or perhaps a patient waiting to be called by the staff. The nonparticipant observer in an ER also is likely to have limited time before being noticed and questioned by hospital staff.

CHECKING RELIABILITY AND VALIDITY

Recall from Chapter 4 that *reliability* refers to "repeatability." *Validity* refers to how accurately a variable corresponds to what it is intended to measure.

The stereotypical critique of qualitative research methods is they can't be verified, they aren't objective, and they aren't repeatable. In short, the criticism is that qualitative observations are neither reliable nor valid. Probably few social scientists make explicit such a strong indictment of qualitative work, but this viewpoint nonetheless is pervasive enough to require attention. In a perceptive book titled *Reliability and Validity in Qualitative Research*, Kirk and Miller (1986) say "Qualitative researchers can no longer afford to beg the issue of reliability. . . . The curious public (or peer reviewer or funding source) deserves to know . . . how data is collected and analyzed" (p. 72).

Reciting some compelling examples, Kirk and Miller build a persuasive case that qualitative research sometimes may be more accurate than quantitative work. They recount a critique of quantitative analysis of survey data about inequality in Sri Lanka. The critique was written by a field researcher who had done on-site observation of villages in the area where the survey was conducted. The survey analysis relied on a definition of a "household" as a group of people "who cook their rice in the same pot" (p. 28). The critique pointed out that the standard in the local villages was for two or more generations to live in the same hut. Each married woman had her own cooking pot so that true households often contained two or more cooking pots—but only one deed to the land. The younger men worked the field and, for practical purposes, owned the land that they would inherit, even though they didn't hold the deed to it. Thus, incorrect definition of "household" in the survey overestimated the percentage of households that were landless.

Another case illustrates the difference between reliability and validity, and also some interesting aspects of the differences between a qualitative and a quantitative approach to generating "data." Kirk and Miller summarize field research about massage parlors. One of the research questions was whether sex-for-hire was part of the operations. The observer on the scene apparently built up a good rapport with the masseuses who consistently told him there were no "extras." Clients of the massage parlors reported the same thing, no sex trade. But based on extensive experience, the principal investigator of the study operated on the theory that "there's always more immorality than you can see." He insisted that the field worker continue to observe and probe. Finally, one informant, apparently assuming the field worker already knew about the sex trade in the massage parlors, opened up. This one instance opened the flood gates of information. Confronted with the "facts," informants who once had denied masseuses took money for sex now "fessed up."

This case brings out three important principles. First, reliable information from interviews (here, repeated reports that the masseuses didn't engage in sex with their clients) is not necessarily correct information. Second, even a numeric calculation of reliability (such as Cronbach's alpha) might be misleading. For example, think of an anonymous survey containing several questions about the relationship between masseuses and their clients, particularly before informants' "confessions." Moreover, what is the likelihood this survey would reveal the correct extent of the sex trade in massage parlors (a validity problem)? Of course, it's really impossible to have a very good idea without doing extensive field work comparing survey responses to assessments based on direct observation. Third, whether qualitative or quantitative research, generating accurate information depends on a "theory." Why did we believe sex-for-hire was commonplace in the massage parlors? Why not compare the reports that denied there were any extras and the reports that said there were extras and go with the report having the higher count, or perhaps create an "average" score of all accounts? The answer clearly depends on a theory about human behavior and what we believe about people concealing their secrets until special circumstances prompt them to "tell all."

Designing concrete, specific methods for achieving accurate observation in qualitative research probably are not possible. And, there are too many contingencies in qualitative observation to justify specific, rigid rules for what to ask, how to phrase it, and what to record. Kirk and Miller (1986) do propose a sensible general approach, however: (1) Field notes should be systematic and abundant. (2) The notes should be shared among field workers. Sharing improves reliability and stimulates observers to take careful and comprehensible notes. (3) Create reliable conventions about recording dates and times, and (4) Clearly separate observations from speculation and comment.

RECORDING FIELD DATA

Observation and ethnography rely on a variety of data sources and methods. Morse (1994, p. 224) compares seven strategies for making observations including ethnography and participant observation. Other data sources are art documents, poetry, diaries, photography, maps, social network diagrams, and videotaped observations. Creswell (1994, pp. 150–151) adds art objects, computer software, and film to this list. As examples in this chapter show, many qualitative researchers use more than one method and several data sources.

In the social network diagram (**sociogram**) shown in Figure 6.2, the goal is to identify the "stars" or persons who take charge of a conversation. Here, the "tail" of the arrow indicates who initiated the conversation, and the head of the arrow points to the recipient. An exercise at the end of this chapter provides an opportunity to identify some strengths and limitations of a sociogram.

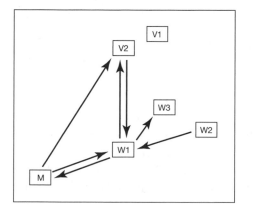

FIGURE 6.2. Sample Sociogram (Hypothetical Example).
(M = manager, W = worker, V = visitor)

For recording conversations in field observations, Creswell (1994, p. 152) suggests designing a note-taking form ("protocol") as a single page divided into two sections, descriptive notes and reflective field notes. **Descriptive field notes** include conversations, the physical setting, and details of activities and events. **Reflective field notes** contain the researcher's thoughts, feelings, ideas, problems and so forth. A sample page is shown in Figure 6.3.

ANALYZING FIELD DATA

Analysis of ethnographic and observational data usually begins by reading the field notes, and paying close attention to major themes and the theoretical framework. During the first reading, look for *patterns or groups of similar themes*

Descriptive notes	Reflective notes

FIGURE 6.3.   Sample Note Sheet.

that will be used to tell the "story." The next step is to decide the *meaning* of the conversational patterns, such as how security in the "Game Room" is managed. With text-based data from interviews, initial readings can be used to identify key words and phrases that will be used to organize the information from all interview notes.

Computer software programs are available to assist with coding, retrieval, theory-building, and other aspects of **qualitative data** analysis. Many of these programs are compatible with word-processing file formats, allowing field notes entered into a word processor to be imported directly into the analysis program. Figure 6.4 shows a simplified example that was produced by *The Ethnograph*, one of many text-analysis computer software programs.

In Figure 6.4, for example, the code word "SHIPTIME" refers to length of time an interviewee spent on board a ship when emigrating from Sweden to the U.S. The researcher may sort the interviews by one or more code words, enabling easy comparison of all text coded with the selected code word(s).

Some software programs accept audio, video and graphics data (Weitzman & Miles, 1995). It's still up to the researcher, however, to determine which words, phrases, character strings, and chunks of text or other information should be coded, what the codes should be, and how the result is related to the research question and to theory. Then the software can help to speed through some of the most tedious aspects of making sense of the data.

```
SEARCH CODE: SHIPTIME

    LINNEA: So then we came over, and it      169 #
    took us 14 days to come over. We came     170 #
    over on a steamer called "Stockholm."     171 #
    It was huge. It was one of Sweden's       172 #
    largest ships. I shouldn't say a          173 #
    steamer, because it was a ship. And       174 #
    usually it took 9-10 days, but it took    175 #
    us 14 because we ran into a terrible      176 #
    storm. And I never was seasick, but       177 #
    my sister was sick the whole trip, and    178 #
    she was so mad at me because I was        179 #
    having so much fun. And I didn't get      180 #
    sick at all.                              181 #

SEARCH CODE: SHIPTIME

    WILLARD: It was a new one. The             82 #
    "Stockholm." Um, it took about six         83 #
    days. In 1948.                             84 #

SEARCH CODE: SHIPTIME

    RAY: We had an awful storm when           405 # $
    I come over. In three days we only        406   $
    went 75 miles. Oh boy, big waves.         407   $
    Every wave came at you like a big         408   $
    mountain, and the boat overtook into      409   $
    it. I never was sea sick. But the         410   $
    rest of them… It took us almost 20        411   $
    days across. We had an awful storm.       412   $

SEARCH CODE: SHIPTIME

    GUNHILDA: The boat was the "Gripsholm."    210 #
    Took about 10 days.                        211 #
```

FIGURE 6.4.   Sample Interview Text from a Code-and-Retrieve Computer Software Program.

WRITING UP THE RESULTS

You've completed the needed observations or interviews and have analyzed your data. Your next task is to write a paper describing what you found. Wolcott (2001) offers several suggestions:

- Begin writing early—even before beginning observations or interviews. Writers who wait until their thoughts are "clear" run the risk of never starting at all.

- Perhaps start by describing the method of your project, the published research you reviewed and the details of how you collected your data. However, most of the write-up of qualitative research should be devoted to the descriptive details and their meanings.

- A good candidate for an opening sentence is, "The purpose of this study is. . . ." If you are stuck here, then the problem likely is lack of focus. Talking to another student or a professor about your research might help define the project. Or, try "freewriting"—write to yourself in order to help pin down your thoughts. Like all writers, you will need to read and revise your written drafts several times (p. 21).

■ You are "telling a story," and your own writing style can be used. However, write for readers who don't know the details of your project.

Integrating Data Collection, Interpretation, and Writing

Qualitative approaches often simultaneously use data collection, data interpretation, narrative report writing, and data analysis (Creswell, 1994, p. 153). Collecting useful qualitative field notes from observing behaviors, examining maps and records, and viewing photographs and documents requires (1) the appropriate descriptive questions (e.g., about values, beliefs, and practices), (2) a familiarity with social science theory, (3) careful attention to details, (4) a willingness to deal with unpredictability, and (5) persistence. As Morse (1994) observes,

> Qualitative research is only as good as the investigator.... Experienced researchers... are persistent, recognizing that good fieldwork is often merely a matter of completing one small task after another. Good researchers are meticulous about their documentation, file methodically, and keep [field] notes up-to-date.... Information must be verified and cross-checked constantly, on an ongoing basis, and researchers must be constantly reviewing notes and other data collected.... it is important for neophyte [beginner] researchers to know they are not alone in experiencing conceptual confusion in the midst of a qualitative project (pp. 225–226).

At the same time, don't forget to contemplate why you are doing all these detailed tasks—it would be easy to get lost in the details, as the phrase "can't see the forest for the trees" illustrates. A good strategy is to reflect about the meaning of what you're recording at every opportunity. Be sure to record these thoughts, too, but clearly distinguish them from factual descriptions.

Janesick (1994, pp. 211–213) compares doing qualitative research to the "metaphor of dance." Both activities have a warm-up period, a total workout stage, and a cool-down period. The warm-up period occurs when the researcher selects the study question, the site, the subjects, and type of research strategies. In the total workout stage, the researcher is immersed in the statements and behaviors of the participants, adjusting the focus of the study, and interpreting the beliefs and behaviors of participants. The cool-down portion includes leaving the field setting, final data analysis, and writing the narrative. Janesick summarizes common "rules of thumb" for the workout stage on which she says most researchers agree.

✓ Look for the meaning and perspectives of the participants in the study.

✓ Look for relationships regarding the structure, occurrence, and distribution of events over time.

✓   Look for points of tension: What does not fit? What are the conflicting points of evidence in the case? (p. 213).

Capturing Meaning and Perspectives: *Tell Them Who I Am*

Keeping these "common rules" in mind, look at the following short excerpt from the book titled, *Tell Them Who I Am: The Lives of Homeless Women*, which is based on participant observation. In his chapter on "Work and Jobs," Elliott Liebow describes the process by which some homeless women maintain a minimally decent, clean work appearance while living out of bags and boxes. Note the clear descriptive character, the meaning of homelessness from the perspectives of these women—and how Liebow helps the reader produce a mental image of the women's daily struggles to get and keep a job.

> . . . [S]ome women do manage to get and keep jobs that require a good appearance. Grace is one of them, but she has the advantage of being able to use her automobile as a clothes closet. She hangs her blouses, jackets, and skirts on a crossbar. Underwear and accessories are piled neatly in a tattered suitcase on the front seat. Each item is tagged and coded so that she can pull out a matching outfit with relative ease. Elise, too, uses her car in this way, but tags and coding notwithstanding, entropy soon takes over. What was order quickly becomes disorder, and full-scale reorganization is required with disheartening frequency (Liebow, 1993, p. 55).

Next, notice how Liebow uses a few well-chosen quotes to portray another point—being labeled "homeless" is even more difficult to manage than maintaining an acceptable image. "One day I was a productive and respected citizen, the next day I was dirt" said Shirley. "People treat the homeless as if they had a communicable disease. They treat them worse than cats and dogs," said Bernice. Julie said she wished she could have a cup of coffee out of her own cup, not a Styrofoam cup, a real cup that was hers alone. Bernice said that most cats and dogs have their own plates to eat out of, and some even have their names on them.

ETHICAL ISSUES IN ETHNOGRAPHIC/OBSERVATIONAL RESEARCH

Chapter 2 raised the question, Should on-site observers inform potential participants that they will be research subjects? Recall that the main tension is between (a) the very important contributions to knowledge often emerging from studies in which observers were *not* known to their subjects as researchers, and (b) the ethical implications of not informing subjects they are participating in a research study.

In addition, there is a real threat to reliability and validity—participant observers become so embroiled in the social life of the community observed that objective reporting is difficult or impossible. Of particular concern is covert (hidden) participant observation. Subjects are likely to accept and trust the researcher as group member, only to find out later that they were research subjects (Tierney, 2001).

Charlotte Allen presents a thought-provoking essay on the topic of covert observation in a 1997 article titled, "Spies like Us: When Sociologists Deceive their Subjects," published in *Lingua Franca*. Allen depicts the nature of the bind confronted by social scientists conducting participant observation—fulfilling research objectives *and* honoring ethical obligations.

As part of her review and discussion about covert observations, Allen recounts the controversy generated from a study by Carolyn Ellis. Ellis investigated social life among a group of Chesapeake Bay "fisher folk," the results of which were presented in her prizewinning book published in 1986. According to Allen, Ellis spent nearly 10 years of summers and weekends studying the fishing community. Initially, she explained to them she was a college student writing a paper on fishing, which she says nearly everyone forgot over time. She secretly tape recorded conversations, eavesdropped on conversations, and pressed respondents for additional information while pretending to visit them socially.

Although Ellis used made-up names in her writing, it became known to the fishing families who had taken her into their homes as a guest that she had used them for research without their knowledge. In addition to descriptions such as "fishy body odor," Allen states that conclusions in Ellis's book about the region were unflattering, because the area was known for its "white-trash backwardness and marshland criminality" (p. 31). The community was decidedly displeased.

In 1995, Allen continues, Ellis published a "remorseful essay" that described her deceptions. But although admitting her guilt, according to Allen, Ellis still was convinced that the success of the project depended on deceiving her subjects:

> I know I did them an injustice. . . . But I couldn't have done the study any other way. My study was predicated on my getting close to them, and if you're constantly reminding people that you're not one of them, you can't do that (Allen 1997, p. 32).

After what Allen (p. 32) calls a "raging debate," the American Sociological Association (ASA) approved stringent new ethics guidelines for professional conduct in the field (see Appendix A for the current ASA guidelines).[1] Although Ellis acknowledged remorse, Allen notes that other researchers insist that scientific research sometimes requires covert techniques—particularly when the payoff is high, and with few negative consequences (p. 32). Ellis, however, apparently has done no additional field work since completing the book (p. 34).

As recounted in Chapter 2, Punch (1986, p. 36) explains there are no easy answers to many situational ethics in ethnographic and observational work. Perhaps Punch's guideline is worth restating: See research subjects as "collaborators" in the research, and behave toward them as we are expected to behave toward friends and acquaintances in our everyday lives (p. 83). But does that mean, no deception ever?

REFLECTIONS ON OBSERVATION AND ETHNOGRAPHIC METHODS

There are two obvious limitations of qualitative research: It's difficult to repeat, and it's difficult to generalize the results. For example, how could the Bourgois study of East Harlem be repeated? To make it repeatable likely would trivialize it to the point that it wouldn't be worth repeating.

But the importance of repeatability is revealed in an interesting question: Suppose a socially conservative businessperson set out to do the same study of the crackhouse. Would the conservative person make the same observations and arrive at the same conclusions? It seems unlikely. Qualitative researchers live in a social world and are subject to social norms, just as are businesspeople. Each is "punished" by peers for being politically incorrect, but the meaning of *politically incorrect* differs markedly between the two groups. The norms of the business world tend to prohibit a businessperson from conducting such a study. Consequently, nearly all the published research omits the business-world viewpoint.

Or, consider generalizing the findings of the nursing-home study to all nursing homes. Diamond's sample was small and selected informally. Although we might strongly suspect his observations are typical, there is little evidence for it in his report. Much depends on our subjective expectation of how much variation there is among nursing homes.

Some argue that qualitative research such as observational methods presents greater challenges to decisions made by institutional review boards (IRBs) for research on human subjects than does quantitative research, such as surveys.[2] For example, Berg (2001) reports that observational studies are more likely to focus on deviant, secret, or difficult-to-locate populations, such as drug smugglers. In working with these populations, written informed-consent slips and probability samples are nearly impossible to manage. Also, qualitative research is likely to be ongoing and evolving, so decisions, such as impartial selection of subjects, become more difficult. However, the role of IRBs also is evolving, with specific details still to be worked out.

Recently the *New York Times* ran an interesting story that illustrates the potential value of qualitative research methods while, at the same time, revealing the controversy that is associated with qualitative methods.

Excerpt: *A Qualitative Study of Slums and Families*

Uchitelle (2001) reports on a study conducted by three economists, two from Harvard University and one from Princeton, who, in contrast to the typical quantitative approach of economists, interviewed poor people in Boston. What the three found was

> . . . slums pull down families, damaging them emotionally . . . counter to current public policy, which tries to improve life in the slums by spending millions on police,

schools and jobs. . . . [But] slums themselves are the problem. The culture of poverty begins to lift only when slum dwellers move to better neighborhoods (Uchitelle, 2001).

This article generated quite a bit of controversy about qualitative methods in an online computer discussion group. The original post identifying the *New York Times* article stated the article may be the "ultimate validation" of qualitative methods. Subsequent posts to the news group quoted the phrase "scientific justification" in the original post, saying it implied we are still "stuck on the idea of justification and verification." Additional commentary criticized the traditional economic viewpoint in rather condescending terms. Others derided the economists for finding what good qualitative researchers have known all along.

In our view, qualitative methods make invaluable contributions that, as the *New York Times* article indicates, wouldn't—and probably couldn't—be learned in other ways. And, we agree with researchers who argue that neither qualitative nor quantitative methods should be exempt from the standards of evidence. It's easy to fault both qualitative and quantitative social research. We need a continuing combination of a variety of approaches.

SUMMARY

This chapter is about qualitative methods, as exemplified by observational and ethnographic approaches. Qualitative research makes much fuller use of all our senses than do quantitative methods. This idea is illustrated in the beginning of the chapter by considering the probable reactions of someone who, returning home expecting an empty house, finds someone in the house.

Findings from qualitative research inform us about the emotional content of human interactions; paint vivid pictures of people's daily lives; describe problems people face and how they cope with them; and work with special populations such as crack cocaine dealers, homeless people, and nursing-home residents. None of this is possible with the methods of data collection and analysis associated with quantitative work. In addition, unstructured observation as qualitative research encourages reporting and interpretation of unexpected events, as illustrated in our review of disaster research.

The chapter reviews three main methods of data collection: ethnography, participant observation, and nonparticipant observation. None of these can be arranged in the way that a survey typically is organized. The study of a crack cocaine house and the study of nursing homes illustrate how the observer must be flexible and inventive. Field work also requires intense attention to detail. Accurate notes must be kept, organized, and analyzed. Constant attention to maintaining data quality is required. The write-up must reflect the particular nature of the study. Writing should start early and continue throughout the field work and after it is complete.

The chapter discusses each component of observation separately, to simplify the presentation. However, qualitative approaches nearly always engage in data collection, data interpretation, narrative report writing, and data analysis as ongoing simultaneous activities.

Qualitative work raises special ethical questions. Often, informing subjects you are researching them makes it impossible to do the research. Written consent forms might be difficult or out of the question in some instances. Also, qualitative research is labor-intensive. It's arguably more difficult in some aspects than most quantitative research, in part because selecting the research site and gaining/maintaining access to subjects generates an ongoing tension.[3]

YOUR REVIEW SHEET: QUESTIONS DISCUSSED IN THIS CHAPTER

1. What are some important similarities and differences between our everyday observations and the observations of social scientists conducting social research?

2. When does the researcher usually choose a site or setting and select the subjects for an observational study?

3. How does a researcher decide which settings and subjects to choose for an observational study?

4. Summarize the difficulties associated with gaining access to subjects in a qualitative research study.

5. Suppose you want to observe the work activities of the mayor of your city or town. Would access be the same during the height of a hurricane as during a typical day? Discuss the similarities and differences.

6. What is an advantage of concealing your identity as a researcher? A disadvantage?

7. What might happen if a nonparticipant observer interacts with the group being studied?

8. Should members of a group be studied without their permission? Look back at the section on "ethics" in Chapter 2 and in Appendix A before answering.

9. Thinking about the observations conducted with nursing home residents, what are some strengths of participant observation? What are some reasons why participant observation might not be the best approach to data collection?

10. Thinking about the observations conducted with couples viewing the two movies, what are some strengths of nonparticipant observation?

11. What are some reasons why nonparticipant observation might not be the best approach to data collection?

12. How is research undertaken on disasters? What does a field researcher do upon arrival at the disaster site?

END NOTES

1. The Policies and Procedures from the Committee on Professional Ethics, American Sociological Association, can be found at *http://www.asanet.org/members/enforce.html*.

2. Recall from Chapter 2 that institutional review board (IRB) is one of several titles for formal committees in research organizations, such as universities and hospitals. IRBs review ethical concerns of proposed research. Usually, research may not proceed without approval of the IRB.

3. This isn't to say that high-quality quantitative data collection is easy—it isn't. A survey, for example, requires often-difficult coordination of the research team and meticulous attention to detail.

STUDY TERMS

access Permission or agreement from subjects and/or agencies to conduct research at an observational or field setting.

announce Divulge to potential subjects that they are part of a research study; opposite of covert (hidden) observation.

complete observer (nonparticipant observer) Field worker whose role as a researcher is not known by the subjects.

descriptive field notes Notes that include conversations, the physical setting, and details of activities and events.

ethnographic research "The direct observation of social realities by the individual observer." Ethnographic research research relies on data that have not been coded into a closed set of categories at the point of data collection. Ethnographers typically investigate a small number of sites for an extended period of time, often years. The goal is to understand, as fully as possible, all aspects of a culture or subculture. They examine the meanings and functions of human actions using verbal descriptions and explanations.

field Location of an observational or ethnographic study.

nonparticipant observer See complete observer.

observational study Unstructured method of data collection in which the researcher visits a field site for an extended time to obtain information by directly watching human social interactions and behaviors.

partial observer Researcher who is observing and participating as a member but is known as a researcher.

participant observer Researcher who is completely immersed in the regular activities of the group under study, and usually is known as a member of the group rather than as a researcher.

qualitative data (meaning-based) Information collected from unstructured observation intended to represent meanings, symbols, descriptions, concepts, and characteristics of people.

qualitative methods Research methods that do not rely heavily on mathematical and statistical analysis. Qualitative research is multi-method in focus, involving a naturalistic approach to subject matter. Qualitative researchers study people in their natural setting, attempting to make sense of phenomena in terms of the meanings that people bring to them.

quantitative methods Research methods that rely primarily on mathematical and statistical analysis of numeric (numbers-based) data.

reflective field notes Notes that contain the researcher's thoughts, feelings, ideas, problems, and so forth.

sociogram Sociometric method of displaying patterns of interaction, such as friendship networks, cliques, and other social networks. It consists of a diagram with circles or squares representing participants, and arrows or lines connecting interacting participants.

target population Collection of all people who are eligible to participate as subjects in a study.

EXERCISES

Exercise 6.1. Participant Observation of a Familiar Group: Unannounced and Announced

Directions: Conduct two types of participant observations of the same group. In your first observation go as an unannounced participant. Then, either later at the same session or at another time, conduct a second observation of the <u>same</u> group as an announced participant.

Before beginning this exercise, review carefully the Code of Ethics forms in Appendix A. *If you are uncertain about any of the ethical expectations, check with your instructor before proceeding with the exercise.* Also, be sure to review relevant chapter sections before planning the observations.

1. Select a group in which you are a current and familiar member. Some groups to consider are your dorm residents, a campus or community club, or your family. Use the same group for each observation.

2. Choose two times that you can observe the group for at least 15 minutes without interruption.

3. Select a specific topic, such as patterns of verbal or nonverbal communication while the group is holding a meeting, watching television, or participating in a sports or game activity. This topic need not be a specific hypothesis as in quantitative research. Observe the same activity and the same group at both times.

4. Use a sample note sheet like Figure 6.3 to record descriptive information and your reflections about the group and its activities. You might need more than one sheet per observation. Conversations should be *recorded exactly*, to the extent possible—don't summarize or skip some words/phrases. Your reflections can be added either during the observation or immediately afterward. Be ready to turn in your original note sheets. For each observation, use a form similar to:

   Type or name of group _____

   Date, time and location of observation 1 (unannounced) _____

   Specific *activity* for observations _____

   Specific *topic* for observations _____

   Date, time and location of observation 2 (announced) _____

Questions

After completing the unannounced observation:

1. How did you arrange yourself in the setting to be able to observe and write your notes? Did anyone ask you to explain what you were doing? If so, what did you say? If not, what do you think their reasons might be?

2. Did you write any notes after completing the observation? If so, why, and what did you write?

After completing the announced observation:

1. How did you arrange yourself in the setting to be able to observe and write notes? Did anyone ask you to explain what you were writing? If so, what did you say? If not, what do you think their reasons might be?

2. Did you write any notes after completing the observation? Why?

After reviewing your answers to the above questions:

3. Which type of observation did you prefer, and why?

4. Was the behavior of the group similar or different for the two observations? If different, provide an example. If the same, briefly explain why.

5. Was your behavior as researcher similar or different for the two observations? Briefly explain.

6. Which observation do you think provides data that are more valid? How can you tell? Refer to the definition of "validity" in Chapter 4.

Exercise 6.2. Nonparticipant Observation of an Unfamiliar Group

Directions: Locate a small group (three to four persons) whose members are unfamiliar to you. Choose a group that will be together for at least 15 minutes, as you will need a few minutes to draw and label the symbols on your sociogram and about 10 minutes for your observation. Refer to Figure 6.2 for a sample sociogram.

Record who initiates verbal communications. Therefore, avoid groups and settings in which participants are likely to have minimal verbal interaction. Be ready to turn in your original sociogram.

Before beginning this exercise, review carefully the Code of Ethics forms in Appendix A. *If you do not understand any of the ethical expectations, check with your instructor before proceeding with the exercise.* Be sure to review relevant chapter sections before planning the observations.

1. Plan in advance the symbols that you will use for your sociogram (e.g., letters, numbers, a combination). Bring several blank sheets of paper for the sociogram. You might need more than one page if there are many verbal interactions.

2. After observing the group briefly:

   a. Decide whether you will record only statements, only questions, only answers, or all verbal communication.

   b. Choose a symbol to represent each member of the group (e.g., "P_1" for "person 1, etc.).

   c. Place each symbol on your blank sheet in the general pattern of group members (e.g., sitting in a circle). Use the entire page, so that there will be enough space to see each arrow when completed.

3. For each verbal communication, draw an arrow to indicate who initiated the verbal communication. The arrow should start at the symbol representing the initiator and point to the recipient(s). See Figure 6.2.

Questions

1. Describe the group and location of the interactions.

2. Who is/are the leader(s) of the communication? Looking at the arrows, how can you tell?

3. If the leader(s) spoke more to some persons, were the respondents more or less likely than other persons to initiate verbal communication?

4. Briefly assess the validity of clearly identifying the group leader(s) from your observations. What additional information might be useful? How difficult would it be to record it reliably?

5. Assess how useful the sociogram was for this exercise; write a short statement pointing out the strengths and limitations (two to four sentences).

6. Would the exercise have been easier or harder if you knew members of the group? If you had announced your project to the group? If you had participated in the group as a member?

7. Construct a tabular layout with one row and one column for each person in your group. Mark row and column headings to identify each person. Use made-up names or symbols. But make notes that permit you to identify mentally each group member later. For example:

		Initiator of Interaction			
		Emily	**Rob**	**Ann-Marie**	**Pinnochio**
Recipient of Interaction	Emily		|||		
	Rob	ЖН ||		||	|||
	Ann-Marie					
	Pinnochio					

Keep track of interactions by placing a mark in the cell of the table for the column of the initiator and the row of the recipient. In the example, Emily initiated seven communications to Rob, and Rob initiated three to Emily.

Exercise 6.3. Evaluating Research: Participant Observation

Directions: Refer to the excerpt on "everyday life in nursing homes" in this chapter to answer the following questions.

Factual Questions

1. How did Diamond become a participant observer? Did he have any trouble in joining the group?

2. What group members did he observe?

3. What was the purpose of the study, as suggested by the findings? How was participant observation a useful method of data collection for this purpose?

Questions for Discussion

1. Describe how Diamond's observations might have been different if he had revealed his identity as a researcher to patients and staff.

2. As a researcher, how might you decide whether or not to disclose your identity?

3. Think of a study in which you believe the accuracy and completeness of the findings would be compromised if subjects knew your identity as a research observer. Briefly

discuss. In this situation, is disclosure of your identity after completing the study an acceptable compromise between (a) disclosing it at the beginning of the study, and (b) not disclosing it at all?

Exercise 6.4. Evaluating Research: Nonparticipant Observation

Directions: Refer to the excerpt on "study of arousal–attraction" in this chapter to answer the following questions.

Factual Questions

1. In what setting did the researchers conduct their study? Where in this setting did they make their observations?
2. Whom did the researchers observe, and what behaviors did they record?
3. Explain the strategy used to record the subjects' behaviors. List at least one advantage and one limitation that might be associated with this strategy.

Questions for Discussion

1. Why do you think the researchers chose nonparticipant observation to obtain their data?
2. Nonparticipant observing in some settings can produce superficial, sketchy conclusions that lead to misperceptions about the social setting under study. What item of information about the couples might be unknown in this research? Briefly explain how not knowing the information might influence the outcome of the study.
3. Observational studies provide firsthand data about behaviors of subjects in a natural setting. However, a limitation of observational studies is generalizability, or the ability to apply the results to other subjects and locations. Comment briefly on the generalizability of the study.
4. Comment on the ethical issue of studying subjects without their consent in this study.

7

INDIRECT METHODS

INTRODUCTION: LOOKING AT HOW THE SOCIAL WORLD WORKS

Sex after Death as a Research Topic?

We *are* being a little facetious—but it's an interesting topic!

A recent study examined gender differences in the inscriptions on cemetery markers. Cemetery markers typically display name inscriptions. Many markers include dates of birth and death, and occasionally events such as marriage, social statuses, and special words, phrases, poetry and other sentiments. Cemeteries also keep written records of interred persons. Before reading further, make a list of possible key words on gravestones that could be used for a study of gender differences. As you read the following excerpt, check off each gender-descriptive word on your list that was used in the study, and list others that you didn't record. You will be asked to review your list in the next section of this chapter.

Excerpt: *Sex after Death? Patterns of Conception, Natality, and Mortality from Cemeteries*

> Gravestones yield social data, including gender, ethnicity (at least as surmised by surname), age . . . marital status and other familial relationships. . . . Inscriptions offer potential insight into the character and demeanor of those buried. Finally, deceased are not often buried randomly but interred in particular (e.g., church) cemeteries because of particular (e.g., religious) affiliations. . . .
>
> William Kephart (1950) first presented empirical evidence of social-class differences from personal interviews regarding Philadelphia funerary and cemetery practices. In 1959, [W. Lloyd] Warner, continuing the Yankee City series in *The Living and the Dead*, with interview and survey data and cemetery documents, presented cemeteries as expressions of community structure and values that reflect class, associational, family, and demographic patterns. . . . Cemetery records, as primary data from which questions must follow, are written on paper or cut in stone. . . .
>
> [W]e focus on [a sample of 10] cemeteries in Coles County, Illinois. . . . All Coles County cemeteries were surveyed in the 1930s by the Sally Lincoln Chapter of the Daughters of the American Revolution (DAR), which recorded all gravestone inscriptions. The survey was updated, beginning in 1979, by the Coles County Genealogical Society, which published three of an expected four volumes in 1984, 1985, and 1996. . . . We reread 110 (5.4 percent) of the stones to assess the reliability of the DAR recordings and found only one discrepancy. . . . The cemeteries span sixteen decades, the 1830s–1980s. The smallest contained twenty-one burials, the

largest, 804. We did not examine a random sample of burials but all burials in the ten cemeteries. . . .

Sociohistorical considerations of gender must acknowledge expressions of inequality, such as gravestones more often identifying females in the context of familial relationships, reflecting male dominance/ownership since historically women were regarded only as complete persons in their relationships to others, particularly adult males. Of the 2,021 marked gravestones, 1,041 (51.5 percent) indicated a familial relationship to another person. While only 371 (34.2 percent) of all males had relationships identified, 657 (71.6 percent) of all females had relationships identified, clearly supporting our expectation. Among males with familial relationships specified, 366 were sons; 3, fathers; 2, husbands. Of the 657 females, 433 were wives; 218, daughters; 4, mothers; 2, sisters. . . . Cemetery type and time period offered no substantial variant pattern. . . .

[Yet, q]uantitative assessment of cemetery data, even rudimentary descriptive parameters, misses the tenderness of the human story. For example . . . [w]as it . . . vows to never part that claimed Elias and Sarah Bisson, married nearly fifty years at their deaths on February 26, 1877? Despite such limitations, these findings advance our understanding of vital events prior to the creation of national birth and death registries (Foster, Hummel, & Adamchak, 1998, pp. 473–485).

This sample illustrates four important general points about indirect sources of data. First, the cemetery data are from a sample that could not have been obtained in any other way. Second, the data collection method is entirely **unobtrusive**—subjects were unaffected in any way by the data-collection method. Third, both qualitative and quantitative analyses are contained in the excerpt. Fourth, comparison of archival records to the actual gravestone inscriptions illustrates the criterion validity check discussed in Chapter 4—whether a variable predicts a criterion or standard.

A second cemetery study of inscriptions on Roman tombstones illustrates some of these general considerations, perhaps even more dramatically. The author notes that age at death is

. . . biased by underrepresentation of children's deaths, exaggeration of ages at death beyond age forty or fifty, and probably by understatement of younger women's ages at death. The inscriptions for males dying between the ages of fifteen and forty-two provide the best basis for mortality estimates (Durand, 1960, p. 365).

He concludes that life expectancy at birth for the total population of the Roman Empire during the first and second centuries probably was about 25 or 30 years.

As the quotation indicates, historical data require careful scrutiny because of the many possible sources of error. And the data are scarce, so they must be taken from whatever sources that can be found—metaphorically speaking, from "outcroppings" (Webb et al., 2000).

Although the research agenda appears to be straightforward description to estimate longevity during the Roman Empire, notice also an implicit comparison.

We likely find tentative conclusions about longevity in the Roman Empire to be startling, because we automatically compare it with current lifetimes that are two and one-half to three times longer in the U.S. Even in areas of the contemporary world with the shortest life expectancy—for example, 38 years in the nations of Malawi, Mozambique, and Zimbabwe in eastern Africa in 2003 (Population Reference Bureau 2003, p. 5)—longevity is higher today than are these estimates for the Roman Empire.

Goals of This Chapter

This chapter examines three types of indirect sources of data: (1) contemporary records (e.g., books, newspapers, magazines, music, TV), (2) archival and historical records, and (3) physical traces.[1] In addition, the chapter reviews the methods of content analysis and unobtrusive observation. Content analysis may be applied to any of the three indirect data sources. For example, the cemetery study relied on archival data (archived gravestone inscriptions) *and* used content analysis to convert the inscriptions into variables.

An important theme of this chapter is how data collected by **indirect methods** complements data collected by **direct methods**, such as surveys and direct observation. It also discusses key issues in obtaining valid and complete information with indirect methods and unobtrusive observation: defining, locating, and selecting objects to study; classifying the information; and analyzing the data. The last section of the chapter reviews the strengths and limitations of indirect methods.

SOURCES OF DATA

Contemporary Records

Do you like hip-hop music? Heavy metal? Country and western? Or, do you listen to music from alternative bands, classic rockers, jazz, or the classics? Regardless of music preferences, you could examine music lyrics from a social science perspective.

However, studying lyrics as sources of data requires clarification about what you wish to know and how you will know when you've heard (or seen) it. For example, suppose you are interested in the extent to which popular culture portrays love relationships as a competition between two people: "love is a game." You decide to focus on musical lyrics as a form of popular culture. To keep manageable limits on the study, you confine the music styles to country and western and classic rock. How might you collect the lyrics data?

One possibility is to record all songs played on a "country and western" radio station and all songs played on a "classic rock" station during a predetermined time period. Then, identify passages indicating "love is a game" by playing back the recordings. This process of converting recorded communication into usable data is an example of **content analysis**.

To conduct a content analysis of the songs, first define the basic items to be classified—the **recording units**. Weber (1990, pp. 21–23) identifies six types of recording units commonly used in content analysis:

- *word*
- word sense—words/phrases that can serve as alternatives for the same meaning (e.g., "applauding" and "clapping") and word units (e.g., New York state)
- *sentence*
- theme—a phrase/sentence that typically has a subject, verb, and object (e.g., "snow covers the grass")
- *paragraph*
- *whole text*—e.g., stories, news articles, songs, etc.

Second, define the criteria for identifying your topic—in the current example, "competition between two people in love relationships." One notion in this example is that, similar to a competitive game, one must watch for cheating in love relationships (Berger 2000, p. 152). To define and select objects for the study, you might examine all relevant words and **word sense** recording units in each audio-taped song that imply "cheating in love." To help you visualize this process, think about your favorite songs—what words or word sense units (words or phrases) suggest cheating in love relationships?

Third, refine the categories. One dimension of cheating in love relationships is deception, such as lying to the other person. Of course, one could choose a few specific words such as lying and deception and their variants (lie, lies, lied; deceive, deceived, and so forth), but you might need other words and phrases that convey the idea of lying. "Being with another" and "saw you with her/him" might impart a visual aspect. What about more symbolic terms such as "hard-hearted" or "evil ways" or "cheating heart?"

In short, you must decide whether to take all lyrics at face value, or broaden the definition to include other words, word sense units, sentences, or even **themes** and paragraphs. Suppose you choose all forms of four word categories: lie (lies, lied, lying), deceive (deceived, deception), betray (betrayal, betrayed), and forsake (forsaking, forsook). A full study might require more than four categories. How do you organize, classify, and analyze these data? Here, a qualitative approach is useful. As described in Chapter 6 in the example of Swedish migration to the U.S., computer software programs can assist with the clerical tasks of qualitative analysis.

Tesch (1990) summarizes some key steps for organizing, classifying and analyzing data using a qualitative approach—

- *Get a sense of the whole.* First, listen to all of the audiotaped songs, perhaps jotting down any ideas that emerge.

- *Pick one song*, such as one that is most interesting to you. Listen to it and *write down what you think is the message or underlying meaning*. Repeat this procedure for several songs.

- *Make a list of topics* from your notes. Past research or theory might be used to determine categories, or to search for patterns in the data.

- *Cluster similar themes, and list them under a few column headings*, for example, "deceit," "lying," "honesty," "happy-go-lucky," "romantic," "sexual innuendo" and so forth.

- Using the list, *listen to each audiotaped song*, replaying sections as needed to accurately understand the lyrics. *Write down each predetermined word, phrase, or theme under the correct column heading.*

- Using the most descriptive words, *turn the list of words, phrases and themes into categories* (e.g., lying, cheating, stealing). Then, condense the list by *grouping categories* (e.g., into "dishonesty").

- *Make final decisions about the material within each category*; replay the songs, if needed.

- *Interpret the results.*

Coding is a qualitative exercise, but the analysis may contain *both* qualitative and quantitative methods. For example, you might want to know whether country–western *or* classic-rock songs contain a higher percentage of references to cheating in love, or you might be interested in whether gender or age of the lead vocalist is related to the content of the lyrics. Berger (2000) suggests several steps in doing a quantitative analysis:

- *Decide on the topic and form a hypothesis about what you expect to find*, based on your theory and past research. *Test your hypothesis* using the lyrics data.

- *Provide definitions in operational (measurable) terms* (e.g., what criteria will define lyrics that refer to "deceit," other than the word itself?).

- Determine whether to include *all audiotaped songs or only a sample*. If a sample, determine a method of selection. *Explain the unit of analysis* (e.g., words, phrases, paragraphs or songs).

- *Determine the classification system. Each category of a variable must be mutually exclusive and, together, the categories must be exhaustive*—each recording unit (e.g., word) must fit into only one category per variable, and there must be a category for each recording unit.

- *Record the data by assigning a numerical value (number) or code to each recording unit.* For example, in each song, record how many times the word *lie* and its variants (lied, lying, etc.) were used. Calculate a test statistic. For example, is the percentage of the words/word sense phrases for "lie" and its variants different for country–western songs than for classic rock?

- *Interpret the results.* Was your hypothesis confirmed? What do the results imply for the theory?

How might one combine qualitative and quantitative research? There are at least three ways: (1) first conduct a qualitative study, followed by a separate quantitative analysis; (2) select one approach to be dominant and the other as the less-dominant, smaller study; or (3) mix both approaches more or less equally throughout the study (Creswell, 1994, pp. 177–178). A mixed-method approach offers a lot of potential, but it requires solid knowledge of both qualitative and quantitative methods. An exercise at the end of this chapter gives you practice in combining qualitative and quantitative approaches. The calculations can be done with a calculator; computer software can be used for more extensive calculations.

Regardless of the specific mix of qualitative and quantitative approaches, notice that none of this could be accomplished by traditional survey or interview methods.

Historical and Archival Data

As Tuchman (1994) points out, "we all live history . . . in the most mundane aspects of our daily lives, . . . [b]ut we often take for granted that structure of feeling" that permeates and guides everyday life (p. 313). In our everyday world:

> All that we take for granted as "natural" is a product of both historical and contemporary processes. Our task as social scientists is to interpret those multifaceted meanings, including their interactions with one another (Tuchman, 1994, p. 310).

Tuchman offers a revealing example of how we take time-specific meanings for granted. The inscription on a cemetery marker for a man who died in his mid-20s in the late 18th century might say, "He lived a useful life." By the 19th century, cemetery markers weren't remarking on "useful lives," but were "remembering" the deceased with "love" (p. 313).

What types of sentiments are chosen for cemetery markers today? If you don't know, the next time you pass by a cemetery, take a few minutes to look at markers placed in the past 20 or so years. Compare what you find to Tuchman's statement about the previous two centuries. And, check the older gravestones; see if you agree with Tuchman's descriptions.

Archival data are recorded information, usually **historical**, stored in repositories such as libraries or museums. These **secondary data** (data collected by someone other than the researcher) or **primary data** (new data collected by the researcher) can be used in historical research.

Suppose you wanted to know what kinds of topics were published in the early years of your high school newspaper or in the major newspaper in your hometown. Someone might already have published a historical study and you could read it as a secondary source of information. More likely, no one has done this, so where would you find primary data about publications in your school newspaper? Libraries often keep newspapers in their archives, usually copied onto tape or in a "micro" format, and increasingly in electronic format. The publishers also probably have archival copies, although accessing their files generally requires permission.

The following excerpt illustrates use of primary historical data. The research questions were: (1) are time period of publication and gender of the author associated with sex-stereotyped parental emotions in child-rearing manuals? If so, (2) can changes over time be identified?

Excerpt: *Emotional Stereotyping of Parents in Child-Rearing Manuals*

As part of a larger study of historical changes in popular American beliefs about emotional development, we examined sex-specific references to emotion in 54 child rearing manuals drawn from six distinctive eras in child rearing philosophy between 1915 and 1980. . . .

We identified six discontinuous periods, each with distinct sociocultural conditions that could be expected to influence popular conceptions of childrearing. The eras, and an abbreviated justification for the selection of each, were: 1) 1915–1922 (child welfare movement; increase in popularity of child rearing manuals); 2) 1927–1935 (period of disciplinary strictness and infant scheduling); 3) 1940–1945 (threat of war and World War II; issues of fear and father's absence); 4) 1947–1957 (early baby boom; prosperity and child-centered culture); 5) 1963–1970 (post-Sputnik; post-pill; period of major social movements); 6) 1974–1981 (increasing participation of women in full-time work force; increasing emphasis on father as caregiver). . . . The final sample for each era included between four and 13 books written for the lay audience. The total sample comprises a list of 54 books. . . . The authors of 21 books were female or female pairs; males or male pairs wrote another 21 books. For the remaining 12 books, author's sex was unknown or consisted of mixed-sex pairs or trios. . . .

In order to discriminate between the general theme of parental influence and the more specific emphasis on a psychodynamic rationale for parental influence, we coded individual books in the final sample for the extent to which they adopted a Freudian explanatory framework. Category 1 (no apparent Freudian influence) included those books which contained no technically accurate use of psychodynamic terminology; Category 2 (some Freudian influence) included those which used psychodynamic terminology that would be familiar to a lay audience (e.g., ego, unconscious), but loosely and without adopting a psychodynamic explanatory framework. Category 3 (strong Freudian influence) included those which used psychodynamic terminology and adopted a psychodynamic explanatory framework. Pairs of undergraduate raters coded each book (interrater reliability = .87 overall). . . . Across all eras, 87 percent of the books sampled were classified as Category 1, 7.4 percent as Category 2, and 5.6 percent as Category 3. . . .

The emotions of mothers and of fathers are evaluated quite differently from one another, whereas little if any distinction is drawn between the emotional reactions of sons and of daughters. Mothers are represented as exhibiting a tendency to be emotional; the expression of this emotion, if it should become "out of control," is construed as a serious threat to the child's achievement of healthy maturity. Fathers are described as having a tendency to respond to their children with less feeling and more "objectivity." These contrasting representations of maternal and paternal emotion are not simply an artifact of psychoanalytic influences on American theories of child rearing, nor are they related to changes in styles of parenting. . . .

We found no differences across eras in the proportion of books containing sex-specific references to emotion. . . . Era differences in proportion of sex-specific passages to all emotion passages . . . also were [statistically] nonsignificant. . . . Author's sex was unrelated to the likelihood of including sex-specific emotion references. . . . Across all eras, mothers' emotions constituted the most frequent sex-specific reference to emotion; daughters' emotions were mentioned least frequently (Shields & Koster, 1989, pp. 44–47).

Notice the interesting mixture of qualitative and quantitative methods. The student coders engaged in a highly qualitative activity to transform what they read into a consistent classification scheme (e.g, level of Freudian influence). Examples of quantitative analysis include (1) the proportion of sex-specific passages across historical eras (and determining the differences that were "statistically nonsignificant"), and (2) the correlation among the coders, which was fairly high (0.87). (Statistical significance is discussed in later chapters.)

The authors of this textbook conducted a study that illustrates how primary historical data can be useful in quantitative research. Our research investigates the effects of inbreeding (reproduction between close relatives, for example, cousins) on infant mortality among the Amish residing in Lancaster County, Pennsylvania. The data consist of records kept by the Amish, an Anabaptist religious group, for purposes entirely unrelated to research.

Excerpt: *Inbreeding and Infant Mortality among the Amish*

Our data are derived from the member directory of the Old Order Amish of the Lancaster county, Pennsylvania Settlement. . . . The directory represents membership and family records collected and printed by the Lancaster Amish for their internal use. The records include data on births, deaths, marriage dates, residence and church district, and family of origin for nearly every member of the Lancaster Settlement (Dorsten, Hotchkiss, & King, 1999, p. 265).

Did you notice that the title of the article mentions inbreeding, but these data don't contain any information about inbreeding? Data to measure the indicator for the variable inbreeding were obtained from a separate source and matched to individuals in the main source. The source of the data on inbreeding is somewhat unique—it provides information to calculate the presence of intermarriages for up to 12 generations of Amish families.

We produced the inbreeding coefficients using information from the Fisher Family History . . . which documents genealogy relationships for descendants of Christian Fisher, one of the founders of the Old Order Amish community in the United

States. . . . More than 90% of the Amish population is included after 1900 (Dorsten, Hotchkiss, & King, 1999, p. 265).

The "inbreeding coefficients" are numbers representing the degree to which an individual's ancestry contains people who are related to the person: the closer the relative and the greater the number of close relatives, the higher the person's inbreeding coefficient. The paper uses a statistical model to predict the effects of inbreeding on infant mortality. The model included statistical controls for birth order, whether first born, gender, survival status of the immediately prior sibling and spacing between the birth of the immediately prior sibling and the infant studied.

We found the higher the level of inbreeding, the greater the chances of dying during the first year for infants who survive the first week of life. More important to social scientists, the findings suggest that several sociodemographic variables—including year of child's birth and church district of residence—predict a greater risk of infant death in the first year of life for those who survive for at least 30 days. Families in some church districts tend to follow more traditional Amish practices and beliefs (e.g., fewer immunizations) than families living in less traditional districts. And economic level differs by church district.

These historical data exhibit three particularly noteworthy features. (1) The records were kept for private use of members of the Amish Settlement with no thought about their use in research. (2) Record keeping was done by a private organization (the Amish) with no large research funding from the government or a private foundation. (3) The overall quality (**reliability** and **validity**) and completeness of the records provide data sufficient to support a comparatively sophisticated quantitative study.

Physical Trace Data

In everyday conversation, the word *unobtrusive* means an action that is low-profile, inconspicuous, and restrained. Similarly, unobtrusive data collection is "inconspicuous" to the research subjects.

One of the useful aspects of unobtrusive data is that measurements are unaffected by the data collection. The observations are made after the behavior of subjects is complete. In contrast, a method such as a personal interview has the potential for influencing respondents to give answers that don't reflect their opinions, or to give deliberately inaccurate accounts of their behavior. Use of **physical trace data** is a prime example of unobtrusive measurement. Examples of trace data include physical evidence left at the scenes of crimes, such as fingerprints, footprints, hair samples, and DNA specimens; broken windows, bullet holes, and other damage to physical facilities; and bruises, broken bones, and other traumas of victims.

Trace data from diverse fields of study inform everyday life in many ways. Environmental conservationists evaluate the effects of different types of human activity on mammals such as deer. They count road kills and record season, type of mammal, geographic location, and other details. Investigators study sunken ships and crashed aircraft to determine the reason for an accident, such as the plane crash of the late John F. Kennedy, Jr., into the Atlantic Ocean in 1999, and the loss of the space shuttle *Columbia* over Texas in February 2003. Soup kitchen workers might count the number of bundles of silverware prior to serving a meal and again at the end of the mealtime to find out how many meals (or persons) they served.

In the social sciences, archaeologists and anthropologists are more likely to rely on trace measures than are other scientists. Arrowheads found in farm fields provide evidence of early human settlements. Well-preserved family Bibles suggest the importance of Christianity to our ancestors.

Trace evidence, especially when combined with other forms of data, can yield important clues about social life and human problems. For example, when one is homeless and lives on urban streets, or conducts business outdoors all day long, and stores and restaurants require a purchase to use their restrooms, how are bodily needs such as urination managed? Duneier's *Sidewalk*, a participant observation study, details the ways in which street vendors and panhandlers in Greenwich Village, New York, solve many problems of daily life. One of the vendors describes his solution for managing urination and offers clues for what might be called a "distinctively aromatic" approach to collecting physical trace data.

Excerpt: *When You Gotta Go.* A former mayor of New York City got a lot of publicity for his public stand about the private matter of bathroom use. Mudrick, a street vendor, recounts his creative approach in response to the city's law.

> "I gotta get me a paper cup and I'm gonna be all right." . . . "Guiliano [Rudolph Guiliani, then the mayor of New York City] says you can't go to the bathroom [directly onto streets, sidewalks and alleys]. I invented this thing. Now everybody out here gets a cup." . . . "I went to Riker's Island jail for [using] the street. . . . Now I get a cup." . . .
>
> While Mudrick pretends to be hailing a cab, he holds the cup and urinates under an untucked shirt. . . . On another occasion, after dumping his urine in the sewer, Mudrick placed the Starbucks cup he had just used in the branch of a tree on Sixth Avenue. . . . I had occasionally noticed paper cups hanging from tree branches but had never thought twice about them. . . . "This is my bathroom. . . . Everybody do's [sic] it" (Duneier, 1999, pp. 173–175).

Using trace data, what clues are in the brief excerpt that might be used to identify the city streets in greatest need of public restrooms? How might you collect the data? One technique for data collection might be visual. Paper cups in trees at certain heights might suggest an inability to access (or dislike for using) public restrooms. However, despite Mudrick's assertion, not all of the men use a cup. Some prefer the sides of buildings, particularly buildings that have an indented section of a wall, and others hide between cars and around, or even in, trash dumpsters.

Of course, counts of paper cups in trees are only suggestive and must be combined with other data before drawing definite conclusions. So, we might need to broaden our potential sources and types of data. What about olfactory cues—might one be able to "follow one's nose" to identify the street locations most frequently used by the men? Would weather affect visual or olfactory cues? Would this study be an invasion of anyone's privacy?

Example: "*Sneaky Measurement*" of Crime and Disorder. In the United Kingdom, Garwood et al. (2000) report that crime "hot spots" aren't well identified, due to imperfect recording of details about location, especially for vehicle crime (p. 159). Moreover, recorded data often do not provide adequate information about time, place, and circumstance to support specific crime-fighting policies. Underreporting can distort the official record of domestic violence and hate crimes, for example (p. 159).

Garwood and her coauthors propose some unobtrusive sources of data they obtained using "sneaky measurement." They argue these sources supplement official crime records and thereby improve the validity of crime information. Examples of some measures they review include:

- *alcohol consumption in public locations*—indicators for the measures include quantity of bottles and cans found in litter containers in parks and other public places

- *vandalism*—indicators include rate of repairs to football stadium seats, bus shelters and telephone booths

- *non-standard maintenance costs in schools* (e.g., losses and damages to books and journals)

- *illegal drug use (heroin smoking)*—indicators include remains of matches and burned foil in bars and public restrooms

- *illegal drug use (amphetamines)*—indicators include high rate of sale of water and soft drinks in clubs (Garwood et al., 2000, pp. 162–63).

Because unobtrusive measures seldom are attached to any single individual, ethical concerns about invasion of privacy are reduced (p. 162). Thinking about your campus or home community, what are some other "sneaky measures" of crime, disorder, or misuse that could be added to this list?

INDIRECT METHODS OF DATA COLLECTION

Unobtrusive Observation

Unobtrusive observation means to observe subjects without the subjects knowing they are being observed. Why not inform subjects they are being watched? The main rationale is to avoid contaminating their behavior or conversation, or to avoid depending on imprecise memories of respondents.

Webb and his coauthors (2000) report an interesting unobtrusive study of drivers' use of turn signals. The main research question was whether drivers conform to the signaling behavior of cars in front of them. Observers were stationed inconspicuously beside the road at an intersection. For a period of 4 weeks they recorded (1) whether drivers used turn signals before turning, (2) direction of the turn, (3) whether a turning car in front used a turn signal, (4) whether another vehicle was driving 100 feet or less behind the vehicle being observed, and (5) gender of the driver. They found more conformity for left turns than for right turns, and more conformity if drivers of both vehicles were female. Follow-up studies found more erratic signaling among drivers of expensive automobiles and in bad weather. Do you think insurance companies might be interested in results from unobtrusive observations such as these?

Content Analysis

Content analysis is a method for coding recorded communication into usable form. Generally, this amounts to creating variables from diffuse communication found in sources such as books, magazines, journals, newspapers, diaries, and other print media and from audio and audiovisual recordings. Content analysis has been used to study a variety of interesting topics such as propaganda, international differences in communication content, cultural patterns of individuals and groups, and even coding of open-ended survey questions (Weber, 1990, p. 9).

More recently, e-mail and electronic text and images, such as those found at computer Web sites and on Web-site "bulletin boards," have been primary source data for content analysis. For example, Baron (1998, pp. 147–148) finds that e-mail writers tend to be more informal and more self-disclosing and feel more socially equal with others than when using pen and paper or a word processor. Indicators of the variables include less careful editing of e-mail than other written documents; more familiar tone in e-mail than in other methods of communication (e.g., use of first names), and use of humor or sarcasm between people who have never met in person. An e-mail project at the end of this chapter will give you an opportunity to do content analysis of e-mail.

We have already reviewed one example of extensive use of content analysis—the historical study of the content of child-rearing books by Shields and Koster (1989). Also, the cemetery study of historic gender differences (Foster, Hummel, & Adamchak, 1998) uses a form of content analysis to transform information from gravestone inscriptions into variables. Here's a third example: a study of political cartoons.

Example: "Cold War" Cartoons. Gamson and Stuart (1992) used content analysis of political cartoons to study two competing points of view during the Cold War: (1) the Soviet threat must be balanced by a strong U.S. military, and (2) the consequences of nuclear war are so devastating that common security and peaceful coexistence with the Soviets was the only sensible policy. Supporters of the strong

U.S. military position were described by the authors as well funded by many wealthy interests and commanding a very large imbalance of resources to promote their viewpoint. Consequently, the authors were surprised to find that, by a small margin, the cartoons reflected the "peaceful coexistence outlook" over the military competition outlook.

The political-cartoons study illustrates some important general points about content analysis. First, not all cartoons could be analyzed, so sampling was required. The authors sampled a sequence of 15 time periods surrounding important events related to the threat of nuclear war. Time-interval examples include (1) detonation of the first Soviet nuclear bomb, (2) launch of the Soviet Sputnik, (3) the Atmospheric Test Ban Treaty, and (4) the summit between President Reagan and Soviet Premier Gorbachev at Reykjavik, Iceland. For each of the 15 time periods, the authors sampled cartoons from 16 large daily newspapers and 3 major news magazines. So there are two levels of sampling: (1) the 16 newspapers and 3 news magazines are a sample of all newspapers and magazines, and from these, (2) only cartoons from selected time intervals were included. The newspapers and magazines and the time intervals were selected purposely to represent top news sources and important periods of time.

Second, a particularly interesting aspect of the study is the coding. The task was to code the diffuse content of the cartoons into consistent recording units, so that each would reflect one of the two views about the competition between the U.S. and the Soviet Union.

> We coded each cartoon for its central idea element—for example, "The Russians are not to be trusted." . . . or "All nations are in the same boat when it comes to nuclear war." The specific codes are clustered into different variations of Cold War [or other] security packages, or in some cases, into other categories (Gamson & Stuart, 1992, p. 65).

Interrater reliability is reported to be 80 percent or higher (interrater reliability was 0.87 overall in the study of childrearing manuals). High reliability generally is reported for content analysis, despite difficult sources of information and complex concepts. Nonetheless, it is not easy to produce reliable content analysis. There's a big difference between superficial knowledge of some general principles and coding items reliably. As Berger points out:

> Do not be surprised if you run into difficulties in doing a content analysis (or any other kind of research, for that matter), and don't be too hard on yourself, either. It takes a good deal of practice and experience to learn how to manage the difficulties that researchers face. The important thing is to think clearly and work carefully, and if you have the opportunity, share what you've learned (Berger, 2000, p. 185).

One way to more clearly understand the difficulties of doing good research and getting some practice in coping with research problems is by completing the exercises at the end of each chapter, which we hope you've been doing.

RELIABILITY AND VALIDITY OF INDIRECT METHODS

Recall from Chapter 4 that *reliability* refers to consistency. A measure is reliable to the extent it yields the same answer each time it is used, in the absence of change in whatever is being measured. In the case of content analysis, for instance, the reliability issue is: Do the coding schemes produce the same research results across different coders?

Validity (accuracy of measuring a construct) is evaluated by three questions: (1) Is there high content validity or general agreement that the variable measures the underlying idea (face validity) and covers all dimensions of the idea (domain coverage)? (2) Does the measure predict a standard (criterion or predictive validity)? (3) Does the measure behave as theory predicts it should (construct validity)?

To evaluate reliability and validity, a variety of ways is appropriate for each of the indirect methods discussed in this chapter. In *Sidewalk*, do descriptive interpretations show sensible relationships with other variables (construct validity)? For example, do only people living or working daily on the street use the cup as a restroom? Is this (and other) behavior consistent with theory underlying the study, for example, about how race or social class defines life for those on the street? How much confidence would you place in observing cups in trees to indicate the need for public restrooms (face validity)?

In the study of cold-war cartoons, more than one coder was used. The agreement among coders, a measure of reliability of the coding process, was reported to be high. In the study of cemetery markers, do the selected words or word units indicate stable patterns across markers predicted by a theory of gender inequality (construct validity)? And did the historical records, the primary data source, agree with the inscriptions on the gravestones (a measure of concurrent validity in the coding)? In the study of child-rearing manuals, do researchers agree that a Freudian framework can be used to evaluate child-rearing manuals spanning different time periods (face validity)?

It appears that reliable information usually can be coded from content analysis of a variety of sources. The reliability could depend more on the accuracy and completeness of the sources, however, than on the ability to train coders to produce reliable results.

ADVANTAGES AND LIMITATIONS OF INDIRECT METHODS

Advantages

There are three primary advantages shared by the indirect methods of data collection. First, they provide access to information not available in other sources. This advantage is amply illustrated by the studies cited in this chapter. How else could we get a glimpse of time differences in infant survival over the past 12 decades other than from historical data? Similarly, content analysis of cultural and political commentary in popular media can be undertaken in ways that couldn't be duplicated by surveys.

Second, indirect methods don't produce reactions from respondents that might contaminate the data. Using your campus, which approach is likely to give the more accurate picture of racial attitudes and racial integration: Counting the number of mixed-race groups at the student center or a survey? The ideal might be to use both.

Third, direct unobtrusive observation can avoid errors that likely would result from usual survey methods. Compare, for example, interviewing people about their use of turn signals to stationing observers in inconspicious locations to watch what actually happens.

Limitations

The primary limitation of indirect data sources is that they seldom contain all the information we need. No information is available on gravestones other than the content of inscriptions. Similarly, unobtrusively observing group behavior at the student center gives limited information about the people who are observed.

In summary, the strengths and limitations of indirect methods reinforce the need to rely on many sources of data, use many methods, be alert to the limitations of each data source and method, and combine information from many sources in imaginative ways.

SUMMARY

This chapter describes several types of indirect sources of data: (1) contemporary records such as music, newspapers, and political cartoons; (2) archival and historical records like child-rearing books, records of gravestone inscriptions, and church records; and (3) physical traces. In addition, the chapter describes two indirect methods of data collection: unobtrusive observation and content analysis.

Indirect methods produce data not available from other sources; this is one primary strength. Also, indirect methods can produce more valid data than from surveys, because indirect methods avoid contamination from respondent reactions or from inaccurate recall.

But issues of validity are important limitations of indirect sources of data, particularly historical data, for which coverage may be incomplete and sources for checking accuracy limited. Even contemporary data sources can be limited—not all recorded music is available (or remembered, even by the artist), and paper cups can blow away. Perhaps the primary disadvantage of indirect sources of data is the limited amount of information they contain. At best, just a few variables can be retrieved from gravestone inscriptions, for example. Historical records are incomplete, and the content of garbage cans doesn't give a full account of the drinking habits of their owners.

YOUR REVIEW SHEET: QUESTIONS DISCUSSED IN THIS CHAPTER

1. What gender-descriptive words did you include in the list you prepared as you read the study of gender differences on gravestones? Briefly evaluate your list.

2. Suppose you plan a study of gender stereotyping in TV commercials. Propose a list of words and phrases you would count as stereotypical of (a) women and (b) men.

3. What words or phrases have you heard recently in songs of any musical type that suggest deception in a love relationship? What are some other words and phrases that convey the idea of "lying" that were not mentioned in this chapter?

4. Briefly explain how and why one might combine qualitative and quantitative approaches in the same study. Include an example to illustrate.

5. Referring to the excerpt on "paper cups," if weather conditions change either visual or olfactory cues, how would the results of the study be affected? Would weather change produce concerns about reliability or validity?

6. Thinking about your campus or home community, what are some "sneaky measures" of crime, disorder, or misuse other than those mentioned in the chapter?

7. Pick an example from this chapter that is used to illustrate reliability. Discuss how the example helps one think about the importance of consistent measures in research.

8. Using one example from this chapter that is used to illustrate validity, discuss how this example helps one think about the importance of using a measure that reflects the idea (construct) it is designed to measure (validity).

END NOTES

1. Adapted from Webb et al. (2000). Webb and coauthors don't mention contemporary recorded sources and divide observation into two categories: (1) simple observation, and (2) contrived observation. In the former, the investigator just watches, unobtrusively. In contrived observation, the investigator intervenes in some way unknown to the subjects.

STUDY TERMS

archival data Recorded information, usually **historical**, that is stored in repositories such as libraries or museums.

content analysis Conversion of recorded communication into usable form, usually variables. Recorded communication is found in print materials (e.g., books and magazines) in audio and visual recordings, and in electronic text and images, such as those found at computer Web sites.

direct methods Method of data collection in which data are obtained personally from subjects or respondents. Examples include interviews, questionnaires, and observation of behaviors. Compare with indirect methods.

historical data Data describing the past. Historical research often is used to examine changes over time, such as in pictures or words.

indirect methods Methods of data collection that don't involve contacts between the researcher and subjects. Compare with direct methods.

physical trace data Data such as paths worn in the grass and fingerprints indicative of subjects' previous activity. Other examples include checking litter containers for cans and bottles to estimate the extent of illegal use of alcohol in public places, and examining rates of repair of public telephones as a measure of vandalism in a community.

primary data Data collected for a specific study. The researcher defines a research question and collects new data tailored to answer the question. Contrast with secondary data.

recording units In content analysis, the basic items to be classified. There are six commonly used types of recording units for text: word, word sense, sentence, theme, paragraph and whole text.

reliability Consistency of a measure; does the same result occur on repeated measurement in the absence of real change?

secondary data Data collected by someone other than the researcher, often for multiple purposes. Prominent examples of secondary data include surveys such as the *General Social Survey* and the U.S. decennial census.

theme In content analysis, a recording unit as subject/verb/object, such as "Snow/covers/the grass."

validity Accuracy with which a measure represents the construct it is designed to measure.

word sense In content analysis, the meaning of words or phrases and phrases constituting a unit (e.g., New York state). Different specific words and phrases often convey the same or nearly the same meaning, for example, "applauding" and "clapping."

unobtrusive observation Watching behaviors in a way that is "inconspicuous" to the research subjects

EXERCISES

Exercise 7.1. Content Analysis: Gender Advertisements

Directions: Select an issue of a popular press magazine that has advertising. Pick at least 30 ads with images of one or more adults. If you don't get 30 ads in one issue, continue through subsequent issues until you get 30.

Code all ads (photographs or drawings) that include images of one or more adults and record the information in a table like the one shown below. For each adult in each ad, record "gender" and assign a code for two additional variables:

Variable 1, Strength: three categories—strong, neutral, weak

Variable 2, Sex object: two categories—yes, no

Be sure to define operational criteria that assign every person in the ads to one and only one of the categories for each variable. Consider strength to include both physical strength and social strength, i.e., "in control of the situation."

For ambiguous images, assign codes and make a note about your decision on a separate sheet of paper. Also, assign an ad number for each ad.

Sample table:

Ad #	Gender	Strength ("In Control of Situation")	Sex Object
1	male	strong	yes
1	female	strong	no
1	male	neutral	no
⋮	⋮	⋮	⋮
30	female	weak	yes

In this example, the first three people were pictured in the same ad. You may have quite a few more observations (rows in the table) than ads.

After recording the data, assign numbers to the "strength" and "sex object" variables as follows:

strength: 1 = weak, 2 = neutral, 3 = strong

sex object: 0 = no, 1 = yes

Then calculate separate averages by gender for both variables:

1. Average "strength" for females: Add up the values of "strength" for females and divide the result by the number of females (*not* the number of ads).

2. Average "sex object" for females: Add up the values of "sex object" for females and divide the result by the number of females. Note that this average is the same as the proportion of females you judged to be sex objects.

3. Average "strength" for males: Add up the values of "strength" for males and divide the result by the number of males (*not* the number of ads).

4. Average "sex object" for males: Add up the values of "sex object" for males and divide the result by the number of males. Note that this average is the same as the proportion of males you judged to be sex objects.

Questions

1. What is the name of the magazine you chose? In this magazine, which gender had the greater number of ads? Taking the type of readership into account, offer a brief explanation.

2. Which gender had the greater average score on "strength"? On "sex object"? Offer a short social-science explanation.

3. Describe any coding problems you encountered and how you solved them. Be specific.

4. Discuss one advantage and one disadvantage of content analysis as a method of data collection, based on this exercise.

5. Did you notice any tendency for the "strength" and "sex object" variables to be more alike in the same ad than they were across different ads? Suppose individuals in the same ad, in fact, were more like others in the same ad than to people in different ads. What effect might this have on generalization to all pictures? (*Hint:* Refer to the discussion of "grouping" in Chapter 5.)

Exercise 7.2. Unobtrusive Analysis: Studying Campus Dorm Windows

Directions: Code and evaluate the types of window decorations of students living in dorms on your campus, as observed from outside the dorm buildings. The research question is: What are the most common symbols hung in dorm windows on this campus? Your instructor will help you with some of the "boundary" decisions, such as whether you should observe all windows in selected dorms and whether to select all dorms.

Before beginning this exercise, review carefully the Code of Ethics forms in Appendix A. *If you do not understand any of the ethical expectations, check with your instructor before proceeding with the exercise.*

As an unobtrusive researcher, do not disturb dorm residents. Do all viewing during daylight hours. View building(s) from as far away as possible and yet collect your data, and avoid any behaviors that might lead residents/others to become suspicious of your presence. Consult your instructor beforehand if you do not understand any field procedure.

Decide what types of symbols to record. For example, will you include all items seen from the outside, such as curtains, window shades, and blinds? You might assign a code for each item (e.g., C = curtains/shades/blinds, G = Greek letters, N = name, P = picture). Construct a table for recording observations similar to the sample table shown below. (You need one column for each dorm in your study and one row for each window.) When you have completed data collection, answer the questions below. Have your table ready to hand in.

	Dorm 1	Dorm 2	Dorm 3	Dorm *n*
Window 1	C, N, N			
Window 2	C, G, P			
Window 3	P, N, N			
Window 4	P, P, P, G			
Window 5				
Window *n*				

Questions

1. Did you code all windows, or only some? Explain briefly how you decided.

2. How many windows did you observe? Did you skip any windows? How might this "boundary" decision affect your conclusions about window decorations on your campus?

3. Briefly describe the decisions you made in coding the decorations.

4. Briefly note any problems you encountered in observing unobtrusively.

5. What is the total number of objects you coded in all windows? If you coded all objects in each window, what is the average number of objects per window? (total number of objects/total number of windows)

6. What was the most common item observed in windows? The least common?

7. What percentage of windows contained no objects? (Number of windows with no objects/total number of windows × 100.)

8. What do you conclude about these patterns of window decorations on your campus, as viewed from outside the building? About unobtrusive research for this project?

Exercise 7.3. Evaluation of Research: Historical Analysis

Directions: Refer to the excerpt on "emotional stereotyping of parents in child rearing manuals" to answer the following questions.

Factual Questions

1. What was the research question of the study?
2. Explain in your own words how the researchers selected specific manuals.
3. Why was the time period divided into eras?
4. Did the researchers find "emotional stereotyping"? Explain.
5. Were there differences in parental stereotyping over time?

Questions for Discussion

1. Did the manuals provide appropriate information for the purposes of this study?
2. List two potential sources of historical information about "emotional stereotyping of parents" other than child-rearing manuals.

Exercise 7.4. E-Project: Social Aspects of E-Mail

Directions:

Step 1: Review the section on content analysis and e-mail. Then, select a topic and write a one-sentence statement about a finding you expect from study of e-mail messages. You can use a qualitative or quantitative approach or a combination of the two. Review relevant sections in this chapter about e-mail as a source of indirect data, and Chapter 3 or other chapters about qualitative and quantitative approaches.

Step 2: Answer questions 1–3 below.

Step 3: Look at the e-mail messages on page 172. Answer questions 4–9. Be prepared to hand in your worksheet.

Questions

1. Before looking at the e-mails, state the topic and your expected finding(s). If you use a quantitative approach, state a testable hypothesis. Be sure to include a comparison group (e.g., another form of communication).
2. Describe the steps of your approach (e.g., Tesch's qualitative, and/or Berger's quantitative).
3. Briefly describe how you decided between a qualitative and quantitative approach. Evaluate the e-mails.
4. Summarize your findings; then consider your findings in relation to what you would expect to find from your comparison group.
5. Summarize what you think are the strong points of your study.
6. Summarize weakness(es) of your study. Mention limitations of the sample of e-mail messages you were able to observe.
7. Describe the most difficult part of the exercise, and briefly explain how you overcame this difficulty.

Sample E-Mail Messages for Exercise 7.4

1. Kim, I am looking for a website or other such source that lists figures for expenditures for things like groceries, transportation, misc. expenditures per family, either in the US as a whole or preferably broken down by state or region. Can you point me in the right direction? Thanks. Tony

2. sue, three women who were part of one of the largest u.s. protests for peace will present a symposium at 7 pm on Tuesday, march 13 in room 138 of the campus center. they will speak about their experiences as members of the women's encampment for a future of peace and justice in romulus, new york during the summer of 1983. at the urging of peace activists in europe and throughout the us, the camp was created to protest the world-wide nuclear arms build-up. members of the camp staged vigils, marches, and even wove webs of yarn on the depot fences in protest. numerous protestors were arrested for acts of civil disobedience and suffered verbal and physical harassment from a minority of local community members. this program is part of the convocation year focus on "a culture of peace" and is an event celebrating women's history month. reception will follow the program. megan

3. Karen, only message I received from U. ;o(Bob
   > > Hi, second test to see if U got my message! :o) Karen

4. hi yourself! Great to hear from you. I'd love to have lunch and catch up. this week is really jammed up for a bunch of silly reasons but how about next week? my date book is downstairs but how about if you give me a few dates when you're available and I'll return the message . . . Suzi

5. hi lindsay, glad you like the p-card. don't you think I look like @@@: ??? found it in a batch of old travel things, and thought you'd have the right sense of humor! let's do our annual reunion at our place. david'll dress up in his special outfit and demonstrate his fawning skills—LOL! david and mary

6. Karen, enjoying some freedom from classes? Got an opinion? Several years ago, as a beginning nursing student, a group of us did a 'pretend' research study on nurse's attitudes toward death and dying. I have half a mind to resurrect it and do a real study. From what I witnessed, there have been few, if any changes over time. Thoughts??? Got notice of the Amnesty meeting too late to go—again :-/ Paula

7. Dear Heather,
   We'd love to have you on the Community Council. I will try to get the notification of the next meeting out to you. I believe it will be at 9:00 am on 12/8/04 in the third floor conference room of the Health Department on the corner of Fourth St. & Central Ave. We can talk about having you come speak with the teens too—that sounds great. I need to get approval from the Alternative Education Supervisor first, so give me a brief overview of what you'd be discussing with them and I'll put together a proposal for her and we can put you on the schedule. That OK with you? Talk to you soon—Patti

8. M, Wasn't sure if the days you are talking about when you will be here, but I thought giving you my schedule might help you make a decision. Tues: reading at the library—morning/afternoon, exercise—afternoon. Wed: reading—morning, class—1-5. Thurs: reading—morning/afternoon, class—2:30-5, group meeting—5:00 until ??? Fri: reading morning/afternoon, exercise—afternoon. Also, would you be able to bring the picture of my apartment you took in June? Love, Me!

9. Hi Sara. Sorry to keep bugging you but now I don't need a ride to the pool. John has arranged to be picked up, so I can drive myself. This is better because I've just realized I have a late afternoon meeting Friday and am not sure when I can leave for the pool. But want to go out for coffee afterwards? Thanks very much for being willing to help out! Roberta

10. Hi Steve . . . Sat PM great :-D going to Pitt on Fri—hope *<{:o}) finds me there—taking my stocking to hang on the fp! Talk w/u toward end of week . . . LUVnXOXOXOX Joy

8 SURVEYS

INTRODUCTION: LOOKING AT HOW THE SOCIAL WORLD WORKS

"I'm thinking of taking your course next semester. What topics will it cover?" Have you ever "interviewed" the professor who is teaching a course before enrolling in it? Students often ask their friends similar questions about a course and instructor. These are examples of informal interviews. The personal interview is one of the main tools for collecting data in a survey. A **survey** is a tool for gathering data by asking questions of many people. Surveys are a familiar way to obtain data in everyday life, and they are used extensively in social science research.

A great deal is known about survey methods (Dillman, 2000). For example, a well-designed survey provides accurate estimate of characteristics of an entire population, based on relatively small samples. Election polls routinely make correct calls of election results using sample sizes of about 1000 to 1500 people—a very small percentage of voters, except in small election districts.

Surveys ask questions about a diversity of topics, including:

- health status (e.g., disabilities, disease history)
- drug, alcohol and tobacco consumption
- criminal behavior
- victimization history (such as victim of violence, victim of robbery)
- attitudes (toward politics, religious minorities, fairness of income inequality, death penalty, civil rights, women's rights, legalizing marijuana, assisted suicide)
- opinions (e.g., about seriousness of the crime problem, foreign aid, mixed-couple dating and marriage, welfare spending, gay marriage).

In addition, many large-scale surveys ask demographic and socioeconomic questions about—

- gender, race, age, and marital status (single, married, divorced . . .)
- number of children (and often ages, sometimes gender)
- education completed
- occupation, income/earnings, employment status
- geographic location (e.g., state, country, or city of residence).

There's little doubt that survey data have revolutionized social research over the past 40 years or so. And, external validity (generalization beyond the study) is comparatively high for surveys. But, as we will see, there are reasons to be cautious when interpreting survey data.

Goals of This Chapter

Three themes guide the discussion in this chapter: (1) the flexibility of survey research for handling many topics, (2) the standards for constructing and evaluating surveys, and (3) the strengths and weakness of survey data.

We'll first consider three excerpts from research journals. Each excerpt shows the process of developing and executing one type of survey, and illustrates some of the strengths and limitations of that survey type. We'll also consider Internet surveys. Then, we'll review some of the principles for conducting valid surveys. The last section presents an excerpt about the effects of parental education and occupation on attitudes toward childrearing. It extends the discussion begun in Chapter 3 about the linkages between theory and research.

THREE FAMILIAR TYPES OF SURVEYS AND A NEWER ONE

Three types of surveys are familiar to most people: personal interview, telephone interview, and mail questionnaire. Internet surveys also are beginning to be used extensively in social research, albeit with some caution.

Personal Interview

Forms of Personal Interviews. It's a beautiful Monday afternoon. You're sitting in the sunshine thinking about what to do next weekend. You know what you'd like to do, see the Dave Matthews Band at the Arena. But you've not been to one of their concerts and decide to get some information from a friend who always attends their concerts, sometimes traveling to nearby states. You start a general conversation:

How did you like the last couple of Dave Matthews concerts?

Your friend describes her recent experiences in some detail; you ask a few more questions, but mostly listen to her descriptions. You're conducting an informal or unstructured interview.

An **unstructured interview** is a "conversation." It's used to learn more about respondents than can be expressed by answers to a few specific questions written in advance of the interview. But, think for a moment about the nature and expectations of this "conversation" (see Figure 8.1). First, it's unlike ordinary exchanges. The interviewer (you) is responsible for providing direction, and the respondent provides

FIGURE 8.1.   Nature and Expectations for Personal Interviews.

the content (Weiss, 1994, p. 207). Second, most of the narrative is provided by the respondent, and the format often isn't question–response, question–response, as it would be in a more formally structured interview. Third, respondents must have some level of trust in you to share their insights (Maxim, 1999). Typically, friends have that trust, developed over a period of time. By comparison, interviewers must gain trust in a very short time. And if the topic is personal or about deviant behavior, extra caution is warranted.

It's later that same afternoon. You meet another friend while walking home and decide to ask him about Dave Matthews concerts. You have the first friend's conversation in mind, and decide to ask more specific questions, including probes, to get additional details. A **probe** is a question or comment used to clarify responses or to request more detail.

YOU: Have you seen the Dave Matthews Band in concert?

FRIEND: Yes.

YOU: What're their shows like? How much do tickets cost? [open-ended probe]

FRIEND: . . . best show I've ever seen.

YOU: Best show you've ever seen? [feedback probe]

FRIEND: This band grew stronger on the road and by word of mouth.

YOU: How did they "grow stronger"? [probe to clarify vague answer]

Although you probably didn't have a written list of questions like an interviewer would have, you're providing more structure to this conversation than the previous one. You've conducted a **semistructured interview**. An interview of this type that includes several people is called a **focus group** or a focused interview (Merton, Fiske, & and Kendall, 1990).

A **structured interview** is a questionnaire administered by an interviewer. It is less flexible than an unstructured or semistructured interview, there is limited probing for additional information, and typically the response categories are provided by the interviewer. The structured interview is designed to return reliable quantitative data for use in statistical analysis.

The following excerpt from a recent journal article uses semistructured personal interviews to examine the pros and cons of open adoption of infants.

Excerpt: *Open Adoption of Infants: Advantages and Disadvantages*

The term *open adoption* refers to a continuum of options that enables birthparents and adoptive parents to have information about and communication with one another before or after placement of the child or at both times. An essential feature of open adoption, regardless of the extent of the openness, is that the birth parents legally relinquish all parental claims and rights to the child. The adoptive parents are the legal parents.

[A]n open letter inviting prospective participants to contact the researcher was included in newsletters of two New England infertility and adoption-support organizations and . . . to all parents who had a recent open adoption in [one New England] state. . . . The letter explained that the interview would be tape-recorded in the respondents' home and that parents would be interviewed jointly as a couple and guaranteed confidentiality. . . .

A semi-structured interview guide . . . was developed and then pretested to assess the instrument's content validity. . . . [S]ome items were added to the questionnaire and others were revised. . . . The interviews . . . lasted from 1 1/2 to four hours, depending on how much the respondents had to say. . . . Twenty-one adoptive couples were included in the sample. . . . All respondents were asked, "What, if any, were your initial fears, anxieties, and concerns about the adoption being open?" and "How did you initially feel about doing an open adoption?" . . .

. . . The parents often noted that the issue of openness was eclipsed by the enormity of four other concerns: coping with infertility; finding a baby; dealing with unresponsive or obstructive social workers, lawyers, and medical personnel; and dealing with the lifelong issues present in all adoptive families. The parents, whatever level of openness they experienced, thought that openness was simply not a matter of much concern . . . (Siegel, 1993, pp. 16–20).

Thinking about the interviews with adoptive parents, what are some strengths of personal interviews? Generally, respondents are more likely to provide answers to questions in a personal interview than in a self-administered questionnaire, and personal interviews produce higher response rates than do other types of surveys. Another important advantage of face-to-face interviewing is that interviewers can follow-up on incomplete, unclear, or unanticipated responses using a probe. For example, a parent who says "finding a baby" was the most difficult part of adoption could be asked—

Could you please explain in greater detail?

Why do you think some people might say, "I don't know" to a question such as:

Before bringing your baby home, about how many times per week did you talk to family or friends about the adoption process?

Even if they don't know the exact number, they likely have a reasonable estimate. But, sometimes people need a bit of time to think about a question. The interviewer, who is face-to-face with the respondent, might probe by saying:

Would you take a moment to think about the question?

or

If you had to choose one answer, what would it be?

Typically, personal interviews are conducted in the respondents' own social settings. Most people probably feel more relaxed in their own homes, but there may be exceptions. A respondent might feel intimidated if the interview is conducted within earshot of an argumentative spouse. Regardless of where the interview takes place, the interviewer must quickly adapt to the respondent and the social setting, so the respondent feels comfortable during the interview.

Personal interviews also allow monitoring of respondents' body language. For example, after observing that a respondent seems confused, bored, or angry, the interviewer might restate or rephrase a question. Also, information can be recorded about body language and social context that might be impossible to obtain otherwise. Face-to-face interviewing also permits easy use of visual aids such as photographs, advertisements, charts, and newspaper clippings. Using a card or list can be an important device for obtaining sensitive information like income, drug use, or sexual behavior. Table 8.1 shows an example of response options for income that can be used on a card handed to respondents.

Limitations and Considerations of Personal Interviews. Why might personal interviews *not* be the best method of data collection? What if the interviewer asked:

Have you ever had a sexually transmitted disease?

Respondents might be hesitant to answer this question in a face-to-face interview. In general, respondents are unlikely to divulge certain types of information, such as deviant or socially questionable behavior.

Also, "being there" during data collection sometimes leads to biased responses. Unlike a self-administered questionnaire, the respondent might choose answers to questions to impress or please (or displease) the interviewer. **Interviewer effect** is bias resulting when a respondent tries to impress the interviewer, or otherwise reacts

TABLE 8.1.   Low-End Response Categories for Income, 1998
and 2000 (General Social Survey).

Dollar Range	Numeric Code	Midpoint
Under $1,000	01	875
$ 1,000 to 2,999	02	2000
$ 3,000 to 3,999	03	3500
$ 4,000 to 4,999	04	4500
$ 5,000 to 5,999	05	5500
$ 6,000 to 6,999	06	6500
$ 7,000 to 7,999	07	7500
$ 8,000 to 9,999	08	9000
$10,000 to 12,499	09	11250
(other response categories not shown)		

Source: *http://webapp.icpsr.umich.edu/GSS*

to the interviewer in a way that produces incorrect or misleading responses. Adapting to the situation may be difficult or impossible, particularly if the interviewer and respondent are poorly matched. For example, a middle-aged, upper-middle class male interviewer might not know how to act with a young unemployed mother. To some extent, interviewers can be matched to respondents, but it is seldom possible to know ahead of time what the respondent will be like.

Finally, the interviewer needs to carefully consider personal appearance and general demeanor. For example, "dressing up" might be appropriate for an interview with a corporate head, but not with an unemployed person living in poverty conditions.

Telephone Interview

Phone surveys are particularly well suited for studying the pace of rapidly shifting attitudes, as illustrated by election and political-opinion polling. They also are well suited for rapid response to major events, as the following study of the shooting of a state governor reveals.

Excerpt: *How Fast Does Shocking News Travel?*

How fast does nationally significant news travel? When a shocking event occurs on a weekday afternoon, which news source do people first use to obtain information about it? Where do people turn for additional information? These are questions that social scientists cannot readily answer. By the time most surveys are fielded, too much time has elapsed for accurate responses to be secured.

The shooting of Governor George Wallace of Alabama on Monday, May 15, 1972, provided an opportunity to obtain tentative answers to these questions. The staff of the Consumer Response Corporation learned of the shooting at approximately 4:40 p.m., while the field department was briefing 12 telephone interviewers. Six interviewers were thereupon transferred from their intended assigned project and were made available to interview people on the shooting.

Concurrent with re-assigning the interviewers, a three-item questionnaire was prepared and printed. . . .

(1) Have you heard the news that Governor Wallace of Alabama was shot today, prior to my telephone call?

(2) From which source did you *first* hear this news?

(3) From which news source will you get additional information about the event?

Interviewing was conducted by telephone throughout New York City. Households were randomly selected from those listed in the New York City telephone directory. Respondents were household heads or spouses of household heads. Interviewing was conducted from 5:00 to 10:00 p.m., and six interviewers conducted a total of 312 interviews. . . .

The data show that information about a nationally significant, weekday afternoon event travels quite fast. By 6 p.m., less than two hours after news of the shooting was first announced to the public through the national media, more than 6 out of 10 respondents (61 per cent) were aware of the event. . . . By 10 p.m., almost every individual contacted knew of the attempted murder of Governor Wallace. . . .

Those informed prior to 6:00 p.m. were almost evenly divided between obtaining the news from the radio (45 per cent) and from a personal acquaintance (44 per cent). Most of those who were informed by an acquaintance had been telephoned. Approximately one in ten (11 per cent) learned of the news from daytime television. Most respondents who learned about the shooting after 6:00 p.m. heard about it on television, particularly on the evening news. . . . Over half the people interviewed intended to turn to both the broadcast *and* print media for further information (Schwartz, 1973–74, pp. 625–627).

In the past several years, telephone interviewing has become automated by a process called **computer assisted telephone interviewing (CATI)**. Using a special type of computer software program, CATI uses random-digit dialing and automated recording of responses to questions. CATI speeds the data-collection process and virtually eliminates transcription errors.

Strengths of Telephone Interviews. Phone interviews are less expensive and less time-consuming than personal interviews. A number of phone calls can be conducted during the time it takes to drive to one respondent's location. The 312 interviews about the shooting of Governor Wallace were completed in just over 5 hours by phone; each interview took about 1 minute.

In telephone interviewing, several interviewers can work in a central location, where a supervisor can be consulted if necessary and can monitor the interviewing process (Groves & Kahn, 1979, p. 7). Lavrakas (1993) argues that supervision is one critical component of ensuring high quality of data collected by telephone interview.

Unlike personal interviews, telephone calls don't require the interviewer to travel into unsafe environments. Suppose you wish to interview residents of a high-risk neighborhood who are working with school officials to ensure the safety of their children. Telephone interviews would produce less risk of harm to the interviewer than visiting the residents in their homes. Also, it's difficult for a researcher to appear relaxed during an interview if personal safety seems threatened.

Limitations of Telephone Interviews. If you or someone you know has held a "tele-marketing" job selling items over the phone, some of the limitations of telephone surveys probably are obvious. It's difficult to ask complicated questions or explore complex topics by phone. For example, how long can *you* keep 10 response categories in mind, particularly if someone reads them to you? Also, some people are reluctant to reveal any information over the telephone to a stranger. Nor can the telephone researcher monitor body language or observe clues about the respondent's social setting. Visual aids can't be used in phone surveys.

Many persons dislike unsolicited calls, particularly during meal times. Some evidence suggests declining response rates to telephone surveys are due to the increasing number of surveys (Maxim, 1999). Bogus "surveys" used to disguise sales pitches add to the difficulties of conducting telephone surveys. Strategies for reducing these problems include: (1) Sending an advance letter about the study and upcoming phone call, (2) calling during time periods less likely to disrupt meals and other routines, and (3) emphasizing the sponsorship and importance of the survey if it is associated with research or education.

Another potential limitation of phone surveys is coverage error. **Coverage error** results from excluding people in the population from the list that is used to select the sample, *and* identify people who are listed more than once on the list. One example of coverage error is using a telephone book to draw a sample of all persons in a community. Not all persons are listed in local telephone books and those not listed are excluded from the sample. On the other hand, some households are listed multiple times because they have more than one phone number. These difficulties were much less a concern in 1972, when the "travel of shocking news" study was undertaken, than they are today. Today, there are more unlisted numbers, cell phones, and multiple phone numbers for a household (or business). Caller ID and call blocking are some of the other services likely to impose limitations on telephone interviewing.

Mail Questionnaire

A third type of survey is conducted by mailing questionnaires to respondents and requesting respondents to return completed questionnaires by mail. A **mail questionnaire** is **self-administered**, that is, there is no monitoring by any member of the research team. On the other hand, a **group-administered questionnaire** is a self-administered questionnaire given to several respondents at the same time, usually (but not always) with a representative of the research team present. An exam for your research methods class is an example of a group-administered questionnaire, usually monitored by the instructor or a teaching assistant. A survey administered in a classroom is another example.

The following excerpt illustrates the use of mail questionnaires to assess behaviors on a highly sensitive topic.

Excerpt: *Identifying Condom Users Likely to Experience Condom Failure*

The rapid spread of the human immunodeficiency virus (HIV) and other sexually transmissible diseases (STDs) during the last decade has led to increased research on the male condom. . . . Anecdotal evidence suggests that a relatively small proportion of condom users are responsible for a disproportionate number of breaks. . . . Because so little is known about the characteristics of such individuals, we cannot predict accurate condom breakage rates for a given user. If simple methods of identifying condom breakers existed, service providers could maximize the impact of their educational interventions by targeting the cohort of users who experience the majority of breaks. . . .

Three hundred couples were recruited for the study from professional organizations and institutions in the Research Triangle Park area of North Carolina. . . . The study protocol required participants and their partners to be in a monogamous heterosexual relationship, at least 18 years old, protected against pregnancy, not practicing behaviors that would put them at risk of STDs (including HIV), and free from known sensitivities to latex. . . .

The 20 study condoms—one from each lot— . . . were mailed to participating couples along with the study questionnaire, a one-page form on which respondents answered a series of questions on slippage and breakage for each condom and filled in an identifying code from the condom packaging. . . . When the investigators received the completed questionnaires, they paid the participating couples for each condom used. . . .

This analysis is based on 177 couples. . . . The median age of the participants was about 30, and the median education was approximately 15 years. . . . Most of the couples (84%) were either married or living together. . . .

Couples with no condom experience in the year before the study and couples who had experienced condom breakage during that period had relatively high rates of condom failure [13.9% and 13.1%, respectively] . . . [but] couples who had used condoms in the year before the study without experiencing condom breakage had a failure rate of 5.6%. . . . Couples who were not living together had significantly higher failure rates than their cohabiting counterparts. If the male partner had a high school education or less, the couples experienced significantly higher failure rates than if he had more education (Steiner et al., 1993, pp. 220–223).

Strengths of Mail Surveys. Recall from the discussion of ethics and human subjects in Chapter 2 that the researcher must understand the expectations for research with human subjects, such as "do no harm," *before* planning a research project. If you've completed a questionnaire, were you informed about how your answers would be protected?

Two levels of protection of information that respondents provide on a survey are confidentiality and anonymity. Mail surveys provide a close approximation to the ideal of complete confidentiality for the respondent. **Confidentiality** means completed questionnaires contain identification such as a name or a code, but the researcher doesn't reveal any answers of any respondents to anyone outside the research project. **Anonymity** means completed questionnaires contain no information identifying respondents; therefore it isn't possible to reveal any individual's answers. Anonymity for respondent and associates is an important consideration for the study of highly personal experiences, illegal activities, and other sensitive topics. For example, suppose someone you know "earned" money for college selling stolen merchandise. How likely is this person to reveal his/her method of financing college in a face-to-face interview? Because of no face-to-face interactions, mail surveys can encourage respondents to share information of a personal or sensitive nature.

It's also cheaper and faster to work with a large sample and cover a large geographic area with a mail questionnaire than with personal interviews, but not so much so when compared with telephone interviews.

Limitations of Mail Surveys. What do you think is the greatest problem with mail questionnaires? If you said, "Not answering it," you're right. A major problem usually accompanying mail questionnaires is nonresponse. The questionnaire goes directly into the "round file"—the wastebasket. But many mail surveys do achieve good return rates (Dillman, 2000; Miller, 1991). Rates vary from as low as 10 to 20 percent to over 90 percent. Much is known about how to achieve a high percentage of returned questionnaires, as reviewed in the final section of this chapter titled "Limitations and Importance of Survey Research."

Low response rates can offset one of the chief advantages of mail surveys—the advantage of *not* revealing sensitive facts in a face-to-face interview. Often people with embarrassing or socially unacceptable answers to sensitive questions are less likely to return the survey. A person involved in illegal drug use, for example, may be much less likely to return a questionnaire than are others. Of course, locating and personally interviewing this same person also may be difficult or impossible.

Internet Surveys

Web and e-mail surveys are used extensively in market research and customer service surveys, and are being used increasingly in academic and government research (Nesbary, 2000, p. 66). At present, there's a lot of enthusiasm for the potential of Internet surveys, particularly surveys completed using a Web browser, such as Netscape or Internet Explorer.

Also, many informal "surveys" on various topics currently appear on the Internet, in which one or a few questions are posed, and respondents are volunteers.

For example, a recent informal CNN poll asked this question of readers at its website *www.cnn.com* (see Table 8.2). Because the data were from volunteers, CNN also posted a disclaimer, stating the poll wasn't scientific and therefore not generalizable to Internet users or to the general public.

TABLE 8.2. Example of an Informal Internet Survey.

Do you think your child has too much homework?

The responses were:

Yes	29%	2227 votes
Just the right amount	21%	1625 votes
Not nearly enough	49%	3746 votes
Total:		7598 votes

Source: www.CNN.com.

Note: Percentages do not total 100% because of rounding.

Schaefer and Dillman (1998) ran an interesting experiment comparing an e-mail administration of a survey to a paper administration delivered by regular mail. They achieved about a 58 percent response rate for both methods. But the email responses were returned much more quickly. Moreover, fewer questions were skipped and a higher percentage of respondents completed the questionnaires. In addition, responses to questions asking for written comments were more frequent and more elaborate with the e-mail version than with the regular-mail version. The authors conclude that a mixed-mode administration, using both e-mail and regular mail, is a promising strategy to improve the response rate.

On the other hand, Schaefer and Dillman describe the difficulties of formatting a questionnaire for e-mail. At the time of their survey, e-mail was all text, so no graphics could be included. Even a simple checkbox such as the one shown in Figure 8.2 wasn't available in e-mail, and respondents couldn't circle their responses; they had to type them on the questionnaire. In this environment, nothing prevents typing answers over the questions, inserting unwanted carriage

1. What is your favorite color?
   - ◯ Red
   - ◯ Blue
   - ◯ Green
   - ◯ Yellow
   - ◯ Black
   - ◯ Other [＿＿＿＿]

FIGURE 8.2. Example of a Simple Checkbox for a Web Questionnaire.

returns into the text, and so forth. However, the problems Schaefer and Dillman had are much less a concern now, because a Web form is a convenient alternative to e-mail. Also, most mail tools support Web documents. With a Web form, respondents complete the survey using a browser such as Internet Explorer or Netscape. Figure 8.2 was constructed as a small Web form.

There are several important advantages of a Web form over e-mail. None of the questionnaire text can be altered, and text boxes can be provided for answers to open-ended questions, as in Figure 8.2 for the "Other" color. Various other devices such as radio buttons (checkboxes) and drop-down menus also are available using a Web browser. Graphics and animated content are possible, and responses can be recorded and tallied electronically.

Strengths and Limitations of Internet Surveys. The advantages of a Web survey are enticing. Here are a few. (1) They eliminate procedures and costs of hiring interviewers and supervisors, producing paper questionnaires and handling mailouts; and reduce costs for distributing/retrieving the completed surveys. Once the survey is up and running, the cost of each additional respondent is nearly zero. (2) Responses may be transferred electronically into a computer data file for analysis, bypassing data entry and essentially eliminating transcription errors. (3) Respondents at distant sites (such as overseas military personnel and civilians living abroad) can be included if they have access to a computer. (4) Graphics, sound, and animation can be attached to a survey. (5) Automated administration of the questionnaire is possible. The browser can check for omitted questions and inconsistent answers. Correct skip patterns can be programmed; for example, the browser can present a question about college major only to respondents who attended college.

On the other hand, many people do not have regular access to the Internet. You might therefore anticipate the primary limitation of Web surveys—coverage error. But there are other limitations, and the list of limitations nearly offsets the advantages (see Best et al., 2001; Dillman, 2000; Sills and Song, 2002). (1) E-mail addresses change often, and usually cover letters, reminders, etc., for Web surveys are sent by e-mail. (2) Response rates are low, even with follow-up. (3) Password or pin protection is required to prevent unwanted survey completions. (4) Selected respondents often consider the e-mail solicitations to be junk mail. (5) The investigator can't predict how the questionnaire will appear to respondents. Different browsers render colors, fonts, and animation differently, and users configure their browsers in many different ways. The differences among browsers sometimes are quite noticeable, particularly when respondents may be using home computers. Many advanced features do not display at all on older systems. The size of the window, the size of the print, and many other formatting features can be set by users and vary substantially among machines. A question that displays nicely on a single screen in a test machine may take two or more screens on an old home computer, for instance.

The limitations of Internet surveys—particularly the coverage problem—remain a serious barrier. Internet access is growing rapidly, however, so we might expect coverage to improve with time. There seems little doubt that important surveys of the general population will be administered at least partially by Web form in the next few years.

CONSTRUCTING THE SURVEY INSTRUMENT

Selecting Questions

If you recall the discussion of measurement in Chapter 4, you'll appreciate that selecting questions for a survey is not nearly as easy as it might seem! How *does* a researcher choose questions for a survey?

Review Past Research. First, learn enough about your topic so you can make intelligent selections of questions. Find out what others have said about the topic, and what questions others have used that might be useful for your survey; questionnaire items seldom are copyrighted. Why spend time reviewing others' research when you'd rather begin your own? It helps to avoid "reinventing the wheel"— repeating errors others have already identified while working on your topic. As you read published studies, look for three important components: (1) theory (how researchers identify the relationship among their selected variables, including the control variables), (2) operationalization (how they turned abstract concepts into variables), and (3) empirical findings (the results of the studies).

Often theory is about general topics that also might include your specific interest. Suppose you're interested in marijuana smoking among preteens. Look for theory about substance abuse more generally, or, more generally still, about deviant behavior of any type, or still more generally, about norms, roles, and sanctions.

Choose Questions Appropriate to the Topic. The next task is to select questions that are related to your research topic. How does one decide which questions to select? (1) Decide what variables are important for your project. (2) Decide what indicators (questions) you need to measure the variables. Remember also that the need for validity and reliability of questions must be balanced against the difficulty of getting people to participate. Be sure to pretest all questions before the actual survey is conducted, as discussed later in this chapter.

Structure of Questions

Questions are divided into two parts: (1) stem and (2) response options. The **stem** asks the question, and the response options contain the answer choices presented to respondents. Questions may be open-ended or closed-ended. In the case of **open-ended questions**, respondents write in an answer, generally in a blank space in the response section of the question. In **closed-ended questions**, respondents are asked to check one (or more) response(s) in a list. The list of responses is called the **response options** (e.g., female/male; yes/no; strongly agree . . . strongly disagree, and so forth).

Figure 8.3 shows two examples of the same question, one with an open-ended response and one with closed-ended responses. Which example do you think is preferable in most studies?

What is your sex (*female or male*)?	————	Open Ended
What is your sex (*check one*)?	Female ☐ Male ☐	Closed Ended

FIGURE 8.3.   Open-Ended and Closed-Ended Options for the Same Question.

The second format is preferable for recording gender and other well-known response options, such as race/ethnicity and age. In general, choose closed-ended response options when possible. They require less respondent effort and ensure uniformity of responses. Uniformity reduces errors and speeds handling of the completed surveys.

A familiar type of open-ended question is the essay question on a test. Essay questions require space for more extensive answers than a word or phrase. In survey research, this type of question is practical only on a self-administered questionnaire or a Web survey, unless responses are tape-recorded. On an Internet Web form, text boxes can be made to automatically expand to accommodate long responses.[1] Regardless of survey type, interpreting answers to open-ended questions is time-consuming. Consider the time it likely takes your professors to read 50 or more half-page answers to one essay question.

Regardless of the structure of questions and responses, be consistent in directions to respondents. Some of the examples in this chapter show checkboxes for responses, and some use a "circle one" instruction. Either method works, but usually it's better not to mix them in one survey, if possible. If you've taken an exam in which a couple of true/false questions are followed by a couple of multiple choice questions, followed by an essay question, followed by a couple of true/false questions, you'll likely appreciate the importance of consistency.

Composing Questions

Many principles apply to writing good survey questions. These include, but are not necessarily limited to, principles in the following summary. Many of the principles discussed in this section are adapted from Dillman (2000), as indicated.

Use Questions from Existing Surveys. As suggested earlier in this chapter, often one can avoid "reinventing the wheel"—dealing with major problems that others have solved—and also make your results comparable to existing surveys. For standard items, like demographics (e.g., race and age of respondent), see how major surveys ask the question. Of course, preexisting questions might not fit the purpose of your survey, or the people you want to survey. For example, a question for adults might not be understood by preteens (or vice versa). And responses on an interview guide might need to be modified for use on a self-administered questionnaire (e.g., deleting a "not applicable" response option). Questionnaires or the full-text of question wording is available online for many major surveys. The URLs for three locations are

ICPSR: *http://www.icpsr.umich.edu/*

General Social Survey: *http://webapp.icpsr.umich.edu/GSS*

National Election Surveys: *http://www.umich.edu/~nes/*

ICPSR is the most general site; it is a distribution center for thousands of data collections (ICPSR stands for Inter-University Consortium for Political and Social Research).[2] Both the GSS and NES sites are linked from ICPSR.

Whether you need to modify some questions or response categories from major surveys or write your own questions, keep the following principles in mind.

Simplify Words and Phrases. And keep the length of questions (and their response options) as short as possible and still communicate your intent. For example, compare the pairs of synonyms in Table 8.3 below (Dillman, 2000, p. 52).

TABLE 8.3. Comparison of Simpler and More Complex Synonyms.

Simple	More Complex
Tired	Exhausted
Honest	Candid
Most important	Top priority
Free time	Leisure
Work	Employment

Also, spend time on sentence structure until the sentences are simple and accurate. For example, simplify

> *We are interested in finding out how satisfied you are with your cable*
> *TV company. There's been a lot of controversy about cable prices lately,*
> *and so this question is very important to us.*
> *[Response categories would follow.]*

to

> *How satisfied or dissatisfied are you with your cable TV company?*
> *[Response categories would follow.]*

Write Complete Sentences. For example, avoid questions like

Highest degree?

    Less than high school .... ☐

    High school degree .... ☐

    Associates degree (2-year college) .... ☐

        [Other response categories would follow.]

Use instead, a complete sentence with explicit instructions to the respondents:

What is the highest educational degree you have completed? (Check one.)

    Less than high school .... ☐

    High school degree .... ☐

    Associate degree (2-year college) .... ☐

        [Other response categories would follow.]

State Both Positive and Negative Sides in the Question Stem. Particularly for rating scales, avoid "How much do you agree with. . . ." Substitute something like "How much do you agree or disagree with. . . ." Otherwise, you probably are leading respondents to agree more than to disagree.

Carefully Phrase Questions about Sensitive Topics. Sensitive topics include child abuse, drug use, sexual behavior, and criminal behavior. Ask about these topics only if they are important to your study, *and* you have approval from your Institutional Review Board or IRB (see Chapter 2). If you do ask about a sensitive topic, phrase your questions carefully—avoid emotionally charged words. Table 8.4 shows two examples given by Dillman (2000, p. 75). Which question is likely to produce less emotional response, particularly if the respondent *has* shoplifted something? The second question obviously is preferred, because it avoids the word "shoplifting."

TABLE 8.4.   Two Examples of a Question on a Sensitive Topic.

Have you ever shoplifted anything from a store?

    ☐   Yes

    ☐   No

Have you ever taken anything from a store without paying for it?

    ☐   Yes

    ☐   No

Also, with sensitive topics, except in rare circumstances, avoid open-ended questions, such as questions about income and wealth. In a personal interview, a card can be handed to respondents showing a complete listing like the partial list in Table 8.1. Respondents are asked to report just a code associated with the dollar range containing their income. This is the procedure used by the GSS.[3] The respondent never mentions a dollar figure, and the interviewer never hears one. Moreover, there is no need to deal with illegible responses such as "30,00" (is the respondent reporting $30 per hour or $3,000 per month, or $30,000 per year?), or illegible digits handwritten by respondents.

Avoid Double-Barreled Questions. Who should provide sex education? Look at the question in Panel 1 of Table 8.5. What is the correct answer if the respondent thinks parents should provide sex education, but schools and churches should not?

TABLE 8.5. Two Examples: One Double-Barreled Question and One Not Double-Barreled.

Panel 1: Double-Barreled Question

Do you think parents, schools, and churches should provide sex education for youth ages 13 to 19? (Circle one.)

Yes

No

Panel 2: Fixed Version of Double-Barreled Question, Separated into Three Questions

Do you think the following groups should provide sex education to youth ages 13 to 19? (Circle yes or no for each group.)

Parents	Yes	No
Schools	Yes	No
Churches	Yes	No

Technically, the correct answer is "No." But many respondents likely will not recognize this, and the researcher probably wants to know the answer for each of the groups. This is an example of a **double-barreled question**. The question should be split into three distinct questions—one asking about parents, one about schools and a third about churches, as shown in Panel 2 of Table 8.5.

Use Specific Quantities in Response Categories, Tailored to Respondents. How much is "a lot " or "some"? In short, avoid questions with vague stems and vague quantities in the response options, as shown in Panel 1 of Table 8.6. The response categories in Panel 1 of Table 8.6 are virtually useless for estimating time on homework. It's difficult to say what the question measures, but probably it reflects frustration with homework as much as the amount of time spent on it. Instead, ask something like the question shown in Panel 2 of Table 8.6.

How should one present response options with time-span questions? The general principle is: Have the same length of time interval for all respondents, and have it cover a comparable time span. For example, "the past four days" span a weekend for some respondents but only weekdays for others, depending on which day of the week they completed the survey. Although estimating for a "typical

TABLE 8.6. Examples Showing Need for Specific Quantities.

Panel 1: Question with Unclear Stem and Response Options.

How much time do you spend on homework?

A lot .... ☐

Some .... ☐

A little .... ☐

Almost none ...... ☐

Panel 2: Improved Version of Question from Panel 1.

In a typical week, Sunday through Saturday, how much time do you spend on homework? (Check your best estimate.)

12 hr or more .... ☐

At least 8 hr but less than 12 .... ☐

At least 4 hr but less than 8 .... ☐

Some time, but less than 4 hr ...... ☐

None at all .... ☐

week" might be difficult for respondents, it's probably best not to mention "last week." Time spent on homework might vary from week to week, depending on when the next exam is, for instance.

Use Nonreactive Response Options. The ad reads: Seventy-five percent of visitors to the World Auto Show rated the NEW "Extreme Machine" as either "thrilling" or "bold"! Perhaps, but did the rating depend on the response options? **Reactive response options** should be eliminated. Also, responses should be comparable to each other and balanced between positive and negative. For example, avoid response options like those shown in Table 8.7.

TABLE 8.7. Example of Reactive Response Options.

What is your reaction to the new 2005 Extreme Machine?

Thrilling .... ☐

Bold .... ☐

Like it a lot .... ☐

Neutral .... ☐

Don't care for it ...... ☐

The question in Table 8.7 violates several important principles that we've discussed: (1) The first two response options are adjectives seemingly designed to "lead" or influence the respondent. And, they aren't comparable or ordered. Which is ranked higher—"thrilling" or "bold"? (2) The options aren't balanced. Three out of five are positive, one is neutral, and only one is mildly negative. (3) The response options aren't mutually exclusive. The machine might be thrilling, bold, *and* the respondent likes it a lot, all at the same time.

Proofread! Spelling errors, typos, and omissions slip past even the best survey researchers. Sometimes this can be embarrassing. Sometimes it can be much worse, leading to potentially serious response errors. For example, suppose you present a list of medical conditions to respondents, asking them to indicate which conditions they have. If diabetes (or any other condition) is omitted from the list, the quality of the survey is seriously degraded.

Table 8.8 presents a summary of each principle for constructing survey questions.

TABLE 8.8.   Summary of Principles for Constructing Survey Questions.

Question Stem	Response Options
Look for questions from major existing surveys, tailored to respondent and/or survey type	Consider response options from major existing surveys, tailored to respondent and/or survey type.
Simplicity	Simplicity
Use complete sentences, with clear instructions to respondent.	
	Use specific response-option quantities tailored to respondents.
	Use balanced-response options.
	Use nonreactive response options.
Avoid double-barreled questions.	
Use care with sensitive topics.	
Use both positive and negative sides of opinions.	Include both positive and negative sides.
Proofread!	Proofread!

LAYOUT OF A QUESTIONNAIRE

As you probably are beginning to understand, writing good questions is hard! Assembling them into a survey form that will convince respondents to answer honestly all of the questions is just as difficult. Think of yourself as a respondent. What does it take to get *you* to go to the trouble of completing a questionnaire or an interview?

In preparing the layout of a questionnaire, consider two types of decisions: (1) In what order should the questions appear? (2) How should the pages and completed document be formatted? The second item has to do with matters such as the layout of questions and pages, where to put instructions, what font and font size to choose, when to use bold or large font, what colors to use, and whether and how to use graphics. It applies mostly to self-administered questionnaires, but a well-laid-out interview guide simplifies the interviewer's task.

Question Sequencing

Remember, *trust is a must for getting survey respondents to share their information.* Therefore, general warm-up questions, even an open-ended question, might encourage rapport with the interviewer (Weisberg, Krosnick, & Bowen, 1996, p. 96) or a positive attitude toward a mail questionnaire. The first question you read on an exam might encourage (or discourage) you about how well you will do, and might even determine whether you complete the exam. Similarly, the first questions on a questionnaire can affect responses to later questions or prompt a prospective respondent not to complete the survey.

Dillman (2000, p. 92) argues that the first question is the most important question on the survey, not necessarily because it provides answers to a key question, but because it often determines whether the survey will be completed. He gives three criteria for selecting it. The first question should (1) be easy, (2) apply to everyone, and (3) be interesting. He mentions age as an example that meets only two of the three criteria; which two? Although Dillman's argument is directed toward self-administered surveys, the point also is applicable to interviews.

Generally, to encourage participation and valid responses, put easy-to-answer questions, nonthreatening questions and interesting items at the beginning of a survey. In general, question sequencing follows the pattern:

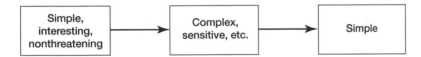

Dillman argues for putting sensitive questions toward the end of the instrument, for two reasons. (1) Respondents should be interested in the questionnaire by the time they get to them, *if* you did your job well. (2) By the end of the questionnaire, respondents have invested sufficient time in it that they are inclined to finish it. Of course, some respondents might quit before they finish, thereby omitting possibly the most important questions.

Figure 8.4 shows an example of a short, self-administered questionnaire about an environmental topic. Question 1 applies to everyone, and it might be at least mildly interesting, but is it easy? Also, is it possible for more than one option to fit some respondents? If so, the response options aren't mutually exclusive. Also, it's not clear what option 3 means. Does "interest/professional affiliation" refer to one reason or two? These response options might make answering the questions a little perplexing.

Questions providing demographic data, such as employment status, age, or level of education, frequently are placed last, as is the case in Figure 8.4. Regardless of the specific order of questions, it usually is important to group questions of a similar topic, perhaps with an introductory sentence such as: Next are some questions about. . . . Be careful here, however; asking several questions in a row *with the same response options formatted into a matrix* can lead respondents to take the "route of least resistence," for example, by checking all "no"

Wind Energy Questionnaire
Survey Research Laboratory
University of Illinois

The Survey Research Center of the University of Illinois is studying public attitudes toward sources of energy, particularly energy machines. As part of this study, would you please fill out this short questionnaire pertaining to wind energy?

(Please circle one code number for each question unless otherwise specified.)

1. Why did you come to see this wind machine? (Circle one.)

Was in the area and heard about it 1
Saw it from the road, was curious 2
Made a special trip to see it because of interest/
   professional affiliation with the subject area 3
Had other business at this base 4
Other (specify) _____
_____

2. If this wind machine were NOT here, would this area be

More pleasing 1
No different 2
Less pleasing 3

•

• (questions omitted here)

•

11. Are you presently

Employed .1
Retired/disabled 2
Homemaker 3
Student 4
Temporarily unemployed 5

THANK YOU FOR YOUR COOPERATION.

FIGURE 8.4.   Example of a Short, Self-Administered Questionnaire (first and last sections).

Source: Sudman and Bradburn, 1982, p. 363.

boxes on a health questionnaire in a doctor's office, regardless of whether one has had the condition, or circling "disagree strongly" to each question about sex education as illustrated in Figure 8.5. Although it's possible this respondent "disagrees strongly" with every question, it's also possible the answers primarily are due to what is called **response set** error—the tendency to select the same answer to many questions when asked in a row, regardless of the question content or accuracy (validity) of the answers.

One approach to avoiding response set is to vary the content of the questions, so that "agree–disagree" has different substantive meanings for some questions than for others. For example, "Strongly agree" to "I love baseball" means just the opposite of "Strongly agree" to "I hate baseball." But be cautious here also—often

Should the following provide sex education for their teen members . . .						
community sports programs?	(Circle 1) Agree strongly	Agree somewhat	Neither agree nor disagree	Disagree somewhat	Disagree strongly
youth clubs?	(Circle 1) Agree strongly	Agree somewhat	Neither agree nor disagree	Disagree somewhat	Disagree strongly
schools?	(Circle 1) Agree strongly	Agree somewhat	Neither agree nor disagree	Disagree somewhat	Disagree strongly
churches?	(Circle 1) Agree strongly	Agree somewhat	Neither agree nor disagree	Disagree somewhat	Disagree strongly
parents?	(Circle 1) Agree strongly	Agree somewhat	Neither agree nor disagree	Disagree somewhat	Disagree strongly

FIGURE 8.5.   Example of Possible "Response Set" Answers from a Matrix Format.

respondents react to whether items express something positive or negative, regardless of the question content.

Formatting Details. The appearance of a survey instrument obviously is more important for a self-administered questionnaire than for an interview guide. But many of the same principles apply to both. The difference is that an interviewer can be trained to negotiate through difficult sections, even if they are not well laid out. But mistakes still are less likely if the interview guide is laid out in an easy-to-follow format.

Dillman (2000) gives dozens of specific recommendations for formatting a self-administered questionnaire. Figure 8.6 illustrates some of these recommendations. The figure shows two of the six questions about liberal–conservative leanings asked on the 2000 National Election Survey (NES). NES data are collected by interview; the guide in Figure 8.6 is a sample questionnaire page adapted from the NES. (The introduction to the six questions remains as originally written.)

In the next several questions, please rate yourself, political candidates and political parties on the seven-point liberal-conservative scale.

1. Where would you place yourself on this scale, or haven't you thought much about this?

- ☐ Extremely liberal
- ☐ Liberal
- ☐ Slightly liberal
- ☐ Moderate; middle of the road
- ☐ Slightly conservative
- ☐ Conservative
- ☐ Very conservative
- ☐ Don't know
- ☐ Haven't thought much about it

1. What about George W. Bush? Where would you place him?

- ☐ Extremely liberal
- ☐ Liberal
- ☐ Slightly liberal
- ☐ Moderate; middle of the road
- ☐ Slightly conservative
- ☐ Conservative
- ☐ Very conservative
- ☐ Don't know

FIGURE 8.6.   Sample Questionnaire Page Adapted from National Election Survey, 2000.

The sample questionnaire page in Figure 8.6 is intended to illustrate some important principles. (1) Use short lines; (2) put instructions immediately before the question(s) to which they apply or, perhaps better yet, within each question; (3) provide sufficient empty space so the pages don't appear too "busy" and (4) use an easy-to-read font size that takes into account the needs of prospective respondents.

The sample in Figure 8.6 may not illustrate all these points equally well; which aspects do you think might be improved?

Finally, be sure to thank the respondent for participating. The thank you could appear in large bold font and centered at the end of the survey, if you can do it without adding another page to the instrument—**Thank You!**

A BRIEF GUIDE TO INTERVIEWING

The following summary of personal interviewing procedures is adapted from the interviewer's manual of the Survey Research Center, University of Michigan (Frankfort-Nachmias and Nachmias, 1996, p. 240). Most of the points apply to both personal interviewing and telephone interviewing.

The opening moments often decide the success or failure of an interview. During that time, the interviewer must legitimize the study and spark enough interest to persuade the respondent to answer accurately all the questions. Therefore, at the beginning of the interview session: (1) Tell the respondent who you are and whom you represent. (2) Tell the respondent what you are doing in a way that will stimulate interest in the survey. (3) Tell the respondent how s/he was chosen. (4) Adapt your approach to the situation, and try to create a relationship of confidence and understanding between the respondent and yourself. Figure 8.7 shows an example of an introduction for a telephone survey (Lavrakas, 1993, p. 102).

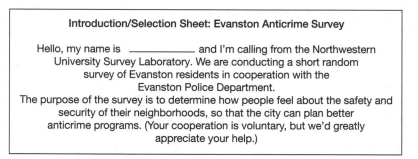

Introduction/Selection Sheet: Evanston Anticrime Survey

Hello, my name is _____ and I'm calling from the Northwestern University Survey Laboratory. We are conducting a short random survey of Evanston residents in cooperation with the Evanston Police Department.
The purpose of the survey is to determine how people feel about the safety and security of their neighborhoods, so that the city can plan better anticrime programs. (Your cooperation is voluntary, but we'd greatly appreciate your help.)

FIGURE 8.7. Example of a Telephone Survey Introduction.
Source: Lavrakas, 1993, p. 102.

During the interview, the interviewer must keep in mind the following techniques.

- *In general, follow the interview guide*—but how closely? The answer to this question depends in part on the form of the interview. Unstructured interviewing is informal; semistructured still permits a fair amount of leeway, and structured interviewing does not permit much deviation from the text. In general, follow the sequence of questions contained on the interview guide; each respondent should be asked the questions in the same order. Ask every question, and repeat any question that is misunderstood. However, the lead researcher(s), often in consultation with interviewers for a project, determines how closely the interview guide must be followed and should communicate the rules to all interviewers.

- *Display a relaxed manner.* The interviewer's style should be relaxed and not suggest a cross-examination or quiz. Read each question slowly and crisply so respondents have time to think about the question and formulate an answer. This is especially important in telephone surveys. The respondent can't watch the interviewer pronounce words.

- *End the interview on a positive note, and thank the respondent.*

PRETESTING THE SURVEY

Would you buy a car never having driven it (or one like it)? Probably not. In survey research, a **pretest** is trying the survey out on some respondents who are similar to those to be included in the main sample. The pretest can help to identify problems with the directions for completing the questionnaire, identify confusing questions and response categories, determine how long it takes respondents to complete the survey, and indicate potential problems with nonresponse.

Researchers sometimes use pretest "think-alouds" to identify problems with questions. Think-alouds ask respondents to describe what they are thinking about each question and its response options as they answer it (Groves, 1996).

Regardless of survey type, the pretest should duplicate all the operations of the main survey as closely as is practical. Select the pretest sample in the same way you intend to select the study sample. For example, if the survey is a random-digit dial telephone survey, use a sample of numbers from the bank (main list) of numbers, and go through the entire interview for a small sample. If the survey is a mail questionnaire, mail it to a small sample drawn from the main sample, and go through the same follow-ups. If the mode is a personal interview, send interviewers to a sample pulled from the main sample. Also, if you're contacting respondents more than once, check your identification system. Be sure you can match responses from the same respondents collected at different times. If you are using a computer for data analysis, check the procedures for getting the data into the computer, and do some preliminary analyses to be sure you haven't left something out or misdefined a variable. Finally, if you make many changes after a pretest, a second pretest is needed!

CONDUCTING THE SURVEY

Legitimizing the Survey

Suppose you received a mail survey from the Oval Office of the While House. Would you answer the survey? How about if a survey came from the local Sewer Board? The point is obvious. The sponsor of the survey has a lot to do with how seriously prospective respondents view it. A nationally recognized organization has more legitimacy than an unknown one. Government-sponsored organizations typically achieve higher response rates than little-known commercial firms (Frankfort-Nachmias & Nachmias, 1996, p. 227). If you're a student doing a survey for your methods class, or for any other course, you can mention your university or college to prospective respondents. If you get permission first, you might be able to use a university letterhead. You need permission because most colleges and universities (and other organizations) restrict use of their logos and letterheads.

A **cover letter** should be sent out, regardless of the mode of administration: telephone, personal interview, mail, or Web form. Time it to arrive during the week prior to the first interview attempt or the arrival date of a mail questionnaire. It should be brief, no more than a page, and contain the following content.

- *Sponsor of the study.* Include this information in the cover letter, questionnaire, follow-up reminders, and thank-you letters. For interview surveys, mention the sponsor in the introduction.

- *Purpose.* How will the survey contribute to the general welfare, advance knowledge, or provide a similar benefit? Two to four sentences should suffice.

- *Voluntary nature.* If the survey isn't required by law, it's voluntary and this should be mentioned.

- *Confidential or anonymous.* Nearly all surveys are at least confidential, and some are anonymous. Be sure to emphasize whichever applies.

- *Questions.* Provide a phone number at which prospective respondents can get more information.

- *Thank you.* Thank prospective respondents in advance.

Follow-up, Follow-up, Follow-up . . .

Low response rate is a chronic problem in survey research. A 100-percent response rate seldom is achieved. It has been found repeatedly that only one attempt to contact prospective respondents leads to unacceptably low response rates, often in the range of 10 to 20% for mail surveys (e.g., Miller, 1991, pp. 145–148). These miserably low numbers can be improved dramatically by follow-up. One reviewer of a selection of studies using questionnaires finds rates from 24 to 90% (Miller, 1991, pp. 146–148). One interpretation is that a mail survey response rate of 50% is adequate and 60% is good, depending on the population and topics (Babbie, 1999, p. 240). Typically today, phone interviews require 20 to 30 follow-ups— a very large increase compared with a few decades ago. For mail questionnaires, a total of five or six attempted contacts, including the cover letter, probably is sufficient (Dillman, 2000). The validity of causal research is not as threatened by nonresponse and coverage errors as are descriptive studies. Why not? If a cause-and-effect relationship based on theory is properly specified, it operates in all subpopulations.

Do inducements such as money, discount coupons, a free item, or a copy of the final report increase response rates? A token money payment, no more than ten dollars paid in advance, has been found to improve response rates, *but follow-up works better*. Other inducements, such as ballpoint pens, contribute to a higher response rate, but not as much as a follow-up or even a token payment (Dillman, 2000). If used, the inducement is announced in the cover letter. Regardless of which survey type is conducted, the principles determining a respondent's decision to participate in any survey are similar (Dillman, 2000). Effective initial-contact strategies for encouraging participation include: (a) Personalizing the contact (e.g., using respondents' names); (b) providing a brief prenotice letter, and a detailed cover letter; and (c) developing and providing a respondent-friendly questionnaire with clear, easy-to-answer questions arranged for easy response (Dillman, 2000, pp. 150–153).

LIMITATIONS AND IMPORTANCE OF SURVEY RESEARCH

The easy availability of survey data has stimulated a massive outpouring of quantitative research in recent decades. Survey research frequently is intended to identify variables that influence important outcomes, such as marital stability and child welfare. There are, however, important limitations of survey data.

Limitations

Nonresponse Error and Coverage Error. Recall that *nonresponse* refers to people selected into a sample who don't complete the survey, and *coverage* refers to excluding people in the population from the list that is used to select the sample and/or listing some people more than once. Nonresponse error is of special concern with mail and Internet surveys, although all surveys are at some risk. Telephone and Internet surveys are especially prone to coverage error.

The concern with nonresponse and coverage error is that people in the sample could be different in important respects from nonrespondents. The differences often affect the conclusions of a study. For example, people omitted from surveys are more likely to be minorities, men, and people with low incomes or very high incomes, and these variables are related to many other variables often measured by surveys.

Sample Attrition. When the same people are contacted just once to complete a survey, it's called a **cross-sectional survey**. The study of individual change, such as attitude change, requires observing the same respondents at least twice. When the same respondents are contacted more than once to complete an additional interview or questionnaire, the survey is called a **panel survey**. A chronic difficulty with panel surveys is **sample attrition** (loss). Some respondents to the first wave of the survey don't participate in one or more subsequent waves. Sample attrition seldom is random. People who change residence are more likely than those who do not move to be missed in follow-up waves. Movers are not a random cross-section of the population. They tend to be younger and more highly educated, for example, than nonmovers. Similarly, people who start drug use while participating in a longitudinal survey on drug abuse are more likely to drop out of the survey, leading to inaccurate explanations of why people become drug users.

Measurement Error. Inaccurate responses to survey questions are examples of *measurement error*—the difference between the observed score and the "true score." Survey measurement errors are due to errors made by the interviewer, respondent mistakes and misrepresentations, a poorly constructed survey instrument, and inappropriate mode of collecting the data (Groves, 1991). Why is measurement error a problem? It typically reduces the correlation between variables. For example, the association between grades in high school and SAT scores generally is lower if grades are self-reported by the students than if they are taken from school records.

Nonexperimental Research. Tobacco companies have repeatedly challenged the conclusion that tobacco smoking is detrimental to health, largely because people can't be randomly assigned to smoke or not smoke. But today, few outside the tobacco industry question the causal connection, and even tobacco executives today acknowledge the risks of tobacco smoke, due in part to extensive survey research. One of the earliest examples is the landmark report of the Surgeon General's Advisory Committee on Smoking and Health (U.S. Public Health Service, 1964), which relied on many surveys (presented in Chapter 12).

SURVEYS AND THEORY

Despite their limitations, complex theories have been developed and hypotheses tested using survey data that would be impossible to obtain otherwise. To conclude this chapter, let's look at an interesting excerpt from a recent national study about parental employment and child rearing. It illustrates the close connections between theory and survey research.

Excerpt: *A Study of Parental Occupation and Attitudes toward Child Rearing*

Based on previous research, Kohn and his collaborators (e.g., Kohn & Slomczynski 1990; Kohn, 1977) proposed a theory that the primary reason for the class differences in child-rearing values is parental education and what they call "occupational self-direction." According to the theory, working-class jobs tend to be repetitive, with little room for variation. In contrast, middle-class jobs require individual decision making:

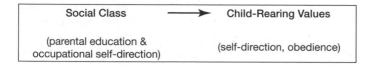

Using personal interviews, Kohn and collaborators conducted a U.S. national survey of 4105 employed men not in the armed services. Closed-ended questions were developed and refined in subsequent pretests. Particular attention was paid to describing parental occupation and to the measurement of child-rearing values. They achieved a fairly good response rate of just over 73 percent.

The main findings support the theory: Working-class parents emphasize obedience for their children, and "middle-class" parents emphasize self-direction. Middle-class parents tend to have more education than do working-class parents, and middle-class parents have jobs permitting/requiring more occupational self-direction than do working-class parents. These differences in education and occupation are reflected in child-rearing values.

Most surveys collect information related to many topics. In contrast, the Kohn National Survey was designed primarily to test a set of theoretical ideas about the relationship between education, work, and child-rearing attitudes. And, despite the limitations of surveys, it's difficult to imagine conducting a national study to test hypotheses without surveys.

SUMMARY

A survey is a method for collecting information about people by directly asking them questions. The three primary modes of administering a survey are personal interview, telephone interview, and mail questionnaire. In addition, in the past few years, some social science surveys have been conducted on the Internet.

The main strength of personal interviews is their flexibility in probing for details; personal interviews also foster high participation rates. But personal interviews are expensive, time-consuming, and not well suited for asking sensitive questions. Compared with personal interviews, telephone interviews are quick and cheap. But they're easier to decline, don't permit visual cues, and aren't well suited for long, complex surveys. Mail questionnaires are well suited for surveys about sensitive topics. Mail questionnaires also are comparatively cheap to administer—there's no labor cost for interviewers. But return rates tend to be low, and the multiple follow-ups needed to achieve an acceptable response rate extend the time it takes to complete a research study using mail questionnaires.

Conducting a survey is relatively easy; however, getting high-quality data from a survey is not easy. The relative advantages of the four modes of survey administration must be evaluated. Questions must be selected with care and composed to ensure accurate and complete responses. The questionnaire, particularly mail questionnaires and Internet forms, must be laid out in an attractive manner. This chapter summarizes several guidelines for writing and formatting a questionnaire. Proofread everything—more than once! Pretesting the survey also is a must.

Nonresponse error, coverage error, attrition in longitudinal surveys, measurement error, and use of nonexperimental data can affect conclusions based on survey data. Nonresponse error comes from differences between individuals who complete and return a questionnaire and those who do not. Coverage error refers to incorrect summaries due to omission of part of the population from the list from which the sample was selected, or to inclusion of some people more than once in the sample frame. Measurement error refers to incorrect answers to questions on the survey. Incorrect attribution of cause and effect due to nonexperimental designs is an ever-present concern with survey data.

The chapter concludes with a review of the Kohn National Survey to illustrate the close relationship between theory, survey data collection, and data analysis. The survey was designed specifically to test some very interesting hypotheses about the relationship between parental social status and child-rearing practices and philosophy. Despite their limitations, surveys provide much valuable data and form the basis for critically important social research.

YOUR REVIEW SHEET: QUESTIONS DISCUSSED IN THIS CHAPTER

1. Thinking about the interviews with adoptive parents, what are some strengths of personal interviews? What are some reasons why personal interviews might not be the best method of data collection? Use the study of adoptive parents as a starting point, but don't confine your answer solely to that setting.

2. State two limitations that a researcher planning telephone surveys would have to consider. Summarize two strengths in your own words.

3. Some people are reluctant to reveal information over the telephone to a stranger. What is a question you wouldn't answer during a telephone interview? How might a researcher obtain this information from you?

4. Write a double-barreled question not discussed in the chapter. Rewrite it to avoid the problem.

5. What are Dillman's three criteria for selecting questions to present first on a survey? Write a question that meets his criteria for a survey about Internet browsing.

6. How might a researcher reduce response-set answers when grouping questions on a similar topic?

7. What is perhaps the greatest problem with mail questionnaires, and why? How can this problem be minimized or overcome?

8. Why is nonresponse a problem for survey researchers? What can be done to decrease nonresponse error?

9. Some researchers prefer to put more complex, sensitive questions at or near the end of the survey form. What is a possible problem with this approach? What are Dillman's arguments in favor of it?

10. How does a researcher determine whether questions designed to measure latent constructs actually measure the attitude or belief they are intended to measure?

11. What can a pretest tell the researcher?

12. Write a balanced assessment of the strengths and weakness of surveys.

END NOTES

1. Another interesting advantage of a survey displayed as a Web form is that long lists such as all 50 states can be put into a drop-down box. As a result, the options don't clutter the survey, but expand when selected so respondents can view the entire list.

2. ICPSR currently holds nearly 5700 collections, and the collection is growing rapidly (Austin, 2003).

3. The column labeled "Midpoint" isn't included on the GSS card. The midpoints illustrate one way to convert the coded categories into numbers representing dollar income. You won't get an estimate of the average income if you take the average of the codes; they are ordinal numbers, not dollars, assigned to the income intervals. Using the midpoints gives a reasonable estimate of the average income, but the estimate *is* sensitive to the value selected for the top open-ended category. Usually a reasonable value can be found, however. On the

other hand, the use of midpoints substantially understates the variation, because all the variation *within* the income ranges is removed from the data.

STUDY TERMS

Anonymity Completed surveys do not contain any information that identifies respondents, either directly or indirectly (respondents are anonymous).

closed-ended question Questions with a short list of predefined answers, usually called response options (e.g., . . . $10,000–$12,499, $12,500–$15,000 . . . for income). A familiar example is a multiple-choice question on an exam.

computer-assisted telephone interviewing (CATI) Phone interview process using random-digit dialing and automated recording of responses; speeds data collection and virtually eliminates transcription errors.

confidentiality Completed surveys contain information identifying the respondents, but the researcher does not reveal any answers of individual respondents (keeps their information in confidence).

coverage error Error due to omitting some part of the population from the sample list, and/or including some people more than once.

cover letter Letter that accompanies or precedes a survey. It describes the purpose of the study and its social contribution, gives the sponsoring agency, tells why the respondent was selected, lists a contact person (for questions and mailback), contains a statement about anonymity or confidentiality, and says "thank you."

cross-sectional survey Survey in which each respondent is surveyed only once. Compare with panel survey.

double-barreled-question Question that is really more than one question. For example: Do you like mom *and* apple pie? The correct answer is yes only if you like them *both*.

focus group (or **focused interview**) A semistructured interview that includes several people.

group-administered questionnaire Self-administered questionnaire completed by several respondents at the same time, for example, in a classroom, usually (but not always) with the researcher present.

interviewer effect Bias resulting when a respondent chooses incorrect answers because an interviewer is present, for example, to impress or irritate the interviewer.

mail questionnaire Type of survey that collects information by mailing a questionnaire to respondents, who return the completed questionnaire by mail.

nonresponse Failure of selected sample members to complete all or part of a survey or interview. Nonresponse error comes from differences between individuals who complete and return a questionnaire and those who don't.

open-ended questions Questions requesting respondents to write in a response. A familiar example is an essay question on an exam. A short open-ended question might ask respondents to write down their age or date of birth.

panel survey Survey in which the same individuals are surveyed at least twice.

personal interview Survey in which data are obtained from respondents while face to face with the interviewer.

pretest Small preliminary survey to check for problems with questions, response options, and procedures. Pretests also are used to determine the length of time needed to complete a survey. The pretest sample should be similar to the target population for the main survey.

probe Follow-up question in an interview used to clarify responses that are incomplete, or elicit a response when one was not offered.

reactive response options Response categories of a question that lead the respondent to an incorrect response.

response options List of responses to a closed-ended question.

response set Tendency of respondents to select the same answer to many questions, irrespective of the question content, for example, answering "strongly disagree" to every question no matter what the respondent's opinion is.

sample attrition Sample loss that occurs when some of those who participated in the first data collection of a panel survey don't participate in later collections (waves). Some reasons for attrition include change of residence, illness or death of respondent, and refusal.

self-administered questionnaire Survey completed by the respondent, usually obtained by mail, in the absence of the researcher, or administered in a group setting such as a classroom.

semistructured interview Face-to-face survey with a set of questions that can be expanded by using probes.

sequencing Determining the order of survey questions in an interview or on a questionnaire.

stem (of a question) The part of a survey item that asks the question. It should be a complete sentence.

structured interview Questionnaire that is administered by an interviewer. Questions are read verbatim to the respondent and answers usually are recorded by the interviewer into one of a set of closed-ended options (although open-ended response categories also can be used).

survey Tool for gathering data in which the researcher asks questions of a sample of individuals. Four types are mail questionnaire, personal interview, telephone interview, and Internet questionnaire.

telephone interview A survey administered by telephone.

unstructured interview A loosely structured survey that might be thought of as a "conversation." The interviewer usually has a list of questions but doesn't necessarily repeat them word-for-word to respondents or use a question–answer, question–answer format.

EXERCISES

Exercise 8.1. Writing Questions

Directions: Find two phone or personal interview questions on an existing major survey about a topic that interests you. These could be found at Internet sites like the GSS or NES (see text).

Questions

1. Write the original questions. Be sure to include the Web site source (URL) for each question.

2. Revise these questions for use in a *self-administered questionnaire*.

3. Explain how you followed good formatting principles for a self-administered survey.

4. What construct are you trying to measure with these questions? How well do you think your questions reflect this construct? Why?

5. Compared with the interview mode of data collection, do you think you need more or fewer questions about the same construct to achieve acceptable reliability and high validity with your self-administered questionnaire? Why?

Exercise 8.2. Unstructured Interviewing

Directions: Decision Resources, Inc., has a client that wants to understand what influences people's TV viewing habits. As part of Phase I of the inquiry, Decision Resources has hired you to conduct four unstructured interviews as a pilot project for a larger study. The objective of Phase 1 is to develop initial insights about how TV viewing habits differ between young people and middle-aged people.

Conduct four unstructured interviews, two with persons who are at least 19 years old but no older than 25, and another two with persons who are at least 40 but no older than 50.

Before beginning this exercise, review carefully the Code of Ethics forms in Appendix A. *If you do not understand any of the ethical expectations, check with your instructor before proceeding with the exercise.* Also, be sure to review carefully the text discussions about unstructured interviews and preparing survey questions.

Careful note taking is important; your notes should be readable. Be prepared to hand in completed interview guides for the four interviews. Don't rewrite these unless your instructor requests.

1. Write a brief interview guide (four to six short one-sentence questions) appropriate for an unstructured interview about TV viewing preferences. Remember, this is a "conversation" with open-ended questions. However, you provide *only* "direction," and the respondent provides the "content." For example, don't suggest an answer, or offer comments about responses (e.g., *don't* say, "I like that too," or "that's good").

Include points you intend to mention if the respondent doesn't mention them spontaneously. Examples include names of shows to ask about, questions about preferred time slots, a question asking whether the respondent has cable or a satellite dish, a list of types of content (e.g., situation comedy, mystery, news, sports), and something about commercials.

2. Prepare a short introduction about the project. Read aloud or paraphrase this introduction at the beginning of each interview. Remember to use "everyday" language and avoid jargon; most respondents are unfamiliar with survey methods terms. Have at least one classmate or your instructor review your introduction before beginning the interviews.

3. For each interview: (a) Record identification information: First name (or pseudonym), age, gender of respondent; date of interview; location of interview. *Be very careful to keep this information confidential.* No one but you should ever be able to connect a

respondent's identity with what the person said during your interviews. (b) Insofar as possible, keep a word-for-word record of the questions and probes you ask and respondents' answers and comments. And, thank your respondent.

Using the following outline write your interview form; make enough copies for each interview—

Interview number: _____ (Write this number at the top of each page of notes for each interview, and number each page after the first.)

Respondent: (first name, age, other relevant information)

Location:

Date:

Introduction:

Interview: (use "I" for Interviewer and "R" for Respondent)—write the exact words.

4. Write a short statement of your findings for Decision Resources, Inc. Include (a) a summary of respondents' TV viewing preferences, (b) an evaluation of whether there are noticeable differences in TV preferences by age, and, if so, (c) a few sentences describing the main differences between young and middle-age respondents.

Note: One strategy for analyzing your notes is to photocopy them and cut the *copies* into parts, one for each comment made by a respondent. First, write the age group on your summary of each comment made by each respondent, so you can identify the age group of each comment after cutting them apart. Or, you could enter your notes into a word-processing program; insert a page break after each comment, and include a header containing all the identifying information such as interviewer number, age, and gender. Again, be very careful not to associate any respondent's true indentity with the notes you enter.

Next, print the notes and sort them into piles so each pile has to do with one idea (e.g., commercials). Then, for each idea, sort the notes into two stacks, one for young respondents and one for older respondents. This permits you to make comparisons between age groups. You may sort the notes more than once, depending on the idea you are analyzing.

5. Summarize what you learned from the pilot study that could be implemented in a larger study using unstructured interviews.

6. Did you find large enough differences between men and women to indicate that you may need separate samples, one for women and one for men? How many interviews do you believe would be needed in the larger study? Why?

Exercise 8.3. Semistructured Interviewing

Directions: Decision Resources liked your work on Phase I of the study of TV viewing preferences and is offering you a small contract to work on Phase II. Your new task is to write a sequence of semistructured questions, based on what you learned from your unstructured interviews during Phase I.

Before beginning this exercise, review carefully the Code of Ethics forms in Appendix A. *If you do not understand any of the ethical expectations, check with your instructor before proceeding with the exercise.* Also, be sure to review carefully the text discussions about semistructured interviews and preparing survey questions.

Be prepared to hand in your original completed interview guides for the four interviews. Don't rewrite these unless your instructor requests you to.

1. Write a sequence of six to eight questions with probes for a semistructured interview, based on your list of activities obtained from the unstructured interview (Exercise 8.2).

2. Next, select four persons, two aged 19 to 25 and two aged 40 to 50, but not the respondents you interviewed for Exercise 8.2. Interview these four people using your semistructured interview guide. Write the *exact words* of the respondent next to your list of questions and probes.

   Respondent: (first name, age, other relevant information)

   Location:

   Date:

   Interview: (use "I" for Interviewer, "R" for Respondent and "P" for probe)—write exact words.

   Introduction: (revise your Introduction from Exercise 8.2, if needed)

3. Briefly summarize your findings.

4. Drawing on these interview experiences, compare the strengths and limitations of unstructured and semistructured interviewing.

Exercise 8.4. Evaluation of Research: Personal Interview

Directions: Refer to the excerpt on "open adoption" in the first section of this chapter to answer the following questions.

   Note: The article combines elements of an evaluation report and basic research, but is discussed here as an evaluation report.

Factual Questions

1. How did the researchers select the respondents to be interviewed?

2. What does *open adoption* mean?

3. How important was open adoption to the 21 respondents in the study? Why?

Questions for Discussion

1. Why might parents refuse to be interviewed for the study? How could nonresponse of parents affect the findings about attitudes toward open adoption?

2. The full article reported that the interviewer read the questions while the respondent followed along on an interview form. In what ways might this strategy assist the interviewer? How might potential problems arise?

3. What types of information might an interviewer be able to observe about adoptive parents during a personal interview that direct questions might not reveal?

4. Suppose a researcher, wearing torn jeans and an old sweatshirt, approaches well-dressed parents. What effects is this likely to have on the interviewing process?

Exercise 8.5. Evaluation of Research: Telephone Interview

Directions: Refer to the excerpt on "how fast does news travel?" in this chapter to answer the following questions.

Factual Questions

1. What led Schwartz to select telephone interviewing?

2. How did questions asked of respondents allow Schwartz to answer his research question? How was he able to estimate the rate at which news travels?

Questions for Discussion

1. Is a short telephone survey advantageous in this study? Briefly explain, taking into account the perspectives of both researchers and respondents.

2. Comment on Schwartz's choice of city and use of telephone directory to collect the data for his study.

3. The phone interviews were obtained between 5:00 and 10:00 P.M. What are the advantages of interviewing during this time? What are the limitations?

4. The interviews were completed with the head of the household or spouse of heads. Was this the appropriate person to interview? Explain.

5. Review potential limitations of this study not mentioned in the previous questions.

6. Briefly describe another nationally significant event that could be examined using a similar approach. If you were to conduct the research, how would you use Schwartz's study to develop your survey?

Exercise 8.6. Evaluation of Research: Mail Questionnaire

Directions: Refer to the excerpt on "at-risk coital partners" in this chapter to answer the following questions.

Factual Questions

1. State the research question in your own words.

2. What group(s) of respondents were selected for the study?

3. How many returned the questionnaires? What is the response rate? Is this a high, medium, or low rate of response for mail questionnaires? Explain briefly.

4. Suggest at least two strategies to increase the response rate for this study.

Questions for Discussion

1. Offer one possible reason why the rate of questionnaire return was not higher than it was.

2. Explain to a person not familiar with survey research methods at least two advantages and two limitations of mail questionnaires.

3. Write a short dialogue for a semistructured interview that would be appropriate for use with respondents who had completed the condom study. Use the rock concert dialogue as a model. (Review semistructured interviewing in the text and in Exercise 8.3.)

9 POPULATION, SAMPLES, AND SAMPLING

INTRODUCTION: LOOKING AT HOW THE SOCIAL WORLD WORKS

Suppose you read in your local newspaper the caption under the picture shown in Figure 9.1. Would you want to know more about the details of the research, such as who provided the views that represent the "U.S. public"?

Research finds the U.S. public increasingly approves of the changing role of women from homemaker to labor market participant.

FIGURE 9.1.   Women at Home and in Paid Employment.

A Sampling Riddle

The caption for Figure 9.1 is paraphrased from the next excerpt. As you read the excerpt, jot down in your own words what you think is the authors' main point and what is their justification.

Excerpt: *Attitudes toward Women in Paid Employment*

> A fundamental and profound shift in public expectations of women's roles at work and at home has been well documented. . . .
>
> Despite minor misgivings . . . , Americans seem generally sanguine [optimistic] about the broadening of women's roles from the home to the workplace and beyond. (Huddy, Neely, & Lafay, 2000, p. 309)

How is this finding justified or documented? It wasn't a question asked on the U.S. census, which attempts to query every U.S. citizen. If no one has obtained information from *all* citizens about attitudes toward women's roles, how can changes in attitudes be "well documented?" The information was obtained from a sample, and sample sizes seldom exceed 2000—to describe some 215 million adults! How can the results from so few generalize to so many? This is the *sampling riddle* for the remainder of the chapter.

Goals of This Chapter

The primary goal of this chapter is to answer the "sampling riddle." The answer is closely related to several additional "little mysteries":

- Why not just study everyone (take a census) to correctly describe a population?

- How is it possible to say anything about how much a sample differs from its corresponding population using information just from the sample?

- How big a sample size is needed? Does the needed sample size depend on the size of its population?

- What is the difference between a "probability sample" like the one used in the above study by Huddy et al. and a "haphazard sample"?

- Why is a probability sample preferred? When can a haphazard sample be justified?

After reading this chapter carefully, you should know the answers to these questions. We begin this chapter with the first little mystery—Why not just study everyone?

WHY NOT STUDY EVERYONE?

Frito-Lay, the snack-food people who bring us "Wavy Lay's" potato chips and other goodies, can't check every single potato that growers might wish to sell to them. There are too many potatoes to test, and it would be too costly. They need to take samples of the potatoes. In many other instances, testing destroys the tested items. For example, testing the life expectancy of light bulbs wears them out, so they can't be sold.

Every 10 years, the U.S. government tries to count every citizen, because the Constitution mandates a census every 10 years. On May 31, 2003, the Web site of the Census Bureau estimated the U.S. population to be 291,111,012 persons (*http://www.census.gov*). Every component of the U.S. decennial census is truly a major operation. Every household in the country must be listed. Every institution that houses people must be identified such as prisons, nursing homes, children's homes, and mental hospitals. Then there are homeless people, who do not live in any dwelling, but by law must be counted. Next, the data must be collected, then processed by computer, then distributed to the many individuals, agencies, and businesses that make use of census data. Even the seemingly minor operation of transferring responses from paper to computer is a massive undertaking when there are over 290 million entries!

The question, "Why take a sample instead of a complete count?" answers itself, for potatoes, light bulbs and people, although the reasons are different. In the case of survey research, usually the choice is between selecting a sample and doing no study, because funding and time constraints nearly always rule out a complete count. Of course, not all populations are as large as the entire U.S. population. But even surveying all persons in smaller populations, such as residents in your hometown, generally exceeds a reasonable budget. Consequently, nearly all surveys are based on samples rather than on a census.

The next few sections of the chapter review the basic concepts needed to understand several aspects of **statistical inference**, meaning to generalize sample information (statistics) to the corresponding population. Later sections of the chapter introduce basic ideas in statistical inference. The final section summarizes different types of sampling methods and draws the important distinction between a probability sample and a nonprobability sample.

BASIC CONCEPTS

The term **element** is a general name referring to the objects to be described, such as people, potatoes, light bulbs, cities, states, church congregations, cemetery markers, magazine ads, newspaper columns and so forth. A **population** is a collection of elements and a **sample** consists of some, but not all, of the elements in a population. In a survey, the elements usually are people, although the elements sometimes consist of groups of people, such as families or households.

The population for a study is defined according to the purposes of the study and often is restricted by practical limitations. Many survey populations are limited to "all U.S. civilian adults, 18 years old and older, living in the continental U.S. and not living in an institution." A study of "Wisconsin high-school graduates" limits the population to people who have graduated from a Wisconsin high school, probably during a specified time interval. As Chapter 7 on "Indirect Methods" illustrates, the population sometimes consists of elements other than people, such as music videos and child-rearing manuals. In qualitative research described in the chapter on "Ethnography and Observation," elements sometimes consist of difficult-to-define entities such as social interactions. Examples include hugging/touching after a movie, or crack house members' comments.

There are two major types of samples: a *probability sample* and a *nonprobability* or *haphazard* sample. Statistical methods for generalizing from samples to populations rely fundamentally on having a probability sample. But, as we'll see later in this chapter, for groups such as homeless people, people in "secret relationships," drug users, and binge drinkers, a probability sample simply isn't feasible.

A **probability sample** is one for which the probability of selection is known and greater than zero for each element in the population. For example, suppose there are 30 students in your research methods class. Your instructor writes each student's name on a separate piece of paper, places the paper slips in a hat, *very* thoroughly mixes the slips, and pulls one out. The lucky winner gets to answer the next question posed by the teacher. What's the chance that *you* get to answer the next question? Obviously, your chance is 1 in 30—a *known probability* of being selected that is greater than zero. This type of probability sample is called a **simple random sample (SRS)**. Each student has the same known chance of selection. There are several other types of probability samples summarized later in the chapter. However, most of sampling theory derives from the reasoning about a SRS.

Probability samples are drawn with the idea of calculating a number called a **sample statistic** to estimate the corresponding population number, called the **population parameter**. Examples of sample statistics include the sample mean (average), sample percentage (alternatively, sample proportion), and the difference between one of these statistics for two groups, for example the difference between the sample average wages of people with and without a college degree. Examples of population parameters include the population mean, population proportion, and the difference between means for two groups in the population.

Sampling error is the difference between a sample statistic and the corresponding population parameter—for instance, the difference between the percentage approving the changing roles of U.S. women in the Huddy et al. sample and the percentage approving in the entire U.S. population.

A **sampling frame** is a list of each element in the population. A sample is drawn from this list. *Every* element must be listed, and listed only *once*. A roster of your methods class should list only once each student enrolled in the course, and not omit any enrolled student.

Perhaps somewhat surprisingly, compiling an accurate sample frame is usually difficult. Often some elements are missing, homeless persons in a city, for example. Also, people move, people get married and divorced, people go to college and come home for the summer, and lists aren't necessarily updated.

What can be done to help ensure a complete sampling frame? The researcher might consult several sources, combining the several sources into a single consolidated sampling frame. Duplicate listings must be eliminated, otherwise the probability of selection for some people is doubled or tripled, or more, without the knowledge of the researcher. It's not easy to eliminate all duplicates in a sampling frame. Names may be listed differently in two sources (e.g., Harry Potter and Potter, Harry) and misspellings occur. Social security numbers frequently are not available in all lists to identify duplicate listings.

No initial list of the population is required for telephone polls relying on computer-assisted random-digit-dialing (e.g., CATI), however. All that's needed is an automated way to dial a number between 000-000-0000 and 999-999-9999.[1] Considerable savings can be achieved by eliminating numbers that don't belong to legitimate respondents. Often pollsters buy numbers in blocks of 100, with each block more or less guaranteed to have some working residential phones. Then automated equipment is used to check for valid numbers before they are placed in the pool of numbers that can be dialed (Ratledge, 2001).

THE SAMPLING DISTRIBUTION

Statisticians are very clever. If they know the probability of selecting each population element from a sampling frame, they can figure out the distribution of a statistic, like the sample mean for all possible samples from that population. A list of each possible value of a sample statistic and its associated probability is called a **sampling distribution**. Statistical tests described in this and the next two chapters are built on the idea of a sampling distribution.

This section addresses three of the little mysteries posed at the beginning of the chapter that are fundamentally dependent on a sampling distribution:

- How is it possible to say anything about how much a sample statistic differs from its population parameter, using information just from the sample?
- How big a sample size is needed?
- Does the needed sample size depend on the size of the population?

A Simple Fish Example: Goldie and Friends

The easiest way to grasp the concept of sampling distribution is to take a simple example. Suppose you have an aquarium with a population of six beautiful goldfish in it, as in Figure 9.2. (*Note:* This fish example *isn't meant to be realistic*; it is much simplified to emphasize the basic logic of using probabilities to generalize from a sample to its population.) The names of your fish and the weight of each, in ounces, are shown in Table 9.1.

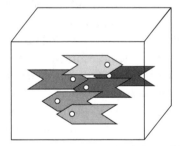

FIGURE 9.2.   Population of Six Beautiful Goldfish.

Imagine you want to know the average weight of the fish, but weighing them is stressful to the fish. So you decide to weigh just two, and use this sample average fish weight to estimate the weight of all six fish. What's the chance you will be in error by more than 1/2 oz?

In case you're stumped, the answer is 8 of 15, or about 0.533. Where did this mysterious number come from? Look at all possible samples for *n* = 2 fish, shown in Table 9.2. Count the number of mean fish weights less than 3 oz *and* the number more than 4 oz. There are four each, making eight in all. Therefore, 8 of the 15 sample means are in error by more than a half ounce.

TABLE 9.1.   Population List of the Six Beautiful Fish and their Weights.

Name	Weight (oz)
Goldie	5
OrangeMan	3
Blackie	2
YellowOne	4
BigOne	6
LittleBrother	1
Population mean (average weight— known only if *all* fish are weighed)	3.5
Variance	2.917
Standard deviation	1.708

TABLE 9.2.   List of All Possible Fish Samples of Size n = 2.

Sample	Fish 1	Wt.	Fish 2	Wt.	Average Weight for the Sample (oz)
			Fish in Sample		
1	Goldie	5	OrangeMan	3	(5 + 3)/2 = 4.0
2	Goldie	5	Blackie	2	(5 + 2)/2 = 3.5
3	Goldie	5	YellowOne	4	(5 + 4)/2 = 4.5*
4	Goldie	5	BigOne	6	(5 + 6)/2 = 5.5*
5	Goldie	5	LittleBrother	1	(5 + 1)/2 = 3.0
6	OrangeMan	3	Blackie	2	(3 + 2)/2 = 2.5†
7	OrangeMan	3	YellowOne	4	(3 + 4)/2 = 3.5
8	OrangeMan	3	BigOne	6	(3 + 6)/2 = 4.5*
9	OrangeMan	3	LittleBrother	1	(3 + 1)/2 = 2.0†
10	Blackie	2	YellowOne	4	(2 + 4)/2 = 3.0
11	Blackie	2	BigOne	6	(2 + 6)/2 = 4.0
12	Blackie	2	LittleBrother	1	(2 + 1)/2 = 1.5†
13	YellowOne	4	BigOne	6	(4 + 6)/2 = 5.0*
14	YellowOne	4	LittleBrother	1	(4 + 1)/2 = 2.5†
15	BigOne	6	LittleBrother	1	(6 + 1)/2 = 3.5
	Mean of the means (average of 15 sample means)				3.5
	Variance				1.167
	Standard deviation (standard error of the mean)				1.080

*Deviates from the population mean by more than 1/2 oz—positive difference.
†Deviates from the population mean by more than 1/2 oz—negative difference.

Why observe every possible two-fish sample, as in Table 9.2? Nearly every research study uses only one sample. To understand the ideas of **statistical tests** in this and the following chapters, you must *imagine* what *would* happen with *repeated samples*, such as in Table 9.2. The list is a step in the reasoning leading up to the idea of a sampling distribution; it's *not* a procedure used in practice!

Notice in Table 9.2 that five of the mean fish weights appear more than once. Table 9.3 presents the sampling distribution for all possible fish samples of size 2, that is, the table lists each distinct fish-weight value and its associated relative frequency. Usually the sample size is designated by the lower-case letter *n*; so in this case *n* = 2. Because of simple random sampling, each of these two-fish samples has the same chance of being selected.

TABLE 9.3.   Sampling Distribution of Fish Mean Weights for Size *n* = 2.

Mean wt (oz)	1.5	2.0	2.5	3.0	3.5	4.0	4.5	5.0	5.5
Probability of Mean									
Fraction	1/15	1/15	2/15	2/15	3/15	2/15	2/15	1/15	1/15
Decimal	0.067	0.067	0.133	0.133	0.200	0.133	0.133	0.067	0.067

In Table 9.3, the top row lists each of the nine possible means for two-fish samples. For example, one sample average is 1.5 oz (Blackie and LittleBrother; see Table 9.2), another sample average is 2.0 oz (OrangeMan and LittleBrother), and so forth. The second and third rows give the probability, in fractional form (which is exact), and in decimal form (which is rounded).

Several important principles about SRS are illustrated by the example of Goldie and her friends.

1. *The number of samples with a specific sample mean declines as the distance increases in either direction between the sample mean and the population mean* (3.5 oz). In Table 9.3, compare the number of samples with specific sample means at each end of the distribution to the number of sample means at the center of the distribution.

2. *An SRS provides unbiased statistics.* When the "mean of all sample means" equals the population mean, the sample mean is an **unbiased statistic**. That is, there is no tendency for samples to overestimate or underestimate the mean of the population from which the sample was taken. For Goldie and friends, the "mean of all sample means"—*and* the population mean are the same—3.5 oz.

3. *When all possible samples are equally probable, as in an SRS, so are all the elements.* In Table 9.3, each individual fish appears five times in the list of 15 pairs. So, the chance of selection for each fish is 5/15 = 1/3 ≐ 0.333.

How Does Sample Size Affect the Sampling Distribution?

Figure 9.3 shows three bar charts, one for the population of six fish, one for all possible samples with *n* = 2, and one for all possible samples for *n* = 3. Panel A shows the distribution of fish weights for the population; there's just one fish at each weight. This is equivalent to samples of size $n = 1$. This distribution in this special example is flat, meaning all the probabilities are the same and the bar chart has a flat appearance. In contrast, the sampling distribution of the sample average weights for two-fish samples shown in panel B isn't flat ($n = 2$); the sample means begin to cluster around the center of the distribution. This clustering is more pronounced for samples consisting of three fish ($n = 3$), shown in panel C.

What does Figure 9.3 illustrate? It shows how the sample size affects the sampling distribution. In the three sample sizes, $n = 1$, $n = 2$, and $n = 3$, the proportion of sample means within 1/2 oz of the true population mean, 3.5 oz, changes from

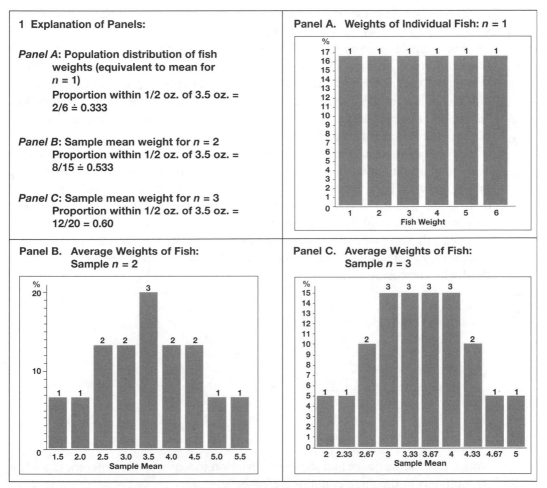

FIGURE 9.3. Bar Charts Showing Distributions of Fish Weights.
Panel A, Population distribution of fish weights (equivalent to mean for $n = 1$). Proportion within ½ oz of 3.5 oz = 2/6 ≐ 0.333. *Panel B*, Sample mean weight for $n = 2$. Proportion within ½ oz of 3.5 oz = 8/15 ≐ 0.533. *Panel C*, Sample mean weight for $n = 3$. Proportion within ½ oz of 3.5 oz = 12/20 = 0.60.

0.333 ($n = 1$) to 0.60 ($n = 3$). In short, Figure 9.3 illustrates the important general principle:

> *As the sample size increases, the mean sample fish weights*
> *cluster closer and closer around the population mean.*

Variance and Standard Deviation

The variance and closely related measure, standard deviation, play a central role in how the sampling distribution is used to generalize from a sample to its population. The **variance** is defined as the average squared distance from the mean. It is a way of measuring how much the numbers in a list differ among themselves. It measures their dispersion or "spread." It gives a condensed indication of dispersion, condensed down into a single summary number.

For example, imagine each fish weighs the same as the population mean, 3.5 oz. Each *difference* between the mean and the weight of one fish therefore is zero. What's the variance in this case? Of course, the variance is *zero*. Now, suppose the *differences* among the weights increase, so that Goldie's weight is 6 oz, rather than 3.5 oz, and LittleBrother's weight is 1 oz, rather than 3.5 oz. The variance increases because the variance summarizes these differences.

A better descriptive measure of variation is called the **standard deviation**. The standard deviation is just the square root of the variance. The square root brings the scale back toward the original scale. There are many possible measures of dispersion, but the standard deviation is the most used and by far the most important, because of its use in generalizing from samples to populations.

The following tabulation shows the mean and both the variance and standard deviation for three distributions, the first with zero variance and the second and third with increasing variability:

	1	1	1
	1	2	2
	1	3	4
	1	4	8
	1	5	16
Mean	1	3	6.20
Var	0	2	29.76
SD	0	1.41	5.46

Notice how the variance and standard deviation increase as the differences among the numbers in the three columns increase.

The standard deviation can be calculated for any list of numbers. When the list is a sample, the result is called a "**sample standard deviation**." It summarizes variation in a single sample. When the list is an entire population, the result is called the "**population standard deviation**," and it summarizes variation in the population of interest. When the list consists of all possible sample means such as in Table 9.2, the result is called the "**standard error of the mean**." It summarizes how much sample means fluctuate around the population mean.

Note: Since the difference between each sample mean and the population mean is one instance of sampling error, the standard deviation calculated for sample means summarizes sampling error. That's why this particular standard deviation has the special name *standard error of the mean*. This is a *very* important idea *and* is easy to miss.

Table 9.1 shows an example of a population standard deviation and variance. For the population of six fish, the standard deviation is 1.708, and the variance is 2.917. Table 9.2 displays an example of the standard deviation (standard error of the mean) and variance for all sample means in the fish example with a sample size of 2. The standard error of the mean is 1.080, and the variance is 1.167.

Extending the Fish Example: The Central Limit Theorem

As Table 9.2 shows, with just six fish in the population, it's fairly easy to list all possible samples containing two fish; there are just 15 of them: Goldie/OrangeMan, Goldie/Blackie, etc. But think of a population of 100,000 fish (in a very large tank). Suppose the new goal is to draw just *one* sample of 100 fish in order to estimate an average fish weight for all 100,000 fish. What is the sampling distribution for all possible sample means with $n = 100$? Clearly, listing all the possible samples, or all the possible sample means, isn't feasible. The number of possible samples (without replacement) of size $n = 100$ is about 2.75×10^{43}! (*Replacement* means returning selected elements to the population before drawing another sample.) However, by using mathematical logic, statisticians have found an especially remarkable rule: the **central limit theorem**:

> *For an SRS (with replacement), as the sample size increases, the distribution of the sample means bunches in the middle to form a normal sampling distribution, regardless of the shape of the population distribution.*

In addition, the mean of this sampling distribution is the same as the mean of the population, and the standard deviation of this sampling distribution equals the standard deviation of the population, divided by the square root of the sample size. (These two relationships do not depend on the central limit theorem.)[2]

The **normal distribution** is symmetric around its highest point, the mean. The vertical axis is proportional to the probability (likelihood) of obtaining a given value listed on the horizontal axis.

There literally are an infinite number of normal distributions, one for each possible pair of mean and standard deviation. One particular normal distribution is used extensively, the **standard normal distribution**, defined to be a distribution

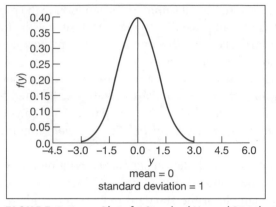

FIGURE 9.4.   Plot of a Standard Normal Distribution.

with mean = 0.0 and standard deviation (and variance) = 1.0 (see Figure 9.4). To convert any variable to standardized form, so its mean is 0 and standard deviation is 1, subtract the mean from each value (e.g., individual fish weight) and divide the resulting difference by the standard deviation (e.g., of fish weights). The result is called a **standard score**, or *z*-**score**, because it often is denoted by the letter *z*.

The normal distribution approximates the distribution of many variables in everyday life, such as heights of people or the timing of students coming to class; a few students are early birds and a few are stragglers, but most come within a fairly short time period before class begins.

The normal distribution also describes the sampling distribution of the sample mean of a probability sample; that's what the central limit theorem says. Areas "under the curve" give probabilities of drawing a sample mean in an interval marked off by the lower and upper boundaries of the interval.

Since the sampling distribution of the mean conforms to a normal distribution, if you know the population mean and variance, you can calculate the complete sampling distribution for a sample of any size. Look back at Figure 9.3. For small sample sizes, the shape of the sampling distribution can be a very poor approximation of a normal distribution, but with $n = 2$ and $n = 3$, the shape already is beginning to bunch in the middle. In practice, with $n = 50$ or more, the shape is similar to a normal distribution for most population distributions. In many cases, the distribution is close to normal with only a dozen or so cases.

But, there still is a wrinkle: How can the central limit theorem help if population numbers are needed before it can be applied? Of course, use sample estimates in their place! By using just two statistics—the sample mean and sample standard deviation—from a single random sample, the entire sampling distribution can be estimated. This result really is quite remarkable! It's the basis for hypothesis testing and other inferential statistics as well. Not all statistics generate a normal sampling distribution, but there are many other distributions to handle quite a variety of statistics. The *t*-distribution is used when the sample standard deviation is substituted

TABLE 9.4. Summary of Sampling Distribution Terms.

Sampling distribution	For a constant sample size, a list of each possible value of a sample statistic from a population and its associated probability.
Central limit theorem	For an SRS with replacement, as the sample size increases, the sampling distribution of the sample mean bunches in the middle to form a normal distribution.
Normal sampling distribution	A specific sampling distribution that is symmetric around the mean of the distribution, sometimes informally called the "bell-shaped curve," but there are many distributions that *look* bell-shaped.
Standard normal distribution	One specific normal distribution with a mean = 0 and a standard deviation (and variance) = 1.0

for the population standard deviation. And Chapter 11 introduces the chi-square distribution and the *F*-distribution.

Table 9.4 summarizes the sampling distribution terms we've discussed.

Applying the Sampling Distribution

The most obvious way to use a sample is to calculate a number, like a percentage or an average, and say the result is the best available estimate of the corresponding population number. For example, the sample data in Table 9.5 show that in 1991, 75.7 percent of the sample approved of the "Women's Movement." This percentage is taken as an estimate of the percentage in the entire U.S. This type of extrapolation from a sample to a population is done all the time. Sample numbers used like this are called **point estimates**.

A point estimate is simple, but it gives no information about the accuracy of the estimate. The primary application of sampling distributions is to assess the accuracy of sample numbers used to estimate corresponding population numbers. The two most used techniques for this purpose are the hypothesis test and the closely related method of confidence interval. The sampling distribution also is used for calculating

TABLE 9.5. Percentage "Very Favorable" or "Mostly Favorable" to the "Women's Movement," by Gender and Year.

Year	Women	Men	Total
1991	77.5	73.9	75.7
(*n*)	(936)	(932)	(1868)
1995	81.6	74.5	79.4
(*n*)	(831)	(368)	(1199)
1998	72.8	73.9	73.4
(*n*)	(556)	(541)	(1097)

Source: Condensed from Appendix A, Table A.1 of Huddy, Neely, & Lafay, (2000, p. 221), with "don't know" responses omitted. The rows designated *n* give the sample sizes.

the sample size needed to accomplish a desired level of sampling accuracy and for determining when the size of the population is an important consideration.

Application to Hypothesis Tests. Suppose you don't know whether men or women have more favorable attitudes toward the women's movement, but you don't think they are the same. So you hypothesize:

> *The percentage of women who report favorable attitudes toward the women's movement is not the same as the percentage of men who report favorable attitudes.*

This hypothesis is an example of a **research hypothesis**. It is just the opposite of the **null hypothesis**, which, in this example, states there is no difference between the genders on attitudes toward the women's movement. Since the research hypothesis doesn't say whether men or women have a more favorable attitude toward the women's movement, it is nondirectional.

The sample statistic for this example is the difference between the percentage of women and men who approve the women's movement. Table 9.5 shows data for 3 years. A percentage difference between women and men can be calculated for each year. Each difference is a sample statistic estimating the corresponding difference in the U.S. population. None of these sample differences is exactly zero, but this does not necessarily mean none of the population differences is zero. A sample difference of 1/10 of a percent, for instance, is not good evidence for a difference in the population (unless the sample size is gigantic).

A statistical test for this example is a mechanism for deciding whether a sample difference is large enough that it is unlikely to be due to sampling error. A probability is calculated. It estimates the chance of seeing a sample difference in either direction at least as large as the observed difference *if* the population difference were zero. If the estimated probability is below a threshold, reject the null hypothesis of no difference. This supports the research hypothesis, but does *not* "prove" it. When the null hypothesis is rejected, we say the difference is *statistically significant*.

The threshold is called the **level of significance**. It is a prespecified probability (**p-value**) required to reject the null hypothesis. The most commonly used level of significance in social research is 0.05 (5 in 100). The calculated p-values for Table 9.5 are:

> 1991: difference = $77.5 - 73.9 = 3.6$; the probability = 0.075
> 1995: difference = $81.6 - 74.5 = 7.1$; the probability = 0.007
> 1998: difference = $72.8 - 73.9 = -1.1$; the probability = 0.682

Only one of these p-values is below the threshold, 0.05. Using the 0.05 level of significance, therefore, the hypothesis of no difference is rejected for 1995, but not

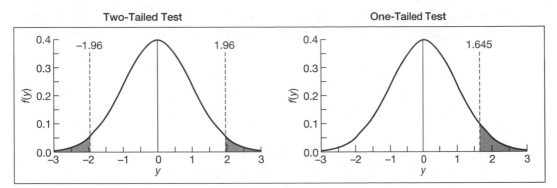

FIGURE 9.5. Standard Normal Distributions with Shaded Areas Corresponding to Probability of 0.05, Two-Tailed and One-Tailed Tests.

for 1991 nor 1998. In general this type of procedure is called a *statistical test* or *test of significance*.

The test for a nondirectional research hypothesis is called a **two-tailed test**. The left and right ends of a distribution are called "tails." With a two-tailed test, the probability associated with the level of significance is split between the upper and lower tails of the sampling distribution, as illustrated in the left-hand panel of Figure 9.5. That is, a difference in either direction large in absolute value leads to rejecting the null hypothesis. Therefore, one-half of the 0.05 must be allocated to negative differences and the other half to positive differences.

For gender differences in attitudes toward the women's movement, a directional hypothesis seems natural—

> *Women are more likely than men to report favorable attitudes toward the women's movement.*

Now the null hypothesis is: Women have no more favorable attitudes toward the women's movement than do men. The null hypothesis, therefore, will be rejected only if the sample percentage of women expressing favorable attitudes exceeds the sample percentage of men by a large enough margin that it is unlikely to be due to sampling error.

Now the entire level of significance is allocated to the upper tail of the sampling distribution, as shown in the right-hand panel of Figure 9.5, and the statistical test is called a **one-tailed test**.

There is an advantage to a one-tailed test. If theory correctly predicts the direction of the relationship, we are more likely to correctly reject the null hypothesis, and thereby support the research hypothesis. In short, a one-tailed alternative hypothesis gives more "statistical power" to detect a correct hypothesis.

Reallocation of the level of significance to one tail of the sampling distribution changes the calculation of probabilities. The revised calculations for Table 9.5 are:

1991: difference = 77.5 − 73.9 = 3.6; probability = 0.038
1995: difference = 81.6 − 74.5 = 7.1; probability = 0.003
1998: difference = 72.8 − 73.9 = −1.1; probability = 0.659

With a one-tailed test and 0.05 level of significance, the null hypothesis is rejected for 1991 and 1995, but still not for 1998. Why not? The direction of difference is wrong for 1998; the percentage of women favoring the women's movement is slightly *less* than the percentage of men favoring the movement. The fact that the null hypothesis is *not* rejected for 1991 using a two-tailed test but *is* rejected using a one-tailed test, illustrates the additional statistical power of a one-tailed test.

Why are the calculated probabilities for one- and two-tailed tests different? For a two-tailed test, the probability refers to the chance of getting a sample difference *in either direction* at least as large as the observed difference. In contrast, the probability for a one-tailed test estimates the chance of seeing a sample difference at least as large as the observed difference *in the direction* predicted by the research hypothesis. As illustrated in Figure 9.5, the probability of a two-tailed test is split between the tails of the distribution, but it is concentrated in one end of the distribution for a one-tailed test.

Application to Confidence Intervals. Probably the most natural way to indicate the estimated size of the sampling error is to report two numbers, a lower boundary and upper boundary, along with a probability the population number lies between the two boundaries. A **confidence interval** is a pair of numbers and an associated probability that the population parameter is between the two numbers. The probability is selected in advance and is called the **level of confidence**. Often the level of confidence is expressed as a percentage, such as a 95 or 99 percent level of confidence. The 0.95 level of confidence corresponds to the 0.05 level of significance for a two-tailed test, and the 0.99 level of confidence to the 0.01 level of significance for a two-tailed test.

To illustrate, look at the 95 percent confidence intervals for the percentage of males in the population calculated from the data in Table 9.5:

Year	Sample Percentage Male	95% Confidence Intervals	
		Lower Bound	Upper Bound
1991	49.89	47.62	52.16
1995	30.69	28.08	33.31
1998	49.32	46.35	52.28

The tabulation shows that for 1991, the probability is 0.95 that the correct percentage of males in the population is between 47.62 and 52.16. For 1995, the probability is 0.95 that the correct percentage of males in the population is between 28.08 and 33.31. In 1998, the boundaries are 46.35 and 52.28. The confidence intervals for 1991 and 1998 contain the known correct percentage of the population which is male (about 49.1%). But the interval for 1995 is way off the mark, suggesting some anomaly in the sampling methods for that year.

The upper and lower boundaries of confidence intervals convey a sense of the precision of the sample statistic in a way not indicated by a statistical test. Notice also the wider boundaries in the estimates for 1995 than for 1991 (for 1995: $33.31 - 28.08 = 5.23$; for 1991: $52.16 - 47.62 = 4.54$). In Table 9.5, there were $n = 932$ males in the 1991 sample, but only $n = 368$ males in 1995, illustrating that sample size is related to the width of the confidence interval: *The larger the sample size, the narrower the confidence interval.*

In brief review, in this section we've addressed the question: How can information in just one sample be used to assess sampling error? The short answer is: With a probability sample, the sample mean and standard deviation can be used as "stand-ins" for the population mean and standard deviation, so that an estimate of the entire sampling distribution—each possible value of a sample statistic from a population and its associated probability—*could* be calculated. In practice, the complete sampling distribution is not estimated. Rather, the calculations are used as the basis of hypothesis tests and confidence intervals.

Our next little mystery is: How big a sample is needed?

How Big a Sample Is Needed? Of course, if you can put up with large sampling errors, only a small sample is needed. However, if small sampling error is required, a larger sample is needed. So, before a sample size can be found, you must decide the size of sampling error that can be tolerated.

Table 9.6 shows the relationship between sample size and sampling error for a percentage when the population percentage is 50%. It displays confidence intervals for sample sizes ranging from 100 to 2000. The first row indicates that for $n = 100$, 95 percent of samples will show a sample percentage between the lower and upper bounds of 40.2 and 59.8 percent. Ignoring the sign (plus or minus), the

TABLE 9.6.   95% Confidence Intervals for Sample Sizes When the Population Percent = 50%.

Sample Size: *n*	Lower Bound (%)	Upper Bound (%)	Sampling Error (%)
100	40.20	59.80	9.80
200	43.07	56.93	6.93
1000	46.90	53.10	3.10
1500	47.47	52.53	2.53
2000	47.81	52.19	2.19

difference between either of these two bounds and the population percentage of 50% is the error: $59.8 - 50 = 9.8$. Also, $50 - 40.2 = 9.8$. So 95 percent of the samples will contain an error of 9.8 or less.

These numbers illustrate why sample sizes seldom exceed one or two thousand. The size of the errors does not go down as quickly as the sample size increases. For instance, doubling the sample size from 100 to 200 does not halve the error: $6.93/9.8 = 0.7071$, which is the square root of 1/2.

In practice, the formula for finding a confidence interval can be used to calculate the sample size needed to reduce the error to a specified number. But, of course, there is no guarantee the error will be less than the specified number, only a specified probability of, for example, 0.95 or 0.99 that it will be smaller than the specification.

Does Size of the Population Matter? The population size enters into statistical inference only if the sample size is a large proportion of the population *and* sampling is done without replacement. A probability sample of 1000 adults gives essentially as good an estimate for the entire U.S. adult population of about 215 million as for a small state like Delaware, which has an adult population of about 600,000.

This conclusion depends on an important assumption, however, that the variation of the variables in the study (e.g., fish weights, attitudes) is roughly the same in Delaware as it is in the U.S. This assumption likely is unrealistic in many research studies. For example, variation in the approval ratings of a newly elected

TABLE 9.7. Summary of Some Terms in Statistical Inference.

Hypothesis test	Formal approach for using sample data to decide whether a statement of fact about the population is correct.
	In social research, hypothesis tests usually are used to decide whether a relationship observed in a sample is large enough that it is a fair bet the variables are related in the population.
Null hypothesis	Testable statement that a population parameter equals a specific value or lies in a specified range. Often the null hypothesis states that the difference between two percentages or means is zero or no greater than zero, sometimes informally called the "no-difference" hypothesis.
Research hypothesis	Usually opposite to the null hypothesis, generally the research hypothesis claims there is a relationship, Often it specifies the direction of the relationship.
Level of significance	Prespecified *p*-value or probability associated with a statistical test. If the calculated probability is no larger than the level of significance, the null hypothesis is rejected. Usually this means the research hypothesis is supported.
Confidence interval	Lower and upper boundary and an associated probability that a population parameter, such as the population mean or percentage, lies between the two boundaries. This probability is called the level of confidence.
Level of confidence	Prespecified probability associated with a confidence interval. The most common level of confidence in social science is 0.95 (95%).

President is likely to be higher across the U.S. as a whole than in any single state because of well-known regional variations in political attitudes.

Table 9.7 summarizes some terms associated with generalizing the results from a sample to a population.

TYPES OF SAMPLES

Using probabilities to make inferences from samples to populations relies fundamentally on having a probability sample. In the real world of social research, however, true probability samples are rare. For many important topics, a probability sample simply isn't feasible. Even samples that start out to be probability samples rarely end up being probability samples. No one knows the probability that people selected into the sample will end up being nonrespondents; this isn't trivial, because response rates usually are well short of 100 percent. And no one knows how many people are omitted from some sampling frames, or included multiple times. Why, then, discuss probability samples at all?

The principles of probability sampling provide benchmarks for evaluating "real-world" samples. Often, samples can be designed as closely as practical to be probability samples and the data collection organized to adhere to the design. In many other instances, such as disaster research or study of homeless populations, it's entirely out of the question to take a probability sample. But it would be excessively rigid to throw out these sources of information because they aren't based on a probability sample.

Probability Sample

A probability sample doesn't require the same probability of selection for each element in the population. It just requires *known probabilities* greater than zero for each element. Only a simple random sample requires equal probabilities.

Simple Random Sample (SRS). The simplest probability sample is a simple random sample (SRS). Recall from earlier discussion in this chapter that a simple random sample is a sample for which every possible sample of a given size has the same chance, greater than zero, of being selected. This definition implies that each element has the same chance of selection as every other element.

The example of a slip of paper for each of 30 students drawn from the professor's hat produces a simple random sample. Also, all the calculations connected with the "story" of Goldie and friends assumed simple random samples. (Both the hat and fish examples use sampling *without* replacement.) One important feature of a simple random sample *with* replacement is that the chance of selecting any element doesn't depend in any way on which other elements already have been selected. The sample elements are said to be *independent* of each other. In contrast, individuals in a sample of households are not independent observations—members of a household are more similar to each other than to the general population.

Systematic Sample. Think of a list of 100 students in order of their student ID number. To get a sample of 10 from the list, choose a random start, and take every 10th student thereafter.[3] In general, take every kth person from the list, where k is the ratio of the population size (N) to the sample size (n): $k = N/n$, rounded down to a whole number. As with an SRS, every element of the population has the same chance of selection with systematic sampling. But, in contrast with an SRS, every sample of size n does not have the same chance of selection. If every 5th person is selected, person 1 will never appear in the same sample with person 2, for instance.

A systematic sampling scheme can work well for small samples. So long as people are listed in random order, a systematic sample is a good strategy, and equivalent to an SRS. But you have to be careful how the list is arranged. Suppose you are taking every 10th person, and the list is composed of couples, with the female always listed first. If the random start is with an odd number, all selections are female; if the start is an even number, all selections are male!

Stratified Sampling. Often, an SRS isn't feasible. Consider a study of the relationship between cancer and church attendance. The research hypothesis is that people currently fighting cancer attend church more frequently than people not fighting cancer. Based on information from the National Cancer Institute (Weir, et al., 2002), an SRS of $n = 500$ from the adult U.S. population would contain 2 to 3 persons who currently have cancer, and they are likely to be 55 years old or older. Clearly, two persons with cancer aren't enough for the study! Moreover, older people are more likely than younger people to have cancer *and* are more likely to attend religious services even if they don't have cancer. So the effects of age and religion are likely to be confounded. What should you do?

This situation calls for a stratified sample. A **stratified sample** is one for which the population is divided into two or more groups, called strata (singular form is stratum), in a way that guarantees each element fits into exactly one stratum. In sampling, strata are variables used for a specific purpose: part of the sample comes from each stratum. For this study, two variables are needed to define the strata: age and cancer. These are "stratification variables." Suppose you divide the population into five age strata, each a 10-year interval, starting at age 20, with everyone aged 70 and older condensed into one open-ended interval, as laid out in Table 9.8. If the sample contains 500 people in each stratum, the total sample size is large, 6000 ($6 \times 2 \times 500 = 6000$).

TABLE 9.8. Sketch of a Table Comparing Age and Cancer Risk.

Cancer	Age Group					
	20–29	30–39	40–49	50–59	60–69	≥70
No						
Yes						

Two stratification variables are needed because both church attendance and cancer risk increase with age. It is essential to compare church attendance for those with cancer to those without cancer *within* each age group, thereby keeping age approximately constant. This stratification scheme with 500 cases per stratum guarantees enough cases in each age category to permit these comparisons.

To make the sample a probability sample, you must know the number of people in each of the 12 strata in the population. This information probably isn't available, but sample estimates do exist (Weir, et al., 2002).

Not all stratified samples require two stratification variables. Decisions about stratification are specific to each survey.

Stratified sampling schemes are used routinely in complex surveys for two reasons: (1) to improve the accuracy of comparisons among strata relative to an SRS, as in the cancer study, or (2) to improve the accuracy of sample estimates for the combined strata. If the number of people in the sample of each stratum is proportionate to the population size of each stratum, the stratified sample is at least as accurate as an SRS for estimating statistics for the entire population (not within strata), and usually it is more accurate.

Cluster Sampling and Multistage Sampling. Imagine assembling a complete list of every person in New York City, or the state of California, or the entire United States! The task is impossibly costly and difficult. By the time such a list is complete, if it could be compiled at all, it's almost sure to be obsolete. For these reasons, nearly all large surveys take something other than individual persons as the **primary sampling unit (PSU)**. Examples of PSUs include households, city blocks, and school districts.

The idea of a **cluster sample** is to sample groups of individual elements called "clusters." For example, the National Education Longitudinal Study (NELS) is a survey of students who were in the eighth grade in 1988 and followed every 2 years through 1994. The study used schools as the primary sampling unit (NCES, 1996). If NELS had surveyed every student in the selected schools, the sample would be called a cluster sample, where a cluster consists of all students in each school.

But in the first year of the project, NELS sampled just 24 students, plus an oversample of two or three Asian and Hispanic students within each selected school. Since a sample of students was taken, rather than all students in each school, the NELS sample is a two-stage sampling scheme. Selection of a sample of schools is the first stage and selection of a sample of students in each selected school is the second stage. The general term for sampling within clusters is **multistage sampling**. These can become complicated. There may be "clusters within clusters," for example, households within city blocks. And stratification may be done within each cluster.

What's the difference between a cluster sample and a stratified sample? A stratified sample is one that selects individuals from every stratum; the strata are not sampled. And a cluster sample is one that samples clusters, rather than taking all of them. This distinction may seem inconsequential, but it isn't. Stratified samples usually are more accurate than an SRS for a given sample size. But cluster and multistage samples are less accurate than an SRS.[4] The reduction in practical problems of collecting data usually more than offsets the loss of sampling accuracy for cluster samples.[5]

Nonprobability Samples

This section answers the remaining three little mysteries introduced at the beginning of the chapter:

- What's the difference between a "probability sample" and a "haphazard sample"?
- Why is a probability sample preferred?
- When can a haphazard sample be justified?

Haphazard Sample. A **haphazard sample** (or convenience sample) is any sample that isn't a probability sample; the probability of selection of each element is not known. When little or no information is available on a topic, a haphazard sample often provides invaluable information. The choice frequently is between a haphazard sample and no sample.

The disaster research cited in Chapter 6 necessarily relies on nonprobability samples. It's impossible to construct a reliable sampling frame for studying people who just survived a disaster like a hurricane or flood, or the destruction of the World Trade Center in New York City. But not to do any research because a probability sample is impossible would result in many valuable insights lost. The alternative might be complete ignorance, or reliance on rumors and speculation.

Excerpt: The Birdhouse Network (TBN). An interesting example of a haphazard sample is the Cornell University Birdhouse Network. Conducted by the Cornell Lab of Ornithology, it is designed to enlist the help of private citizens in carrying out research about the natural habits of birds. Part of the overview posted on the Web site associated with the project reads:

> The Birdhouse Network is a citizen-science monitoring program in North America. It is intended for people of all ages and backgrounds who provide birdhouses (nest boxes) for cavity-nesting birds and then observe and record the lives of these fascinating birds up close throughout the breeding season. (Cornell Lab of Ornithology, 2004).

Would you use this sample to generate precise estimates of the number of eggs laid per nest, the number of fledglings, or the number of times per year birds nest in the wild? Probably not, but the data still provide very useful information to ornithologists at Cornell. The researchers certainly have a better idea of these numbers with the data than with no data. And it probably is impossible to get a probability sample of birds.

A cluster sample might work, but observing every bird, or taking a probability sample within each cluster, would be difficult, if not impossible. Moreover, the size of the sample generated by The Birdhouse Network is much larger than the research team could collect on its own.

Theoretical Sample. In theoretical sampling, field researchers record observations about an event, look for patterns or regularities in the observations, and often propose generalizations of the patterns they have observed in specific settings. The generalizations are used to develop theory. Sometimes theoretical sampling is called "grounded theory," because the theory is derived from (grounded in) the observed behaviors of social life. Research based on other data collection strategies, such as personal interviews, sometimes relies on theoretical sampling procedures. An example is Diamond's research of "everyday life in nursing homes" in Chapter 6.

Snowball Sample. Another type of nonprobability sample is a **snowball sample**. The name loosely describes the strategy used to recruit participants. A few participants are used to locate others, who in turn provide additional leads, until the target sample size is reached. The procedure is particularly useful when the population cannot be defined in advance, but a few initial contacts can be located who fit the study criteria and who will provide additional leads.

Excerpt: *Secrecy and Status in Forbidden Sexual Relationships.* An interesting study of secret relationships used snowball sampling.

> A feature of cross-sex secret, forbidden sexual relationships is that they are typically constructed between *status unequals*. One status imbalance usually exists: age, class, or marital status. . . .
>
> The data come from intensive interviews with 65 single women who had or were having long-term (over a year) intimate relationships with married men. The interviewees came from three sources. First, whenever I attended a public or social occasion, I mentioned the project, and women I met in these settings volunteered to be interviewed. Second, a respondent would occasionally suggest other potential interviewees. Third, women, hearing of the project, requested to be interviewed.
>
> The frequently reinstituted "snowball" sampling procedure generated an extensive list of potential interviewees from a wide variety of social networks. After 48 interviews with a diverse set of women over a period of five years, saturation was experienced. Since I was fairly accurately predicting the women's accounts, I discontinued interviewing. During the analysis and writing stages, though, I followed 17 women who contacted me during the early stages of their liaisons. . . .
>
> [T]wo stages of intimacy emerge: (1) exchanging secrets about the self or "Becoming Confidantes" and (2) creating mutual secrets or "Becoming a We." The man's marital status, reinforced by his gender and socioeconomic status, has major effects concerning time constraints, expectations of temporariness, and privacy. These

lead to intense feelings, idealization, and trust, which enhance the woman's commitment to perpetuating the relationship. The relationship is perpetuated through the construction of mutual secrets (rituals and property), which are imbued with intense symbolic significance. The strategies used to conceal the relationship increase the woman's dependence on it and reduce her power within it. Secrecy protects the interests of the powerful. (Richardson, 1988, pp. 209–211)

Without a prior sample size in mind, when does snowball sampling end? Usually when all leads have been exhausted, the pattern of findings suggests replication of information from previous respondents ("saturation"), a predetermined number of participants has been obtained, or some combination of these situations occurs. As a nonprobability sample, the findings properly apply only to the sample studied and not to a larger population.

The observations in a snowball sample obviously are dependent on each other; each person after the first suggests whom to include next. Standard methods for generalizing to a population depend on the assumption of independent observations. Hence, standard statistical tests are likely to be misleading. We must depend on informal judgments, or work with a sampling expert to see if a realistic scheme for computing statistical tests can be devised. With a snowball sample, be on the lookout for evidence suggesting most respondents come from a tight-knit group, which would bias the conclusions if generalized beyond the sample.

Quota Sample. Suppose your methods instructor assigns a project calling for study groups in the class to collect data from undergraduates on the campus. The research hypothesis is

Married students are less likely than single students to engage in "binge drinking."

You decide to interview 100 students. Because most students are not married, the group decides to interview 50 married and 50 single students, to ensure including enough married respondents. So far, this procedure sounds like a stratified sample, stratified by marital status. What's the difference? With a **quota sample**, individuals within the "strata" aren't sampled at random. Interviewers sample haphazardly; all that's required is to get a predetermined number of interviews from each of the "strata."

This procedure can lead to poor results. Suppose, for example, your group decides to go to the local pub to do the interviews. You interview all 50 of your quota of single students, and only two married students, because there were only two married students in the pub. So you fan out the next night and knock on doors in the married-student housing units. This strategy doesn't violate any rule of quota sampling. All that's required is 50 single and 50 married students. Not surprisingly, the result is overwhelming support for the hypothesis. But, of course, the sample estimate of the difference between married and single students is seriously biased!

Hopefully in practice, few quota samples are this extreme. But they do tend to underrepresent "reluctant" respondents. For example, in a telephone survey, just keep calling until you complete your 10 interviews with black male high school students. The potential for bias in this strategy is obvious. But it's a lot cheaper than repeated attempts to contact 10 specific respondents selected at random from a sampling frame.

Purposive Sample. Suppose you need information about drug use and AIDS risk. Could you identify a population of all drug users? A **purposive sample** often is selected to meet specific criteria. A purposive sample is justified for studies in which it is impossible to list all elements of the population. A purposive sample also can be advisable in very small samples, where random sampling error is likely to be unacceptably large.

A study reported by Schilling, El-Bassel, and Gilbert (1992) describes the risk behaviors and attitudes of an urban soup-kitchen population. The research team chose a kitchen that serves meals to food-stamp recipients in the Manhattan section of New York City.

> According to soup kitchen staff, about 60 percent of the clients are drug users or alcoholics. The majority are not in treatment and spend their days on the street. At night they live in shelters, sleep in subways and doorways, or stay with friends. (Schilling, El-Bassel, & Gilbert, 1992, p. 353)

A primary task of the counselors working at the soup kitchen is to refer clients with alcohol or drug problems to treatment and community services. Schilling et al. relied on the counselors to refer to the research study clients who had a history of drug use. Although Schilling et al. provide a clear rationale for their sampling strategy and used counselors as knowledgeable "experts" for identifying members of the sample, the results properly apply only to the sample studied. Generalizing the findings beyond the sample relies on informal judgment.

It is a rare sample that is of interest for its own sake; we nearly always intend some sort of generalization beyond a particular sample. But, a nonprobability sample is nearly certain to be biased and to generate larger sampling error than a probability sample. Most of them probably also contain substantial bias. Kalton (1983) gives a succinct summary of the disadvantages of nonprobability sampling. He is particularly hard on quota samples.

On the other hand, as shown in this chapter, nonprobability samples often provide useful information that would not be available to purists who insist on a probability sample or nothing. So, be extra skeptical of findings from nonprobability samples, but don't necessarily dismiss them.

SUMMARY

This chapter begins with a sampling riddle: How can the results from a sample of a few thousand or so observations be generalized to a large population like all U.S. adults, some 215 million people? Using statistical procedures to generalize from a sample to the population is called "statistical inference." The idea of a sampling distribution is the foundation of statistical inference. To understand the concept of sampling distribution, you must imagine many repeated samples from a population. Of course, real-world studies seldom take more than one sample, but understanding the theory depends on imagining what would happen *if* repeated samples were taken.

Sampling distributions describe how specific sample statistics, such as the sample mean, vary over repeated samples. One of the amazing results of sampling theory is that the entire sampling distribution of the sample mean, and many other statistics, can be estimated from one sample. The normal sampling distribution depends on just two numbers, the population mean and population standard deviation. Moreover, the sample mean and standard deviation can be used as "stand-ins" for an unknown population mean and standard deviation, and an estimate of the sampling distribution can then be calculated. But, practical interest doesn't focus on the entire sampling distribution. Rather, the calculations are used as the basis of the two main types of statistical inference: hypothesis tests and confidence intervals.

The idea of a statistical test is to see if a sample difference is big enough so we are willing to bet it didn't arise from chance fluctuations in sampling. The procedure starts with a null hypothesis that usually states there is no relationship between two variables in the population. The research hypothesis states there is a relationship. A probability called a "*p*-value" is calculated, giving the chance of finding a sample relationship at least as large as the observed sample relationship, if there were no relationship in the population. If that probability is small enough, reject the null hypothesis. The probability, or *p*-value, is called the "level of significance." In social research, the level of significance typically is 0.05 or below. If the calculated *p*-value is at or below the level of significance, reject the null hypothesis, thereby (usually) supporting the research hypothesis.

When the research hypothesis indicates a relationship isn't zero but doesn't state a direction, the associated hypothesis test is a two-tailed test. The *p*-value is split between the lower and upper tails of the sampling distribution. When a direction is indicated, the hypothesis test is a one-tailed test, and the *p*-value is concentrated in one tail of the sampling distribution: in the upper tail if the hypothesized difference is positive and the lower tail if it is negative.

A second formal method of statistical inference is called a "confidence interval." A confidence interval presents a lower and an upper boundary and an associated probability. The probability states the chance the population parameter lies in the interval between the lower and upper boundaries. This probability is called the level of confidence.

A probability sample is a sample for which the probability of selecting each element in the population is known and greater than zero. A simple random sample (SRS) is the most elementary probability sample; for any sample size, *n*, the probability of selection is the same for each element of the population *and* for each combination of *n* elements.

A stratified sample is one in which the population is divided into two or more strata (groups) so that each element fits into exactly one stratum. Elements are selected from each of the strata.

In a cluster sample, the population also is divided into groups, called clusters, so that each element fits into just one cluster. In contrast to a stratified sample, some, but not all, of the clusters are included in the sample. All elements in selected clusters are in the sample. In a multistage sample, elements are sampled within the clusters.

Usually, stratified samples give better sampling accuracy than an SRS of the same size, and an SRS generally produces better sampling accuracy than cluster samples of the same size.

Several types of nonprobability or haphazard samples are used in social research: theoretical, snowball, purposive, and quota samples. Haphazard samples are likely to contain bias, and even if they don't, we have no way to know that they don't. Consequently, generalizing from a sample to its population isn't, strictly speaking, justified. However, a probability sample often is nearly impossible to select. So the choice is between no information (no study) and some information—perhaps a lot of information from a nonprobability sample. Data from nonprobability samples obviously should be considered with caution, but should seldom be rejected as "worthless."

YOUR REVIEW SHEET: QUESTIONS DISCUSSED IN THIS CHAPTER

1. In your own words, explain why we take a sample instead of a complete count.

2. Suppose there are 20 students in your research methods class. Your instructor writes each student's name on a separate piece of paper, places the paper slips in a hat, thoroughly mixes the slips and pulls one out. What is the probability (in fraction and decimal form) that your name is drawn? Show your calculations.

3. Explain why it is important to avoid interpreting every relationship observed in sample data as if it were "real" in the population from which the sample was drawn. Explain how statistical tests help to protect against this kind of overinterpretation of data.

4. Define *probability sample*.

5. Distinguish between the terms *statistic* and *parameter*. Give an example of each.

6. Define *sampling distribution*. Explain why sampling distributions indicate the chance a sample statistic will be in error by as much or more than any specified amount.

7. What can be done to help ensure an accurate sampling frame? Consider both duplicate elements and omissions.

8. Define simple random sample (SRS), systematic sample, stratified sample, and cluster sample.

9. Why choose stratified sampling? Mention two main reasons.

10. What is the difference between a cluster sample and a stratified sample? What is the main reason for using each type? List some typical social science variables used to define strata and clusters other than those in this chapter.

11. What is the difference between a "random" sample and a haphazard sample?

12. Why is a probability sample preferred over a haphazard sample? Is a nonprobability sample worthless? Summarize the shortcomings and strengths of nonprobability samples.

13. When can a haphazard sample be justified? (Refer to your answer to #12.)

14. Although the soup-kitchen study of drug risk provides a clear rationale for the sampling strategy and appropriate use of the counselors as knowledgeable persons, it is difficult to know how well the results generalize to the population. It's even difficult to define what the population is. Why?

15. In the fish example, why aren't there 15 different sample mean weights? There are 15 distinct samples.

16. Suppose the differences among the fish weights increase. What happens to the variance? Why?

17. How can the central limit theorem help us if we need to know the population standard deviation before using it?

18. When do you use the normal sampling distribution, and when might you need another distribution?

19. In a standard normal distribution, where do the numbers, -1.96 and $+1.96$ come from?

20. Does the needed sample size depend on the size of the population? Briefly explain.

END NOTES

1. In practice, this procedure is impossible. There are 10 billion possible numbers. Some of the prefixes may be allocated to businesses, colleges, universities, hospitals, and the like, so these prefixes are eliminated. Some households have more than one phone number, and one number may be dedicated to a computer, fax, or children. Moreover, many people now have caller ID, and/or answering machines, and may refuse to take a call unless they recognize the caller's number.

2. In most real-world situations, the population is so large that there is no practical difference between sampling with and without replacement. The rule given in the text for finding the standard error of the mean applies to sampling *with* replacement or to sample sizes that are a very small fraction of the population size. In the fish example, though, sampling was done *without* replacement and the sampling fraction is quite large, $2/6 = 1/3$. The text formula has to be modified to take this into account. For the variance of the mean, multiply the population variance by $(N - n)/(N - 1)$ and divide by $n = 2$ to get the variance of the sample means: $(6 - 2)/(6 - 1) \times 2.917 \div 2 = (4/5) \times 2.917 \div 2 \doteq 1.167$. The standard error of the mean is the square root of the variance: $\sqrt{1.167} \doteq 1.080$. Note that the calculated variance and standard deviation in Table 9.2 match exactly these theoretical formulas.

3. With a fractional k (e.g., $144/10 = 14.4$), one approach is to choose a random start between 1 and 144 and treat the list as circular until 10 units are selected. In this example, if the random start is 1 through 4 and you take every fourteenth person, you don't need to wrap around to the beginning of the list. For higher starting numbers you do.

4. The accuracy of a stratified or cluster sample is measured by comparing the sampling variation for sample statistics like the mean or percentage to sampling variation of the same statistic calculated from an SRS.

5. Sample designs like stratified samples, cluster samples, and multistage samples complicate the statistical analysis. Unbiased estimates of population parameters like the population mean reading score in the NELS, for example, require sampling weights. And correct estimates of p-values require specialized software.

STUDY TERMS

central limit theorem For an SRS (with replacement), as the sample size increases, the distribution of the sample mean bunches around the population mean to form a normal sampling distribution. The mean of the sampling distribution is the mean of the population, and the standard deviation is given by the standard deviation of the population divided by the square root of the sample size. But these latter two facts do not depend on the central-limit theorem.

cluster sample Groups of individual elements are sampled instead of individual elements. The groups are called "clusters." Each individual in selected clusters is included in the sample. Schools might form the clusters for a sample of students, for example.

confidence interval Lower and upper boundary and an associated probability that a population parameter, such as a mean or percentage, lies between the boundaries. This probability is called the level of confidence. The boundaries are estimated from sample data, given a specified level of confidence.

element Objects comprising a population. Examples of elements include people, families, households, cities, states, church congregations, cemetery markers, magazine advertisements, and fish.

haphazard sample (or convenience sample) Any sample that isn't a probability sample. The probability of selection of the elements is unknown.

hypothesis test Formal approach for using sample data to decide whether a statement of fact about the population is correct. In social research, hypothesis tests usually are used to decide whether a relationship observed in a sample is large enough that it is a fair bet the variables are related in the population.

level of confidence Prespecified probability associated with a confidence interval. The most common level of confidence is 0.95 (95%).

level of significance Prespecified probability giving the *p*-value required to reject the null hypothesis. The most commonly used level of significance is 0.05 (5 in 100). If the estimated probability from the data is smaller than the level of significance, reject the null hypothesis. Otherwise, do not reject it. Rejecting the null hypothesis generally supports the research hypothesis.

multistage sampling Sampling clusters and elements within clusters, for example, households within city blocks.

nonprobability sample A sample for which the probability of selection of each element is not known.

normal sampling distribution Sampling distribution that is symmetric around the mean of the distribution. It is defined by a specific mathematical formula.

null hypothesis Testable statement that the population statistic from which a sample was drawn equals a specific value. In social research, the null hypothesis usually states there are no differences in a dependent variable among levels of an independent variable, sometimes informally called the "no difference" hypothesis.

one-tailed test A hypothesis test of a relationship in which the direction of the relationship is predicted in advance of the test. For example, women express more favorable attitudes toward the women's movement than do men. The entire probability of the level of significance is put in one tail of the sampling distribution rather than being split between the two tails. A one-tailed test gives more statistical power to reject a false null hypothesis.

point estimate A single sample statistic such as a sample mean used to estimate the corresponding population mean. Contrast point estimate to a confidence interval where two boundaries are calculated and a probability is given that the population parameter lies between the boundaries.

population Collection of elements to be described—for example all people comprising a religious group, all fish in a fish bowl—or elements of any other known collectivity.

population parameter (parameter) A number such as a percentage, mean, or the difference between percentages describing the entire population.

primary sampling unit (PSU) A collection of elements, such as people or fish, to be sampled as a single unit. Examples of PSUs include households, city blocks, and schools. In cluster sampling, PSUs are sampled rather than individual elements.

probability sample Sample for which the probability of selection is known and greater than zero for each element in a population.

purposive sample Nonprobability sample selected to meet specific criteria of a study, such as all drug users in a soup-kitchen population.

***p*-value** Estimate of the probability of observing a sample statistic with a greater deviation from the null hypothesis than the observed statistic if the null hypothesis were correct.

quota sample Nonprobability sample that takes a prespecified number of elements from each of several subgroups of the population, e.g., 100 male and 100 female, or 33 male and 67 female. The subgroups are comparable to strata. A quota sample differs from a stratified sample because the elements are selected haphazardly within each subgroup with quota sampling, but are selected by probability sample with stratified sampling.

research hypothesis Usually opposite to the null hypothesis. In most instances, the research hypothesis states that there is a relationship.

sample Some part of a population, generally selected with the idea of calculating a sample statistic to estimate the corresponding population parameter.

sample statistic Number calculated from a sample, such as the sample mean (average), sample percentage (or sample proportion), or the difference between sample means or percentages for two groups.

sampling distribution List of each possible value of a sample statistic from a population and its associated probability.

sampling error Difference between a sample statistic and population parameter when a sample is used to describe the population, for example, the difference between the average number of children in families in a sample of the U.S. population and the correct, but usually unknown, average in the population.

sampling frame Complete list of each element in the population. A sample is drawn from this list. Consequently, getting a probability sample depends on the list being complete, with no duplicate entries.

simple random sample (SRS) The most elementary probability sample; every possible sample of a given size has the same chance of being selected.

snowball sample Nonprobability sample obtained by relying on a few participants to identify other participants, who in turn provide additional leads, until the target sample size is reached.

standard deviation Measure of dispersion of a variable. The standard deviation is the square root of the variance. A *sample* standard deviation summarizes variation in a single sample. A *population* standard deviation summarizes variation in the population.

standard error A special name given to the standard deviation when the numbers are a sample statistic, like the sample mean.

standard normal distribution Normal distribution with a mean = 0.0 and a standard deviation (and variance) = 1.0.

standard score (*z*-score) A variable transformed to ensure that it has a mean of exactly zero and a standard deviation of exactly one, obtained by subtracting the mean of the original variable from each value and dividing the result by the standard deviation of the original variable.

statistical inference Technical term for using probability methods to generalize sample statistics to population parameters (e.g., to generalize a sample percentage to the population percentage).

statistically significant Term used to describe a sample statistic whose *p*-value is less than or equal to the level of significance.

statistical test A procedure usually used to decide whether an observed sample relationship is big enough to justify the conclusion that a relationship exists in the population. Statistical tests sometimes are used for other purposes, for example, to test whether the average height of U.S. men equals 5 feet 10 and one-half inches.

stratified sample Sample taken by selecting elements from each of two or more groups called strata (singular form, stratum). The strata are defined so that each element fits into exactly one stratum. So strata define a variable used for a specific purpose of sampling.

theoretical sample Nonprobability sampling strategy often used by field researchers who directly observe social events, often used to develop a theory to guide future research. Sometimes called "grounded theory," because the theory is derived from (grounded in) the observed behaviors of social life.

two-tailed test Statistical test for a nondirectional hypothesis. The probability associated with the level of significance is split between the upper and lower tails of the sampling distribution.

unbiased statistic Statistic whose "expected value" (mean of all sample means) equals the corresponding population parameter. Unbiased implies no systematic tendency to overestimate or underestimate the population parameter.

variance Measure of how much the numbers in a list differ among themselves (dispersion). It is defined as the average squared distance from the mean.

EXERCISES

Exercise 9.1. Taking an SRS (without Replacement).

Directions: Below is a list of the social science and natural science faculty at small but prestigious AP University, located in the mythical state of North California.

Suppose you want to know whether social science (SS) or natural science (NS) faculty members are more likely to ask students questions during class lectures. You have resources to observe the classes of only a small number of faculty members, so you must rely on a sample.

(SS) Nadia Adams	(SS) Charles Criscione
(SS) Timothy Ames	(SS) AmyJo Domst
(SS) Nancy Ames	(SS) Joyce East
(NS) Denise Antosh	(NS) Ronald Ensign
(SS) Quinn Ardillo	(NS) Len Fenniello
(NS) Gordon Bak	(NS) Arlene Fintzel
(SS) Walther Barreca	(NS) Grace Germaine
(NS) Heath Battaglia	(NS) Lea Goo

(NS) Julia Belliotti	(NS) David Gora
(NS) Brian Benkelman	(NS) George Griffiths
(SS) Anita Bentham	(NS) James Huyck
(SS) Betty Berry	(NS) Vivian Johnson
(SS) Carol Bleecher	(SS) Robert Joseph
(SS) Fritz Bohlen	(NS) Margaret Krzal
(NS) Carolyn Boorady	(SS) Alexis Lagana
(NS) Nancy Benton	(SS) Gary Lanze
(SS) William Branicky	(NS) Sandy Liedke
(SS) Linda Brescia	(SS)Marcia Mackay
(SS) Glenn Cave	(SS) Anthony Maitland
(NS) Bonny Christner	(NS) Karen Paige

1. Assign a number to each member of the population of faculty. (Assign numbers down the columns.) How many faculty members are in this population?

2. Select a 20% SRS (without replacement) from this population. How many faculty members will be in the sample? Show your calculation.

3. Use the table of random numbers in Appendix B. Using a random start (e.g., drop a pencil point on the page without looking, selecting the closest number as the start—not really random, but good enough), select enough random numbers for the 20% sample. How many digits do you need in each of the random numbers? (*Hint:* If the number of faculty in the population is less than 10, you need one digit, if 10–99, two digits needed. . . .)

4. Write down all the numbers you select from the random numbers table, then cross out numbers you can't use (i.e., zeros (00), numbers that are larger than the population size, or numbers that are duplicates). Then, make a list of the name, science area, and number of each faculty member in your sample.

5. How many SS and how many NS faculty members are in your sample?

6. What makes this sampling scheme "sampling without replacement"?

7. Would a stratified sample be better than your SRS for comparing social-science to natural-science classrooms? Briefly explain.

Exercise 9.2. Stratified Random Sample

Directions: A stratified sample is one for which the population is divided into two or more groups, called strata, in a way that guarantees each person (or other element) fits into exactly one stratum. Part of the sample comes from *each* of the strata. The strata themselves are not sampled. For this exercise, the population is defined as all SS and NS faculty members. Faculty in other disciplines are excluded from this population.

1. Suppose you want to know whether SS or NS faculty members at AP University ask more questions of students during class lectures. You decide to sample an equal number of SS and NS faculty members. What is your stratification variable and what are its strata?

2. Sort the list into two lists, one for NS and one for SS. Number each consecutively starting at 1.

3. Using the random numbers table, take a 20% random sample of *each list separately.* (You need to select two sets of numbers from the random numbers table.) How many faculty members are in each sample? Write the names and numbers of selected faculty members in your stratified sample.

4. Compare your stratified sample to the SRS of Exercise 9.1. What is the most obvious difference between the two samples? (If no differences were found, what is the most obvious difference one would expect between the two sampling strategies?)

5. Looking at the faculty list of names, what potential problem might you have in trying to stratify by gender?

6. Suppose the sample size were large enough (and you could resolve the potential problem suggested by Question 5), how could you arrange the faculty list to stratify by science field *and* gender? How would you select the sample?

Exercise 9.3. SRS and the Sampling Distribution

Directions: The central limit theorem and Goldie the fish's experience tell us that as the number of observations in an SRS increases, the sample means bunch close to the population mean. When the SRS increases are plotted on a graph, the sampling distribution looks like the normal distribution.

1. Using the population of student ages below, draw 20 or more simple random samples (SRSs), each with $n = 5$. The drawings should be *with* replacement—each selected age should be put back into the "pot" before the next drawing (so it is available for selection into more than one sample).

A Population of Student Ages ($N = 45$)

19	22	20	27	44	21	21	24	23
20	24	23	20	21	26	24	23	19
21	20	25	21	23	23	19	31	27
22	20	38	21	21	22	24	23	20
20	21	22	21	19	36	23	23	27

2. Calculate the sample mean for each sample, preferably using a calculator. Round each mean to the nearest whole number.

3. Write each mean on a separate line of ruled paper.

4. Calculate the mean of your sampling distribution (add all sample means and divide by the number of samples, N_s). This is the "mean of all sample means."

5. On the sampling distribution on the next page, the vertical axis represents the number of means (1, 2, ... N_s) and the horizontal axis represents the numeric value of a sample mean you calculated. Plot all sample mean scores. Use a column of Xs to represent each frequency, as shown in the following example.

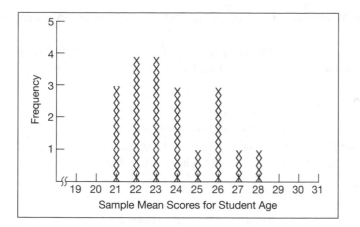

6. Looking at the shape of the curve, estimate (informally determine) the population mean for student age.

7. Now, calculate the actual population mean (here, the population is known, with $N = 45$).

8. A statistic is unbiased if and only if its mean over all possible samples equals the mean of the population. How close is the population mean to the mean of the sampling distribution you created? (numeric difference between the calculated mean and informally estimated mean)

9. Compute the standard deviation (SD) of the sampling distribution (the sample means are the scores for student age x). Use one of the formulas below. (*Note:* N_s [your 20 or more] refers to the number of samples, not the sample size [5].) The SD of the *population* is 4.9955. Divide it by the square root of 5 and compare the result to the SD of your sampling distribution. The two numbers should be approximately the same, but you have relatively few (just 20 or a few more) samples, so there is room for some difference.

$$SD = \sqrt{\frac{\Sigma(x_i - \bar{x})^2}{N_s - 1}} = \sqrt{\frac{\Sigma x_i^2 - N_s \bar{x}^2}{N_s - 1}}$$

10. Summarize in your own words the purpose of this exercise.

Note: If your exercise didn't turn out the way it should have, (a) you don't have enough samples, (b) your sampling method isn't random, (c) you made a mistake in the calculations, and/or (d) you were very unlucky. Try again!

Exercise 9.4. Evaluation of Research: Nonprobability Sample

Directions: Refer to the excerpt on "secrecy and status in forbidden relationships" in this chapter to answer the following questions.

Factual Questions

1. Describe the study participants. Why do you think these individuals were selected?

2. How were initial participants located?

3. What evidence does the author give to suggest that the snowball procedure provided an adequate sample?

4. How does the author characterize the generalizability of the study? To what population (if any) do you think the results generalize? Briefly defend your answer.

Questions for Discussion

1. Briefly describe the sampling strategy in your own words.

2. Evaluate the usefulness of the sampling strategy to address the study topic. Are there other strategies that might be more useful? Why or why not?

3. How did the author decide to end sampling? Briefly discuss pros and cons of this approach.

4. Why does a snowball sample produce dependence among the sample elements? Why is this a problem for statistical inference?

DATA PREPARATION AND BASIC ANALYSIS

INTRODUCTION: LOOKING AT HOW THE SOCIAL WORLD WORKS

Now comes the fun part—data analysis! Here we get to see what the data reveal about how the social world works. Take the question of violence between two people as an example. After reviewing past research on the topic, you might propose a theory predicting gender differences in the rate of victimization to violence, and state the following general hypothesis:

> *Women are more likely than men to be victims of violence.*

The rationale might be that women are economically and physically more vulnerable to violence than men are.

Consider one type of violence—being hit by another person. The hypothesis of gender difference can be translated into a diagram. The diagram gives a useful picture of the hypothesis, but it doesn't indicate whether women *or* men are more likely to be hit.

> *gender → hit*

The hypothesis mentions violence generally. Hit is just one manifestation of violence. This illustrates the nature of theory; it usually is more general than the specific hypotheses we test.

Table 10.1 displays the relationship between gender and "ever hit," using data from the General Social Survey (GSS), a nationally representative sample of the U.S. adult population.[1] The question asked of GSS respondents is, "Have you ever been punched or beaten by another person?" These data support the hypothesis that the chance of ever being hit depends partly on gender, *but* the *direction* of the difference is just the opposite of the hypothesis: Men are more likely to have been hit than are women.

A good summary of Table 10.1 is:

> *Men are more likely than women to have been hit at some time in their lives. Over half of the men have been hit at least once (53.1%), whereas only a little more than a fourth of the women have ever been hit (26.2%).*

TABLE 10.1. Percentage "Ever Hit," by Gender.

Ever Hit by Anyone?	Male	Female	Total
Yes	53.1	26.2	38.2
No	46.9	73.8	61.8
Total %	100.0	100.0	100.0
(Total n)	(228)	(282)	(510)

Source: 2002 General Social Survey, cumulative data file 1972–2002 (Davis, Smith, & Marsden, 2003). This table is for the year 1994.

Main table entries are percentages. Numbers in parentheses are the numbers of respondents.

The percentage difference is a useful measure of the strength of a relationship: $53.1\% - 26.2\% = 26.9\%$, although percentage differences usually aren't shown in tables. This is a moderately strong relationship. The percentage difference is used as a measure of **social significance** (sometimes called **substantive significance**)— that is, an interesting, "socially important" association exists between the variables. It's important to distinguish between *substantive* importance and *statistical significance*. With a very large sample, a trivial substantive difference might be statistically significant, that is, probably not due to sampling error.

The original research hypothesis is not supported; it predicted women would be more likely than men to be victims of violence. One possible reason why men are more likely to be hit than women is that cultural norms accept and even encourage physical violence among men more than among women. Another possibility is that men are more likely than women to abuse alcohol and illegal drugs, and substance abuse predisposes people to be victims of violence.

These explanations are ad hoc—that is, made up after seeing the data. Consequently, they're not very convincing. It's easy to think up explanations for something you've already seen but a lot more difficult to predict it in advance! The next chapter shows an intriguing extension of the relationship between gender and hit by using a three-variable table.

Goals of This Chapter

This chapter continues discussion of *comparison* in research. It shows how to use tables to display a relationship between two variables, such as between gender and hit. The chapter also looks at the similarities between formal data analysis and everyday analysis, and how they differ.

A second important goal of this chapter is to strengthen your skills for evaluating competing claims that you encounter daily, such as the belief in wearing a magnet to reduce carpal-tunnel pain, as reviewed in Chapter 3. To help avoid jumping to (false) conclusions, it's essential to recognize the claims you hear. The structure of a two-variable table like Table 10.1 is a useful "box" for helping to recognize the nature of claims. And there are more general boxes summarized in this chapter and in Chapter 11.

A third goal of the chapter is to recognize what data are needed to make a persuasive case. Unfortunately, most important questions can't be answered definitively with any data that conceivably could be obtained, but none of us can wait for a definitive answer before making all our decisions. We just have to go with what we have at decision time, and try not to fall into the "sticky theory" trap.

A fourth goal of the chapter is to introduce basic procedures of data analysis. Often important insights arise from a step-by-step understanding of a technical process. However, it's easy to get lost in the details as the popular phrase "can't see the forest for the trees" suggests. Still, it's necessary to learn some details about data analysis in order to gain an appreciation of the research enterprise as a whole.

Finally, some of you might choose to continue your education as graduate students in one of the social sciences. Moreover, a growing number of jobs in finance, government, and private business require quantitative skills. A foundation in data analysis can help prepare you for graduate education, and for employment in many professional jobs.

We begin our study of data analysis by examining the arrangement of data in a data matrix. A small example of a data matrix is used in subsequent sections to illustrate how to prepare data summaries.

DATA MATRIX

Data analysis starts with the **raw data**, which is a listing of the value of every variable for every observation. The raw data are assembled into a two-dimensional table or matrix called the **data matrix**. The data matrix nearly always is stored electronically; it contains too much detail to be very informative by itself. However, it's important to understand its organization so you can effectively summarize it.

In a data matrix, the term *column* has a special meaning. Unlike most other contexts, such as spreadsheet software and printed tables, *a column in a data matrix is just one character (number or letter) wide.* Any one-digit number takes just one column, any two-digit number requires two columns, etc. A variable like gender represented by one-digit codes (e.g., 1 if the person is female and 2 if male) requires just one column. But a variable like age spans two or, possibly even three, columns in a data matrix.

A **field** is a sequence of adjacent columns used to represent a single variable; a field *is* like a column in a spreadsheet or a printed table. A field may contain either numeric data, like age, weight, number of siblings, or "character data," such as a name, or comments from open-ended survey questions.

Table 10.2 shows an example of a small data matrix containing 10 variables (including "caseid" or "case identification number") and 30 cases from a randomly drawn sample from the GSS for year 1994 (Davis, Smith, & Marsden, 2003).

TABLE 10.2. Example of a Small Data Matrix with 30 Cases and 10 Variables (Including the Identification Number in the First Two Columns) (GSS, 1994).

```
0---+----1----+----2 (column ruler, not part of data matrix)
01211012299999921
0212400 1 2375031
0311210 399999975
041110121 3750046
051240012   75019
062121021  450025
0712400 1  350026
0822400 1 2750055
092110121 2375039
101110121 4500044
112240021 2750031
12224002399999954
132240011 2125027
1422400 1 2750044
1512400 399999981
162121023  200024
1722400 399999978
181131121 4500043
191110121 2750028
202240011 2125028
212240021 3750048
221110111 4500041
2312400 399999973
24224002399999963
252240012 1375050
2622400 399999967
2722400 2  450050
281131111  900032
29224002399999938
3022400 399999989
```

The layout of the data matrix generally follows the format of Table 10.2. Each row of the matrix contains information for a different observation (case), and each field represents a different variable. In the GSS dataset, each observation is a person. Observations also can consist of units like classrooms, schools, school districts, households, and geographical units like states, cities, or countries.

Column(s)	Variable	Description/Values
1–2	caseid	Identification number
3	gender	Gender of the respondent
		1 = male
		2 = female
4	hit	Ever punched or beaten by another person?
		1 = yes
		2 = no
		8 = don't know
		9 = no answer
		BK = not applicable (BK stands for blank)
5	hitwhen	Ever punched or beaten by another person & when?
		1 = yes, when a child only
		2 = yes, when adult only
		3 = yes, both when a child and an adult
		4 = never
		8 = don't know
		9 = no answer
6	hitadult	Ever punched or beaten by another person when an adult?
		0 = no
		1 = yes
7	hitchild	Ever punched or beaten by another person when a child?
		0 = no
		1 = yes
8	drunk	Ever drink more than you think you should?
		1 = yes
		2 = no
		8 = don't know
		9 = no answer
		BK = not applicable
9	wrkstat	Work status
		1 = Working full time
		2 = Working part time
		3 = Other (e.g., attending school, retired, keeping house)
10–15	persinc	Annual personal income (earnings) (estimated from income ranges)
16–17	age	Age of respondent in years

FIGURE 10.1. Codebook for Table 10.2.

Of course, these numbers are useless without some indication of what they mean. The **codebook** provides a key that defines the meaning of the numbers and codes, and their location in the data file. An abbreviated codebook for the GSS sample of Table 10.2 is shown in Figure 10.1. For each variable, the codebook identifies the columns spanned (field), gives a short name, includes a short description and defines the meaning of each value. The digit 9 or a sequence of 9s is used to represent "no response," which is missing data. The short names, like gender, hit, hitwhen, . . . usually are used in statistical software to identify the variable.

Summarizing data sometimes is called **data reduction**. Examples of summaries include frequency distributions, means (arithmetic averages), tables, and many other statistical methods. Some of the basic procedures of data reduction are explained in this chapter, and some more advanced procedures are reviewed in Chapter 11.

UNIVARIATE STATISTICS

Suppose you had to summarize the findings of a survey with 50 questions and 200 respondents. How many numbers would you have to examine? The answer is: $200 \times 50 = 10,000$ different numbers, and 200 respondents is a small number for a survey! Chances are you'd never make much sense of it. A few well-chosen statistics provide summaries of data that would be impossible to garner by looking at the raw data. Examination of summary statistics one variable at a time is called **univariate analysis**.

A **frequency distribution** is the most-often reported univariate summary for nominal data and sometimes is used for ordinal variables. The distribution usually includes the count and percentage for each category of the variable. Sometimes, categories for numeric variables such as respondent's age are collapsed into a few intervals and summarized by counts and percentages (e.g., for age intervals 18–24, 25–39, . . .). Table 10.3 shows two **univariate frequency distributions** compiled from the data matrix in Table 10.2, one for gender and one for the variable "hitwhen."

A **percentage** is obtained by counting the number of cases for each category of a variable, dividing by the total number of cases, and multiplying by 100. The result is frequency "per 100," or *relative frequency*. Note that *percentages permit comparisons among groups with unequal counts of respondents,* such as the sample in Table 10.3 with "12 males" and "18 females." If 10 people in both gender groups say they have been hit, it would be misleading if you didn't compare relative frequencies, like percentages: 10 of 12 = 83% and 10 of 18 = 56% (rounded to whole numbers). An example about SUVs in the next section reinforces the importance of using percentages with unequal sample sizes.

Univariate summaries for interval or ratio variables include (1) **measures of central tendency** such as the mean, median, and mode; and (2) **measures of dispersion** (or scatter), such as the standard deviation.

TABLE 10.3. Frequency Distributions for "Gender" and "Hitwhen."

Gender	Frequency	Percentage
1 Male	12	40.0
2 Female	18	60.0
Total	30	100.0
Hitwhen		
1 As child only	6	20.0
2 As adult only	3	10.0
3 Both times	2	6.7
4 Never	19	63.3
Total	30	100.0

The most-often used measure of central tendency is the *mean*. It's the arithmetic average: Add up the values for all observations (e.g., persons) and divide by the number of observations. A second measure is the *median*, the number that divides the distribution in half when values are arranged in order, low to high. The median is particularly useful when a distribution is **skewed**, that is, a distribution that has more observations at one end of the distribution than at the other. The *mode* is defined as the most frequent value. (A distribution can have more than one mode.)

Recall from Chapter 9 that the *standard deviation* is the most-often used measure of *dispersion* or how much the values of a variable differ from the mean. The *variance* is the average of the squared differences between the mean and each value; the standard deviation is just the square root of the variance. The more the individual observations differ from the mean, the higher the variance and standard deviation. The variance and standard deviation also measure how much the values differ from each other. If they differ from the mean, they *must* differ from each other.

The mean, median, and standard deviation properly are calculated only for interval and ratio variables, but in practice they are used to describe ordinal variables as well. The mode is appropriate for any type of variable.

Calculations for the median, mean, mode, and standard deviation are shown below for the variable "age" in the sample of 30 observations given in Table 10.2.

1	2	3	4	5	6	7	8	9	10	11	12	13	14	15		16	17	18	19	20	21	22	23	24	25	26	27	28	29	30
19	21	24	25	26	27	28	28	31	31	32	38	39	41	43	|	44	44	46	48	50	50	54	55	63	67	73	75	78	81	89

↑

Median = 43.5 (middle value for age)   Median

Mean: $\bar{x} = \dfrac{\Sigma x}{n} = \dfrac{1370}{30} = 45.67$ (arithmetic average for age)

Mode = 28, 31, 44, 50 (most frequent, each has frequency = 2)

Pop. estimate, standard deviation: $= \sqrt{\dfrac{\Sigma(x - \bar{x})^2}{n-1}} = \sqrt{\dfrac{11064.67}{29}} = 19.53$

Notice $n - 1$ is used instead of n in the denominator of the calculation for the variance and standard deviation, but the sample variance is defined as the average of the squared deviations from the mean, implying n is the denominator. Using $n - 1$ gives an unbiased estimate of the population variance.

(Σ stands for "add," and $\sqrt{}$ stands for "square root.")

BIVARIATE TABLE

A **bivariate table** shows the relationship between two variables. It is a special case of a cross-tabulation. In general, a **cross-tabulation** displays the joint frequencies or percentages of two or more variables. In a bivariate table, nearly always one of the variables is considered to be the independent variable and the other the dependent variable. The essential part of the table displays univariate percentage distributions of the dependent variable side by side, one for each category of the independent variable.

Look back at Table 10.1. The first column shows the distribution of the variable hit for men, and the second column shows the distribution of hit for women. Now, look for the two univariate distributions in Table 10.1. They are displayed on the "margins" of the table, one at the right edge or margin, and one at the bottom margin of the table. They are called **marginals** (or *marginal frequency distributions*). The last column shows the distribution of "ever hit" for both genders combined. It's called the **row marginals**, because it displays row totals at the edge or margin of the table. The last row of the table is called the **column marginals**, because it contains the totals for each column. What do these two marginal distributions show? They show univariate frequencies and/or percentages for each of the two variables.

Note that the two marginal distributions don't display the same type of information. The marginal for the dependent variable, "Ever hit," displays a univariate percentage distribution. But, the marginal for the independent variable, "gender," displays frequency counts of male and female instead of percentages. The only percentages displayed here are 100%, which indicates that the column percentages add to 100%.

Tally Sheet

To construct a bivariate table from raw data, first do a tally of responses for each case, then convert the tally marks to frequencies and calculate percentages. Table 10.4 shows a completed **tally sheet** for the crosstabulation between gender and hit using the data matrix in Table 10.2.

The small paired numbers enclosed in parentheses in the upper right of each cell in Table 10.4 are *cell labels*, for example [1,2]. The first number in each pair designates the *row number*. The second number designates the *column number*. These numbers do not appear in published tables, but they are useful identifiers for learning about tables.

Note that there are no 8s and no 9s in Table 10.4 for "ever hit" in the sample of 30 cases, although the codebook lists them as possible values. There is only a

TABLE 10.4. Tally Sheet 1 Using Data from Table 10.2.

Hit?	1 (Male)		2 (Female)	
1 (Yes)	⦀⦀ ‖	[1,1]	‖‖	[1,2]
2 (No)	⦀⦀	[2,1]	⦀⦀ ⦀⦀ ‖‖	[2,2]
8 (don't know)		[3,1]		[3,2]
9 (no answer)		[4,1]		[4,2]

handful of 8s and 9s in the entire 510 cases for 1994 who answered the hit questions, so it's fairly unlikely to get even one in a sample of just 30.

To see exactly how to make a tally, take the first two lines in Table 10.2:

```
----+----1----+----2--
01211012299999921
0212400 1 2375031
```

As the codebook in Figure 10.1 indicates, columns 1 and 2 are reserved for the "caseid," which is just an arbitrary identification number (e.g., person 01, person 02, . . .). For person "01", the first row, "gender" = 2 (female) in column 3, and "hit" = 1 (yes) in column 4. Therefore, this case should be tallied in cell [1,2]—females who were hit. Person "02," second row, has "gender" = 1 and "hit" = 2, so should be tallied into cell [2,1]—males who were not hit, and so forth. (The last two rows of Table 10.4 are discarded because they are empty.)

After the tally is completed for all cases, count the marks in each cell and enter the total in the cell. This is the *bivariate frequency*. Next, add the entries in each row and in each column to produce the row and column marginals. Table 10.5 shows the completed tally, with tally marks converted to numbers and with marginal frequencies included.

Check your calculations. The sum of the row marginals must equal the sum of the column marginals. In Table 10.5, the column marginals are 12 and 18, and the row marginals are 11 and 19. Both add up to 30, the total number of cases.

Percentage Calculation

Conversion to percentages is essential as noted earlier in this chapter, and here's why. Suppose you have a sample of 25 men and 50 women. You find that 5 men approve of buying a new SUV and 10 women approve. When you look only at the raw numbers, you might misinterpret the results and say: *Women are more likely than men to approve of buying an SUV.* After all, 10 women are more than 5 men. But, the percentages are the same: 20% of women and 20% of men approve:

Men: $5/25 = 1/5 \Rightarrow 20\%$
Women: $10/50 = 1/5 \Rightarrow 20\%$

TABLE 10.5. Tally Sheet 2 Using Data from Table 10.2.

Hit?	1 (Male)		2 (Female)		Total
1 (Yes)	ⲾⲾⲾⲾⲾ || [1,1] 7		|||| [1,2] 4		11
2 (No)	ⲾⲾⲾⲾⲾ [2,1] 5		ⲾⲾⲾⲾⲾ ⲾⲾⲾⲾⲾ |||| [2,2] 14		19
Total	12		18		30

Converting frequencies to percentages standardizes the frequencies to show how many per 100 (percent). In Table 10.1 the number of women (282) isn't the same as the number of men (228). The percentages tell how many men per 100 men were ever hit, and how many women per 100 women were ever hit.

Rules for Percentages. The total number that is divided into the frequencies to produce percentages is called the "percentage base." For example, in $6/24 \times 100 = 25\%$, 24 is the percentage base. In a two-variable table, there are three possible percentage bases—

- *row totals* (11 and 19 in Table 10.5)
- *column totals* (12 and 18 in Table 10.5)
- *grand total* (30 in Table 10.5).

Each base tells something about the data, but in nearly all cases, only one indicates directly what we really want to know: *how the dependent variable differs among categories of the independent variable.* Two rules determine how to calculate and interpret the percentages.

Rule 1: Calculate percentages within categories of the *independent* variable. Rule 1 eliminates using the grand total! *Rule 1 requires looking at the table, deciding which is the independent variable and observing whether the independent variable is the column or the row variable.* In Table 10.1, the percentage base is the column total, because gender is the independent variable and it's the column variable—the value of gender changes across the columns. Why not use the row totals? Because the intent is to compare how many males per 100 said "yes" to how many females per 100 said "yes." (One can compare percentages in the "no" row or "yes" row. But only one of the two comparisons is needed, because the percentage differences are the same, except for reversal of the ± sign.)

To find the *cell percentages*, divide each **cell frequency** by the percentage base for that cell (in this case, the column total) and multiply by 100. The calculations (rounded to one decimal place) for Table 10.5 are

Cell (1,1): percentage = $(7/12) \times 100 \cong 0.583 \times 100 = 58.3\%$
Cell (1,2): percentage = $(4/18) \times 100 \cong 0.222 \times 100 = 22.2\%$
Cell (2,1): percentage = $(5/12) \times 100 \cong 0.417 \times 100 = 41.7\%$
Cell (2,2): percentage = $(14/18) \times 100 \cong 0.778 \times 100 = 77.8\%$

The calculations for row marginals are:

Row margin 1: percentage = $(11/30) \times 100 \cong 0.367 \times 100 = 36.7\%$
Row margin 2: percentage = $(19/30) \times 100 \cong 0.633 \times 100 = 63.3\%$

TABLE 10.6. Percentage "Ever Hit" by Gender, Subsample.

Ever Hit	Male	Female	Total
Yes	58.3	22.2	36.7
No	41.7	77.8	63.3
Total %	100.0	100.0	100.0
(n)	(12)	(18)	(30)

Source: Subsample of 30 cases for 1994 from the 1996 GSS data file.

After doing the tally and calculating the percentages, assemble the results into a presentation-quality table, like Table 10.6.

Notice that Table 10.6 doesn't display cell frequencies. Most published tables drop the cell frequencies to avoid an excessively busy appearance and to save space; however, the percentage bases should always be reported. Why report percentage bases in tables? The reader can reproduce each cell frequency by multiplying the percentage by the percentage base and moving the decimal back two places to the left (although with large sample size, this generally produces quite a bit of rounding error). More important, the size of the base for each percentage is an indication of how stable the sample estimate of the population percentage is.

Did you notice the differences between the percentages in Table 10.1 and Table 10.6? These differences are examples of *sampling errors*. The data for Table 10.1 are compiled from the full GSS for the 1994 survey, and the data for Table 10.6 are a simple random sample of the full 1994 GSS.

Table 10.7 shows what the computer software program SAS (*www.sas.com*) does by default with Table 10.1. The labels under "Ever Hit" at the top left in the table are defined as:

"Frequency": The top entry in each cell is the cell frequency, or the number of observations in the cell; for example, the cell [1,1] frequency is 121.

"Percent": The second number in each cell is a percentage using the total number in the table ($n = 510$) as the percentage base. For example in cell [1,1]: $23.73 \doteq (121/510) \times 100$. As we've just seen, this seldom is a good choice.

"Row Pct": The third number in each cell is a row percentage. This means the row marginals are used as the percentage base; for example in cell [1,1]: $62.05 \doteq (121/195) \times 100$.

"Col Pct": The last number in each cell is the column percentage. The column marginals are used as the percentage base, for example for cell [1,1]: $53.07 \doteq (121/228) \times 100$. These percentages are the ones we have been considering thus far.

Remember Rule 1: We want to compare the percentage of males to the percentage of females who were ever hit. Therefore, compare the "Col Pct" percentages across columns, but *not* across rows. Comparing within each column provides no comparisons between men and women.

TABLE 10.7. SAS Computer Printout of Data in Table 10.1 ("Ever Hit" by "Gender").

EVER HIT	GENDER		
Frequency | Percent | Row Pct | Col Pct |	(male) 1|	(female) 2|	Total
(yes) 1 |	121 | 23.73 | 62.05 | 53.07 |	74 | 14.51 | 37.95 | 26.24 |	195 38.24
(no) 2 |	107 | 20.98 | 33.97 | 46.93 |	208 | 46.67 | 66.03 | 73.76 |	315 61.76
Total	228 44.71	282 55.29	510 100.00

Look again at the row percentages in Table 10.7 (third entry in each cell). Suppose you said:

The percentage of those who have been hit who are males is 62.05, whereas the percentage of those who have not been hit who are males is 33.97.

Technically, this comparison is correct. The size of the difference is a measure of the strength of the relationship (indicator of social or substantive significance), because the comparison is across categories of the percentage base. Only if this percentage is zero is there no relationship in the table (perfect independence between the two variables.) However, the interpretation doesn't give an immediate picture of the relationship between hit and gender. This example illustrates why there is a strong convention for using categories of the independent variable for the percentage base.

In contrast to SAS, the cross-tabulation procedure in another prominent statistical software package, SPSS (*www.spss.com*), displays cross-tabulations with joint frequencies and *no* percentages. It's easy to specify the contents of the cells in either package, but you have to know what to specify and how to tell the software what you want.

Arranging Variables in a Table

Some published tables are arranged with the independent variable as the row variable. In this case, following Rule 1, how would you calculate the appropriate percentages?

Rule 1 says: "percentage within categories of the independent variable." So, use the *row* totals as the percentage base. The table below shows what Table 10.1 looks like transposed, with gender as the row variable and hit as the column variable. Now, the totals add to 100% in each row instead of each column.

Percentages "Ever Hit" by Gender (Transposed Table).

Gender	Ever Hit: Yes	Ever Hit: No	Total	*n*
Male	53.1	46.9	100.0	(228)
Female	26.2	73.8	100.0	(282)
Total	38.2	61.8	100.0	(510)

In this table, compare percentages across *rows*: 53.1% − 26.2% = 26.9%, exactly the same numbers as before. The table above is just the "transpose" of Table 10.1. ("Transpose" means to interchange the rows and columns, so that column 1 in Table 10.1 is row 1 in this table, and so forth.)

Comparing these two tables illustrates another important point in reading tables:

Check for the percentage base before reading the rest of the table!

In Table 10.1, the correct comparisons are between columns. In the table above, the correct comparisons are between rows. To read either table, follow Rule 2:

Rule 2: Compare percentages across categories of the percentage base. *If* Rule 1 is followed, this translates into: Compare percentages across categories of the independent variable. Hopefully you will not see many instances in which Rule 1 is violated, but published tables occasionally do violate it. Failure to pay attention to Rule 2 leads to entirely bogus interpretation of a table!

PREPARING THE DATA FOR ANALYSIS

Coding the Data

Data coding refers to converting responses into numbers or codes (numeric or otherwise). With short questionnaires, closed-ended questions and a small sample of respondents, it's possible to print the codes directly on the questionnaires. Then either prepare a data sheet or enter the data directly into a computer file, such as a spreadsheet. The codes for each response option can appear in parentheses at the end of the response option, or in the margin. The latter style is called "edge coding." Figure 10.2 shows an example. The researcher can look at the questionnaire to see how the data are represented in the computer.

```
A. What is your gender (check one):
        [ ] Female                      (1)
        [ ] Male                        (2)

B. Do you consider yourself (check one):
        [ ] Strong Republican           (1)
        [ ] Weak Republican             (2)
        [ ] Independent                 (3)
        [ ] Weak Democrat               (4)
        [ ] Strong Democrat             (5)
        [ ] No party identification     (9)
```

FIGURE 10.2.   Portion of a Sample Questionnaire, with Edge Coding.

Cleaning the Data

Immediately after coding, data *always* contain errors. Whatever the method used to collect the data (audiotapes from personal interviews, mail surveys, personal interviews, coding sheets in content analysis), the coded data must be checked carefully for errors before proceeding to the next step.

Data frequently are described as "clean" or "dirty." "Dirty" data contain errors such as incorrect reading of responses on a questionnaire, incorrectly transcribing a personal interview comment, assigning a wrong code to a response category, and other human errors. If entering data using a computer program, the data should be entered twice, and the two files compared by a computer, although this double-entry step often is skipped in practice.[2]

Often errors are detected quickly by looking at univariate frequencies. Therefore, before doing any analysis such as that shown in Table 10.1, check the univariate distribution for each variable. Out-of-range codes are among the most frequent errors and are easy to spot in a frequency distribution. For example, if you have assigned a score of 1 for female and 0 for male and find a case with a score of 3 for gender, it's an obvious error. Another way to look for errors is to check for inconsistent answers to similar questions, when feasible. Suppose a completed questionnaire contains the following questions and responses:

Question 1: Do you ever drink alcoholic beverages?

    [✓] No, never (total abstainer)

    [   ] Yes

Question 2: Do you ever drink alcoholic beverages more than you think you should?

    [   ] No

    [✓] Yes (at least sometimes)

If there is a discrepancy like the one between these two questions, and there is no third question to help you resolve the discrepancy, you probably should treat the questions as if the respondent had skipped them, set their values to "missing."[3] An example of a third question that might help resolve this discrepancy is: "How many alcoholic beverages do you consume in a week?"

All data-cleaning procedures should be described in the report for the reader to evaluate.

Data Transformations: Creating New Variables, Modifying Codes

Often data preparation includes calculation of new variables or modification of the original variable codes. Two frequently used transformations are: combining variable categories and creating composite variables.

1. *Combine (collapse) variable categories.* Researchers often combine categories of a variable. Some surveys allow six or eight response options for a question about race and 20 or 30 for ethnicity. Such large numbers of response options usually must be collapsed into a few homogeneous categories for analysis and presentation. Why combine variable categories? Consider trying to evaluate a table containing 30 rows and 30 columns, for example, even if there were an adequate number of cases for each cell. However, avoid combining heterogeneous (diverse) categories. Although you probably wouldn't combine ages 1–4 with 9–12, consider another example. Racial categories "white" and "nonwhite" frequently were used in the past, but seldom are today, because of the increasing heterogeneity among racial groups other than Caucasian. The nonwhite category is too heterogeneous.

But combining categories hides details, such as how many respondents report a particular ethnic background. Sometimes the lost detail masks important patterns. Part of the "art" of doing research is condensing excessive detail without losing essential information.

You can combine categories, but it's impossible to "uncombine" them. Therefore, no matter how variables are collapsed for analysis, the original data set should always retain all the original detail (minus any errors). The best strategy is never to change the original file after the errors are removed. A "working data file" can contain all the data transformations. Even in the working data file, it's usually better to define new variables for collapsed versions of the original variables they are based on and keep both versions in the file.

2. *Create composite variables, such as an index or scale.* Another frequently used operation is creating new variables by combining more than one variable. Recall from the measurement chapter (Chapter 4) that one type of **composite variable** is called an **index** or **scale**. Which variables might one combine? Items to create an index are chosen for their *face validity* to measure a construct; that is, they *appear* to measure components of the same concept. For instance, if there are six questions asking whether respondents own various electronic devices like a laptop computer, a cell phone, a DVD player, . . ., each scored (1 = yes) or (0 = no), and a person answers "yes" to all six, the score for the composite measure is six; if five "yes" and one "no," the score is five, and so on. The new variable is then included in the analysis. For example, you might want to know the association between owner's age and the number of electronic items owned.

Items used to define an index sometimes are weighted unequally, and the weighted scores added together. Differential **weighting** of items comprising an index sometimes is done to reflect the importance of the items in measuring the construct. Suppose you decide to create an index of "violence victimization" based on reports of incidents like "ever hit," being "severely beaten," or being "attacked with a weapon." You judge these incidents to be of unequal severity. You could assign a score of 4 to being "attacked with a weapon," 3 to being "severely beaten," and 1 to "ever hit." Then, add the weighted scores for each individual to form an index of "violence victimization"—a new variable.

Many questionnaire items use the Likert-scale format. For example:

I often drink more than I should (circle one).
strongly agree——agree——uncertain——disagree——strongly disagree

Typically, five to seven response options are provided, and the respondent is asked to choose one. A score is assigned to represent the intensity of the attitude about drinking behavior. For example, assign 1 through 5 for "strongly disagree" to "strongly agree," respectively. (In some studies the neutral category "uncertain" is omitted, because there might be either "too many" or "too few" uncertain respondents, making the frequency distributions appear distorted.)

Now for the fun part—data analysis!

SUMMARY

This chapter opens with a simplified example of a research question: "Are men or women more likely to be victims of violence?" A single indicator of violence illustrates the idea: "Ever punched or beaten by another person" (shortened to "ever hit" or "hit" in most of the chapter). A bivariate table reveals a surprising result: Men are more likely to have been hit at some time in their lives than women are. The data for this example illustrate details related to data handling and analysis throughout the rest of the chapter.

The second section describes the organization of the data matrix. Regardless of whether one uses computers or hand calculations, the data matrix is the starting point for data preparation and for the analyses. The data matrix is a rectangular array, one observation listed on each row and one variable listed in each column, or sequence of adjacent columns called a "field." A field in a data matrix is like a column in a spreadsheet. The codebook is the key for deciphering the data matrix. It gives the names and descriptions of every variable, the meaning of each value of the variable (e.g., 1 = strongly disagree . . . 5 = strongly agree) and specifies the field where it appears in the data matrix.

The "Univariate Statistics" section shows how to use the data matrix and its codebook to construct a univariate percentage distribution and calculate univariate statistics like the mean and standard deviation. The section called "Bivariate Table" illustrates how to construct and read a two-variable table. The main purpose of a bivariate table is to check for a relationship between two variables. It is laid out to compare distributions of the dependent variable between categories of the independent variable. Converting frequencies to percentages in bivariate tables "standardizes" them to indicate how many per 100 (relative frequency).

The final section of the chapter explains how and why data are cleaned, and how to do elementary transformations on the raw data in preparation for data analysis. A univariate percentage table of all variables is a good way to begin the checks for errors in the data; look for out-of-range values for each variable.

YOUR REVIEW SHEET: QUESTIONS DISCUSSED IN THIS CHAPTER

1. Propose at least one social science explanation for the relationship between gender and "ever hit" that is not discussed in the chapter.

2. Because of the extreme complexity of the social world, the social sciences seldom, if ever, find a definitive answer to questions they raise. In your own words, what do they offer?

3. What is the first step in data preparation? Provide specific examples.

4. How should one handle inconsistent answers, like this example?

   Question 1: *Do you ever drink alcoholic beverages?*

   [✓] No, never (total abstainer)

   [　] Yes

   Question 2: *Do you ever drink alcoholic beverages more than you think you should?*

   [✓] Yes (at least sometimes)

   [　] No

   Explain, in your own words.

5. What is the purpose of a tally sheet? How should it be set up?

6. Summarize typical data transformations and describe the purpose of each.

7. Why collapse categories of a variable? Describe an example from Table 10.8 (in the "Exercises" section).

8. No matter how variables are collapsed for analysis, the master dataset always should retain all detail. Why is this important?

9. Describe procedures for creating an index of violence victimization based on a few specific indicators or examples of violence.

10. Even knowing what each number stands for, a data matrix is not very informative by itself, particularly when there are many observations and many variables. Why not?

11. Why assign a row/column for each response category (e.g., for "don't know") in the tally of Table 10.4?

12. If column totals are the percentage base, the percentages may be compared across *columns*, but not across *rows*. Why? State the two rules for reading a bivariate percentage table. What is the rationale for each rule?

13. In Table 10.1 the percentage base is the column total. Why not use the row total?

END NOTES

1. These data were tabulated from the 2002 cumulative data file of the GSS. This data file contains observations for all years in the GSS (1972–2002). The GSS sample is taken from the adult population of U.S. residents. The data for this chapter are for 1994 only. The question, "Have you ever been punched or beaten by another person?" was not asked of the entire sample. There were nearly 3000 respondents in the 1994 survey, but many questions were asked of only part of the sample, so that more questions could be asked without undue

burden on any one respondent. The variable called "gender" was recorded by the interviewer and not asked directly of respondents.

2. The SAS statistical package includes a procedure designed for comparing every value in two files. Data entered into a spreadsheet are easy to read into a SAS dataset. Other statistical packages, such as SPSS, can be programmed to compare files.

3. A quick way to check for inconsistencies like this is to examine a cross-tabulation between variables that are related by definition, like the two in this example. Look for nonzero entries in the inconsistent cells, for example, the cell showing responses for the "no" category of question 1 and the "yes" category of question 2.

STUDY TERMS

bivariate table Cross-tabulation of two variables. See cross-tabulation.

cell frequency Number of occurrences of an event defined by the intersection between a column and a row in a cross-tabulation (e.g., the number of women who ever were hit).

codebook A listing of all variables in a data collection with each variable accompanied by (1) a short "variable name," (2) a brief description, (3) the location (field or columns spanned), and (4) the meaning of each value.

column marginals Totals for each column, shown in the last row of a table containing a cross-tabulation.

composite variable Variable created by adding, averaging, or combining in some other way two or more other variables. See index (one type of composite variable).

cross-tabulation Table displaying the frequencies and/or percentages for every combination of values of two or more variables.

data coding Conversion of information from the form it was collected into predefined values of variables, usually from words or answers on a questionnaire to numbers in a computer file.

data matrix Two-dimensional table used to organize and retrieve raw data. Rows represent observations; fields (composed of one or more adjacent columns) represent variables.

data reduction Summarizing one or more variables, for example, percentage distribution, mean, standard deviation.

field Sequence of adjacent columns in a data matrix containing the values of a single variable.

frequency distribution A univariate summary including the count and percentage for each category of a nominal, ordinal, or collapsed interval variable.

index Composite measure often created by averaging or summing two or more variables.

marginals (or marginal frequency *distributions*) Univariate frequency distributions for variables in a cross-tabulation that are displayed at the edges, or margins, of the cross-tabulation.

measure of central tendency A statistic or parameter that summarizes where numbers in a distribution tend to concentrate. Examples include the mean, median and mode.

measure of dispersion A statistic or parameter that summarizes how much numbers in a distribution are spread out. Examples include the standard deviation and variance.

percentage Frequency per 100, obtained by counting the number of cases in each category of a variable, dividing by the total number of cases for all categories, and multiplying the quotient by 100.

raw data A listing of the value of every variable for every observation.

row marginals Row totals shown in the last column of a table containing a cross-tabulation.

scale Group of response options to a question that are arranged in order of intensity or importance (contrast to index).

social significance (or substantive significance) Importance of an observation for practical applications or social theory. In a cross-tabulation, one indicator of social significance is the magnitude of the percentage difference. Contrast with statistical significance (Chapter 9).

tally sheet Blank table with labels for the variable categories, used to prepare cross-tabulations manually.

univariate analysis Examination of statistics such as the mean, standard deviation, and frequency distribution, which describe one variable at a time.

univariate frequency distribution List of the number and percentage in each category of one variable, as in Table 10.3.

weighting (of a variable) In calculating an index, multiplying each component by a different numeric constant before calculating a sum or average. The constants are the weights and are chosen to reflect the importance of each component for defining the index.

Exercises

Exercise 10.1. Univariate Analysis 1

Directions: Use the information in Table 10.8 to produce the univariate distributions for Table 10.9. Be sure to review the rules for calculating percentages. Show your calculations.

TABLE 10.8.   A Data Matrix of 50 Cases from the GSS.

ID	SEX	HIT	HITWHEN	HITADULT	HITCHILD	DRUNK	WRKSTAT2	PERSINC	HRLYWGE
01	Male	No	Never	No	No	Yes	Full-time	100.000	27.47
02	Male	Yes	Both	Yes	Yes	Yes	Other		
03	Female	No	Never	No	No	No	Part-time	5.500	5.29
04	Male	No	Never	No	No	Yes	Full-time	67.500	25.96
05	Male	No	Never	No	No	No	Full-time	32.500	16.45
06	Male	Yes	Both	Yes	Yes		Full-time	18.750	31.25
07	Female	No	Never	No	No	Yes	Full-time	18.750	9.01
08	Male	No	Never	No	No	No	Other	32.500	
09	Female	No	Never	No	No	No	Other		
10	Male	Yes	As child	No	Yes	Yes	Full-time	100.000	32.05
11	Female	No	Never	No	No	No	Other	27.500	13.22

ID	SEX	HIT	HITWHEN	HITADULT	HITCHILD	DRUNK	WRKSTAT2	PERSINC	HRLYWGE
12	Male	No	Never	No	No		Full-time	3.500	1.68
13	Male	Yes	Both	Yes	Yes		Full-time	27.500	6.78
14	Female	No	Never	No	No	No	Other		
15	Male	Yes	Both	Yes	Yes	Yes	Full-time	55.000	22.04
16	Female	No	Never	No	No		Other		
17	Male	No	Never	No	No	Yes	Full-time	32.500	15.63
18	Female	Yes	As child	No	Yes	No	Part-time	7.500	7.32
19	Female	No	Never	No	No		Full-time	6.500	5.70
20	Male	No	Never	No	No	No	Full-time	55.000	19.23
21	Female	Yes	As adult	Yes	No		Part-time	11.250	8.65
22	Male	Yes	As child	No	Yes	No	Full-time	21.250	9.08
23	Female	No	Never	No	No	No	Full-time	16.250	7.81
24	Female	No	Never	No	No	No	Other		
25	Female	No	Never	No	No		Full-time	13.750	6.61
26	Male	Yes	As child	No	Yes	Yes	Full-time	18.750	9.38
27	Male	No	Never	No	No	No	Full-time	37.500	14.47
28	Female	Yes	As adult	Yes	No		Full-time	45.000	21.63
29	Male	Yes	As child	No	Yes	No	Full-time	27.500	10.58
30	Female	No	Never	No	No		Other		
31	Male	No	Never	No	No	No	Part-time	0.750	0.87
32	Female	No	Never	No	No	No	Full-time	11.250	6.79
33	Female	No	Never	No	No	No	Full-time	16.250	5.21
34	Male	Yes	Both	Yes	Yes	Yes	Full-time	9.000	4.79
35	Female	No	Never	No	No	No	Other	5.500	9.17
36	Male	No	Never	No	No		Other		
37	Male	No	Never	No	No	Yes	Full-time	27.500	11.25
38	Female	Yes	As adult	Yes	No		Full-time	27.500	13.22
39	Male	Yes	As child	No	Yes	Yes	Full-time	21.250	6.81
40	Male	Yes	As child	No	Yes	No	Full-time	2.000	4.55
41	Female	Yes	As adult	Yes	No		Full-time	16.250	32.50
42	Male	Yes	Both	Yes	Yes	Yes	Full-time	5.500	1.26
43	Male	No	Never	No	No		Full-time	27.500	10.58
44	Male	Yes	As child	No	Yes	No	Full-time	55.000	14.69
45	Male	No	Never	No	No		Full-time	27.500	13.22
46	Female	Yes	Both	Yes	Yes	No	Full-time	32.500	13.59
47	Female	No	Never	No	No		Other		
48	Male	Yes	As adult	Yes	No	Yes	Full-time	9.000	4.33
49	Female	No	Never	No	No	No	Other	0.750	
50	Male	No	Never	No	No		Other		

TABLE 10.9.   Univariate Analysis.

Gender	Frequency	Percentage
1 Male	_____	_____%
2 Female	_____	_____%
Total	_____	100.0%
Hitwhen		
1 As child only	_____	_____%
2 As adult only	_____	_____%
3 Both times	_____	_____%
4 Never	_____	_____%
Total	_____	100.0%
Drunk		
1 Yes	_____	_____
2 No	_____	_____
Total	_____	100.0%

Exercise 10.2. Univariate Analysis 2

Directions: Use the information in Table 10.8 to produce the following univariate statistics. Be sure to review the rules for calculating percentages. Show your calculations.

Mean wage

Median wage

Frequency and percentage distribution for gender

Frequency and percentage distribution for hit2

Frequency and percentage distribution for wrkstat2

Mean, variance and standard deviation of female. Create a "dummy" variable by assigning a 1 to females and 0 to males. Call this variable "female" (categories are yes = 1, and no = 0).

$$\text{variance:} \quad s^2 = \frac{\Sigma(x - \bar{x})^2}{n}$$

The variable x is the value of female (0 or 1) for each observation; $\bar{x}$ is the mean of female, n is the number of observations ($n = 50$ in Table 10.8), and Σ stands for "add up." (The standard deviation is just the square root of the variance.)

Note: Most statistical texts use $n - 1$ instead of n in the denominator of the formula for the variance. Also, nearly all software uses $n - 1$. Using $n - 1$ produces an unbiased estimate of the population variance. It's not the sample variance, although it often is defined loosely as such. The instructions use n here for a definite reason (see Question 2 on page 267).

Questions

1. Compare the mean of the variable called "female" to the percentage distribution for gender. What correspondence do you see?

2. Multiply the mean of female by [1 − the mean]. Compare this to the variance. If they aren't the same you made a mistake—check your numbers.

3. Suppose you had constructed a variable called "male" instead of female, and assigned a 1 to males and 0 to females. What do you predict about the mean and variance for male?

Exercise 10.3. Preparing a Bivariate Table

Directions: Use the data in Table 10.8 to prepare the bivariate tables below. Table 10.10 should show your tally marks, cell frequencies, and row and column totals (column totals go inside the parentheses). Table 10.11 requires calculating percentages. Show all calculations. Then, answer the questions below.

TABLE 10.10. Tally for Hit by Gender.

Hit?	1 (Male)	2 (Female)	Total
1 (Yes)	(1,1)	(1,2)	
2 (No)	(2,1)	(2,2)	
Total			

TABLE 10.11. Percentages Hit by Gender.

Hit?	Male	Female	Total
Yes	%	%	
No	%	%	
Total	100% (n =)	100 % (n =)	100% (n =)
n	( )	( )	( )

Questions

1. Write a concise summary of the relationship (if any) you observe in Table 10.11.

2. Why should Table 10.11 display column percentages instead of row percentages or percentages based on the total number of observations in the table?

3. Compare the relationship in Table 10.11, based on 50 cases, to the relationship in Table 10.1. How close are they? Why are they different?

4. Explain how you calculated the percentages in Table 10.11.

Exercise 10.4. Evaluation of Research: Univariate Analysis

Directions: Refer to the excerpt on "condom users likely to experience condom failure" in Chapter 8 to answer the following questions.

Factual Questions

1. How many couples in the analysis were married or living together? How many were not married or living together? Show your calculation.

2. The 177 couples included in the analysis used 1947 condoms. Of these condoms, 5.3% broke (1.6% nonclinical; 3.7% clinical) and 3.5% slipped off during sex, resulting in a clinical failure rate of 7.2% and an overall failure rate of 8.8%.

   a. How many condoms broke? How many slipped off? Show your calculations.

   b. Which problem, breakage or slippage, was a greater concern?

Questions for Discussion

1. Briefly explain in your own words the rationale for examining univariate statistics. What univariate statistics are included in the excerpt?

2. In Question 2, can one compare either percentages or frequencies to determine which problem (breakage or slippage) was of greater concern? Briefly explain your answer.

3. Although percentages often are used in univariate analysis, not all percentages are univariate. Offer an example of a percentage that doesn't provide univariate information, and briefly explain why it doesn't.

INTRODUCTION: LOOKING AT HOW THE SOCIAL WORLD WORKS

Women are more likely than men to be victims of violence. This hypothesis appears at the beginning of the previous chapter. But for one type of violence, "ever hit," the General Social Survey (GSS) data show just the opposite! Men are more likely than women to report having been "punched or beaten" at some time in their lives. Over half of the men (53.1%) reported having been hit at least once; whereas, only a little more than a quarter of women (26.2%) say they have been hit.

Table 10.1 from the previous chapter is reproduced as Table 11.1. (Unlike Table 10.1, Table 11.1 displays marginal row frequencies in parentheses, to be used for some calculations later in the chapter.) First, look at the title of the table. Note that in the tables in this chapter (and Chapter 10) the dependent variable (ever hit) is listed first, followed by the independent variable (gender). Although not all tables follow this convention, it simplifies reading the tables and will be used in this text. Therefore, read the title of a table first. If there is a **control variable**, as in some tables later in this chapter, it will be stated last in the title.

TABLE 11.1. Percentage "Ever Hit" by Gender.

Ever Hit by Anyone?	Male	Female	Total	
Yes	53.1	26.2	38.2	(195)
No	46.9	73.8	61.8	(315)
Total %	100.0	100.0	100.0	
(*n*)	(228)	(282)	(510)	

Source: 2002 General Social Survey, cumulative data file 1972–2002 (Davis, Smith & Marsden, 2003). This table is for the year 1994.

Main table entries are percentages. Numbers in parentheses are the numbers of respondents.

Why are men more likely to have been hit than women? One speculation in Chapter 10 is that men drink more alcohol than women, and alcohol consumption "paves the way" for violence. This hypothesis can be checked by observing the relationship between gender and hit while holding constant or *controlling* for drinking behavior, a procedure discussed in this chapter.

Another possibility has to do with *when* a person is hit: as a child, as an adult, or both. Remember the question used to create the variable "ever hit" is

Have you ever been punched or beaten by another person?

The question refers to an entire lifetime. Therefore, another possibility is that there are differences according to whether the hitting happened when the respondent was a child or an adult. Because women are more likely to suffer domestic abuse than men, a good possibility is that the gender difference is not nearly so large, or might even reverse, for adults. The GSS did ask a follow-up question to the "ever hit" question. It reads as follows:

Did this happen to you as a child or as an adult?

By combining the answers to these two questions, Table 11.1 can be expanded to include additional detail. Table 11.2 displays the result.

The table is very informative. First, look at the row labeled "Child Only." It reveals that males are much more likely to be hit only as children than females are (27.6% − 8.2% = 19.4%). But, the percentages of males and females hit only as adults are nearly equal (9.6% − 13.5% = −3.9%). Although women are slightly more likely to be hit when adults than men are, this difference is so small that the gender difference isn't likely to be statistically significant. **Statistically significant** means that the difference between women and men calculated from the sample is unlikely to be due to sampling error.

TABLE 11.2. Percentage "Ever Hit" by Gender, Using an Expanded Measure of "Ever Hit."

Ever/When Hit	Male	Female	Total
Never	46.9	73.8	61.8
Child Only	27.6	8.2	16.9
Adult Only	9.6	13.5	11.8
Both	15.8	4.6	9.6
Total %	100.0	100.0	100.0
(*n*)	(228)	(282)	(510)

Source: 2002 General Social Survey, cumulative data file 1972–2002 (Davis, Smith, & Marsden, 2003). This table is for the year 1994.
Main table entries are percentages. Numbers in parentheses are the number of respondents.

The percentages in Table 11.2 for "Both" (hit both as child and as adult) also show a comparatively large difference between men and women (15.8% − 4.6% = 11.2%). Table 11.1 appears to mask important detail!

We clearly have two competing reasons for the finding that males are more likely to be hit than females.

1. The relationship between gender and hit is due to alcohol consumption; men drink more alcohol, and this "causes" them to get entangled in situations in which they are more likely to be hit than women are.

2. Men are more likely to be hit as children, and this accounts for the gender difference in adulthood.

These two possibilities provide great examples of the need to include control variables. This chapter introduces methods for implementing the controls.

Goals of this Chapter

Recall from Chapter 10 that a *cross-tabulation* is a table displaying the frequencies and percentages for every combination of values of two or more variables. This chapter continues the study of cross-tabulation. We expand a bivariate table similar to Table 11.1 to include one more variable—a control variable. The result is a **trivariate** (three-variable) **table**. The critical importance of extending analyses beyond bivariate relationships is revealed by the new results that emerge for the gender-hit association.

The basic idea of *statistical control* is fairly easy to grasp with three-variable tables. The chapter presents the use of statistical controls using tables as a foundation for understanding other methods. Cross-tabulations are too cumbersome for complex data analysis, however. Later sections of the chapter give an overview of more advanced methods of analysis, including comparisons among means and regression analysis. The last few sections present a short introduction to statistical tests for (1) checking a relationship in a table, (2) simultaneously comparing several means, and (3) regression analysis.

At the end of this chapter, you should have an overview of what is possible in data analysis. However, a thorough understanding of these methods requires more detailed study than can be included in a beginning methods course.

THE TRIVARIATE TABLE: ADDING A "CONTROL" VARIABLE

Chapter 10 shows how a bivariate table displays a univariate distribution within each category of the independent variable. A trivariate table shows a bivariate table within each category of a third (control) variable. Each of the bivariate tables shows a **partial relationship**; sometimes these are called **partial tables**.

The process of studying two variables by observing their relationship within each category of one or more other variables is called **elaboration**. In everyday language, elaboration means "the process of expanding on." In table elaboration, a bivariate table is expanded by checking it within each category of at least one additional variable.

Hit, Gender, and Alcohol

Table 11.3 displays an example of a trivariate table showing the relationship between "ever hit" and gender for each category of the control variable, "drinking behavior."

TABLE 11.3.   Percentage "Ever Hit" by Gender, Controlling for Drinking Behavior.

	Drink Too Much?					
	Yes			**No**		
Ever Hit?	**Male**	**Female**	**Total**	**Male**	**Female**	**Total**
Yes	70.4	39.6	58.2	43.5	22.9	31.0
No	29.6	60.4	41.8	56.5	77.1	69.0
Total %	100.0	100.0	100.0	100.0	100.0	100.0
(*n*)	(81)	(53)	(134)	(147)	(227)	(374)

Source: 2002 General Social Survey, cumulative data file 1972–2002 (Davis, Smith and Marsden, 2003). This table is for the year 1994.

The table displays two bivariate distributions side-by-side: (1) one cross-tabulation between hit and gender for respondents who say they sometimes drink too much, and (2) a second cross-tabulation for those who claim they never drink too much.

Here's the key to understanding partial tables: The partial relationship between hit and gender in each of these two subtables cannot be due to drinking behavior, because drinking behavior is constant among observations in each subtable. To see this point more clearly, first cover the right-hand side of the table with your hand. Look at the left-hand side. It is a bivariate table showing the relationship between hit and gender for those *who drink too much*. In this "drink too much" group, the gender difference for "ever hit" remains high: 70.4% − 39.6 = 30.8%.

Next, cover the left-hand-side table. Now you see the relationship between gender and hit for respondents *who never drink too much*: 43.5% − 22.9 = 20.6%. This percentage difference also is fairly high, though not quite as large as the difference for those who report drinking too much.

Although the differences in Table 11.3 are not precisely the same in the two partial relationships, the gender–ever hit relationship remains when drinking behavior is controlled (percentage difference in the two partial tables = 30.8% and 20.6%). How do we interpret this finding? Drinking behavior does *not* explain the gender difference in ever being hit. We haven't discovered the answer to the question: "Why are men more likely to report being hit than women?" This type of result of elaboration analysis is called **replication**. The bivariate relationship approximately replicates, or is unchanged, in each partial table.

Hit, Gender, and Age

Table 11.2 shows evidence that the gender difference in being hit occurs mostly in childhood. Maybe there is a chain reaction: Gender affects the chance of being hit as a child, and being hit as a child carries over into adult years. In the chain-reaction view, there is no direct impact of gender on being hit as an adult. That is, gender operates *indirectly* by creating during childhood the circumstances that make one vulnerable to being hit as an adult. This hypothesis implies being hit as a child is an **intervening variable**, intervening between gender and being hit as an adult—

gender → hitchild → hitadult

The diagram uses shorthand names for the two variables:

hitchild = respondent was hit as a child: 1 = yes, 0 = no
hitadult = respondent was hit as an adult: 1 = yes, 0 = no

The chain-reaction view implies that the relationship between hitadult and gender is zero or near zero when hitchild is controlled. The hypothesis is testable: Check the relationship between hitadult and gender, controlling for hitchild.

There are no variables in the GSS master data file defined exactly like hitchild and hitadult. But it's possible to create them from the two questions quoted in the introduction to the chapter. The new variables are derived from the original questions using the rules laid out in Table 11.4.

TABLE 11.4.   Original Questions from the GSS Dataset for "Ever Hit" and "Hit When."

"IF YES: A. Did this happen to you as a child or as an adult?"	"Have you ever been punched or beaten by another person?"	
	Yes	No
Child	hitchild = 1 hitadult = 0	
Adult	hitchild = 0 hitadult = 1	hitchild = 0 hitadult = 0
Both	hitchild = 1 hitadult = 1	

*Questions quoted verbatim from the GSS codebook (Davis, Smith, & Marsden, 2003).

First, look at the bivariate relationship between gender and hitadult shown in Table 11.5. This is the relationship we now are trying to explain—whether one was ever hit as an adult.

TABLE 11.5.   Percentage "Hit When an Adult," by Gender.

Hit When Adult	Male	Female	Total
Yes	25.4	18.1	21.4
No	74.6	81.9	78.6
Total %	100.0	100.0	100.0
(*n*)	(228)	(282)	(510)

Main table entries are percentages. Numbers in parentheses are the
numbers of respondents.

The table shows men are more likely than women to have been hit during their
adult years, but note that the relationship is not as strong as the one in Table 11.1;
the percentage difference is just 7.3% (25.4 − 18.1%).

Next look at the bivariate cross-tabulation between gender and hitchild in
Table 11.6. The table shows 43.4% of males report being hit as a child, but only
12.8% of females say they were hit when they were children, more than a 30%
difference.

TABLE 11.6.   Percentage "Hit When a Child," by Gender.

Hit When Child	Male	Female	Total
Yes	43.4	12.8	26.5
No	56.6	87.2	73.5
Total %	100.0	100.0	100.0
(*n*)	(228)	(282)	(510)

Main table entries are percentages. Numbers in parentheses are the
numbers of respondents.

Finally, the three-variable table for hitadult and gender, controlling for
hitchild, appears in Table 11.7. The finding is remarkable! The "chain-reaction"
hypothesis is supported—there's almost no relationship between hitadult and gender when hitchild is controlled. It's unusual to find support for a hypothesis as
clear as this. (Exercise 11.4 asks you to combine GSS data from all years in which
the hit questions were asked to see whether this finding is retained.)

This type of elaboration analysis is called **interpretation**. The variable hitchild
interprets the relationship between hitadult and gender. Because hitchild intervenes
between gender and hitadult, hitchild is called an **intervening variable**.

Note that the format of Table 11.3 is identical to that of Table 11.7. Both tables
contain two bivariate tables, side by side. As before, first cover the right-hand side
of Table 11.7. The bivariate table on the left side (left partial table) shows the relationship between gender and hitadult for those who were hit when a child. In this
table, the relationship between hitadult and gender is very close to zero: 36.4% −
36.1 = 0.3%. Covering the left-hand side of the table, the bivariate table on the

TABLE 11.7.   Percentage Hit When Adults by Gender, Controlling for Hit When Child.

| Hit When Adult? | Hit When Child? | | | | | |
| | Yes | | | No | | |
	Male	Female	Total	Male	Female	Total
Yes	36.4	36.1	36.3	17.1	15.4	16.0
No	63.6	63.9	63.7	82.9	84.6	84.0
Total %	100.0	100.0	100.0	100.0	100.0	100.0
(*n*)	(99)	(36)	(135)	(129)	(246)	(375)

Main table entries are percentages. Numbers in parentheses are the numbers of respondents.

right shows the same relationship for those who were not hit when a child. The relationship in this table also is close to zero, $17.1\% - 15.4 = 1.7\%$. Neither partial relationship is close to being statistically significant.

We conclude that being hit as a child is important in understanding the original relationship between gender and ever hit. The evidence indicates that the root cause of the gender difference goes back to childhood, but it doesn't explain *why* boy children are substantially more likely to be hit than girl children. The analysis does give potentially important clues, however, about where to focus future research on the topic.

Classifying Three-Variable Relationships

When a control variable is added to a bivariate relationship, four outcomes of the elaboration process are possible.

1. ***Replication:*** *Each partial relationship matches the original bivariate relationship—the control variable does not modify the original relationship.* The relationship "stands up" under the control; the bivariate relationship is replicated in the partial tables. Look back at Table 11.3. It's not a perfect example, but it's fairly close. The bivariate relationship for those who "drink too much" is a little stronger than the bivariate relationship in Table 11.1, and the relationship for those who "never drink too much" is a little weaker. But, statistical tests show that the difference between the two relationships isn't large enough to attribute it to anything other than random sampling error.[1]

2. ***Interpretation:*** *The partial relationships are zero and the independent variable affects the control variable.* When the partial relationships all are zero (or near zero) *and* the independent variable affects the control variable, it's called "interpretation." The analysis of hitadult, hitchild and gender in Table 11.7 is a "near perfect" illustration of an interpretation; both partial tables show no relationship. The control variable is hitchild, and it intervenes between gender and hitadult.

3. ***Explanation:*** *The partial relationships are zero and the control variable affects the independent variable.* The relationship between hair length (long, short) and wearing a dress (yes, no) is an example of explanation; here, the control variable is gender. A three-variable table would display two partial tables of the relationship between hair length and wearing a dress, one for females and one for males. We say that gender "explains away" the observed bivariate relationship between hair length and wearing a dress. There is a *spurious association* between hair length and dress.

Note: The partial relationships are zero for *both* interpretation and explanation. The difference between the two depends on the causal order of the independent and control variables. Figure 11.1 shows a picture diagram distinguishing between interpretation and explanation.

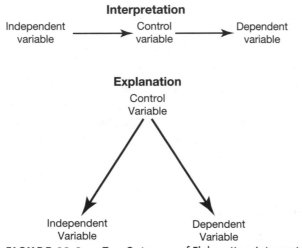

FIGURE 11.1.   Two Outcomes of Elaboration: Interpretation and Explanation. The partial relationships are zero.

4. ***Specification (Statistical Interaction):*** *The partial relationship is different in one level of the control variable than in at least one other level.* When the relationships differ in different partial tables, the result is called **specification**. The findings specify the strength and direction of the relationship in each category of the control variable. In one type of "perfect case" with a two-category control variable, one partial relationship is zero, and the other partial is stronger than the original bivariate association. In a still more extreme "perfect case," the bivariate relationship is zero, or close to it, and the relationships in the two partial tables "emerge" (have strong bivariate associations), but in opposite directions.

A more common term than specification for describing different partial relationships is **statistical interaction**. Don't confuse statistical interaction with the terms "interpersonal interaction" or "relationship." Relationship refers to an association, usually bivariate. Statistical interaction refers to variation among relationships between two variables within categories of one or more control variables.

The age–crime–job relationship in Chapter 5 is another example of statistical interaction.

Limitations of Cross-Tabulation

Imagine a table cross-classifying age by years of schooling. To cross-tabulate all ages and years of education, a table likely would contain more than 1000 cells! An obvious strategy is to collapse the values of age and schooling down to manageable size. Age could be split at the median, and schooling at 12 years to produce a 2×2 table.

But a lot of potentially important detail is covered up when variables are collapsed, particularly when they are collapsed to this extreme degree. More importantly, a sequence of three-variable tables, one for each control variable, isn't good enough. The idea of control demands *simultaneous controls*. What's needed is one table showing the joint cross-tabulaton of the dependent variable, independent variable, and *all control variables*. Imagine what the cross-tabulation might look like with only a few control variables—two categories for gender, two categories for ever hit, two for drinking behavior, two categories for age and two for urban/rural residence produces a table with 32 cells. Each additional two-category variable doubles the number of cells. So, six two-category variables require 64 cells, seven require 128 cells, and so on. Clearly, some simplifications are essential. The next section briefly reviews methods other than cross-tabulation for summarizing relationships.

ADDITIONAL ANALYSIS METHODS

Bivariate Table of Means

If the dependent variable is **numeric** (numbers-based), like time or earnings, and the independent variable is **categorical**, like gender or race, a useful device is to calculate the dependent-variable mean score for each category of the independent variable. A simple diagram of a hypothesis with a numeric and a categorical variable is:

gender → *earnings*

Table 11.8 shows an example using "annual earnings" as the dependent variable and gender as the independent variable.[2] (To avoid unnecessary complication later, the sample used to construct Table 11.8 includes only people who were working full-time or working part-time.)

Table 11.8 reveals a substantial difference between the average annual earnings of men and women in 1994: $33,190 − 21,300 = \$11,890$ per year. The number of cases (n) is displayed for each mean in the table. Without the number of cases included in a table, the reader can't determine whether the sample used to produce the table has few or many cases (e.g., 1 of 10 = 10%, and 100 of 1000 = 10%).

TABLE 11.8. Annual Earnings for 1994 by Gender (×$1,000).

Income	Males	Females	Total
Mean	33.19	21.30	27.16
(*n*)	(848)	(872)	(1720)

Source: 2002 General Social Survey cumulative data file (Davis, Smith, & Marsden, 2003). The data are from 1994 sample. Mean income is in $1,000. *n* is the numbers of respondents.

Note: The sample consists of those who were either working full-time or working part-time. Others are excluded.

Table 11.8 is comprised of sample means, but is comparable to Table 11.1, which uses percentages. Table 11.8 shows a bivariate association between gender and annual earnings. Annual earnings is a numeric (ratio) variable. Table 11.1 shows a bivariate association between gender and ever hit. The dependent variable, ever hit, is a categorical (nominal) variable.

More about Elaboration

Gender is not the only possible determinant of being hit; likewise, gender is not the only variable that affects earnings. What is one variable that might account for the gender difference in earnings?

One possible variable is work status, which is defined in the next few examples as a nominal variable with two categories: "work full-time" and "work part-time." The hypothesis is:

Men earn more than women because they are more likely to work full-time than women are.

The initial (bivariate) hypothesis was: "Men earn more than women." Gender is the independent variable and the dependent variable is annual earnings. The revised hypothesis implies the gender difference in earnings disappears under control for work status. Table 11.9 shows the relationship between gender and earnings separately for full-time and part-time workers.

The table shows how work status specifies the bivariate relationship between gender and earnings. The specifications are:

- For full-time workers, the bivariate relationship is unchanged: Men earn an average of $35,690 and women earn an average $23,860, which is a difference of $11,830 more per year for men, close to the dollar difference in the bivariate table, Table 11.8.

- But, for part-time workers, the partial relationship is much smaller than in the bivariate relationship: $13,370 for men and $10,630 for women, a difference of just $2,740 per year.

TABLE 11.9.   Annual Earnings for 1994 (× $1,000) by Gender,
Controlling for Work Status.

Work Status	Male	Female	Total
Full-time	35.69	23.86	29.98
(n)	(753)	(703)	(1456)
Part-time	13.37	10.63	11.62
(n)	(95)	(169)	(264)
Total	33.19	21.30	25.9
(n)	(848)	(872)	(1720)

Source: 2002 General Social Survey cumulative data file (Davis, Smith, & Marsden, 2003).
The data are for the 1994 sample.

Income is in $1,000. Numbers (n) are the numbers of respondents. The sample consists
of those who were either working full-time or working part-time. Others are excluded.

No simple path diagram can be drawn to represent this situation. In fact, it requires
two diagrams. One diagram is needed for full-time workers, showing an impact of
gender on earnings, and another diagram is needed for part-time workers, showing little or no impact. This pattern of differing relationships in partial tables is
another example of statistical interaction.

There's a "built-in" relationship between earnings and whether one works full-
time or part-time, because earnings is defined by wage × hours. Economists often
use wage instead of earnings. Suppose we study hourly wage instead of annual
earnings. Are there still gender differences in pay? The GSS data permit only a
very rough estimate of hours worked in a given year; consequently, the analyses
with wage as reported next should be viewed as an illustration.

Table 11.10 reports hourly wage by gender, controlling for work status. It
shows that men earn about five dollars more per hour than women; this difference
is nearly constant between full-time and part-time work. The relationship between
wage and gender remains, but the statistical interaction (differing relationship in
the partial tables) so prominent in Table 11.9 is gone.

What general principle emerges from the comparison between annual earnings and wage as dependent variables? The comparison illustrates the importance
of the conceptual aspect of research. The findings in these two cases clearly
depend on the way the dependent variable is defined. Neither result is wrong, but
you may prefer one over the other. We prefer the analysis using hourly wage. A
separate analysis of the determinants of hours worked might be combined with the
analysis of wage to predict annual earnings.

Regression Analysis

The 1994 earnings variable in the GSS contains 21 income ranges. Imagine a cross-
tabulation with 21 categories for earnings, two for gender and two for work status:
$21 \times 2 \times 2 = 84$ cells. Clearly, such a table is too big to evaluate readily. Using

TABLE 11.10.   Estimated Hourly Wage for 1994 by Gender and "Work Status."

Working Full/ Part-Time	Male	Female	Total
Full-Time	$17.63	$12.53	$15.16
(*n*)	(750)	(702)	(1452)
Part-Time	17.91	12.94	14.70
(*n*)	(93)	(169)	(262)
Total	$17.66	$12.61	$15.09
(*n*)	(843)	(871)	(1714)

Source: 2002 General Social Survey cumulative data file (Davis, Smith, & Marsden, 2003). Data are for the 1994 sample.

The method of estimating yearly hours worked is to multiply weeks worked by the number of hours worked last week for those working and by "usual hours worked" for those on vacation or sick leave. This estimate is crude.

The result produced some outliers. Consequently, estimates above $50/hour were omitted from the analysis.

Note: The sample consists of those who were either working full-time or working part-time. Others are excluded.

average earnings reduces the table to four cells (see Table 11.9). This is an obviously useful simplification. But almost any dependent variable you can think of probably is influenced by many factors, as the ever hit–gender example illustrates. Therefore, realistic data analysis must include many control variables, and they must be included as *simultaneous* controls. Ten or even 20 variables is a modest number when considering the complexity of the social world. What can be done?

Some further simplifying techniques are essential. The business of science is simplification—extract the essential patterns out of what otherwise looks like chaos.

The most basic and still the most-often used simplification is a statistical method called **linear regression analysis**, usually shortened to just "regression analysis" or "regression."

Don't confuse regression analysis with the threat to internal validity described in Chapter 5 called "regression to the mean." Regression to the mean refers to observations at either extreme of a distribution drifting back toward the mean on repeated measurements (e.g., test scores, temperatures in different cities).

Regression analysis is a method of predicting the value of the dependent variable using at least one "predictor variable." The term *control variable* is used infrequently in regression; predictors in a regression include all variables other than the dependent variable. When one variable is the focus of attention, it is the independent variable, and all other predictor variables are control variables. Technically, however, in regression analysis there's no difference between an independent variable and a control variable. The only difference is in the researcher's focus.[3]

How does regression analysis handle the predictor variables? All values of all predictors are combined into a single number predicting the dependent variable. For example, suppose we wish to use *age*, education (*educ*), and gender (*female*) to predict hourly wage. Predicted hourly wage is calculated by a straight-line (linear) equation:

$$predicted\ hourly\ wage = a + b_{age}\ age + b_{educ}\ educ + b_{fem} female$$

The symbols, $a, b_{age}, b_{educ}, b_{fem}$, stand for constant numbers. The constant number represented by the letter a is called the "intercept." The intercept indicates where the prediction line intercepts the vertical axis on a plot with the dependent variable on the vertical axis. It generally plays no role in the interpretation of the results but is essential to get accurate predictions. The constants symbolized by the letter b with a subscript are called "regression coefficients" or "partial slope" coefficients. Each coefficient gives an estimate of the effect of the predictor variable on the dependent variable, simultaneously controlling for all other predictor variables in the model.

Where do the constants—the intercept and regression coefficients—come from? They are estimated from the data by picking the values that give the most accurate predictions for the entire sample. "Most accurate" is defined by minimizing the sum of the squared prediction errors. Details of their calculations are beyond the scope of this book; however, the constants are easy to obtain using statistical software.

The linear equation in this example says: Multiply the value of each predictor variable (age in years, years of schooling completed, and female) by its corresponding regression coefficient, and add their products to the intercept to get the predicted hourly wage.

For example, the regression coefficient for education (years of schooling) is 1.48. This means, controlling for both age and gender, the predicted wage increases by $1.48 an hour for each year of additional schooling (1994 dollars).

Regression analysis is a flexible tool. It can be adapted to many nonlinear patterns in data, and easily accommodates categorical variables. Linear regression works when the categorical variables are the predictors. For categorical dependent variables, a type of regression called logistic regression is the most-often-used alternative.

"Dummy" Variables in Regression Analysis. Let's look at an example showing how to use regression analysis to estimate the effects of gender and work status on hourly wage. A **dummy variable** is a nominal variable with only two categories for which the two codes are the numbers 0 and 1. To do this analysis, define two dummy variables:

female = 1 if the respondent is female, 0 if the respondent is male

part-time = 1 if respondent is working part-time, 0 if working full-time.

[Others (e.g., retired) are omitted from this analysis.]

These are the two predictor variables in the equation predicting wage for this example:

$$predicted\ wage = a + b_{fem}\ female + b_{pt}\ parttime$$

In the regression, include a dummy variable for female *or* male, but *not* both. Including both is redundant; if you know a respondent is female, you know she is not male. For the same reason, include a dummy variable for part-time work *or* full-time work, but not both.[4]

Table 11.11 displays the predicted wage from this regression using the GSS data. The regression equation appears at the top of the table in three formats. The last one shows the numerical constants for the intercept and the two predictors. The column labels display both the value of the dummy variable, female (0,1), and the categories of male and female. The same double-labeling appears in the row labels for work status. The cells of the table show the predicted wage for each combination of *female* and *parttime*.

TABLE 11.11. Predicted Hourly Wage for 1994 Using a Regression with *Female* and *Parttime* as Independent Variables.

predicted wage = intercept	+	slope$_1$ × female	+	slope$_2$ × parttime
= a	+	b$_{fem}$female	+	b$_{pt}$parttime
= 17.62	−	5.08 female	+	0.363 parttime

Work Status	Male (female = 0)	Female (female = 1)
Full-time (*parttime* = 0)	17.62	12.54
(*n*)	(750)	(702)
Part-time (*parttime* = 1)	17.98	12.90
(*n*)	(93)	(169)

Source: General Social Survey, cumulative data file 1972–2002 cumulative file (Davis, Smith, & Marsden, 2003). This table is for the survey year 1994. Main table entries are predicted wages. Numbers enclosed in parentheses are the numbers of respondents.

The estimate of hourly wage is very rough. It was calculated by dividing annual earnings by a very rough estimate of annual hours worked. The result produced some outliers. Wages above $50/hour were omitted from the analysis.

The value of the regression coefficient for *female* is −5.08. This means, controlling for full-time or part-time work, the regression analysis procedure estimates women earn $5.08 less per hour than men.[5]

MORE ABOUT STATISTICAL TESTS

The cross-tabulations used in this chapter, along with the means and regression coefficients, all come from a single sample, the GSS data for 1994. You can be quite sure none of these sample statistics, such as average age or wage, exactly equals the corresponding parameter in the entire U.S. population. The same questions about **statistical inference** introduced in Chapter 9 (generalizing from a sample to its population) arise here:

1. *In a cross-tabulation*, how can one decide whether the relationship is large enough to rule out the possibility that it is due to sampling error?
2. For *differences among several mean scores*, how can one decide whether differences are large enough to rule out the possibility that they are due to sampling error?
3. With *regression coefficients*, how can one decide whether the relationship is strong enough to rule out the possibility that it is due to sampling error?

The solution to these questions lies in the use of statistical tests. Except for chi-square, details about how to calculate statistical tests are beyond the scope of this textbook. But we'll look briefly at three types of tests:

1. chi-square test for a two-variable table
2. *t*-test and *F*-test to compare means
3. *t*-test and *F*-test for the results from regression analysis.

These descriptions are intended only to introduce you to the basic concepts in statistical inference for tables, means and regression, and give you some exposure to the terminology.

Chi-Square Test for Cross-Tabulations

There are three ways the term *chi-square* is used:

- *chi-square test*—a statistical test based on using the chi-square statistic with the chi-square probability distribution
- *chi-square statistic*—a statistic calculated from a sample table (and sometimes from other types of sample data)
- *chi-square distribution*—a probability distribution used in the chi-square test, analogous to the normal distribution but with a different shape.

The **chi-square test** is used with cross-tabulations. The term *chi-square* (pronounced "kī") comes from the Greek letter *chi* and from a sum of squared numbers. It is denoted by χ^2 in statistics.

The chi-square test is carried out by calculating the **chi-square statistic** from cell frequencies of a cross-tabulation using data from a sample. The calculated

TABLE 11.12. Chi-Square Calculations for Table 11.1.*

Cell	"Observed" Cell Frequency	"Expected" Cell Frequency	Squared Difference $(O - E)^2$	Squared Difference/ Expected Freq.
(1,1)	121	$228 \times 195/510 = 87.2$	$(121 - 87.2)^2 = 1144$	$1144/87.2 = 13.1$
(2,1)	107	$228 \times 315/510 = 140.8$	$(107 - 140.8)^2 = 1144$	$1144/140.8 = 8.1$
(1,2)	74	$282 \times 195/510 = 107.8$	$(74 - 107.8)^2 = 1144$	$1144/107.8 = 10.6$
(2,2)	208	$282 \times 315/510 = 174.2$	$(208 - 174.2)^2 = 1144$	$1144/174.2 = 6.6$
Sum				$\chi^2 = 38.4$ $p < 0.0001$ (with 1 degree of freedom)[6]

*Numbers are rounded.

chi-square statistic is used with the **chi-square distribution** to find the *p*-value (probability value). Most statistics textbooks include an appendix of probabilities for the chi-square distribution, and nearly all statistical software prints *p*-values for chi-square. If the *p*-value is below the level of significance (most often 0.05), reject the null hypothesis of no relationship in the table. Nearly always, rejecting the null hypothesis supports the research hypothesis.

Table 11.12 shows the calculations of the chi-square statistic for the gender × "ever hit" table, Table 11.1. Look at column 3, labeled "Expected" Cell Frequency. These are the frequencies that would occur if all the percentage differences in the table were exactly zero, that is, if there were no relationship between the variables in the table. The formula for expected frequency is:

Expected frequency = row total × column total/total sample n.

The chi-square statistic measures the difference between observed and expected frequencies. The larger the chi-square statistic, the stronger the relationship in the table. However, chi-square depends on the sample size and the number of cells in the table, so it is not a good measure of the strength of a relationship. For the data in Table 11.12, the chi-square statistic is: $\chi^2 = 38.4$ with an associated *p*-value very close to zero. This means the probability is very small of obtaining a χ^2 as large as 38.4 for a 2 × 2 table if there were no relationship between "gender" and "ever hit" in the population. Therefore, declare the relationship in Table 11.1 to be statistically significant—a good bet there is relationship between "gender" and "ever hit" in the population.

T-Test and *F*-Test for Comparing Means

Recall that Table 11.8 shows the difference in average annual earnings between women and men to be $11,890 per year. Is the difference big enough to be due to something besides sampling error? The *t*-statistic can be used to test the significance of the difference between two means. For the difference between annual earnings of women and men, the *t*-statistic is $t = 12.39$, $p < 0.0001$ (calculation omitted). This means the chance of finding a difference of \$11,890 between men and women is less than 1 in 10,000 (much less) if the two genders had equal annual earnings in the U.S. population. This difference is statistically significant, meaning unlikely due to sampling error.

What should be done when there are more than two means to be compared simultaneously? Stated another way, the question is: "Do a set of means differ from each other?" The *F*-statistic is designed for this type of test. The analysis of variance (ANOVA) is a statistical method that, in part, organizes groups of *F*-statistics and associated calculations involving comparisons of several means.

Table 11.13 reports an example containing five means, one for each of five categories of educational degree. The question is: Do these five means differ enough to attribute the differences among them to something besides sampling error? An **F-test** (and its *p*-value), reported at the bottom of the table, indicates that their differences are very unlikely to be due to sampling error. Not surprisingly, annual earnings *is* related to the highest educational degree one has completed.

TABLE 11.13. Average Annual Earnings by Highest Educational Degree Completed (× \$,1000).

	Highest Educational Degree				
	Less than High School	**High School Diploma**	**Associates Degree (Two-Year College)**	**BA Degree**	**Graduate Degree**
Average earnings	16.71	22.39	26.44	36.32	46.65
(*n*)	(169)	(916)	(128)	(347)	(158)

$F = 89.78$, $df = 4$, $p < 0.0001$.

Source: 2002 General Social Survey cumulative data file (Davis, Smith, and Marsden, 2003)

T-Test and *F*-Test for Regression

The same ideas for statistical tests among means apply to regression analysis. There is an **F-test** indicating whether *any* of the regression coefficients is significant. A **t-test** is associated with *each* regression coefficient. For the coefficients, these tests indicate whether the associated effect is statistically significant. The *F*-test in regression is the same test used in ANOVA.

The *F*-tests for the regression using age, number of years of schooling, and gender to predict wage, and the second regression using just gender and work status to predict wage, both are highly statistically significant—that is, their *p*-values are much below 0.05.

SUMMARY

This chapter continues the example begun in Chapter 10 examining an important social science question: Are men or women more likely to be victims of violence? Using cross-tabulations and one measure of physical violence ("Ever hit by another person?"), Chapter 10 reports a substantial bivariate relationship: Men are more likely than women to be hit.

Chapter 11 examines two possible reasons for this relationship. The first is straight-forward. Men are more likely to drink to excess and this accounts for their being hit more often. This hypothesis is not supported, so we tried a second approach. The second analysis is more complicated. "Ever hit" is split into two variables: "hit as child" and "hit as an adult." The data show that males are much more likely than are females to be hit during childhood, and this vulnerability carries over into adult years. Controlling for "hit as child," there is nearly zero relationship between gender and being hit as an adult. Hit as a child intervenes between gender and hit as an adult.

The next section of the chapter introduces two comparatively advanced methods of data analysis: (1) comparisons among means and (2) regression analysis. The research question is: "Do males have higher earnings (or higher hourly wages) than females?" Regression analysis and its extensions are designed for research involving simultaneous analysis of many variables.

The final sections of the chapter present a brief introduction to using statistical tests with tables, comparisons among means and regression. Statistical tests provide a method for making inferences from a sample to its population based on probability calculations. The chapter briefly introduces three types of statistical tests: The chi-square test for a bivariate table, the F-test and t-test applied to analyses of means, and the F-test and associated t-test applied to regression.

This chapter further illustrates the central role data analysis plays in understanding our social world. The exercises that follow allow you to gain additional practice in data analysis: calculating and reading percentage tables and evaluating a data table.

YOUR REVIEW SHEET: QUESTIONS DISCUSSED IN THIS CHAPTER

1. Why not compare percentages within categories of the independent variable, (i.e., within the percentage base)?

2. How are univariate distributions used in social science research?

3. In a bivariate or trivariate table, where are the cell frequencies?

4. In Table 11.1, can "gender" be the row variable and "ever hit" the column variable? Explain.

5. How can the title of a table provide clues about which are the independent and dependent variables? the control variable?

6. Why not just construct a new three-variable table for each new control variable?

7. What is the key to understanding Table 11.7, and trivariate tables in general?

8. Can variables with more than two categories be included in a cross-tabulation to study a relationship? Briefly explain.

9. What is a good strategy for studying a relationship when the dependent variable is numeric and the independent variable is categorical?

10. Suppose you want to examine simultaneously the effects of "age," "gender," and "work status" on "wage." What analysis method is appropriate? Briefly discuss.

11. Explain what it means to declare the relationship in Table 11.1 "statistically significant."

12. What feature of Table 11.9 indicates there is statistical interaction present? Summarize the interaction in Table 11.9.

13. In your own words, what function do statistical tests serve?

14. Suppose the total sample size is 1000. What is the average cell frequency in a $3 \times 2 \times 5$ cross-tabulation? Do you think all the cells would have the same frequency? Why or why not?

END NOTES

1. Both a linear regression and a logistic regression including the interaction between drinking and gender show p-values for the interaction term well above 0.05.

2. Annual earnings is an estimate of the total earnings ($\times$ $1,000) from one's principal occupation for 1994. Respondents were presented a list of income ranges and asked to check the range that contained their income. Dollar estimates were calculated by taking the midpoint of each interval. The estimate for the top interval was set to 100 ($100,000). The estimate for the bottom interval was set to 0.75 ($750), on the assumption that those in that interval ($0 to $1,000) are closer on average to $1,000 than to $0.

3. This is true of multi-way tables as well, but it's not apparent from the way they are laid out in this chapter. If you compare column one to column four in Table 11.7, for instance, you see the relationship between hitchild and hitadult for males, and comparing column two to column five shows the relationship between hitchild and hitadult for females. But the relationship between hitchild and hitadult is not the focus of attention in the analysis.

4. It's just as acceptable to define a dummy variable *male*: 1 = male, 0 = female. Using *male* instead of *female* reverses the sign of the regression coefficient. Using *female* indicates how much less females earn than males, controlling for *parttime*. Using *male* instead indicates how much more males earn per hour than females. Similarly, a dummy variable can be constructed indicating full-time work instead of part-time work. Again, the only difference in the results is a sign reversal on the regression coefficient.

Generally, a nominal variable with any number of categories can be used as an independent variable in regression by including a dummy variable for each category except one. Because of the rule that the categories of a variable must be mutually exclusive and exhaustive, at most, one of these dummy variables can be 1; the rest must be 0. If they all are 0, then the respondent must be classified into the category without a dummy variable in the regression. Either way, the computer knows which category fits the observation.

5. Note how close the predicted hourly wage in Table 11.11 is to the average hourly wage in the corresponding cells in Table 11.10. The differences are because the regression is defined so that the statistical interaction is exactly zero. Since there is very little interaction in Table 11.10, it matches the predicted values from the regression quite closely. This is one of the main ways regression analysis simplifies a display of means for every combination of categories of many predictor variables, by assuming statistical interactions to be zero.

6. Degrees of freedom are calculated: df = (rows − 1) × (columns − 1).

STUDY TERMS

categorical variable (or nominal scale) Variable with a few (usually) unordered categories.

chi-square distribution A theoretical probability distribution used in many applications for statistical inference, including testing for a relationship in a bivariate table.

chi-square test Statistical test done by calculating the chi-square statistic for a sample cross-tabulation and comparing it to the probability from the chi-square distribution.

chi-square statistic Number calculated from the sample frequencies for a cross-tabulation. (The chi-square statistic and chi-square test apply to many situations other than cross-tabulations, but these other applications are not reviewed in the chapter.)

control variable Variable used to check a bivariate relationship within each category of the control variable.

dummy variable Two-category variable that takes a value of 0 or 1, often used as an independent variable in regression analysis.

elaboration Process of studying the relationship between two variables by observing their relationship within each category of one (or more) control variables.

explanation (type of elaboration) Bivariate relationship exists only due to a control variable that is "causally prior" to both the independent and dependent variables. In the perfect type, the bivariate relationship between the original independent variable and the dependent variable is zero within categories of the control variable (e.g., the sex–beard–dress relationships). The bivariate relationship is called spurious; that is, it is not due to cause and effect.

***F*-test** Statistical test to assess whether sample differences among two or more means are likely due to sampling error.

inference See statistical inference.

interpretation (type of elaboration) A bivariate relationship exists due only to a control variable that intervenes between the independent and dependent variables. In the perfect type, the bivariate relationship between the original independent variable and the dependent variable is zero within categories of the control variable (e.g., gender–hitchild–hitadult relationships). Contrast with explanation.

intervening variable A variable that is affected by the independent variable and affects the dependent variable. In the pure intervening-variable case, the original relationship between the independent variable and the dependent variable vanishes (is zero) when the intervening variable is controlled statistically, as in a three-variable table.

linear regression analysis (regression analysis, regression) Method of predicting the value of the dependent variable using a linear formula and one or more independent variables, such as: *predicted hourly wage* $= a + b_{age} age + b_{educ} educ + b_{fem} female$. Usually, the regression analysis is done with a computer statistical software program, such as SPSS or SAS.

numeric variable Interval and ratio variables (sometimes ordinal variables); the numerical values are given their natural mathematical meaning (compare with categorical variable).

partial relationship Association between the independent and dependent variables within a category of one or more control variables; in tabular analysis, a partial table, in regression, a partial slope coefficient.

replication (type of elaboration) Each partial relationship matches the original bivariate relationship within categories of the control variable (or variables) (control variable has no effect on the bivariate association).

specification (type of elaboration) Finding that the relationship between the independent and dependent variable is different in different categories of one or more control variables. Also called statistical interaction.

statistical inference Process of drawing conclusions about a population using data from a sample of that population.

statistical interaction Variation among relationships between two variables within categories of one or more control variables.

statistically significant Sample statistic deviates from the null hypothesis by a large enough amount to trigger rejection of the null hypothesis. The size of the difference required to reject the null hypothesis is determined by a probability (p-value). If the calculated p-value is no larger than the level of significance, reject the null hypothesis. In social research, the most-used level of significance is 0.05.

statistical test A procedure for making a decision as to whether a population value of a statistic is some stated value, called the null hypothesis. Usually the null hypothesis states no relationship between two variables. Statistical tests are the primary technical method of statistical inference.

***t*-test** A statistical test used for many statistics, e.g., to compare two sample means or test a regression coefficient against a null hypothesis that it is zero (no partial relationship).

trivariate table A table that includes three variables: independent, dependent, and control.

EXERCISES

Exercise 11.1. Preparing a Trivariate Table

Directions: Use the data in Table 10.8 to prepare the trivariate tables below. Show tally marks, cell frequencies, and row and column totals in a table laid out like Table 11.14. Tabulate column percentages and column totals in a table like Table 11.15. Show your calculations. (Column totals go in the parentheses.)

1. Summarize the relationships in Table 11.15.
2. Looking at the cell percentages, what difficulty with multivariate tables emphasized in the chapter does Table 11.15 illustrate?

TABLE 11.14. Tally Sheet for "Hit When Adult" by Gender, Controlling for "Hit When Child."

Hitadult	Hitchild = Yes		
	Male	Female	Total
1 = yes			
2 = no			
Total *n*			

Hitadult	Hitchild = No		
	Male	Female	Total
1 = yes			
2 = no			
Total *n*			

TABLE 11.15. Percentage "Hit When Adult" by Gender, Controlling for "Hit When Child."

Hit When Adult	Hit When Child?					
	Yes			No		
	Male	Female	Total	Male	Female	Total
Yes						
No						
Total %	100.0	100.0	100.0	100.0	100.0	100.0
(*n*)	( )	( )	( )	( )	( )	( )

TABLE 11.16. Attitudes toward Women in Military Combat by Religion (Hypothetical Data).

Religion	Percent Approving	Percent Disapproving
Catholic	42.2%	57.8%
Protestant	39.4	60.6
Other	56.0	44.0

Exercise 11.2. Reading a Percentage Table

Directions: Refer to Table 11.16 when answering the following questions. Review the rules for calculating and reading percentages.

Factual Questions

1. What is the independent variable in Table 11.16? What is the dependent variable?
2. What is the percentage base (row totals, column totals, total *n*)?
3. Are the percentages in Table 11.16 calculated correctly? Explain, using Rule 1 for calculating percentages.
4. Summarize the findings shown in Table 11.16.

Questions for Discussion

1. Provide a brief social science explanation for the findings.
2. What entries are omitted from Table 11.16 that should be included in a publication-ready table?

Exercise 11.3. Using the General Social Survey to Study "Ever Hit" and Gender

Directions: Table 11.17 contains the frequencies for the hitadult × hitchild × gender for all survey years the hit questions appeared in the GSS. Construct a three-variable percentage table from these frequencies. Be sure you are clear about the identity of the dependent variable, independent variable and control variable, before beginning. Then answer the questions below.

The finished table should look something like Table 11.18.

TABLE 11.17. Frequencies of Hitadult × Hitchild × Gender, All Survey Years the Questions Were Asked in the GSS.

	hitchild = yes gender = male	hitchild = yes gender = female	hitchild = no gender = male	hitchild = no gender = female
hitadult = yes	1147	391	1161	1241
hitadult = no	2140	709	3905	8621

Source: General Social Survey, cumulative data file 1972– 2002 cumulative file (Davis, Smith, & Marsden, 2003). This table is for survey years: 1973, 1975, 1976, 1978, 1980, 1983, 1984, 1986, 1991, 1993 and 1994. Table entries are joint frequencies.

TABLE 11.18. Percentage Reporting Being Hit as an Adult by Gender, Controlling for Hit as a Child.

Hit as an Adult	Hit as a Child (Yes)		Not Hit as a Child (No)	
	Male	**Female**	**Male**	**Female**
Yes				
No				
Total %				
(*n*)				

Factual Questions

1. Summarize the relationship between hitadult and gender for those who *were* hit when they were children.

2. Summarize the relationship between hitadult and gender for those who were *not* hit when they were children.

3. What is/are the major difference(s) between your new table and the three-variable table for the same relationship for the 1994 survey year (Table 11.7)?

Questions for Discussion

1. What do you think is/are the main technical reason(s) Table 11.18 differs from Table 11.7?

2. Summarize the revised findings in one or two concise sentences.

3. Explain why you think the findings appear as they do (i.e., how you think the process actually works).

Exercise 11.4. Coding Data, Preparing Data Tables, and Evaluating "Substantive Significance"

1. **Selecting Variables:** Select three variables from Table 10.8, one dependent variable (*Y*), one independent variable (*X*), and one control variable (*Z*). Exclude all four "hit" variables. List the name of each variable and how you classify it (dependent, independent, control).

2. **Null Hypothesis:** State the null hypothesis using your *X* and *Y* variables.

3. **Research Hypothesis:** State a research hypothesis—one that will permit a one-tailed statistical test. (Typically, first you would read up on your topic, in part to reduce the chance of choosing the wrong direction for your test.)

4. **Cleaning Data and Modifying Variables:** Develop a coding scheme applicable to tabular analysis for each of your variables. To have sufficient frequencies in each table cell, use two categories per variable. Collapse the categories of each variable that has more than two categories. For a continuous variable, each category of the recoded variable should stand for an interval of the original variable. Be sure the intervals do not overlap *and* do not leave any gaps.

Write the original variable categories for categorical variables with more than two categories and the lowest and highest values for each interval of a continuous variable. Next to the original values, write the categories for the collapsed variable.

a. My *X* is _____ Its categories were _____.
I coded the first category(ies) _____ as _____
_____, and the second category(ies) _____ as
_____.

Rationale for recode _____

b. My *Y* is _____. Its categories were _____
_____

I coded the first category(ies) _____as _____
_____, and the second category(ies) _____ as _____
_____,

Rationale for recode _____

c. My *Z* is _____. Its categories were _____
_____.

I coded the first category(ies) _____ as _____
_____, and the second category(ies) _____ as
_____

Rationale for recode _____

5. **Calculating Percentages and Reading Tables:**

a. Prepare a bivariate percentage table for your *X* and *Y* variables (independent and dependent variables, respectively). Include all items needed for percentage tables. (Check the rules for calculating percentages.)
Referring to your hypothesis, what finding emerged? _____
_____
Use "≥ 10% difference" to determine whether your relationship is "substantively significant." Is it?

b. Using your *Z* variable, prepare a trivariate table, properly labeled, to conduct an elaboration analysis. What finding emerged? _____
_____
Use "≥ 10% difference" to determine whether your relationship is "substantively significant." Is it? What do you conclude about *Z*'s influence on the bivariate relationship?
_____
What type of elaboration pattern (replication, interpretation, explanation, specification) did you find between *X* and *Y* after adding *Z*? _____
Draw it, using a cause-and-effect arrow diagram.

Exercise 11.5. Advanced Evaluation

Evaluation of Research Article: Data Tables

Note: Some students can benefit from reading a complete journal research article. One article using trivariate tabular analysis is Fiorentine and Cole (1992).

Directions to students: Read the article referenced above and answer the questions below. Your instructor will provide instructions for obtaining the article.

Factual Questions

1. What is the dependent variable in Table II in the article? What is the independent variable? What is the control variable? Explain the reason for your answers.

2. How many males perceive their chances of medical school admission as excellent if they had a high GPA? How many females? Show your calculations (*Hint:* Convert percentages into frequencies).

3. How many partial tables are shown? Briefly describe each, using the control variable category name for each.

Questions for Discussion

1. Look at the percentages in the "competitive GPA" category for males and females and the frequencies obtained for Question 2 for each gender. Briefly explain the advantage of calculating percentages for cross-tabulations versus looking at the frequencies.

2. Assume that a percentage difference of 10% or greater indicates a "substantively important" relationship between the two variables. Is there a substantively significant relationship between gender and estimates of admission?

3. Based on your answer to the previous question, do you agree or disagree with the authors that "there was no gender difference in estimating the chances of admission to medical school"? Explain your answer.

12 PREPARING THE REPORT

INTRODUCTION: LOOKING AT HOW THE SOCIAL WORLD WORKS

"She looked at the lips that seemed to suggest. . . ."

Unlike romance novels, detective stories and many forms of popular writing, which are produced for the pleasure of individuals, writing about research results is undertaken to contribute to general human knowledge and welfare. For example, the disaster research reviewed in Chapter 6 found that procedures followed "on the ground" often don't conform to plans for managing disasters (Quarantelli, 1997). Victims are likely to be transported by private vehicles to the most familiar hospital, regardless of disaster plans, resulting in an uneven distribution of patients among hospitals. At the hospitals, the less seriously injured usually arrive first and therefore tend to be treated first. Also, new groups providing emergency medical services often emerge during disasters, and established institutions such as hospitals often are underutilized.

Findings about services during disaster times are potentially very useful for community leaders and the general public. The heightened concern about public security after September 11, 2001 reinforces the need for successful management of disasters, whether human or natural in origin. But without appropriate research and dissemination of the findings, knowledge about disasters would be known only to the disaster victims, a few of their family and friends, and local relief workers.

Suppose the research findings don't support a well-formulated hypothesis or theory; should they be reported? Yes. Negative findings tell researchers where not to look, and inform policymakers what doesn't work (Harrison & McNeece, 2001, p. 502). This important point generally is overlooked in the popular press, and often by journal editors and reviewers. It is much easier to publish a paper based on "positive findings" than one in which the theory is not supported by the data.

Goals of this Chapter

When you set out to complete a term paper, what questions come to mind? Probably two questions are: "What should I write about?" and "How should I organize it?"

This chapter summarizes the final step in the research process: **dissemination** of scientific research results. It illustrates an important contrast between the way common sense information spreads among individuals and the public nature of science. The chapter also describes key issues encountered by authors of scientific reports, and gives instruction about how to write a scientific report for this course and other courses—or for publication.

Most people find it difficult to write. Where does one learn how to write a scientific report? Start by reading what others have written, such as the journal articles and monographs excerpted in this textbook. Often finding a topic and getting organized are the most difficult parts. This chapter offers advice on both counts.

RESEARCH REPORTS: FOUR EXAMPLES

This section summarizes and describes the organization of (1) an empirical journal article, (2) an evaluation report, (3) a monograph, and (4) a government document. The summaries are intended to convey three key aspects of report writing:

1. the importance and variety of formal research reports
2. the organization of the reports
3. the content of the reports.

Of course, there are many types of scientific reports besides the four mentioned here, far too many to summarize them all; these four provide an overview.

Also, you will learn about a newer type of research dissemination that is increasingly important in class activities and at professional conferences, the poster display.

Journal Articles and Similar Papers

Perhaps the most prestigious and important way to disseminate research results in most social science disciplines is publication in a scholarly **refereed journal** (Thyer, 2001, p. 504). Refereed journals publish only papers that have passed an intensive review process called "peer review." **Peer review** means each submission to the journal is evaluated by a panel of experts for importance and accuracy. Reviewers include scholars closely associated with the academic discipline of the journal. For example, a sociologist might review articles in *Marriage and the Family*, *Criminology* or *Social Problems*.

A few examples of scholarly journals and their social science discipline are:

■ *American Sociological Review, Social Forces* (sociology)
■ *Social Work* (social work)

■ *Criminology, Journal of Research on Crime and Delinquency* (criminology/criminal justice)

■ *Marriage and the Family, Journal of Social Issues* (family and human relations)

■ *Addiction, Social Problems* (human services)

■ *American Economic Review, Journal of Human Resources* (economics)

■ *American Political Science Review, Journal of Politics* (political science)

In contrast, articles published in popular-press magazines such as *Time, Newsweek, Sports Illustrated, Ebony,* and *YM,* typically are not subject to the formal peer review used by scientific journals. Popular-press magazines (1) contain articles about current issues for the general public, (2) seldom are based on original scholarly research, and (3) typically have no list of sources used by the author to write the article. Most articles in the popular press do undergo informal review by an editor and possibly one or two others, but they are not subject to the lengthy formal review process required for publication in a refereed journal.

Who chooses the experts to review journal articles submitted to refereed journals? The journal editor does, based on specializations needed to evaluate each specific article. For example, a qualitative research article on "social-class inequality in education" submitted for publication to the journal *Social Forces* calls for reviewers with expertise about class inequality, education, and the relationships between education and class inequality. Also, reviewers may be selected, in part, for their expertise in specialized methods used in the article, whether qualitative or quantitative.

The chief job of reviewers is to evaluate the article. They identify strengths and weaknesses, suggest revisions, and recommend to the journal editor whether to publish the paper. Reviews often are critical. Rarely does a paper make it to publication without substantial revision. Often papers are revised multiple times before publication, and many are not published. It can take up to a year or longer to obtain a publication decision from a journal. Of course, few authors like to hear that additional work is needed (and probably that includes most student writers). However, the goal of the peer review process is twofold: (1) select only the best submissions for publication and (2) improve the quality of selected papers.

Of course, the review process is imperfect. It is based on the notion that the process of review, critique, and revision is self-correcting over time; and no one knows of a better method.

Example of a Journal Article: *Inbreeding and Infant Mortality among the Amish, Revisited* As described in Chapter 7, this study investigates effects of inbreeding on infant mortality among the Amish residing in Lancaster County, Pennsylvania (Dorsten, Hotchkiss, & King, 1999). It relies on data for up to 12 generations of Amish families.

The research paper appeared in the scholarly journal *Demography*, published by the Population Association of America (PAA). According to the PAA Web site:

> *Demography* is the official journal of the Population Association of America. It is an interdisciplinary peer-reviewed periodical that publishes articles of general interest to population scientists. Fields represented in its contents include geography, history, biology, statistics, business, epidemiology, and public health, in addition to social scientific disciplines such as sociology, economics, psychology, and political science. Published quarterly, it includes theoretical and methodological articles, commentaries, and specialized research papers covering both developed and developing nations. (*http://www.jstor.org/journals/paa.html*)

The findings of the paper are interesting: The higher the level of inbreeding, the less likely a newborn is to survive the first year of life. But more important to social scientists, sociodemographic variables such as parents' church district of residence and year of child's birth also influence the risk of infant death, even with statistical control for inbreeding. Although the findings properly apply to the Amish community, the research likely was published in the journal *Demography* because it extends accumulating knowledge about the effect of sociodemographic variables on infant mortality.

What are the components of a scholarly article like the inbreeding study? As with nearly all scholarly papers, the inbreeding article contains an **abstract**. The abstract is a summary of the research report. The rest of the paper follows a fairly standard format. The major sections are shown as run-in headings in the next paragraphs.

Introduction. The introductory section doesn't display a heading. It begins by identifying a gap in current knowledge, and states how the paper contributes to filling the gap.

> An unresolved issue in research on child survival is the extent to which familial mortality risk in infancy is due to biological influences net of sociodemographic and economic factors, such as household economic status, household health-related knowledge and attitudes, parental competence in child rearing and genetic viability. . . .
>
> We extend prior research on familial mortality risk in the first year of life by using the inbreeding coefficient to predict perinatal, neonatal, and postneonatal mortality. (Dorsten, Hotchkiss, & King, 1999, 263)

Usually the introduction is brief. The entire introduction in this paper contains just two short paragraphs. Readers and reviewers are knowledgeable in the field and don't need an extended review. Even though the typical introduction is short, it must focus precisely on a known issue, or present a concise explanation for *why* readers should be interested in a new issue.

"Unobserved Measures and Recent Familial Mortality Research." This is the "literature review," even though it's not called that. In fact, the paper doesn't contain a complete review of research about infant mortality. It reviews earlier papers investigating possible bias in estimating the effects of socioeconomic variables on infant mortality due to omission of an explicit measure of inbreeding.

In short, the literature review focuses narrowly on the main "reason for being" of the paper. The research question for the paper is: *Has past research overestimated effects of variables like education and earnings on infant mortality, due to lack of control for genetic influences like inbreeding?* To find out, the partial solution is to include an explicit measure of inbreeding in the analysis.

"Data and Methods." This section describes the sample. The sample was taken from church records of the Old Order Amish. All cases of infant death were included, plus a sample of survivors. The section is split into two subsections:

"Coefficient of Inbreeding"	Explains the calculation and meaning of the main independent variable, "inbreeding."
"Other Independent Variables"	Summarizes alternative "causes" of mortality other than inbreeding that are controlled by a specialized regression method (Cox proportional hazards regression).

The data and methods section includes discussion about the data: How the sample was collected, how many cases it contains, and how many potential cases were eliminated and why. It also describes each variable, so that readers know exactly how it's defined. The description must do more than just list the names of variables, even if the variables are familiar. For example, it is not sufficient to list gender as a variable without describing how it is defined for the study. Readers must know what code is assigned to male and female in order to interpret the results. The *Demography* article identifies the coding of gender in the first table. One of the row labels of the table is "Female (1 = yes)." (It's understood that 0 = no, because of universal practice in defining dummy variables.)

"Findings." The summary of findings is organized around a sequence of tables fairly typical in journal articles.

- *Table 1.* The first table presents univariate statistics for each variable in the study: mean, standard deviation, and minimum and maximum values.
- *Table 2.* The second table shows bivariate relationships between the inbreeding coefficient and the three time periods of infant mortality: Perinatal mortality, neonatal mortality, and postneonatal mortality.[1]
- *Table 3 through Table 5b.* The remaining tables display the main findings, which are estimates of the effects of inbreeding and the other independent variables on

three outcomes: perinatal, neonatal, and postneonatal deaths, respectively. Table 5b presents alternative estimates for postneonatal deaths.

"Discussion." The final section of the paper summarizes the findings. The data indicate that inbreeding affects neonatal and postneonatal mortality but not perinatal mortality. The discussion section emphasizes the main point and offers possible reasons for the exception for perinatal mortality. The final conclusion of the study is:

> In summary, we find that inbreeding increases the risk of neonatal and postneonatal mortality. Yet, the findings of the present study also reaffirm the relevance of incorporating social, demographic, and cultural measures in studies of child survival. We find clear evidence of the impact of these measures, even in a population [with a high level of intermarriage] in which biological influences are expected. (p. 270)

Evaluation Reports

Recall from Chapter 2 that *applied* or *evaluation research* assesses the effectiveness of social programs. Unlike basic research, evaluation research focuses on whether intended outcomes of policy and practice were achieved in a specific setting. The **evaluation report** disseminates the results from an evaluation, primarily to practitioners and policy makers. However, remember the cautionary note in Chapter 2—individuals involved with a social intervention ("stakeholders") don't necessarily agree on an outcome, its definition and measurement, or even the length of time required to achieve it. An evaluator must consider viewpoints of those involved, such as appropriate outcomes and how to measure them, how to implement the intervention, and variables other than the intervention needed for the analysis.

Example of an Evaluation Report: *Evaluation of a School-Based Pregnancy Prevention Program, Revisited* Chapter 2 describes a social-intervention program designed to make pregnancy-prevention information and contraceptive technology available to inner-city adolescents (Zabin et al., 1986). The evaluation was designed to assess the school-based intervention by comparing changes in knowledge, attitudes, behaviors, and pregnancy rates between (1) students who were offered pregnancy-prevention services and (2) students who were not offered these services. Students in the schools with the pregnancy-prevention program were in the "experimental group." The rest were in the "control group." Data were collected from students through self-administered questionnaires. The excerpt suggests that the two school-based clinics did influence student behaviors and attitudes, as anticipated. The primary goal of the evaluation was to assess the contributions from the specific program included in the evaluation, but the researchers conclude other schools might benefit from similar programs.

The Zabin et al. article appeared in the professional journal *Family Planning Perspectives* (now *Perspectives on Sexual and Reproductive Health*), published by the Alan Guttmacher Institute:

> *Perspectives on Sexual and Reproductive Health* (formerly *Family Planning Perspectives*) provides the latest peer-reviewed, policy-relevant research and analysis on sexual and reproductive health and rights in the United States and other industrialized countries. For over three decades, *Perspectives* has offered unique insights into how reproductive health issues relate to one another and their implications for policy, programs and people's lives. In addition to articles and special reports and forums, each issue brings you staff-written summaries of recent findings and developments in reproductive health and rights. (*http://www.guttmacher.org/journals/aboutper.html*)

The evaluation article doesn't contain an abstract. The several parts of the paper are described briefly; the sections of the paper are shown as run-in headings below.

Introduction. As with the *Demography* paper, the introduction is not preceded by a heading, but it's much longer than the introduction to a typical journal article. It describes in detail the participating schools, the characteristics of the sample of students, the survey instrument, sample attrition (dropout), and the components of the pregnancy-prevention program. Remember, evaluations assess specific programs in specific settings. Therefore, a detailed description of the setting is needed.

"Some Methodological Problems." This section describes methodological problems of the study and notes that these problems are typical in school evaluations. The survey was administered four times, about a year apart, to the same students. The evaluation was designed to measure changes in knowledge, attitudes, and behaviors related to pregnancy prevention. As you might expect, one of the methodological problems was student absence from school on the days the surveys were administered. Another problem was students in the study moving in and out of the school attendance areas. In addition, the four schools aren't equivalent in important respects. The demographic composition varied among the four study schools, for example. And demographic variables such as parental education and occupational level are related to sexual practices.

"Changes in Knowledge and Attitudes." The paper contains no section titled "Findings." The findings are split into three sections. "Changes in Knowledge . . ." is the first one. It reports differences between experimental and control schools in changes of attitude and knowledge over the 4 years of the study. The findings are mixed, but appear to show small positive effects of the program on knowledge about contraception and reproductive health, and little or no effects on attitudes.

"Changes in Behavior." Changes in sexual behavior are reported in this section. Three outcomes were studied: (1) age at first sexual intercourse, (2) attendance at the birth-control clinic, and (3) use of oral contraceptives. Effects on age at first coitus were small, but effects on attending the clinic and use of contraceptives were substantial. Remember a particularly interesting finding from the excerpt? Junior-high boys in the experimental school made as frequent use of the clinic as did girls.

"Pregnancy Rates." The final section summarizing the findings focuses on the likelihood of becoming pregnant. The data indicate a strong impact of the program on the risk of pregnancy among sexually active females; the program reduces pregnancy risk.

"Conclusions." The authors conclude the program was effective. Appropriate for an evaluation, they mention the specific location and time of the evaluation:

> The brief, though intensive, pregnancy prevention program introduced in two Baltimore schools has demonstrated significant changes in several areas of adolescent knowledge and behavior—changes that have major implications for the formulation of public policy and for program design. (p. 124)

They generalize the findings beyond the Baltimore schools in the study and recommend:

> In conclusion, these findings suggest the efficacy of a program with pregnancy prevention as an explicit objective. Such a model requires a program and a staff capable of addressing a wide range of reproductive health issues. (p. 125)

"Appendix." The appendix displays special tables to assess the impact on the study findings of students moving in and out of the study areas.

Monographs and Books

Translated literally, a **monograph** means "one writing." For social science research, this terse definition translates into: A book-length publication that focuses on a narrow research issue, often based on a large research project. How does a monograph differ from a book? A monograph usually is shorter in length. Monographs and books are prepared by some researchers so that they have a complete collection of their work in one place, rather than as 6 to 10 articles in different journals, although some also publish individual articles from a study (Thyer, 2001, p. 506).

Example of a Monograph: *Sidewalk*, Revisited. Chapter 6 presents an excerpt from Duneier's (1999) study titled, *Sidewalk*, published as a monograph. Recall that Duneier shows how street vendors and panhandlers in Greenwich Village, New York, solve many problems of daily life, including lack of access to public restrooms. The general progression of the chapters is from descriptions of specific subgroups of people to their daily life on the city streets. This monograph is divided into three sections, which the author calls "parts."

Part 1: The Informal Life of the Sidewalk
Three chapters: "Book Vendors," "Magazine Vendors," and "The Men without Accounts."

Part 2: New Uses for Sidewalks
One chapter: "How Sixth Avenue Became a Sustaining Habitat."

Part 3: The Limits of Informal Social Control
Four chapters: "Sidewalk Sleeping," "When You Gotta Go," "Talking to Women," and "Accusations: Caveat Vendor?"

Duneier shares two concerns with his readers: Should he use pseudonyms (aliases) to protect the privacy of the people he wrote about, and how could he assure each person the right to an "informed decision" about whether to be in the book. He decided to use the real names of his subjects:

> I have decided to follow the practice of the journalists rather than the sociologists. I have not found that the people I write about ask to have their identities disguised. . . . Moreover, it seems to me that to disclose the place and names of the people I have written about holds me up to a higher standard of evidence. Scholars and journalists may speak with these people, visit the site I have studied, or replicate aspects of my study. So my professional reputation depends on competent description. . . . (pp. 347–348)

Duneier didn't conduct covert (nonparticipant) observation, but his method of getting "informed consent" nevertheless is quite interesting:

> I brought the completed manuscript to a hotel room and tried to read it to every person whose life was mentioned. . . . [However, m]ost people were much more interested in how they looked in the photographs than in how they sounded or were depicted. (Duneier, 1999, pp. 347–348)

Government Reports

The last example of a research report is particularly noteworthy. It illustrates how research sometimes offers cause-and-effect conclusions about critically important topics that can't be examined using controlled experiments, due to ethical and practical constraints.

Example of a Government Report: *The U.S. Surgeon General's Report on Smoking and Health.* The report of the Surgeon General's Advisory Committee on Smoking and Health, published in 1964, is a landmark government publication. It relied on data from many sources, including questionnaires and interviews; retrospective data from the subjects' histories; and studies that followed subjects contacted before the onset of disease and followed until their death or the study ended. The Committee also consulted autopsy studies revealing damage to internal organs of people and controlled experiments with animals. In addition, it relied on members' expertise related to medicine, biology, chemistry, psychology, and statistics.

The Surgeon General's report resembles a monograph in many respects: it's monograph length and focuses on a narrow range of research questions. It consists of two parts, 15 chapters, and 387 pages. But there are important contrasts to a monograph as well. First, it's rare for more than three or four authors to collaborate on a monograph. The Surgeon General's report lists 10 members of the Surgeon General's Advisory Committee on Smoking and Health plus the Surgeon General, Luther L. Terry as ex officio chair, and the Assistant Surgeon, James M. Hundley, as ex officio vice-chair. Second, **government reports** generally do not contain original research. The Surgeon General's report is based on research existing prior to the time of its publication. This is a distinctive difference between a government report and a monograph.

The committee consisted of highly capable experts in a mix of fields such as internal medicine, mathematical statistics, clinical pathology, genetics, cancer biology, and cardiopulmonary disease. The description of their activities in Chapter 1 of the report summarizes the sources of information, the meetings and the debates about the validity of data, the meaning of causation and the criteria for accepting a causal relationship. The report is too lengthy to summarize in detail. But you can get a sense of the breadth and depth of it by looking at its table of contents:

Foreword

Acknowledgments

Part I. Introduction, Summaries and Conclusions

Part II. Evidence of the Relationship of Smoking to Health

Chapters 3 and 4 of the report are of particular interest. They contain a lengthy review of the struggle with the issue of identifying causation between smoking and health in the absence of controlled experiments. The arguments concerning the causal effects of tobacco smoke convey a sense of the serious work that can go into a government document, and they provide a good review of a central theme in this textbook, and in all scientific research. The argument starts by noting an association between tobacco smoke and the likelihood of an early death.

> The array of information from the prospective and retrospective studies of smokers and nonsmokers clearly establishes an association between cigarette smoking and substantially higher death rates. (U.S. Public Health Service, 1964, 30)

But, the survey data consulted by the Committee exhibited the typical problems we have discussed in several previous chapters. For example, the average nonresponse rate was 32% for the seven prospective studies. The Committee estimated that nonresponse may have inflated the relationship between smoking and health problems. The Committee, nonetheless, concluded in specific instances that a causal connection does exist between tobacco smoke and disease. For example:

> Cigarette smoking is causally related to lung cancer in men; the magnitude of the effect of cigarette smoking far outweighs all other factors. The data for women, though less extensive, point in the same direction. (U.S. Public Health Service, 1964, 31)

In the absence of experiments with humans, how was the committee able to draw these types of conclusions? Certainly, the variety of evidence was an important factor. In addition—and this is critical, as you've seen in previous chapters—*research must* control, *as far as possible, variables that might cause people both to smoke and to contract diseases associated with tobacco smoke*. The Committee reviewed studies with controls for a number of possible confounding variables, including age, occupation, urban–rural residence, exercise, drinking habits, and religion. Finally, it's pretty clear that lung cancer doesn't cause people to smoke. So another possible explanation of the association, reverse direction of cause, isn't plausible. The balance of evidence fairly strongly indicates a causal connection between smoking tobacco and various ailments.

Other Forms of Reports

Posters. Have you ever looked at posters in school projects or on display in public places like supermarkets? What do you recall about their appearance?

A common tendency with posters is clutter! Posters should be as sparse as possible, yet convey all the information that is necessary to understand the project.

Unnecessary items should be omitted. At a **poster presentation**, the researcher usually is present to answer questions during viewing.

Should you include mathematical equations and similar project details? Consider your audience. These details allow a clearer understanding of the actual steps involved and might be needed for some audiences, but not for others.

Typically, posters include:

- Name and affiliation of the researcher(s)
- Objectives of the research
- Theory and hypothesis (if relevant to the project)
- Background information (e.g., sample/population and field site, if applicable)
- Data, method of data collection, and method of analysis (keep these brief)
- Results (generally limit to easy-to-read graphs or simple tables)
- The most important conclusions from the study, highlighted.

Each of these topics can be separate sections of the poster put on letter-sized paper. Each section should have a heading. Use easy-to-read print. Some presenters use colored construction paper to matte each poster section; others use colored paper or color printers to print the individual posters. See the sample illustration in Figure 12.1.

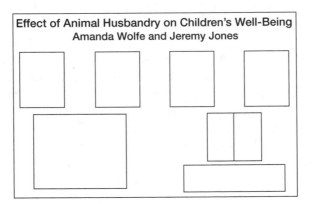

FIGURE 12.1.   Example of a Poster Layout.

Neatly display each individual poster section with a logical progression of ideas. Place a title in a "banner" format near the top. If possible, hang individual sections near eye level, particularly those most important to explain the research. Find out in advance whether you need to bring a large piece of posterboard to display your individual poster sections, push pins, tape, etc. Additional details about poster presentations are included in a later section of this chapter.

A BRIEF GUIDE TO REPORT WRITING

Getting Started—and Following Through

Chapter 6 offers some suggestions about writing reports about qualitative research, derived from Wolcott's (2001) book titled, *Writing Up Qualitative Research*. Because the suggestions generally apply to most scholarly writing, it's instructive to look at them again.

1. *You are "telling a story," and your own writing style can be used.* If you don't have a writing style (or don't know whether you have one), a good approach is to think about what *you* would need to know in order to understand your own project if someone else were describing it to you. How can you make your topic interesting to your readers? You aren't writing a novel or a poem, so your creativity is limited. Try stating your research problem in the form of an interesting question, for example:

"Are children who are taught to assume responsibility for care of pets more likely than other children to develop a sense of personal control?"

Or, you might get started with:

"The purpose of this study is. . . ."

As Wolcott points out, if you are stuck here, then perhaps the problem is "focus," meaning your topic likely is too broad. If you said something grandiose like "The purpose of this study is to solve the crime problem," you definitely lack focus. The "broad topic" problem is common among undergraduate students. Take time at the beginning to narrow your topic; it will save much frustration. Remember, knowledge advances in "baby steps." And look at published research articles as models. You don't want to "re-invent the wheel."

2. *Begin writing early, even before beginning data collection.* You always can change words, sentences, paragraphs, and sections of a paper. Use short sentences and paragraphs. Perhaps start by describing existing research you reviewed and the details of how you plan to obtain the data. Wolcott suggests writing an early draft, even before beginning the research. You don't have to show it to anyone. Just getting some ideas on paper (or in the computer) helps to clarify your thinking. Writing down some ideas also reduces the potential to get overwhelmed by the "blank canvas" problem that some painters face, the worry that the first brush stroke is so important it must be "perfect." Having something on paper, even if most of it is changed, will encourage you to work on it.

What about talking to another student or a professor about your research? These are good ideas. Explain your goals, and how you plan to collect data. Or, try writing to yourself in order to help pin down your thoughts. For example, if your goal is to describe adoptive parents' perceptions of the infant adoption process, how will you locate adoptive parents, how will you obtain data from them, and what do you think you might find?

In addition, be sure to: (1) use headings and subheadings, (2) check all references for accuracy, and (3) identify the citation style needed. Headings help to organize ideas. Look at the headings and subheadings of this chapter, or any other chapter in this book. Headings and subheadings also communicate the outline of what you have to say to the reader. Consider the difficulty of making sense of this book or any of your textbooks without headings! Check with your instructor about the use and preferred style of headings. It is likely that the headings for the journal article and evaluation report summarized in this chapter come closer to what you need for a student paper than the headings in a textbook.

Keep an accurate record of what you read and the full **citation** information for each source. One approach is to put all potentially usable information, including direct and indirect quotes, on individual note cards with all citation information. Or, you might create a computer file. The format of **references** varies somewhat from one publisher to another, although most now follow a convention similar to the one used in this book. Check the references in this chapter for one example, but follow the directions provided by your instructor. And, check all the references and citations for accuracy—it's very easy to make errors!

Avoid **plagiarism** "like the plague." What is plagiarism? Here is what *The Sociology Student Writer's Manual* (2002) says about it:

> Plagiarism is the using of someone else's words without giving that person credit. While some plagiarism is deliberate, . . . much of it is unconscious, committed by writers who aren't aware of the varieties of plagiarism or who are careless in recording their borrowings from sources. Plagiarism includes
>
> Quoting directly without acknowledging the source
>
> Paraphrasing without acknowledging the source
>
> Constructing a paraphrase that closely resembles the original in language and syntax. (Johnson et al., 2002, p. 118)

Cite *all* sources of ideas, quotes, and information not widely known, everything other than your own thoughts and information that is "common knowledge" (e.g., there are seven days in a week) and basic knowledge presented in many sources.

The **bibliography** of a social science research report includes all sources explicitly cited in the paper, books, monographs, journal articles, and government reports, as well as general periodicals and newspapers, encyclopedias and dictionaries, Internet resources, and personal communication. Usually the bibliography is titled "References." It appears at the end of the report. A guide such as the *Style Guide* published by the American Sociological Association (ASA) is essential. The ASA publication guides the preparation of materials for courses in sociology and related disciplines, such as criminal justice. It also serves as a reference to authors preparing manuscripts for all ASA journals and publications, such as the *American Sociological Review, Journal of Marriage and the Family*, and *Annual Review of Sociology*.

The ASA guide includes chapters titled "Some Matters of Style," "Some Mechanics of Style," "Preparing Your Manuscript for Submission: Details," and "Submitting Your Manuscript." Other information in the guide includes reference sources, and an appendix containing explicit examples of reference list formats (e.g., for citing books, journal articles, republished works, government sources, and archival sources). *The Sociology Student Writer's Manual* (Johnson et al., 2002) also contains a chapter on citations based primarily on the ASA *Style Guide*.

Like all writers, you need to read and revise your written drafts several times. Also, be sure to use "spell-check" in your word-processing program. But don't use it blindly. A recent report found that good students made fewer spelling errors when they did *not* use spell-check!

Components of a Qualitative Report

The organization of qualitative research reports varies considerably by topic and theoretical preferences of the author. And, there is considerably more variety in writing qualitative reports than quantitative ones. Consequently, the content of sections about methods and analysis of qualitative reports generally are comparatively long narrative accounts.

Lofland and Lofland (1995) present an outline that resembles the major topic headings of most qualitative scientific reports. The sections presented by Lofland and Lofland are:

- *Abstract:* The abstract contains a succinct, paragraph-length summary of the paper.
- *Introductory paragraphs.* The introductory section of the report states the main theory or thesis. Lofland and Lofland advocate stating it in the form of a proposition or relationship, using nontechnical terminology. In addition, the early paragraphs often state the relationship of the topic to social problems.
- *Early overview.* Following the statement of the thesis, inform the reader about the organization and content of the rest of the report.
- *Literature review.* Include a review of studies similar to yours, and tell how they relate to the research you are reporting.
- *Data sources.* This section is important. Field work is highly varied and most definitely not routinized. Inform readers how you identified your sample or social setting, how you gained access, whether you informed participants you were

doing research about them, about social conflicts between you and your subjects, about your emotional reactions and feelings of stress, about emotional entanglements between you and your subjects, and how you recorded your observations. As implied by this long list of topics and their complexity, this section may require several pages or, in a monograph, may take an entire chapter.

■ *Main body.* This section presents a summary of observations and some type of analysis. Clearly describe how the data and your analysis of it relate to the main thesis/theory stated in the introductory section. Make the connection explicit for the reader. Subdivide this section as required, and reorganize the subheadings until you "get them right."

■ *Summary and conclusions.* Include a titled section that summarizes the study, states your conclusions, discusses implications for theory, and proposes additional research to complement what you've done. Mention both the strengths and weaknesses of your research.

■ *References.* List complete references for each citation in the text. Verify that each reference is complete, accurate, and follows the prescribed format.

Components of a Quantitative Report

If you've collected quantitative (numbers-based) data, follow the outline for journal articles shown in the subsection in this chapter titled "Journal Articles and Similar Papers." You don't need to follow the headings exactly. Your report must include all the components, however.

An abstract is optional. Ask your instructor whether one is required. In either case, cover the following topics using specific headings that fit your paper.

■ *Introduction.* This section should give a succinct overview of the purpose of the study.

■ *Focused literature review and theory.* Make your case in this section. Cite only studies directly relevant to your paper. Perhaps a good general motto is: When in doubt, leave it out.

You might split this discussion into two or three sections, each with its own heading, depending on the nature of the study. For example, if there is controversy in the literature about some aspect of your study, you may need to devote a short section to describing the controversy and how you resolved it. Finally, state your hypotheses.

■ *Data.* Describe your data. If you developed a questionnaire or completed interviews, describe the questions for your key variables and explain how they reliably measure what you intend them to measure (validity). Describe the sample. How did you (or others) select it, and how were the data collected—by mailed questionnaire, by telephone interview, by in-person interview, or by observation? If you are doing secondary analysis using data from a large dataset like the General Social Survey, some of these details can be omitted. Instead, cite the documents related to the data (e.g., the codebook).

Precisely define each variable so the reader knows exactly what the numerical values mean. This means stating the code representing each value of categorical variables and the scale of continuous variables. For example, "marital status" (1 = married, 2 = divorced, 3 = widowed), and "age" measured in years. If you collapse age into a few categories, explain how you combined categories, what ages the new categories include, and explain how you determined the age intervals (e.g., split age at its median).

- *Method.* Describe the method(s) of analysis you used. This description should be brief, but show that you know what you're doing.

- *Findings.* Put your numerical results in tables. Just as in a journal article, "Table 1" should display univariate statistics like means, standard deviations, and frequencies for each variable in the study. For nominal-scale variables with many categories (e.g., 10 ethnic groups), include a frequency distribution, but display it compactly.

  For a student paper, the remainder of the tables likely are two- and three-variable cross-tabulations. Include chi-square tests of significance for each table. You might also try some more advanced statistics, with guidance from your instructor.

  Write some text summarizing the results you've put in the tables. Highlight the major results; do they support your hypotheses? What are the major exceptions, if any? Novices often repeat in the text every number in every table. This is *very* boring, and unnecessary—would you be interested in such detail? Summarize the results in a table so readers can see at a glance what you've found.

  Use the "table" function in your word processor to make the data tables. It's definitely worth the trouble to learn it!

- *Discussion and conclusions.* Start by reviewing whether your main hypotheses are supported. If they are, discuss the implications. If they aren't, speculate about possible reasons, but don't be too sure about the reasons. Remember: One study never "proves" anything. What you say is tentative and subject to further investigation. Discuss reasonable "next projects" to extend what you've done, or to test your speculations about why your theory was not supported.

- *References.* Find out the format required by your instructor for a quantitative report and follow it carefully. See additional discussion in the "Bibliography" section.

THE CLASS OR PROFESSIONAL CONFERENCE PRESENTATION

Experienced presenters will tell you that all materials for a presentation should be completed at least one week prior to the presentation date. You'll have time to attend to any last-minute details and can arrive at the session confident you are ready.

Papers presented at professional conferences generally are written in a format appropriate for a journal article. Sometimes these are read, but it's often better to give an oral presentation that isn't read word for word. If you have the software and time to prepare it, an electronic slide show outline provides a good set of notes for you and the audience. A one-page outline is shown in Figure 12.2.

Effect of Inbreeding on Early Childhood Mortality:
Twelve Generations of an Amish Settlement

Introduction
　　Overview of Lancaster Amish Settlement
Recent Familial Mortality Research
Data and Method of Analysis
Findings
Conclusions and Implications
　　Next Steps

FIGURE 12.2. One-Page Outline of a Paper for Presentation.

　　Prepare in advance to answer questions; be knowledgeable about your project. How can you prepare for questions others might ask? Think what you might ask if *you* were in the audience, and consider answers that would satisfy you. Also, ask your instructor, classmates, or another person to serve as a "practice audience." Practice will help you become comfortable discussing the details of the project. Your practice audience might ask some tough questions about your research; that's part of its function. Make notes of topics you are unsure how to answer, and do a little "prep work" on these topics before the presentation. Students who have presented papers and posters say that prior practice does help on the day of the presentation.

　　Find out the time allotted to your presentation, and practice staying within that time limit. You want to keep your audience "wishing to know more." For poster presentations, lay out the individual posters to approximate the way they will appear for the presentation. Remember to keep to the size allotted for poster displays. Check with your instructor or the organizer of the poster session. Get to the site early and, if possible, look over the room assigned for your presentation or poster displays. Early arrival also will allow time to manage the unexpected, should it arise. "Expect surprises" is a good motto.

　　Make copies of the study abstract to hand out. Include the title of your presentation, your name, institutional affiliation, and e-mail address. Particularly at professional conferences, sometimes an audience member asks for an abstract describing a study, in this case, your study.

　　Maybe you will become famous!

SUMMARY

This chapter summarizes the final step in the research process: The report of findings. It illustrates an important contrast in the way individuals learn compared with the way scientific knowledge accumulates. As we have emphasized repeatedly, a critical feature of science is that the findings are public and subject to formal peer review.

The primary focus in the chapter is on the written report. The written report is the most important mode of dissemination; other forms of reports typically begin with a written draft. The chapter begins with four examples of the major types of written reports. It also describes the poster display, a visual presentation increasingly seen at professional and student social science research conferences.

The next section of the chapter discusses insights and general guidelines for getting started and following through with the writing process. Next, the chapter reviews components of two types of reports, reports of qualitative research and reports of quantitative research. The chapter ends with some considerations for oral presentations in class and at professional conferences.

YOUR REVIEW SHEET: QUESTIONS DISCUSSED IN THIS CHAPTER

1. Suppose the findings of a study about how the social world works are judged to be statistically or clinically "not significant"—are they useless? Explain your answer.

2. What are the main forms of written documentation of social science research described in the chapter? Briefly describe each.

3. Where could one look to learn how to write a scientific research report?

4. What questions come to mind when you set out to write a "term paper" for a course? In social science research, where do answers to these questions come from?

5. About how long does it take to get a journal article published after submission? Explain why.

6. Why are scholarly journals probably the most important and prestigious sources for publishing research results?

7. What are the components of an empirical journal article using quantitative data? Summarize briefly the contents of each component.

8. Evaluation reports do not follow the same format as empirical journal articles like the *Demography* paper. Summarize the main ways they differ.

9. What is a monograph? How does a monograph differ from a book and from a book-length government report?

10. Describe some strategies for developing your own writing style.

11. Where can one look to find out what already is known on a topic? Be specific.

12. Why do writers use headings (and subheadings) in a paper?

13. What is a very common "error" in summarizing data tables?

14. What can be learned about presenting professional posters from looking at everyday examples?

15. What information should be included on a poster for a professional poster session?

16. In getting ready for a class or conference presentation (including poster displays), how can one prepare for questions that others might ask?

17. What is plagiarism? What steps should you take to avoid plagiarism?

END NOTES

1. Perinatal death refers to death in the first week for infants born alive. Neonatal death refers to death of infants who survived the first week but died within a month of birth. Postneonatal death refers to death of infants who survived the first month but died within the first year after birth.

STUDY TERMS

abstract Summary of the research; if used, it is presented at the beginning of a research report and seldom exceeds a paragraph or two in length.

bibliography A list of all sources explicitly cited in a paper—books, monographs, journal articles, and government reports, as well as general periodicals and newspapers, encyclopedias and dictionaries, Internet resources, and personal communications.

citation Reference in the text of a paper to a source of an idea, fact, or quotation—any material or idea that isn't "common knowledge" or the writer's own thinking. Sources include journal articles, evaluations, monographs, government documents, and so forth. Compare with references.

dissemination Spread or diffusion. In science, dissemination refers primarily to informing the scientific community and practitioners about research findings.

evaluation report Written document summarizing findings of an evaluation. The primary audience usually consists of professionals with an interest in the social intervention.

government report Written document produced or sponsored by a government agency. Usually it does not contain original research. Rather, it reviews research existing prior to the time of its publication. This is a distinctive difference between a government report and a monograph.

monograph Literally translated, "one writing." More precisely, a monograph is a book-length document written on one scientific topic. In social research, a monograph presents a detailed report of an extensive research program of study.

peer review The process through which each submission to a journal is evaluated by a panel of experts for importance and accuracy.

plagiarism Quoting or summarizing in writing someone else's ideas without crediting the source.

poster presentation Dissemination method using posters to summarize research findings, usually at a professional conference; the researcher usually is present during viewing of the poster to answer questions.

refereed journal Scholarly periodical that publishes only peer-reviewed papers. Issues are published several times a year, usually monthly, bimonthly, or quarterly.

references Alphabetized list of sources cited, appearing at the end of a document; compare with bibliography and citation.

EXERCISES

Exercise 12.1. Writing a Research Report Using Quantitative Data

Directions: Choose one of the exercises from earlier chapters in this book for which you collected data, or use an exercise that your instructor assigns. If you have not collected data for an exercise in this course, you may use data you collected for another course; check with your instructor. Otherwise, use the data in Table 12.1.

Table 12.1 contains frequencies for three variables: gunchild, gunadult, and gender. The two variables, gunchild and gunadult, are derived from the GSS questions:

Have you ever been threatened with a gun, or shot at? (1 = yes, 2 = no)
IF YES: Did this happen to you as a child or as an adult? (1 = child, 2 = adult, 3 = both)

TABLE 12.1.   Frequencies of Gunadult × Gunchild × Gender, for all Survey Years
These Questions were Asked in the GSS.

	gunchild = yes gender = male	gunchild = yes gender = female	gunchild = no gender = male	gunchild = no gender = female
gunadult = yes	152	20	2148	925
gunadult = no	358	145	5685	9868

Source: General Social Survey, cumulative data file 1972–2000 cumulative file (Davis, Smith, & Marsden, 2003). This table is for survey years: 1973, 1975, 1976, 1978, 1980, 1983, 1984, 1986, 1991, 1993, and 1994. Table entries are joint frequencies.

These two questions were used to create the variables gunchild and gunadult, just as the pair of questions for "ever hit" were used to create hitchild and hitadult in Chapter 11.

If you use the data in Table 12.1, report the following tabulations in your paper:

1. Univariate frequencies:

   gender

   gunchild

   gunadult

2. Bivariate tables:

   gunchild × gender

   gunadult × gender

   gunchild × gunadult

3. Trivariate table:

   gunadult × gender × gunchild.

Prepare a short report of your research in the format of a journal article. The paper should include (1) an introduction, (2) a statement of the research question and thesis (or hypothesis), (3) description of the method of data collection, (4) how you analyzed the data, (5) your findings, (6) what you conclude about your research, and (7) limitations of your study, as discussed in the relevant chapter(s) in this book.

If your instructor requests, add a title page, references and brief literature review. If your paper is based on a previous exercise or data collection for another course, include these items as an Appendix.

Exercise 12.2. WebProject: Locating Online Journals

Directions: Perform the following searches and obtain the requested information. Write a paragraph describing what you have learned about locating online journals. Print your search results and be ready to hand it in with this exercise.

1. **Search 1.** Connect to the Internet and go to the google search engine (*www.google.com*). Conduct a search for "social sciences index/abstracts with full text: journal list." How many full-text journals are listed at this site? Write the names of three full-text journals that are professionally reviewed.

2. **Search 2.** Type in the following URL: *http://www.loc.gov/*. What organization sponsors this Web site? Click on "Index A-Z", then go to "S." Then go to "Newspapers and Current Periodicals Reading Room." Find and list two magazine and newspaper sources with full text available online.

3. **Search 3.** Return to *www.google.com*. Conduct a search to find out: What journals does the University of California Press publish? Which are e-journals? Which e-journal was online first, and what was the date?

13 APPLYING PRINCIPLES OF "SCIENCE LEARNING" TO EVERYDAY LEARNING

INTRODUCTION: LOOKING AT HOW THE SOCIAL WORLD WORKS

A "skull-and-crossbones-type" picture on the cover of a popular magazine—although it is perhaps eye-catching, would you expect a sober, balanced assessment of an important social issue in the lead article?

A recent cover of *Sports Illustrated* (*SI*) shows a baseball crossed with two hypodermic needles, suggesting that steroid use in professional baseball is widespread—and that it's a big problem. It seems to imply a *big, bold* exclamation point**!** But what is the evidence for these implications? What does such a cover picture have to do with the use of steroids? And how much credibility are you willing to put in the "confessions of an MVP (most valuable player)?" This *is* only the cover however. Maybe the story presents enough supporting evidence to justify the hype. Part of this chapter reviews the content of the story, with the intent of evaluating how well it backs up the implications of the cover.

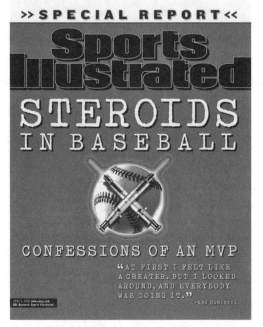

Sports Illustrated Cover, June 3, 2002.
James Porto / Sports Illustrated

Every day each of us is bombarded with numerous claims and counterclaims about many issues—steroids in baseball, global warming, the impact of violent TV programs on real violence in our culture, immigrants and immigration, universal health care, and a bewildering assortment of consumer choices. Whether commercial advertising for breakfast cereal or political arguments about "welfare," these claims share important features: (1) it's generally impossible to find definitive evidence in support of one view over all competing views, and (2) usual sources of information generally have some "ax to grind."

Goals of this Chapter

The study of methods in the social sciences teaches how to conduct *and* evaluate credible research. But do the standards of evidence apply only to formal research? No. Deciding whether 0 percent or 50 percent of professional baseball players take steroids has to do with sampling accuracy and measurement accuracy, topics that we've examined in earlier chapters.

Specifically, what can be learned from "science learning" that applies to everyday learning? This chapter isn't a definitive guide to everyday decision making. Rather, it attempts to achieve two objectives: (1) reinforce your developing skills about how to look for important criteria in decision making, and (2) illustrate the generalizability of basic principles of social-research methodology. The principles of evidence in social science research provide benchmarks for assessing the many claims we hear each day. Very often, the demands of evidence indicate we should withhold judgment—probably more often than most of us do. On the other hand, it's usually not possible to wait for convincing evidence before something must be decided.

The chapter summarizes five everyday situations. It reviews some of the basic terms in methodology, and the exercises at the end of the chapter ask you to break down each situation into the social-research components we've looked at in this book. *We strongly suggest you read the exercises first, then make notes about how to answer the exercises as you read—or answer the exercises as you read—* because the situations and related exercises are examples of fundamental principles about how to evaluate claims in everyday life.

STEROIDS IN BASEBALL

What are steroids, and why might they be a problem? A steroid is a complex chemical substance consisting primarily of hormones. Anabolic steroids are the class of steroids taken by athletes to improve their performance. *Stedman's Medical Dictionary* (1995) defines anabolic steroid as follows:

> *anabolic s[teroid].* A s[teroid] compound with the capacity to increase muscle mass:
> compounds with androgenic properties which increase muscle mass and are used in

the treatment of emaciation. Sometimes used by athletes in an effort to increase muscle size, strength, and endurance. (*Stedman's*, 1995, p. 1676)[1]

Side effects of steroids can be serious. WebMD summarizes potential side effects for one particular form of anabolic steroid—androstenedione, popularly known as "andro," infamous because of its use by the great home-run hitter, Mark McGwire.

Q: Since AN [androstenedione] is widely available and the FDA hasn't stopped stores from selling it, why is there so much concern about it, as reflected in the media?

A: Because AN is classified as a dietary supplement, it is not regulated by the FDA the way prescription drugs are (WebMD, 2002).

This same WebMD web page goes on to catalog the many serious risks associated with AN:

- The quantity of AN in dietary supplements varies, ranging from none to excessive dosage. Product labels do not indicate the quantity of AN.

- In high dosages typically used by athletes, AN may lead to numerous threats to the user's health, including problems with the liver, behavioral problems, sexual dysfunction, infertility, increased risk of heart disease, reduced supply of HDL (the "good" cholesterol) and muscle disorders.

- AN is likely to combine with other drugs users may be taking to produce still more medical complications.

There are at least two issues implied by the *Sports Illustrated* lead story: (1) how widespread (prevalent) is the use of steroids in professional baseball? and (2) how dangerous is their use to the health and welfare of the player?

Prevalence of Steroid Use

The title and headline for the *Sports Illustrated* article reads:

Totally Juiced

With the use of steroids and other performance enhancers rampant, according to a former MVP and other sources, baseball players and their reliance on drugs have grown to alarming proportions. (Verducci, 2002, p. 34)

Are these claims thorough and balanced? Neither the wording nor the content of the opening statement gives us much confidence that they are. The evidence consists solely of a sequence of testimonials and lengthy quotes from ballplayers, both major and minor league. Ken Caminite, the MVP referred to in the excerpt, is quoted estimating that 50% of players do it, but he later retracted that estimate

(*New York Times*, 2002). Jose Canseco is quoted as estimating that 85% use some kind of enhancer.

In short, the article doesn't contain an accurate estimate of the prevalence of steroid use in baseball.

What would an accurate estimate require? A probability sample of professional baseball players combined with repeated medical tests for many drugs. Since the tests aren't always correct, they ideally would be supplemented by anonymous self-reports from players. Careful development of a questionnaire or interview schedule combined with extraordinary efforts to gain the confidence of the players in the sample also would be required. Obviously, a popular magazine like *Sports Illustrated* isn't going to conduct such a study, though it might have commissioned one from a reputable research institution.

How damaging to the main theme of the story is the absence of a good numerical estimate of the prevalence of steroid use? Our study of sampling and qualitative methods suggests that much useful information isn't readily quantifiable and doesn't derive from a probability sample. A *New York Times* editorial judges the *Sports Illustrated* story to be credible, however, and calls for action based on it—

> Ken Caminiti, the former major league infielder, has backed off from his assertion in this week's *Sports Illustrated* that fully one-half of all major league baseball players use illegal steroids. But as the magazine demonstrates in compelling detail, Caminiti's underlying point is certainly true: The use of performance-enhancing drugs is far more widespread than previously suspected. It is also clear that the owners and the players' union, currently engaged in talks aimed at averting a strike, should move the drug issue much higher on their agenda. Unlike professional basketball and football, Major League Baseball has no steroid policy or testing program for big-league players. (*New York Times*, 2002, p. A14)

Why is the *New York Times* editorial staff convinced? Of course, we don't know, but we can surmise that it's because of extensive quotes from ballplayers and others in the sport. Some of the descriptions of how to obtain steroids and other drugs, based on interviews with players, contain so much detail that it's not likely that they were concocted on the spot for the reporter. It appears that "something is going on out there," even if we aren't able to quantify it exactly.

Still, *Sports Illustrated* doesn't document its methods. How did it select the sample of players it interviewed? How many players refused to be interviewed? Were the questions leading ones? Is the sample of players interviewed large enough to give a reliable assessment of the prevalence of steroid use in baseball?

We don't know the answers to these questions. But we do know that *Sports Illustrated* and the journalist have a vested interest in reporting spectacular findings. Maybe reporters selected pockets of players they already knew informally were steroid users. Given the high-pressure environment of the media, this is a plausible scenario—but, again, we don't know. Nonetheless, the article convinces us that there's some problem with steroid use in baseball, but we reserve judgment about whether it's serious enough to merit all the excitement.

Dangers of Steroid Use

The *SI* article mentions two types of health risks associated with steroid use: (1) injury and, (2) impaired body functions. The evidence of these risks comes primarily from (a) anecdotal (personal story) cases of specific players, (b) interviews with doctors who specialize in sports medicine, (c) informal citation of research findings, and (d) league statistics showing an increase in time and money spent on disability.

Caminiti, for example, won the MVP award in 1996, the year he started taking steroids. In the years after 1996, he was injured a high percentage of the time and never approached the MVP level of performance again. A lengthy, graphic quote from Caminiti recounts the problems he encountered because his body virtually shut down production of natural testosterone.

More generally, and more convincingly, *SI* cites medical research indicating steroid consumption damages the heart and liver, leads to hormone imbalance, is associated with strokes and aggressive behavior, increases cholesterol levels and diminishes sexual function (Verducci, 2002, p. 36).

But most of the article is devoted to anecdotal information and doesn't convey a good indication of how widespread these problems likely will be given the usual dosages taken by ballplayers.

The article also attributes increased player injuries and days on the disabled list to steroid use. It cites four types of evidence: (1) opinions of a couple of sports managers and an orthopedic physician, (2) an increase in the number of players on the disabled list, (3) a 20% increase in the average number of days on the disabled list comparing the 2001–2002 season to 1997, and (4) a 130% increase over 4 years in the cost to owners for pay to players who were unable to play due to injuries (Verducci, 2002, p. 44).

How convincing is this evidence of health risks? Each piece, taken separately, is only moderately convincing. Particularly the data on sports injuries is spotty and could be due to many variables not under **physical** or **statistical control**. Only one comparison year is used in each mention of a percentage increase, generating some suspicion that the comparison year might have been picked deliberately to emphasize the main point. In particular, it would be useful to know the natural rate of variability in these rates from year to year, and to see trend lines over several years. Is the trend markedly up, despite yearly fluctuations?

The *SI* article by itself is, at best, suggestive, but the evidence appears sufficient to justify drug testing in baseball, as in other major sports, the NCAA, and Olympic competition. Even if no more than 10 or 15% of players use/abuse steroids, we know from pervasive medical evidence of the dangers of steroids (not just the limited data cited in the *SI* article) that prohibiting steroid use and enforcing the ban by testing probably is justified.

You might say we've been too hard on *Sports Illustrated*, expecting the magazine to be something it obviously isn't—a research journal. In spite of reservations about the *Sports Illustrated* story, we do conclude that action probably is warranted. This conclusion illustrates a second important point—practical decisions nearly always must be made before all the evidence is in. But our critique brings out a very important principal—we shouldn't relax our standards for making decisions because good evidence is difficult to find.

GBL (GAMMA-BUTYROLACTONE)

The Web search of WebMD for information about steroids turned up another interesting issue: Presence of gamma-butyrolactone (GBL) in dietary supplements. GBL is a strong chemical used in household and industrial solvents. It also is found in dietary supplements where it is claimed to produce many "miracles"—relieve insomnia, produce growth hormones, reduce stress, improve sexual potency. The article makes some serious claims about the dangers of GBL:

Q: What does GBL do to the body?

A: So far, one person who consumed a product containing GBL has died, and 55 others have experienced side effects ranging from vomiting, aggression, and tremors to slowed heartbeat, impaired judgment (causing at least one traffic accident), seizures, breathing difficulties, and coma (WebMD, 2002).

There are two reasons for interest in the GBL article. First, it illustrates the potential importance of reliable information. Know your sources, and heavily discount sources with a vested interest in convincing you of something. In particular, know that most health supplements are not regulated, many are advertised in a manner implying that they produce "miracles," and many are quite dangerous. The article mentions several product names and listings of chemical ingredients, but it does not give a certain identification scheme, just a list of products and a list of possible chemical ingredients. This is important. New products containing GBL could appear at any time, and old products could reappear under a new name.

Secondly, the WebMD article itself is deficient. It states: ". . . one person who consumed a product containing GBL has died, and 55 others have experienced side effects?" What is the relevance of these figures? Probably one person who *did not* consume GBL also died and 55 others probably experienced the "side effects" during the same time interval referred to in the quote from WebMD. To make an informed judgment, compare the *incidence* of death and of the 55 other ailments among GBL consumers to the *incidence* among non–GBL consumers, preferrably controlling for other risk factors such as age, general health, and gender.

What is called for fits into a bivariate table. Think of a table with two categories of GBL—users and nonusers—and assume that GBL is the column variable. The dependent variable is died (yes, no) within a specified period of time. The percentages convert counts into rates that can be compared between users and nonusers, between columns.

The article doesn't even tell us what the base number is for the 1 death and 55 other ailments. Did 1 person die and 55 get sick out of 56, 100, 1000, 2000 . . . who took GBL? The answer makes a big difference in our assessment of the risk; in fact, it's impossible to assess the risk at all without the base number. As the article stands, we are left to assume that probably the numbers would not have been posted if the experts didn't have sufficient information for concern, a weak presumption.

Omission of the base of comparison is a frequent shortcoming in public discussions. For example, an architect specializing in building skyscrapers was interviewed soon after the World Trade Center was destroyed by terrorists. He was asked to assess the argument that few new skyscrapers should be built because they are vulnerable to air crashes

In response, he argued that high-rise building should not be restricted because most airplanes that crash into buildings do not hit skyscrapers. So what? There are a lot more short buildings than skyscrapers to hit, but there probably also is more air traffic around tall buildings.

This argument is missing a fundamental ingredient: a comparison. We need to know whether the *risk* of being hit by an airplane is related to the height of a building. This certainly seems like a plausible hypothesis, but the interviewer didn't even notice the lack of a comparison.

PONCE DE LÉON AND THE "FOUNTAIN OF YOUTH": HORMONE THERAPY AND WOMEN'S HEALTH

Ponce de Léon was a Spanish explorer who sailed the Caribbean seas searching for the mythical "fountain of youth." He didn't find the fountain of youth, but he did discover Florida. However, Ponce de Léon's exploits illustrate an important aspect of **sticky theory**. People believe what they want to believe and act on those beliefs.

Medicine is an arena particularly likely to generate inflated hopes and beliefs, probably because stricken people so fervently desire to be cured. A best-selling book titled *Feminine Forever* (Wilson, 1966) apparently was a major source of the idea that women can achieve everlasting youth and beauty by taking estrogen supplements at the onset of menopause. Wilson claimed a great medical discovery: Menopause is a curable disease—just take estrogen supplements! He traveled extensively promoting this idea and published his findings in reputable medical journals such as *JAMA* (*Journal of the American Medical Association*). The dust jacket of his book proclaims:

> A fully-documented discussion of one of medicine's most revolutionary breakthroughs— the discovery that *menopause is a hormone deficiency disease, curable and totally preventable*, and that every woman, no matter what her age, can safely live a fully-sexed life for her *entire* life. (Wilson, 1966, emphasis in the original)

A number of observational studies appeared to support this viewpoint. But it soon was found that estrogen supplements were associated with increased risk of uterine cancer. And later, Wilson's son reported that *Feminine Forever* and Wilson's research were financed by the Wyeth pharmaceutical firm—manufacturer of one estrogen supplement called Prempro (Kolata, 2002). However, evidence suggested that reducing the dosage of estrogen and combining it with progesterone reduces the risk of uterine cancer to near normal level. Therefore, estrogen alone was recommended for women who had had hysterectomies (removal of the uterus), and estrogen plus progesterone (usually a synthetic called progestin) for women with a uterus.

What was the basis for recommending hormone supplements? Numerous observational studies suggested a variety of benefits to combined estrogen and progestin supplements in postmenopausal women, including improved cardiovascular health and increased bone density. But none of these early studies were based on careful controls using random assignment to treatment and nontreatment groups. Instead, each woman (and her doctor) decided whether she should take the supplements. Women who self-selected themselves to take the supplements were, on average, of higher income, healthier, less prone to overweight, and less likely to smoke (Kolata, 2002). This self-selection of healthy women into the group who took hormone supplements created a positive relationship between hormone supplements and various health benefits. Self-selection created another example of a *spurious relationship*, as illustrated in Figure 13.1.

The Women's Health Initiative Study

In the late 1990s (1997–98) the Women's Health Initiative (WHI) began two clinical trials to assess the potential benefits of hormone supplements. The treatment in one of the studies combines estrogen and progestin, and the treatment in the other is estrogen alone, limited to subjects without a uterus. However, on May 31, 2002, the WHI suddenly halted the estrogen–progestin study, some 3 years before its scheduled completion. The research team judged that the risks of the supplements outweighed the benefits. They found slight, but statistically significant, elevations in the risk of breast cancer, heart attack, stroke, and blood clots in the lungs

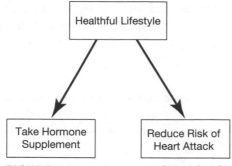

FIGURE 13.1. Spurious Relationship from Observational Studies of Potential Medical Benefits of Hormone Therapy in Postmenopausal Women.

and legs of those taking the supplements instead of the placebo (WHI, 2002). The difference between the risks of supplements versus placebo were very small, however. The biggest difference was an 18 in 10,000 (0.18%) increased risk for blood clots from taking the supplements. These small effects showed up as statistically significant because of the large sample size.

But the study didn't evaluate the short-term benefits of estrogen–progestin supplements in reducing the often severe symptoms of menopause—hot flashes, vaginal drying and thinning, and urinary-tract infections and incontinence (lost ability to control bladder). Since the increased risks associated with estrogen-progestin don't appear for several years and are very slight, the short-term benefits still may exceed the risks.

The halting of the estrogen–progestin study was a shock to much of the medical community. Previously, the standard had been to recommend hormone supplements for postmenopausal women. These recommendations were based on the extensive observational studies noted earlier (Kolata, 2002). Why did the WHI study more than offset earlier evidence of benefits of hormone supplements?

Subjects in a clinical trial are assigned at random to the treatment and control groups. In the WHI study, over 16,600 women were assigned at random to take either (1) a combination of estrogen and progestin supplements or (2) a placebo. Neither the subjects nor the research team knew who was taking the supplements and who was taking a placebo (Writing Group, 2002).

With random assignment, *all* factors that influence outcomes, like heart attack or bone density are, on average, the same at the beginning of the study for both those who did and those who did not take the supplements. With over 8000 women in each group, average differences between the experimental and control groups due to random variation are highly likely to be quite small. We "expect" them to be zero. Given appropriate **statistical tests**, differences in health outcomes between those who took supplements and those who took a placebo can be attributed with high confidence to effects of the supplements. But, remember, high confidence isn't the same thing as certainty.

GAMES OF CHANCE AND "OVERDUE" EVENTS

Our fourth application of science principles to everyday life is in the area of games of chance. Many believe events in games of chance depend on recent outcomes in the game—"I'm overdue" (for good luck), or "I'm on a run" (of good luck).

Sometimes recent events in games of chance do affect the next outcome. For example, if you have drawn 45 cards *without replacement* from a 52-card deck and have yet to draw a queen, your chance of getting a queen on the next draw is much higher than it was on the first draw: 4 out of 7 versus 4 out of 52. In contrast, the chance of getting a six on the next toss of a single die is unrelated entirely to what has happened in recent rolls of the die. It doesn't even depend on whether the die is "fair." What happens on the next toss is entirely unaffected by what happened on previous tosses. Similarly, the chance of getting a head on the next coin toss is exactly the same, no matter what the sequence of heads and tails on the previous tosses was. Those who believe otherwise are prone to lose money in games of chance. Such beliefs also are likely to overinterpret "slumps" in sports. What's a "slump"? Usually, it's just a random string of poor performances—no more unusual than a string of several tails in a row in the toss of a coin.

True to "sticky theory" predictions, even some very intelligent people keep meticulous records of the frequencies of numbers occurring in lottery jackpot drawings. However, look at Figure 13.2; it shows a typical frequency distribution for lottery-number picks from 1 through 49. It's clear you *should* bet on 45, and probably on 40 and 11, and you *shouldn't* bet on 13, 14, 30, 33—right?

Wrong! Don't forget there's natural variation in random events. If you doubt the "natural variation" argument in lotteries and other games of chance, look where the numbers in Figure 13.2 come from. They were generated by a computer random-number generator—a "pure chance" technique! A statistical test supports that these numbers were drawn at random (without replacement for each set of 5), with exactly the same chance for each number, from 1 through 49. Another sample of 490 numbers will produce similar "evidence" of numbers to avoid or to bet on, but they will be different than the numbers suggested by Figure 13.2.[2]

The case of the lottery-number picks illustrates some of the fundamental ideas in the sampling chapter.

- *Any one sample contains* sampling error—*probably more error than you expect.* In the "population" of lottery numbers, the proportion of each number is exactly 1 in 49. In any sample of 490, then, the "expected" frequency is exactly 10 for each possible number, 1 through 49. But, there is considerable variation among the frequencies, entirely due to random variation in the sample.

- *When you can't be sure, a* statistical test *is a device for making a decision.* In the case of the lottery numbers, the question is: Is the method of drawing winning numbers "fair"? Fair means each number has the same chance of selection every time. No matter how many instances of drawings you observe, however, some

Pick		Frequency
1	|***********************	11
2	|************************	12
3	|********************	10
4	|**************************	13
5	|****************	8
6	|****************************	14
7	|******************	9
8	|****************	8
9	|******************	9
10	|**********************	11
11	|********************************	16
12	|****************************	14
13	|**********	5
14	|**********	5
15	|******************	9
16	|**************************	13
17	|**********************	11
18	|******************	9
19	|********************	10
20	|****************	8
21	|******************	9
22	|********************	10
23	|**********************	11
24	|********************	10
25	|********************	10
26	|******************	9
27	|********************	10
28	|**************	7
29	|********************	10
30	|**********	5
31	|**************	7
32	|******************	9
33	|**********	5
34	|**********************	11
35	|****************	8
36	|**************	7
37	|******************	9
38	|****************************	14
39	|************	6
40	|********************************	16
41	|****************	8
42	|************	6
43	|************************	12
44	|**********************	11
45	|**************************************	19
46	|**********************	11
47	|**********************	11
48	|**************************	13
49	|**********************	11

FIGURE 13.2. Frequency Distribution of Lottery Number Picks: 1, 2, . . . , 49.

numbers will be selected more than 10 times in a sample of 490, and some less. A statistical test is based on a calculated probability that any sample of 490 numbers deviates from fair so much that the lottery likely is not fair. If the probability is not below some arbitrary threshold, typically 0.05 (or less), then make the practical decision to act as if the lottery *is* fair.

None of us make practical decisions by conducting statistical tests of significance. Moreover, there's little you can be certain about in life; yet you have to decide. Good judgment might boil down to an ability to make accurate intuitive probability assessments—judgments about the likelihood of what will happen if. . . . Those with "good judgment" might very well stand a better chance of "success" in life!

CAR RELIABILITY

How easy is it to find good information about the reliability of cars? A major source of car repair data is *Consumer Reports* (*CR*). *CR* publishes data annually from surveys describing the reliability of most makes and models, including separate reports for different engine and drive-line options (two-wheel drive vs. four). These data are extensive; how useful are they?

Consumers Union (CU) is a nonprofit organization. It accepts no commercial advertising. This is a major advantage over most other sources of information about automobile performance. Nearly all other magazines about automobiles are full of automobile ads.

The CU sample is very large (over 675,000 vehicles for the 2003 survey), but it's a nonprobability sample of subscribers. Moreover, some subscribers didn't return a completed questionnaire, and the response rate is not reported. Also, ratings are derived from respondent answers to questions about their vehicles and therefore are subject to "recall error," which translates into measurement error. *CR* readers are given no information about how serious measurement error might be.

Data are reported for overall reliability and for a list of 14 categories of problems like "Engine," "Cooling," "Fuel," "Ignition," "Transmission," etc. (*Consumer Reports* Annual Auto Issue, 2004, p. 82; *Consumer Reports Buying Guide*, 2004). Each vehicle is rated in each category by a system of small colored circles (or black and gray in the Buying Guide), as described in Figure 13.3. The percentages are percentages of respondents who reported problems they considered serious in the 12-month period prior to the survey.

What can be learned from ratings like this? The number of surveys returned for each make/model/configuration is much less than the total sample size. The sample size for each make/model isn't reported; *CR* doesn't publish the data if the sample size is below some threshold, but we don't know what the threshold is. The average sample size appears to be about 400 to 500. But the number obviously varies substantially among models since some makes and models are much more popular than are others. At least as important, there's no indication of the costs of the repairs. The difficulty of obtaining good cost data doesn't change the fact that we would like to know costs. In addition, the data contain very little indication of how many miles a vehicle will run before it's entirely worn out. This is an important factor for those who keep a vehicle for most of its useful life. The most recent

Most reliable	Category 1:	2.0% or less
•	Category 2:	2.0% to 5.0%
•	Category 3:	5.0% to 9.3%
•	Category 4:	9.3% to 14.8%
Least reliable	Category 5:	More than 14.8%

FIGURE 13.3. Consumer Reports Rating System for Auto Reliability.

Note: Consumer Reports uses a system of small red and black circles to designate the categories. But Consumers Union, publisher of *Consumer Reports*, refused permission to reproduce the chart as it appears in their publications. Notice that the category boundaries overlap. Does 2% go in category 1 or in category 2, for example. The categories are not mutually exclusive.

issue of the Annual Auto Issue, however, does present a couple of useful charts (*Consumer Reports* Annual Auto Issue, 2004, pp 16–17).

Finally, the data don't control for probable **selection bias** in the purchase of a vehicle. Why is the Honda Civic, for example, rated more reliable than the Chevrolet Corvette? Are Civic drivers more diligent about routine maintenance? Do they drive more conservatively than Corvette owners? Granted, control for "hard use" would be difficult or impossible to implement. But, again, the difficulty of implementing a procedure is irrelevant to its importance in evaluating the data. On balance, however, it seems likely that accurate statistical control for driver "personality" would have a modest impact on the ratings.

Do all these criticisms mean the *CR* car reliability data are useless? No! It just means they aren't as useful as we would like. The fact that *CR* doesn't accept any commercial advertising is an important consideration. No data are perfect, but "not perfect" isn't the same as useless. The standards of evidence you learn in formal science provide benchmarks to evaluate how skeptical you should be of information you use to make everyday decisions. You always should be skeptical to some degree or another. In short, consult the *CR* data and consult other sources too. Then, as usual, make the best choice you can make in the absence of full information.

SUMMARY

Several important principles of social science methods are illustrated in this chapter. Probably the most important single idea is that everyone faces "mega" information overload and must therefore depend on others for information. Judgments about the quality of that information are crucial. Three important criteria are illustrated:

- Evaluate the expertise/credentials of your sources.
- Pay close attention to possible vested interests—product sponsors, sticky theory devotees, someone with an "ax to grind," and so forth—that might affect what is claimed.
- Consider how fully and carefully the methods of inquiry are documented.

The point about credentials and vested interests go hand in hand. Several examples in this chapter emphasize these two considerations. The *Sports Illustrated* story about steroids in baseball obviously was motivated by an interest in selling advertising and copies of the magazine.

In the case of hormone replacements, **cause-and-effect** claims must be subject to independent review by people with enough expertise to evaluate the claims *and* without vested interest in the outcome. Given the substantial monetary incentives for persuading people they need to purchase something, it's not surprising that often it isn't easy to spot "tainted" information. In contrast, *Consumer Reports* auto repair data aren't motivated by any direct commercial interest in selling one make of automobile instead of another, but it must sell subscriptions to continue its operation.

When in doubt, recall important principles you've learned in this text—

- Look for a **spurious relationship** and understand the power of **random assignment** to avoid misinterpreting an incidental association as if it were due to cause and effect. Think of the hormone supplement case as one example (Figure 13.1).

- Insist on a *base of comparison*—raw numbers seldom are useful reported in isolation. Percentages, for example, tell "how many per 100" died who took GBL. And this should be compared to how many per 100 died who did *not* take GBL.

- Develop good judgment about *sampling variability*—how results can vary from sample to sample (**sampling error**) without being due to any systematic process such as bias in a lottery.

- Pay close attention to potential sources of *survey error*, such as **non-response error** and respondent misreport (**measurement error**).

- Develop a good sense of the roles of **qualitative** and **quantitative data**. Many aspects of human affairs are nearly impossible to quantify where qualitative observation may provide a lot of insight. But qualitative observation is difficult to replicate.

As a final point, *begin to notice how the same themes about quality of information run through many real-world situations*. The critical principles in social science methods apply to nearly every situation—in both research and everyday learning—in which a decision must be made based on information.

YOUR REVIEW SHEET: QUESTIONS DISCUSSED IN THIS CHAPTER

1. Summarize how formal social science standards and procedures apply to everyday learning.

2. Summarize the evidence presented by *SI* that steroid use is widespread in major league baseball. What procedures would be needed to produce accurate estimates of the percentage of players who use steroids? Does *SI* meet these standards? If not, could one devise a study that would? Explain briefly.

3. Summarize and evaluate the evidence relating to sports injuries presented by *SI*.

4. Why was the evidence weak indicating that women should take hormone supplements after menopause? Why is the Women's Health Initiative study using random assignment strong enough to offset prior evidence indicating benefits of the hormone supplements?

5. What basic principle of science is violated by the connection between the author of *Feminine Forever* and the pharmaceutical industry, and, more generally, by sources of information about medicinal drugs?

6. How is a "run" of good luck in cards similar to a hitting "streak" in baseball? How is this point illustrated in Figure 13.2?

7. What sampling principles are illustrated by the simulated lottery numbers in Figure 13.2?

8. What are the main strong points of the *CR* data on car reliability? What are the weaknesses? What important general principle does the text claim is illustrated by the strengths and weaknesses of the *CR* data?

9. In your own words, what are the five principles of a scientific approach with which to judge the quality of information encountered in everyday life?

STUDY TERMS

cause and effect Change of the cause is followed by a change in the effect, "everything else being equal," as illustrated by *if . . . then* statements.

control To "hold constant" one or more variables that might be related to both the presumed cause and the presumed effect.

measurement error Difference between an observed value and the "true" value of a variable.

nonresponse Failure of selected sample members to complete all or part of a survey. *Nonresponse error* comes from differences between individuals who complete and return a questionnaire and those who do not.

overgeneralization Concluding that a pattern observed in a too-small number of instances is typical of many/all other situations that you have not observed. For example, you observe in 100 lottery drawings that the number 22 turns up more often than any other number, and conclude that future drawings are more apt to turn up 22 than any other number.

physical control Control in which the researcher determines the values of all causes thought to affect the outcome. Social researchers have limited ability to use physical controls and must rely on statistical control.

qualitative data Information collected from unstructured observation intended to represent meanings, symbols, descriptions, concepts, and characteristics of people.

quantitative data Information collected from comparatively structured research in which the observations are converted into numbers.

random assignment A "pure chance" procedure used to determine which subjects are in the treatment group and which subjects are in the control group. The purpose is to improve *internal validity* (did the treatment have the effect attributed to it?).

sampling error Difference between a sample statistic and population parameter when a sample is used to describe the population.

selection bias People decide for themselves whether to engage in an activity such as taking estrogen. The basis of their decision, such as healthy lifestyle, affects an outcome such as a heart attack. The result is a spuriously low incidence of heart attack among women who took estrogen.

spurious association Noncausal relationship between two variables, generated by their common dependence on at least one other variable.

statistical control An approximation of physical control in which a relationship between two variables is observed within constant levels of control variable(s).

statistical test A procedure for making a decision as to whether a population value of a statistic is some stated value, called the "null hypothesis." Usually the null hypothesis states no relationship between two variables. Statistical tests are the primary technical method of *statistical inference* (process of drawing conclusions about a population using data from a sample).

sticky theory A phrase we invented to try to capture the widespread observation that people sometimes hold ideas so strongly that they refuse to acknowledge evidence that contradicts their ideas.

END NOTES

1. *Androgenic* refers to any substance (e.g., testosterone) that stimulates the development of secondary male sex characteristics.
2. This scenario roughly follows the rules of the PowerBall game, which now specifies a pick of five numbers from 1 through 53 plus a pick of one "PowerBall" in the range of 1 through 42.

EXERCISES

Exercise 13.1. The Critical Consumer—Issue 1

Directions: Answer each of the questions by referring to the *SI* story about "steroid use in professional baseball."

1. In a brief sentence, define the population for the steroid story.
2. The primary variable in the steroids story is consumption of anabolic steroids. Write two operational definitions of this variable: (a) as a numeric variable, and (b) as a categorical variable with two categories (dichotomous).

3. Write a brief discussion of the difficulties you might encounter getting accurate measurements of steroid use in a survey, and with medical tests.

4. The steroid story is primarily a descriptive study, the goal being to describe the extent of use/abuse of steroids in professional baseball. But it also discusses the relationship between steroid use and various health problems. One outcome of steroid use mentioned in the story is reduced production of testosterone. Assume you collapse testosterone production into a dichotomy: (a) normal or above, and (b) below normal. Use the dichotomous version of your steroid-use variable (Question 2) to produce a (hypothetical) 2 × 2 table showing percentages supporting the view that steroid use reduces testosterone production to below-normal levels. (Assume a sample of males.) Describe the relationship in one or two sentences.

5. Suppose the relationship you produced in your answer to Question 4 is observed in real data. Identify and discuss variables that might generate this relationship even if steroid use didn't affect testosterone production. Or argue that it's difficult to explain away this relationship as spurious even if it's not observed in a randomized experiment.

Exercise 13.2. The Critical Consumer—Issue 2

Directions: Answer each question referring to the story about "hormone therapy and women's health."

1. Identify the dependent variable(s) and primary independent variable in the hormone-supplements example. Identify at least one potential control variable.

2. In your own words, describe why early research showing health benefits of estrogen or estrogen–progestin supplements probably mistook a spurious relationship to be a causal relationship. In your answer, first define a spurious relationship and draw a path (arrow) diagram illustrating this idea. Then, fill in the path diagram with the names of the variables in the hormone supplement debate.

3. Explain why a randomized clinical trial isn't subject to the same criticism about spuriousness that applies to observational studies.

4. The WHI halted its very large clinical trial ($n > 16,000$) early because of small elevations in health risks for women assigned to take the hormones instead of the placebo. The biggest elevation of risk was for the risk of blood clots: 34 of 10,000 for women taking the supplement versus 16 of 10,000 for women taking the placebo. Why is such a small difference still statistically significant? (*Hint:* If there had been only 1000 women in the study do you think this difference (34 vs. 16 in 10,000) would be statistically significant?)

5. Discuss the practical (logistics and funding) and ethical issues you think might arise if a large clinical trial were undertaken to test the following two hypotheses:

   a. There's an interaction between hormone supplements and a healthful lifestyle (consisting of a "preferred" diet and regular vigorous exercise). The interaction is such that the hormone supplements are beneficial for those with the "healthful lifestyle" but detrimental for those who don't follow the healthful lifestyle.

b. The observed health risks of the hormone supplements in the WHI study accelerate over time such that the risk goes up much faster after the first 5 years than it did in the initial period.

6. On balance, based on your current limited information, do you judge either hypothesis in Question 5 to be worth the expense? If so, which one (or both), and why? Do you think a study to test these hypotheses would pass the IRB (human-subjects review board)? Why or why not?

Exercise 13.3. The Critical Consumer—Issue 3

Directions: Answer the following questions referring to the discussion about "*CR* auto reliability data."

1. Consider the auto reliability data as a relationship between two variables: (a) make of automobile, and (b) frequency of repairs. Which of these two variables is the independent variable? The dependent variable?

2. Which type of variable is make of automobile: nominal, ordinal, interval, ratio? Explain why.

3. Construct a (hypothetical) two-variable table for make of automobile and cost of repairs, with make of automobile as the column variable. Show a strong relationship in the table. Use just two makes of automobile, and choose one make that has a large, powerful engine and one that has a small engine and gets high fuel economy. What essential feature of a variable is missing from your automobile-make variable?

4. Explain how the difference in repair costs between the two makes in your example might be due to something other than the quality of the make of automobile—that is, to the driving "personality" of the car owners. Construct a three-variable table illustrating your argument.

5. Put on your "imagination hat." Suppose you were to do a randomized field trial to study the inherent reliability built into five makes/models of automobile. Describe the procedures for this study. What records would you require participants to keep? First, discuss how you would operationalize the concept of "inherent reliability." Then explain how the random assignment of the make/model of automobile to subjects in your experiment gets around the potential for spuriousness described in Question 4.

Exercise 13.4. The Critical Consumer—Issue 4: Independent Peer Review in Everyday Learning

Directions: Write a brief essay about the role of independent peer review in science and how it might apply to practical decisions. Address the following issues:

1. Why is it so difficult to identify a cause-and-effect relationship?

2. Draw on examples in this chapter to illustrate some of the subtle and not-so-subtle ways vested interests may influence conclusions about causation.

3. Contrast the norm of independent review with the influence of vested interests.

TABLE 13.1. Hitting Streaks—Rookie Big-League Player (0.300 batting average).

Total at Bats	Length of Streak	Streak									
10	10	Out	Out	Out	Out	Out	Out	Out	Out	Out	Out
11	1	Hit									
13	2	Out	Out								
17	4	Hit	Hit	Hit	Hit						
18	1	Out									
19	1	Hit									
21	2	Out	Out								
22	1	Hit									
23	1	Out									
24	1	Hit									
26	2	Out	Out								
27	1	Hit									
30	3	Out	Out	Out							
33	3	Hit	Hit	Hit							
34	1	Out									
35	1	Hit									
37	2	Out	Out								
38	1	Hit									
46	8	Out	Out	Out	Out	Out	Out	Out	Out		
47	1	Hit									
48	1	Out									
50	2	Hit	Hit								
54	4	Out	Out	Out	Out						
55	1	Hit									
61	6	Out	Out	Out	Out	Out	Out				
63	2	Hit	Hit								
66	3	Out	Out	Out							
67	1	Hit									
68	1	Out									
70	2	Hit	Hit								
71	1	Out									
73	2	Hit	Hit								
81	8	Out	Out	Out	Out	Out	Out	Out	Out		
82	1	Hit									
86	4	Out	Out	Out	Out						
87	1	Hit									
88	1	Out									
90	2	Hit	Hit								
91	1	Out									
93	2	Hit	Hit								
98	5	Out	Out	Out	Out	Out					
99	1	Hit									
102	3	Out	Out	Out							

Exercise 13.5. Batting Slumps and Hot Streaks

Directions: Consider Steve Steroidal Massif, a rookie major-league baseball player with a 0.300 lifetime batting average (he has, in the past, hit safely 3 times for every 10 times at bat). Steve has a stellar minor-league record and has just been "brought up" to his major-league parent club to help revive it from its current standing in the cellar of its division. Table 13.1 shows Steve's first 102 at-bats. (This is a little less than 1/5 of a season for a starter.)

1. Suppose you are the manager of this ball club. After Steve's first 10 at-bats, would you (a) bench him, (b) send him back to the minor leagues, (c) stick with him at least for the rest of the season? Explain why.
2. Identify the streaks that you consider to be "slumps" in Steve's first 102 at-bats.
3. Identify the streaks which you think are "hot streaks" in Steve's first 102 at-bats.
4. Explain why the "slumps" are longer than the "hot streaks."
5. Suppose the hitting records in Table 13.1 were generated at random—as they were, in fact. What implications does this fact have for your answers to Questions 2 and 3? Offer a definition of a streak. (*Hint:* Base your definition on the idea that the chance of getting a hit depends partly on how well the hitter has done in recent at-bats.)

TABLE 13.2. Hitting Streaks—Veteran Big-League Player (0.300 lifetime batting average).

Career at Bats	Length of Streak	Streak									
398	18	Out	Out	Out	Out	Out	Out	Out	Out	Out	Out
		Out	Out	Out	Out	Out	Out	Out	Out		
537	6	Hit	Hit	Hit	Hit	Hit	Hit				
565	15	Out	Out	Out	Out	Out	Out	Out	Out	Out	Out
		Out	Out	Out	Out	Out					
997	15	Out	Out	Out	Out	Out	Out	Out	Out	Out	Out
		Out	Out	Out	Out	Out					
1320	25	Out	Out	Out	Out	Out	Out	Out	Out	Out	Out
		Out	Out	Out	Out	Out	Out	Out	Out	Out	Out
		Out	Out	Out	Out	Out					
1583	5	Hit	Hit	Hit	Hit	Hit					
2559	22	Out	Out	Out	Out	Out	Out	Out	Out	Out	Out
		Out	Out	Out	Out	Out	Out	Out	Out	Out	Out
		Out	Out								
2905	18	Out	Out	Out	Out	Out	Out	Out	Out	Out	Out
		Out	Out	Out	Out	Out	Out	Out	Out		

Exercise 13.6. Batter Up!

Directions. Table 13.2 shows a selection of "streaks" for a veteran player, Grant Greybeard. Grant has a lifetime big-league batting average of 0.300 (same as rookie Steve). Answer the questions below referring to Table 13.2. Remember, the numbers in Table 13.2 were made up to look like batting averages using a random number generator.

1. Explain why Grant has more long streaks and slumps than Steve. (*Hint:* Consider number of career at-bats in your answer.) Does your answer contain a definite guarantee that Grant will have longer streaks than Steve? Why?

2. Note that out of at least 2905 career at bats for Grant, only 8 are displayed in Table 13.2. How many more hitting "slumps" as long as 25 do you think might have occurred in Grant's career? Answer in qualitative terms (none, one or two, a few, several, etc.). Explain why.

3. How often do you think people mistake an unusual sequence of events, like a hitting slump or streak, for some mysterious, or not so mysterious, unseen "force" (causal mechanism)? Describe an example you have seen that might illustrate this point, or make up a realistic example if you can't think of one you have seen.

APPENDIX A
CODE OF ETHICS

This appendix contains selected excerpts from the Code of Ethics of the American Sociological Association and from the Code of Ethics of the American Anthropological Association.

The American Sociological Association Code of Ethics consists of four major parts:

Introduction

Preamble

General Principles

Ethical Standards

The excerpts in this appendix include the first paragraph of the Introduction and the entire section on General Principles.

The Code of Ethics of the American Anthropological Association contains eight sections:

I. Preamble

II. Introduction

III. Research

IV. Teaching

V. Application

VI. Epilogue

VII. Acknowledgments

VIII. Other Relevant Codes of Ethics

This appendix contains Section III, Research.

AMERICAN SOCIOLOGICAL ASSOCIATION CODE OF ETHICS

The American Sociological Association's (ASA) Code of Ethics sets forth the principles and ethical standards that underlie sociologists' professional responsibilities and conduct. These principles and standards should be used as guidelines when examining everyday professional activities. They constitute normative statements for sociologists and provide guidance on issues that sociologists may encounter in their professional work.

General Principles

The following General Principles are aspirational and serve as a guide for sociologists in determining ethical courses of action in various contexts. They exemplify the highest ideals of professional conduct.

Principle A: Professional Competence. Sociologists strive to maintain the highest levels of competence in their work; they recognize the limitations of their expertise; and they undertake only those tasks for which they are qualified by education, training, or experience. They recognize the need for ongoing education in order to remain professionally competent; and they utilize the appropriate scientific, professional, technical, and administrative resources needed to ensure competence in their professional activities. They consult with other professionals when necessary for the benefit of their students, research participants, and clients.

Principle B: Integrity. Sociologists are honest, fair, and respectful of others in their professional activities—in research, teaching, practice, and service. Sociologists do not knowingly act in ways that jeopardize either their own or others' professional welfare. Sociologists conduct their affairs in ways that inspire trust and confidence; they do not knowingly make statements that are false, misleading, or deceptive.

Principle C: Professional and Scientific Responsibility. Sociologists adhere to the highest scientific and professional standards and accept responsibility for their work. Sociologists understand that they form a community and show respect for other sociologists even when they disagree on theoretical, methodological, or personal approaches to professional activities. Sociologists value the public trust in sociology and are concerned about their ethical behavior and that of other sociologists that might compromise that trust. While endeavoring always to be collegial, sociologists must never let the desire to be collegial outweigh their shared responsibility for ethical behavior. When appropriate, they consult with colleagues in order to prevent or avoid unethical conduct.

Principle D: Respect for People's Rights, Dignity, and Diversity. Sociologists respect the rights, dignity, and worth of all people. They strive to eliminate bias in their professional activities, and they do not tolerate any forms of discrimination based on age; gender; race; ethnicity; national origin; religion; sexual orientation; disability; health conditions; or marital, domestic, or parental status. They are sensitive to cultural, individual, and role differences in serving, teaching, and studying groups of people with distinctive characteristics. In all of their work-related activities, sociologists acknowledge the rights of others to hold values, attitudes, and opinions that differ from their own.

Principle E: Social Responsibility. Sociologists are aware of their professional and scientific responsibility to the communities and societies in which they live and work. They apply and make public their knowledge in order to contribute to the public good. When undertaking research, they strive to advance the science of sociology and to serve the public good.

Source: American Sociological Association Code of Ethics. Available at: http://www.asanet.org/members/ecointro.html#intr. (Accessed May 30, 2004.)

CODE OF ETHICS OF THE AMERICAN ANTHROPOLOGICAL ASSOCIATION

In both proposing and carrying out research, anthropological researchers must be open about the purpose(s), potential impacts, and source(s) of support for research projects with funders, colleagues, persons studied or providing information, and with relevant parties affected by the research. Researchers must expect to utilize the results of their work in an appropriate fashion and disseminate the results through appropriate and timely activities. Research fulfilling these expectations is ethical, regardless of the source of funding (public or private) or purpose (i.e., "applied," "basic," "pure," or "proprietary").

Anthropological researchers should be alert to the danger of compromising anthropological ethics as a condition to engage in research, yet also be alert to proper demands of good citizenship or host–guest relations. Active contribution and leadership in seeking to shape public or private sector actions and policies may be as ethically justifiable as inaction, detachment, or noncooperation, depending on circumstances. Similar principles hold for anthropological researchers employed or otherwise affiliated with nonanthropological institutions, public institutions, or private enterprises.

A. Responsibility to people and animals with whom anthropological researchers work and whose lives and cultures they study

1. Anthropological researchers have primary ethical obligations to the people, species, and materials they study and to the people with whom they work. These obligations can supersede the goal of seeking new knowledge, and can lead to decisions not to undertake or to discontinue a research project when the primary obligation conflicts with other responsibilities, such as those owed to sponsors or clients. These ethical obligations include:

- To avoid harm or wrong, understanding that the development of knowledge can lead to change which may be positive or negative for the people or animals worked with or studied
- To respect the well-being of humans and nonhuman primates

- To work for the long-term conservation of the archaeological, fossil, and historical records

- To consult actively with the affected individuals or group(s), with the goal of establishing working relationships that can be beneficial to all parties involved

2. Anthropological researchers must do everything in their power to ensure that their research does not harm the safety, dignity, or privacy of the people with whom they work, conduct research, or perform other professional activities. Anthropological researchers working with animals must do everything in their power to ensure that the research does not harm the safety, psychological well-being or survival of the animals or species with which they work.

3. Anthropological researchers must determine in advance whether their hosts/ providers of information wish to remain anonymous or receive recognition, and make every effort to comply with those wishes. Researchers must present to their research participants the possible impacts of the choices, and make clear that despite their best efforts, anonymity may be compromised or recognition fail to materialize.

4. Anthropological researchers should obtain in advance the informed consent of persons being studied, providing information, owning or controlling access to material being studied, or otherwise identified as having interests which might be impacted by the research. It is understood that the degree and breadth of informed consent required will depend on the nature of the project and may be affected by requirements of other codes, laws, and ethics of the country or community in which the research is pursued. Further, it is understood that the informed consent process is dynamic and continuous; the process should be initiated in the project design and continue through implementation by way of dialogue and negotiation with those studied. Researchers are responsible for identifying and complying with the various informed consent codes, laws and regulations affecting their projects. Informed consent, for the purposes of this code, does not necessarily imply or require a particular written or signed form. It is the quality of the consent, not the format, that is relevant.

5. Anthropological researchers who have developed close and enduring relationships (i.e., covenantal relationships) with either individual persons providing information or with hosts must adhere to the obligations of openness and informed consent, while carefully and respectfully negotiating the limits of the relationship.

6. While anthropologists may gain personally from their work, they must not exploit individuals, groups, animals, or cultural or biological materials. They should recognize their debt to the societies in which they work and their obligation to reciprocate with people studied in appropriate ways.

B. Responsibility to scholarship and science

1. Anthropological researchers must expect to encounter ethical dilemmas at every stage of their work, and must make good-faith efforts to identify potential ethical claims and conflicts in advance when preparing proposals and as projects

proceed. A section raising and responding to potential ethical issues should be part of every research proposal.

2. Anthropological researchers bear responsibility for the integrity and reputation of their discipline, of scholarship, and of science. Thus, anthropological researchers are subject to the general moral rules of scientific and scholarly conduct: they should not deceive or knowingly misrepresent (i.e., fabricate evidence, falsify, plagiarize), or attempt to prevent reporting of misconduct, or obstruct the scientific/scholarly research of others.

3. Anthropological researchers should do all they can to preserve opportunities for future fieldworkers to follow them to the field.

4. Anthropological researchers should utilize the results of their work in an appropriate fashion, and whenever possible disseminate their findings to the scientific and scholarly community.

5. Anthropological researchers should seriously consider all reasonable requests for access to their data and other research materials for purposes of research. They should also make every effort to insure preservation of their fieldwork data for use by posterity.

C. Responsibility to the public

1. Anthropological researchers should make the results of their research appropriately available to sponsors, students, decision makers, and other non-anthropologists. In so doing, they must be truthful; they are not only responsible for the factual content of their statements but also must consider carefully the social and political implications of the information they disseminate. They must do everything in their power to insure that such information is well understood, properly contextualized, and responsibly utilized. They should make clear the empirical bases upon which their reports stand, be candid about their qualifications and philosophical or political biases, and recognize and make clear the limits of anthropological expertise. At the same time, they must be alert to possible harm their information may cause people with whom they work or colleagues.

2. Anthropologists may choose to move beyond disseminating research results to a position of advocacy. This is an individual decision, but not an ethical responsibility.

Source: American Anthropological Association Code of Ethics. Available at: http://www.aaanet.org/committees/ethics/ethicscode.pdf. (Accessed May 30, 2004.)

APPENDIX B
RANDOM NUMBERS TABLE

To select a sequence of random numbers, select a starting point more or less at random. Move along the table selecting only numbers in the interval you need.

Example: Suppose you need 100 numbers in the interval 1 to 50, inclusive, and you begin with row 7, column 5. The first three two-digit numbers are 65, 02, 43. Discard 65 since it is out of range. Continue in the next *column* (78, 00, 82), or next *row* (67, 83, 44) until you have 100 two-digit numbers with values 1 or more and 50 or less. If you continue in the next *column* (78, 00, 82), discard all three numbers, because they all are out of range. If you go to the next row (67, 83, 44), discard 67 and 83 but keep 44.

547857	496038	784760	299502	851758	932493	806415	736667
598468	534028	354552	768698	914010	095604	897400	996895
870202	077750	460232	404114	219769	957246	205525	635094
354974	529215	112441	433642	025069	772063	586542	580751
182983	394227	068065	939192	212603	389630	427041	773515
713900	932525	297335	723956	762908	119432	895944	174988
616308	573693	937577	005379	650243	780082	530708	749178
225087	635372	930911	884602	678344	973758	380845	996777
657451	588074	581305	723636	988669	145165	650369	486021
164541	251208	351871	284285	216030	589167	877150	539773
315238	675740	433578	473041	595719	338420	890908	379281
676442	982750	339642	561394	999312	595885	223757	848839
881443	962575	451749	678496	112867	378954	326887	277493
850765	103340	386832	349406	205124	949795	844560	095201
074351	105262	609006	749360	218378	099366	721385	612013
014617	594500	005835	804689	523450	225873	399027	305492
587423	125512	208907	512185	703842	911664	891234	829322
718335	355549	609486	864109	893593	160174	908978	418575
177269	321163	450220	097151	172184	936909	239568	866222
415808	023537	105589	358430	323822	647459	557302	895008
375166	735870	203549	307084	551954	084628	750431	894228
321793	990894	142855	794080	439666	617698	913570	877756
588863	313263	018840	604945	364271	564930	673017	018390
149087	962287	751896	465155	424528	910735	202217	101670
229504	659695	034352	896204	923668	921413	994354	235201

820314	556780	428850	650645	099170	213221	226478	493143
306055	024519	518603	042758	918014	544581	584075	021236
502063	152045	210332	906664	831783	492162	039316	442335
084474	679844	584096	488837	077028	961135	179521	235111
504204	270915	442253	174235	664374	927071	263153	568883
765950	320226	155399	164501	883678	490388	457211	549015
990542	085225	858380	418055	463637	746182	121286	137485
205735	830855	798938	005698	228646	016715	147876	810011
487402	936262	115666	077702	798192	376416	175627	220030
638333	452325	973180	569962	497361	579333	282622	040115
525247	860954	251586	964360	911007	990991	285251	555679
438408	581097	849002	612365	182130	459728	309556	015240
086168	367444	189431	178167	187199	597675	330241	365588
987726	863029	393318	721358	456479	647820	365536	963197
526120	050771	708261	168321	013919	230449	569609	655896
499410	865459	750373	828724	828026	862151	902485	097174
948782	855328	269455	268403	051687	441005	996975	814158
892229	450015	482389	939828	258981	388390	963450	338193
514629	302015	922068	470031	025674	924809	488499	234889

APPENDIX C
INTRODUCTION TO THE GENERAL SOCIAL SURVEY (GSS)

The General Social Survey (GSS) is a repeating survey of U.S. households designed for use by the entire community of social-science scholars and students. In this respect it is unusual, if not unique, in the United States (Davis, Smith, & Marsden, 2003). Most surveys cover a restricted scope of topics such as consumer attitudes, aspects of aging, drug abuse and income and wealth. And, they are collected primarily for use by the principal investigator or for scholars in a narrow range of academic specialities. So the word "General" in the title carries a definite meaning.

The GSS is conducted by personal interview by the National Opinion Research Center (NORC). NORC is a nonprofit survey research corporation affiliated with the University of Chicago.

The initial survey was done in 1972. The interview schedule was short, consisting of just 20 questions. It was conducted primarily to validate the concept. In 1973, the National Science Foundation began funding an annual survey with a complete battery of questions. Each survey contains hundreds of questions. Annual surveys continued through 1993. Subsequently, the sample size was nearly doubled and the survey was conducted biannually. No surveys were conducted in 1979, 1981, and 1992, however, because of lack of funding. In the years before the biannual survey, sample sizes ranged from 1372 to 1860. Thereafter, sample sizes lie in the interval 2,765 to 2,992.

Current funding support comes from several agencies:

American Jewish Committee

Andrew Greeley

Centers for Disease Control and Prevention

Carnegie Corporation

Lilly Endowment Fund

Mellon Foundation

National Institutes of Health

National Science Foundation

Office of Naval Research

Smith-Richardson (NORC, 2003)

A new GSS sample is drawn for each survey; each respondent is interviewed just once. Consequently, study of individual change over time is not possible, but the GSS does permit study of aggregate trends in the repeated variables.

According to the NORC Web site (NORC, 2003), there are at least 7000 documented research applications of the GSS. In addition, it frequently is used in undergraduate and graduate college and university classes and by the news media.

Survey Content

A guiding principal of the GSS is replication. A large number of core questions are repeated in each survey, with the same wording. Repeated variables include demographic and stratification variables such as:

- Age
- Gender
- Race
- Marital status
- Education
- Occupation (prestige, D.O.T. [a description of type of work])
- Industry
- Income
- Hours worked per week
- Employment status
- Residence (region, size of city/town/rural area)
- Geographic mobility (change of residence)
- Nativity (born in U.S.?)
- Household composition
- Status variables like education, occupation and income
- Spouse's status variables like education, occupation and income

The GSS also contains many questions about a variety of social and political topics. Examples include:

- Party identification (Democrat, Independent, Republican)
- AIDS
- Alcohol consumption
- Alienation
- Race relations and attitudes
- Arrests
- Military (many questions related to the military)
- Attitudes and habits related to the "fine arts"
- Voluntary associations (many questions)

■ Religion

■ Civil liberties

■ Attitudes toward authority

■ Attitudes toward social issues like abortion, pornography, women's rights, minorities, euthanasia

■ Consumer behavior (e.g., auto purchase, garage sale, price haggling)

■ Family finance

■ Sign of the zodiac

The last item is kind of amusing. The GSS is designed and executed with the benefit of continual advice from many highly regarded scientists. So why does the GSS data contain the astrological sign of each respondent? Do the experts advising the GSS staff believe researchers might find scientific support for astrology? The Web site says—

Note 2: The data set contains the respondent's zodiac sign, calculated from the question on date of birth. The item was included to allow users to make an objective test of a widely held superstition. Alas, some critics have argued that we are encouraging anti-scientific ideas by including it. Either way, no one has yet found a reliable correlation with the item. (GSS Overview, 2003)

Beginning in 1985, a sequence of topical modules has been included. These modules do not appear on each survey but may be replicated periodically. Examples of topics include:

■ Political participation

■ Religion

■ Intergroup relations and conflict (questions about, e.g., protest movements, causes of poverty, group wealth)

■ Civic duty

■ Work and employment (questions about, e.g., corporations and unions, supervision, job control, pay)

■ Culture—fine arts

■ Multiculturalism

STUDENT PAPERS

NORC sponsors a pair of annual student-paper competitions, one for undergraduate students and one for graduate students. One winner is selected in each category by the principal investigators of the GSS, James A. Davis and Tom W. Smith, assisted by a panel of experienced scholars. College graduates are eligible for 1 year after graduation, so senior theses and master's theses are eligible for a time after leaving school.

Submissions must meet several criteria:

- Be original unpublished research
- Be authored by a student or recent graduate (1 year or less since graduation)
- Be based on GSS data or data in the affiliated international data bank called the International Social Survey Program (ISSP, 2003)
- Be 40 pages or less, including all tables, figures, and references

Submit two copies to Tom Smith by February 15—

Tom W. Smith

General Social Survey

National Opinion Research Center

1155 East 60th St.

Chicago, Il 60637

Check the Web page for further information (http://www.norc.uchicago.edu/projects/gensoc5.asp).

Papers are judged for:

- Contribution to understanding U.S. social life
- Quality of theory and data analysis
- Sophistication in application of methodological principles and statistical analysis
- Clarity of expression

Judging is completed in late April each year. Winners are awarded a $500 cash prize, a commemorative plaque, and a base package of the statistical software package SPSS.

GSS Data

The GSS data file contains coded responses to each question asked for every survey year. It is organized exactly like the example data matrices shown in Chapter 10, one field for each variable and one row for each respondent. Values for questions not asked in a given year are coded missing for every respondent in the years when the questions were not asked. The 1972–2002 data file contains nearly 44,000 observations. This is the sum of the number of completed surveys for all survey years combined up to and including 2000 (see Table AC.1).

Response rates have been about 77%, with the lowest 70% in 2000 and the highest 82% in 1993. These rates are among the best that can be expected with a large

TABLE AC.1.   GSS Sample Size and Response Rate by Year

Year	Frequency	Percentage	Response Rate (%)
1972	1613	3.7	N/A
1973	1504	3.4	N/A
1974	1484	3.4	N/A
1975	1490	3.4	76
1976	1499	3.4	75
1977	1530	3.5	77
1978	1532	3.5	74
1980	1468	3.4	76
1982	1860	4.3	78
1983	1599	3.7	79
1984	1473	3.4	79
1985	1534	3.5	79
1986	1470	3.4	76
1987	1819	4.2	75
1988	1481	3.4	77
1989	1537	3.5	78
1990	1372	3.1	74
1991	1517	3.5	78
1993	1606	3.7	82
1994	2992	6.8	78
1996	2904	6.6	76
1998	2832	6.5	76
2000	2817	6.4	70
2002	2765	6.3	70
Total	43698	100.0	

national survey. The interview currently runs about 90 minutes. So achieving this high response rate is good evidence of the dedication and talent of the NORC survey team. Table AC.1 reports sample sizes for all years and response rates for most years.

GSS Web Site

As you learned in Chapter 10, you need a codebook before the data are usable. The GSS Web site contains a complete online codebook (GSS Homepage, 2003).

http://webapp.icpsr.umich.edu/GSS

The codebook includes the exact wording of each question, the meaning of each value, the field spanned by the coded variable, a univariate frequency distribution and several lengthy appendices explaining details about the data collection and coding.

The site permits download of selected variables (click "Extract"). It also offers limited online data analysis (click "Analyze"). Figure AC.1 shows a screen shot of the Analyze facility. If you click "Extra Codebook Window, " as suggested at the bottom of the screen, a GSS codebook opens in a new window, leaving the Analyze screen viewable. The two windows permit cutting and pasting variable names from the Codebook into the "Analyze Dialog" boxes.

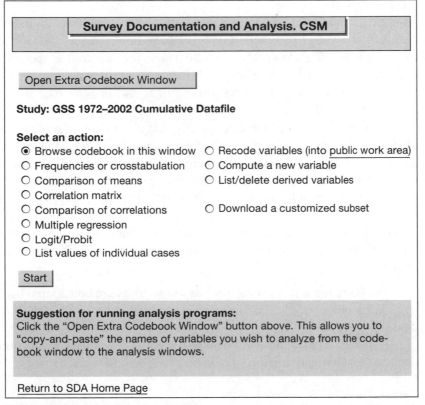

FIGURE AC.1.   GSS Analyze Window.

As seen, the facility provides for several types of analysis, and some capacity to recode variables and create new variables. Recoding includes operations like collapsing categories. For example, the GSS variable called wrkstat contains nine categories:

- Working full-time
- Working part-time

- Temporarily not working due to vacation, sickness, or other
- Unemployed or laid off
- Retired
- In school
- Keeping house
- Other
- NA

For the examples in Chapter 11 comparing the average income/wage of women and men, this variable was collapsed into full-time and part-time, leaving others out of the analysis.

A typical example of "compute a new variable" is creation of an index by taking the sum or average of several GSS variables. For instance, the GSS contains 18 variables indicating answers to attitudinal questions about free speech, e.g., "If such a person wanted to make a speech in your (city/town/community) against churches and religion, should he be allowed to speak, or not?" (Davis, Smith, & Marsden, 2003, p. 117).

After careful analysis of the face validity and checks for reliability, you might decide to take the average of some or all of these items as an indication of respondent attitude toward free speech. The calculations automatically exclude the missing-data categories, but check to be sure it is doing what you want it to do. Look at all the univariate frequencies of the items to see if everything is coded missing the way you want it.

Check the wording of each question. Some of them are worded so that a positive answer means just the opposite of the meaning of a positive answer in other questions. For example:

76. There are always some people whose ideas are considered bad or dangerous by other people. For instance, somebody who is against all churches and religion . . .

A. If such a person wanted to make a speech in your (city/town/community) against churches and religion, should he be allowed to speak, or not?

Response option	Code
Yes, allowed to speak	1
Not allowed	2
Don't know	8
No answer	9
Not applicable	BK (Blank)

80. Consider a person who advocates doing away with elections and letting the military run the country.

C. Suppose he wrote a book advocating doing away with elections and letting the military run the country. Somebody in your community suggests that the book be removed from the public library. Would you favor removing it, or not?

Response option	Code
Favor	1
Not favor	2
Don't know	8
No answer	9
Not applicable	BK (Blank)

A code of 1, "Yes, allowed to speak," for Question 76 indicates the respondent favors free speech, but a code of 1, "Favor," for question 80 means the respondent opposes free speech.

SDA Tables Program
(Selected Study: GSS 1972-2002 Cumulative Datafile)
Help: General / Recording Variables

REQUIRED Varible names to specify
Row:

OPTIONAL Variable names to specify
Column:
Control:
Selection Filter(s):   *Example: age (18–50)*
                                  gender (1)
Weight: No Weight

Percentaging: ☑ Column ☐ Row ☐ Total

Other Options
  ☐ Statistics ☐ Suppress table ☐ Question text
  ☑ Color coding ☐ Show Z-statistic

  Run the Table   Clear Fields

Change number of decimal places to display
For percents: 1
For statistics: 2

FIGURE AC.2.   GSS Frequencies and Cross-Tabulation Screen.

The nines and blanks should be coded missing for both questions. You may code eight missing or you may want to code it to a middle value, between "Yes" and "No" and "Favor" and "Not favor." If you code it missing in both questions, recode one of the two so that the numbers 1 and 2 mean the same thing substantively for both questions. For example if you reversed the scoring on question 76 so that "Yes, allowed to speak" = 2, and "Not allowed" = 1, then the higher numeric code in both questions indicates an attitude in favor of free speech.

If you decide to set 8 to a middle category, a set of recodes that would work is—

Question 76:   1 = No   Question 80:   1 = Favor
                2 = Don't know   2 = Don't know
                3 = Yes   3 = Not favor

This coding scheme assigns high numbers to those who favor free speech and low numbers to those who do not.

Figure AC.2 shows a screen shot of the "Frequencies and Cross-tabulation" facility. Note that, for cross-tabulation, the user is given the choice among three percentages. Except in rare circumstances, be sure the "Total" is *not* selected. Otherwise, select "Column" *or* "Row" but not both. Use the rules given in Chapter 10 to determine which percentage to select. Categories of the *independent* variable should be the percentage bases.

GLOSSARY

abstract Summary of the research; if used, it is presented at the beginning of a research report and seldom exceeds a paragraph or two in length.

access Permission or agreement from subjects and/or agencies to conduct research at an observational or field setting.

announce Divulge to potential subjects that they are part of a research study; opposite of covert (hidden) observation.

anonymity The researcher does not know the identity of respondents, and the researcher therefore cannot link data to specific individuals (compare with confidentiality).

applied (evaluation) research Investigation of a social intervention designed to find out whether it works. Evaluation is a goal or objective, rather than a method of data collection (compare with basic research).

archival data Recorded information, usually historical, that is stored in repositories such as libraries or museums.

basic research Investigation for which the goal is to expand the level of knowledge rather than to change or evaluate a social intervention or social policy. The study of the possible effects of maternal schooling on child health is an example (compare with applied research).

bibliography A list of all sources explicitly cited in a paper—books, monographs, journal articles, and government reports, as well as general periodicals and newspapers, encyclopedias and dictionaries, Internet resources, and personal communications.

bivariate relationship Association between two variables; for example, a bivariate table displays the relationship between just two variables.

bivariate table Cross-tabulation of two variables. See cross-tabulation.

case One instance of the unit being studied, such as persons, couples, social groups, and organizations like schools. In this use of the term, for example, each respondent in a survey is a case, and so is each subject in an experiment.

categorical variable A variable with a finite number of categories. The categories are different, but one category is not greater or less than any other category (e.g., gender contains two categories).

categories (of a variable) Classes of a variable; values of a nominal variable, for example, state of residence, with categories: Alabama, Alaska, . . . Wisconsin, Wyoming.

causal inference Conclusion that an observed relationship is due to the effect of the independent variable on the dependent variable (see also internal validity).

causal relationship A relationship that occurs where current knowledge of the cause reduces uncertainty about the effect some time in the future.

cause and effect Change of the cause is followed by a change in the effect, "everything else being equal," as illustrated by *if . . . then* statements.

cause-and-effect relationship Manipulation of the cause is followed by a change in the effect, "everything else being equal," as illustrated by *if . . . then* statements. The study of cause and effect is called explanatory research.

cell frequency Number of occurrences of an event defined by the intersection between a column and a row in a cross-tabulation (e.g., the number of women who ever were hit).

central limit theorem For an SRS (with replacement), as the sample size increases, the distribution of the sample mean bunches around the population mean to form a normal sampling distribution. The mean of the sampling distribution is the mean of the population, and the standard deviation is given by the standard deviation of the population divided by the square root of the sample size. But these latter two facts do not depend on the central-limit theorem.

chi-square distribution A theoretical probability distribution used in many applications for statistical inference, including testing for a relationship in a bivariate table.

chi-square statistic Number calculated from the sample frequencies for a cross-tabulation. (The chi-square statistic and chi-square test apply to many situations other than cross-tabulations.)

chi-square test Statistical test done by calculating the chi-square statistic for a sample cross-tabulation and comparing it to the probability from the chi-square distribution.

citation Reference in the text of a paper to a source of an idea, fact, or quotation—any material or idea that isn't "common knowledge" or the writer's own thinking. Sources include journal articles, evaluations, monographs, government documents, and so forth. Compare with references.

classical experimental design (pretest-posttest control group design) Experimental design in which pretest–posttest changes for the experimental group $\overline{O}_2 - \overline{O}_1$ are compared with changes for the control group $\overline{O}_4 - \overline{O}_3$, and subjects are assigned at random to the treatment or control group.

closed-ended question Questions with a short list of predefined answers, usually called response options (e.g., . . . \$10,000–\$12,499, \$12,500–\$15,000 . . . for income). A familiar example is a multiple-choice question on an exam.

cluster sample Groups of individual elements are sampled instead of individual elements. The groups are called "clusters." Each individual in selected clusters is included in the sample. Schools might form the clusters for a sample of students, for example.

codebook A listing of all variables in a data collection with each variable accompanied by (1) a short "variable name," (2) a brief description, (3) the location (field or columns spanned), and (4) the meaning of each value.

column marginals Totals for each column, shown in the last row of a table containing a cross-tabulation.

complete observer (nonparticipant observer) Field worker whose role as a researcher is not known by the subjects.

composite variable Variable created by adding, averaging, or combining in some other way two or more other variables. See index (one type of composite variable).

computer-assisted telephone interviewing (CATI) Phone interview process using random-digit dialing and automated recording of responses; speeds data collection and virtually eliminates transcription errors.

concepts (constructs) Variables that are not directly measurable; examples include prejudice, self-esteem, occupational status, and intelligence.

confidence interval Lower and upper boundary and an associated probability that a population parameter, such as a mean or percentage, lies between the boundaries. This probability is called the level of confidence. The boundaries are estimated from sample data, given a specified level of confidence.

confidentiality The researcher knows respondents' identities, but does not reveal information in any way that can be linked to individual respondents (keeps their information confidential) (compare with anonymity).

confounding variable A variable producing a spurious (noncausal) association between two variables.

constant A measure with only one category; all cases fit into one category (compare with variable).

construct validity Method of evaluating validity by observing whether measurements of constructs exhibit relationships with other variables as predicted by theory.

content analysis Conversion of recorded communication into usable form, usually variables. Recorded communication is found in print materials (e.g., books and magazines) in audio and visual recordings, and in electronic text and images, such as those found at computer Web sites.

content validity Method of evaluating validity that relies on researchers' judgments about whether procedures reflect the construct they are designed to measure.

continuous variable Variable whose values correspond to numbers that lie at any point along a straight line.

control To "hold constant" one or more influences that might be related to both the presumed cause and the effect. The purpose of using controls is to avoid mistaking an incidental or chance "relationship" for a causal relationship (see physical controls and statistical controls).

control group In an experiment, the group that receives no treatment; it is included simply for comparison.

control variable A variable that is held constant; a constant is a measure with one category, and all cases fit into one category (e.g., female gender).

controlled experiment The experimenter determines what is changed, by how much and what is not changed (kept constant).

correlation (Pearson product-moment correlation) Number ranging from -1 to 1, which measures the degree of linear relationship between two variables. A correlation of 1.0 indicates a perfect positive linear relationship. A correlation of -1 indicates a perfect negative linear relationship; a negative relationship means that values of the variables change in opposite directions (one increases as the other decreases). A correlation of 0.0 indicates no linear relationship.

cover letter Letter that accompanies or precedes a survey. It describes the purpose of the study and its social contribution, gives the sponsoring agency, tells why the respondent was selected, lists a contact person (for questions and mailback), contains a statement about anonymity or confidentiality, and says "thank you."

coverage error Error due to omitting some part of the population from the sample list, and/or including some people more than once.

criterion validity Method for assessing validity by testing whether a variable predicts a criterion or standard. For example, does self-reported age predict the age calculated from one's birth certificate?

Cronbach's alpha Most general single measure of reliability based on internal consistency. It is calculated by using all of the two-variable correlations between scale items.

cross-sectional data A collection of variables measured at the same time for each case.

cross-sectional survey Survey in which each respondent is surveyed only once. Compare with panel survey.

cross-tabulation Table displaying the frequencies and/or percentages for every combination of values of two or more variables.

data coding Conversion of information from the form it was collected into predefined values of variables, usually from words or answers on a questionnaire to numbers in a computer file.

data matrix Two-dimensional table used to organize and retrieve raw data. Rows represent observations; fields (composed of one or more adjacent columns) represent variables.

data reduction Summarizing one or more variables, for example, percentage distribution, mean, standard deviation.

dependent variable "Outcome" variable or effect; it *depends* on the independent variable(s).

descriptive field notes Notes that include conversations, the physical setting, and details of activities and events.

descriptive research Research intended to present a profile of subjects' characteristics, one at a time, such as in the campus drug study. This drug study does not present comparisons designed to identify causes of drug use.

direct methods Method of data collection in which data are obtained personally from subjects or respondents. Examples include interviews, questionnaires, and observation of behaviors. Compare with indirect methods.

discrete variable Variable with a finite number of categories or whose categories correspond to whole numbers (compare with continuous variable).

dissemination Spread or diffusion. In science, dissemination refers primarily to informing the scientific community and practitioners about research findings.

domain coverage Degree to which a set of variables measures the entire range of content (domain) of a construct. A math test for third-graders should cover all the math operations they have learned, not just addition, for example.

double-barreled question Question that is really more than one question. For example: Do you like mom *and* apple pie? The correct answer is yes only if you like them *both*.

dummy variable Two-category variable that takes a value of 0 or 1, often used as an independent variable in regression analysis.

elaboration Process of studying the relationship between two variables by observing their relationship within each category of one (or more) control variables.

element Objects comprising a population. Examples of elements include people, families, households, cities, states, church congregations, cemetery markers, magazine advertisements, and fish.

empirical test Testing an idea by observing what happens in the physical world.

ethnographic research Investigation based on a broad perspective that emphasizes looking for the meaning attached to social settings by the participants. Ethnographic research is not confined to any method of data collection. But it typically is based on a small number of cases and depends on intensive open-ended interactions with them. The goal is to reveal the meanings and functions of human actions and interactions.

evaluation report Written document summarizing findings of an evaluation. The primary audience usually consists of professionals with an interest in the social intervention.

exhaustive categories Set of categories that accommodate every person or object; no person or object is left unclassified.

experiment Investigation in which a researcher manipulates or changes at least one variable and observes what happens to at least one other variable. The objects of the manipulation in experimental research with people are called subjects.

experimental group In an experiment, the group that receives some type of "treatment."

explanation (type of elaboration) Bivariate relationship exists only due to a control variable that is "causally prior" to both the independent and dependent variables. In the perfect type, the bivariate relationship between the original independent variable and the dependent variable is zero within categories of the control variable (e.g., the sex–beard–dress relationships). The bivariate relationship is called spurious; that is, it is not due to cause and effect.

explanatory research Research with the goal of identifying cause-and-effect relationships (e.g., residence affects contraceptive use). Compare to descriptive research, which does not attempt to discover cause-and-effect relationships.

external validity Degree to which findings are generalizable beyond the experimental or research setting. Random selection is done to improve external validity.

F-test Statistical test to assess whether sample differences among two or more means are likely due to sampling error.

face validity Judgment of researchers about whether a specific item measures at least part of the construct it is intended to measure. An addition test for third-graders measures skills in addition but not multiplication.

falsifiable Hypothesis formulated so that observations might show it is wrong.

field Location of an observational or ethnographic study. Also, sequence of adjacent columns in a data matrix containing the values of a single variable.

focus group (or focused interview) A semistructured interview that includes several people.

frequency distribution A univariate summary including the count and percentage for each category of a nominal, ordinal, or collapsed interval variable.

generalization To extend what has been observed to situations or persons not observed.

government report Written document produced or sponsored by a government agency. Usually it does not contain original research. Rather, it reviews research existing prior to the time of its publication. This is a distinctive difference between a government report and a monograph.

group-administered questionnaire Self-administered questionnaire completed by several respondents at the same time, for example, in a classroom, usually (but not always) with the researcher present.

grouping effects Increased sampling variability when experiments are run with intact groups of subjects, due to dependence among subjects in the same group.

haphazard sample (or convenience sample) Any sample that isn't a probability sample. The probability of selection of the elements is unknown.

historical data Data describing the past. Historical research often is used to examine changes over time, such as in pictures or words.

historical research Study based on data in historical records, typically focusing on changes over lengthy periods of time.

history Events or circumstances occurring between a pretest and posttest other than the treatment that might account for observed changes in the outcome, a threat to internal validity in the absence of a comparison group.

human subjects review board See institutional review board.

hypothesis Speculation about how the world works. In science it's usually a proposed causal relationship that, at least in principle, can be checked by observation.

hypothesis test Formal approach for using sample data to decide whether a statement of fact about the population is correct. In social research, hypothesis tests usually are used to decide whether a relationship observed in a sample is large enough that it is a fair bet the variables are related in the population.

independent variable Variable assumed to generate or "cause" variation in another variable.

index (or scale) Variable defined by combining two or more other variables, usually by adding or averaging the values of the components (for each person or observation).

indicators Observable variables such as a survey question that partially measure complex, abstract concepts (constructs) such as "self-esteem" or "parental support."

indirect methods Type of observation that does not involve direct contacts between the researcher and the subjects. Examples include content analysis, historical research and unobtrusive observation. Compare with direct methods.

inference See statistical inference.

informed consent Formal statement obtained from research subjects prior to starting the research. The statement affirms that the subject agrees to participate with full understanding of the risks and benefits of participation.

institutional review board (IRB) A formal committee that examines research proposals for potentially harmful impacts on research participants (social, psychological, emotional, physical). The IRB advises researchers about needed changes before research may begin. On college campuses, this group might be called the human subjects review board (or human subjects committee).

instrumentation Change in the measuring instrument between pretest and posttest that is mistaken for a treatment effect; a threat to internal validity.

interaction The possibility that selection into the treatment and control groups occurs in such a way that subjects in the treatment group react differently to some factor than do those in the control group.

internal consistency Comparing more than one measurement of a construct when all the measurements were taken at the same time.

internal validity Degree to which the treatment did, in fact, have the effect attributed to it in the experimental setting; random assignment is undertaken to protect internal validity.

interpretation (type of elaboration) A bivariate relationship exists due only to a control variable that intervenes between the independent and dependent variables. In the perfect type, the bivariate relationship between the original independent variable and the dependent variable is zero within categories of the control variable (e.g., gender–hitchild–hitadult relationships). Contrast with explanation.

interval variable A continuous variable whose values are numbers but which does not include a natural zero, such as the Fahrenheit temperature scale.

intervening variable A variable that is affected by the independent variable and affects the dependent variable. In the pure intervening-variable case, the original relationship between the independent variable and the dependent variable vanishes (is zero) when the intervening variable is controlled statistically, as in a three-variable table.

interviewer effect Bias resulting when a respondent chooses incorrect answers because an interviewer is present, for example, to impress or irritate the interviewer.

items Term used to refer to the individual components of an index.

level of confidence Prespecified probability associated with a confidence interval. The most common level of confidence is 0.95 (95%).

level of significance Prespecified probability giving the p-value required to reject the null hypothesis. The most commonly used level of significance is 0.05 (5 in 100). If the estimated probability from the data is smaller than the level of significance, reject the null hypothesis. Otherwise, do not reject it. Rejecting the null hypothesis generally supports the research hypothesis.

linear regression analysis (regression analysis, regression) Method of predicting the value of the dependent variable using a linear formula and one or more independent variables, such as: *predicted hourly wage* $= a + b_{age} age + b_{educ} educ + b_{fem} female$. Usually, the regression analysis is done with a computer statistical software program, such as SPSS or SAS.

mail questionnaire Type of survey that collects information by mailing a questionnaire to respondents, who return the completed questionnaire by mail.

mail survey A survey that collects information by mailing a questionnaire to respondents.

marginals (or marginal frequency distributions) Univariate frequency distributions for variables in a cross-tabulation that are displayed at the edges, or margins, of the cross-tabulation.

maturation Observed changes in subjects between a pretest and posttest that would have occurred with or without the treatment or any other external event(s); maturation may be mistaken for treatment effects and therefore is a threat to internal validity.

measure (or variable) Operational version of a concept; an indicator (e.g., a survey question) with each response assigned a *unique* category or value.

measure of central tendency A statistic or parameter that summarizes where numbers in a distribution tend to concentrate. Examples include the mean, median, and mode.

measure of dispersion A statistic or parameter that summarizes how much numbers in a distribution are spread out. Examples include the standard deviation and variance.

measurement error Difference between an observed value and the "true" value of a variable.

model A simplification of reality designed to promote understanding by summarizing essential elements and reducing complexity.

monograph Literally translated, "one writing." More precisely, a monograph is a book-length document written on one scientific topic. In social research, a monograph presents a detailed report of an extensive research program of study.

multiple methods More than one method of data collection used in combination to measure one variable. The objective is to reduce or eliminate many of the shortcomings associated with each individual method.

multiple-treatment interference Situation that occurs when multiple treatments are administered to the same subjects, and the effects of early treatments persist longer than the time between treatments. A threat to external validity.

multistage sampling Sampling clusters and elements within clusters, for example, households within city blocks.

mutually exclusive categories Set of nonoverlapping categories defined so no person or object fits into more than one category.

negative relationship Relationship in which values of two variables move in opposite directions. As the value of one variable increases, the value of the other variable decreases, and vice versa.

nominal variable (categorical variable) Variable that classifies objects or elements into one and only one class or category; the classes simply are different (e.g., color).

nonparticipant observer (complete observer) A researcher who makes observations, usually in public settings, without the subjects being aware they are being studied.

nonprobability sample A sample in which the probability of selecting each element is *not* known, usually due to lack of a comprehensive list of elements.

nonresponse Failure of selected sample members to complete all or part of a survey or interview. Nonresponse error comes from differences between individuals who complete and return a questionnaire and those who do not.

nonresponse error Errors in sample statistics due to differences between individuals who complete and return a questionnaire and those who do not. Those who fail to return a completed questionnaire (nonrespondents) might be different from respondents in ways that influence the results of the study.

normal sampling distribution Sampling distribution that is symmetric around the mean of the distribution. It is defined by a specific mathematical formula.

null hypothesis Testable statement that the population statistic from which a sample was drawn equals a specific value. In social research, the null hypothesis usually states there are no differences in a dependent variable among levels of an independent variable, sometimes informally called the "no difference" hypothesis.

numeric variable Interval and ratio variables (sometimes ordinal variables); the numerical values are given their natural mathematical meaning (compare with categorical variable).

observation The term observation is used in three ways: (1) to indicate a process for getting information by looking to see what happens, (2) to indicate a profile summary of variables for one individual or other unit (case) such as a college, and, (3) to indicate observational analysis, which means, roughly, to go out and talk to people, see what they do, stay for a while, and see what develops. This latter sense of observation is associated with ethnographic and other qualitative approaches to research.

observational study Unstructured method of data collection in which the researcher visits a field site for an extended time to obtain information by directly watching human social interactions and behaviors.

observed score Value of a variable obtained through procedures such as personal interview or observed behaviors (compare with true score).

one-group pretest–posttest design Design with no control group or comparison group; the researcher observes change between a measurement taken before an event occurs and a second measurement taken after it.

one-shot case study Most basic design, consisting of one observation after an event has occurred or a treatment administered; usually, informal or implicit comparisons are made between the observations in the study and other information not gathered as part of the formal study.

one-tailed test A hypothesis test of a relationship in which the direction of the relationship is predicted in advance of the test. For example, women express more favorable attitudes toward the women's movement than do men. The entire probability of the level of significance is put in one tail of the sampling distribution rather than being split between the two tails. A one-tailed test gives more statistical power to reject a false null hypothesis.

open-ended questions Questions requesting respondents to write in a response. A familiar example is an essay question on an exam. A short open-ended question might ask respondents to write down their age or date of birth.

operational definition Collection of rules for obtaining observations that will become a variable.

operationalization Process of converting abstract concepts (e.g., academic achievement, self-esteem) into measurable variables.

ordinal variable One type of categorical variable defined by a set of categories, each of which is either greater than or less than each of the other categories, but with no indication of the magnitude of the differences among the categories (e.g., agree–disagree questionnaire item).

overgeneralization Concluding that a pattern observed in too small a number of instances is typical of other situations not observed. For example, you observe in 100 lottery drawings that the number 22 turns up more often than any other number, and conclude that future drawings are more apt to turn up 22 than any other number.

***p*-value** Estimate of the probability of observing a sample statistic with a greater deviation from the null hypothesis than the observed statistic if the null hypothesis were correct.

panel survey Survey in which the same individuals are surveyed at least twice.

parsimony Simplicity; in science, the simpler theory is preferred when two theories make the same predictions.

partial observer Researcher who is observing and participating as a member but is known as a researcher.

partial relationship Association between the independent and dependent variables within a category of one or more control variables; in tabular analysis, a partial table, in regression, a partial slope coefficient.

participant observer Researcher who is completely immersed in the regular activities of the group under study, and usually is known as a member of the group rather than as a researcher.

peer review The process through which each submission to a journal is evaluated by a panel of experts for importance and accuracy.

percentage Frequency per 100, obtained by counting the number of cases in each category of a variable, dividing by the total number of cases for all categories, and multiplying the quotient by 100.

perfect relationship Relationship for which knowledge of one variable reduces uncertainty about the other variable to zero.

personal interview A method of data collection in which information is obtained from each respondent in a face-to-face meeting with the interviewer.

physical controls The researcher determines what is changed, by how much, and what is not changed (i.e., kept constant). Contrast physical control to "control" by random assignment, for which only the expected differences among means of variables are controlled.

physical trace data Data such as paths worn in the grass and fingerprints indicative of subjects' previous activity. Other examples include checking litter containers for cans and bottles to estimate the extent of illegal use of alcohol in public places, and examining rates of repair of public telephones as a measure of vandalism in a community.

placebo Nonreactive agent, such as the sugar pill given in medical research, to provide a "baseline" comparison group in experiments.

plagiarism Quoting or summarizing in writing someone else's ideas without crediting the source.

point estimate A single sample statistic such as a sample mean used to estimate the corresponding population mean. Contrast point estimate to a confidence interval where two boundaries are calculated and a probability is given that the population parameter lies between the boundaries.

population Collection of elements to be described—for example all people comprising a religious group, all fish in a fish bowl—or elements of any other known collectivity.

population parameter (parameter) A number such as a percentage, mean, or the difference between percentages describing the entire population.

positive relationship Relationship in which values of two variables move in the same direction. As the value of one variable increases, the value of the other variable also increases.

poster presentation Dissemination method using posters to summarize research findings, usually at a professional conference; the researcher usually is present during viewing of the poster to answer questions.

posttest Measurement of the outcome in an experiment taken *after* the treatment is administered. The posttest must use the same, or equivalent, data-collection procedures as used for the pretest.

posttest-only control-group design Random assignment design comparing differences between the experimental group and the control group after the treatment is administered to the treatment group. Subjects are assigned at random to treatment and control groups.

pretest Small preliminary survey to check for problems with questions, response options, and procedures. Pretests also are used to determine the length of time needed to complete a survey. The pretest sample should be similar to the target population for the main survey.

primary data Data collected for a specific study. The researcher defines a research question and collects new data tailored to answer the question. Contrast with secondary data.

primary sampling unit (PSU) A collection of elements, such as people or fish, to be sampled as a single unit. Examples of PSUs include households, city blocks, and schools. In cluster sampling, PSUs are sampled rather than individual elements.

probability sample Sample for which the probability of selection is known and greater than zero for each element in a population.

probe Follow-up question in an interview used to clarify responses that are incomplete, or elicit a response when one was not offered.

purposive sample Nonprobability sample selected to meet specific criteria of a study, such as all drug users in a soup-kitchen population.

qualitative data Information collected from unstructured observation intended to represent meanings, symbols, descriptions, concepts, and characteristics of people.

qualitative methods Research methods that do not rely heavily on mathematical and statistical analysis. Qualitative research is multi-method in focus, involving a naturalistic approach to subject matter. Qualitative researchers study people in their natural setting, attempting to make sense of phenomena in terms of the meanings that people bring to them.

qualitative research ("meaning-based" research) A relatively unstructured approach to social science, involving an interpretive, naturalistic method, attempting to make sense of, or interpret, phenomena in terms of the meanings people bring to them.

quantitative data Information collected from comparatively structured research in which the observations are converted into numbers.

quantitative methods Research methods that rely primarily on mathematical and statistical analysis of numeric (numbers-based) data.

quantitative research ("numbers-based" research) Comparatively structured research that emphasizes causal relationships among variables, using data represented by numbers.

quota sample Nonprobability sample that takes a prespecified number of elements from each of several subgroups of the population, e.g., 100 male and 100 female, or 33 male and 67 female. The subgroups are comparable to strata. A quota sample differs from a stratified sample because the elements are selected haphazardly within each subgroup with quota sampling, but are selected by probability sample with stratified sampling.

random assignment A "pure chance" procedure used to determine which subjects are in the treatment group and which subjects are in the control group. The purpose is to improve internal validity (did the treatment have the effect attributed to it?).

random selection A "pure-chance" procedure for including subjects in a study. The purpose is to improve external validity.

ratio variable Variable defined by values that are natural numbers *and* zero indicates the absence of some real-world quantity (e.g., wage).

raw data A listing of the value of every variable for every observation.

reactive arrangements Umbrella term covering a variety of experimental manipulations that may not mirror real-world settings; a threat to external validity.

reactive response options Response categories of a question that lead the respondent to an incorrect response.

recording units In content analysis, the basic items to be classified. There are six commonly used types of recording units for text: word, word sense, sentence, theme, paragraph, and whole text.

refereed journal Scholarly periodical that publishes only peer-reviewed papers. Issues are published several times a year, usually monthly, bimonthly, or quarterly.

references Alphabetized list of sources cited, appearing at the end of a document; compare with bibliography and citation.

reflective field notes Notes that contain the researcher's thoughts, feelings, ideas, problems, and so forth.

regression (to the mean) Average for extreme scores at the pretest (either very high or very low) moves closer to the middle score at the posttest, because of imperfect but positive correlation between pretest and posttest scores. Regression to the mean threatens internal validity when subjects are selected for their extreme score, often for remedial treatment, and subjects are not assigned at random to the treatment.

relationship (or association) A relationship exists between two variables when knowing the value of one variable reduces uncertainty about the value of the other variable. Knowledge of gender, for example, reduces uncertainty about hair length.

reliability Consistency of a measure; does the same result occur on repeated measurement in the absence of real change?

replication (type of elaboration) Each partial relationship matches the original bivariate relationship within categories of the control variable (or variables) (control variable has no effect on the bivariate association).

research hypothesis Usually opposite to the null hypothesis. In most instances, the research hypothesis states that there is a relationship.

respondent An individual who answers the questions on a survey; analogous to case in ethnographic/observational research and subject in experiments.

response options List of responses to a closed-ended question.

response set Tendency of respondents to select the same answer to many questions, irrespective of the question content, for example, answering "strongly disagree" to every question no matter what the respondent's opinion is.

row marginals Row totals shown in the last column of a table containing a cross-tabulation.

sample Some part of a population, generally selected with the idea of calculating a sample statistic to estimate the corresponding population parameter.

sample attrition Sample loss that occurs when some of those who participated in the first data collection of a panel survey don't participate in later collections (waves). Some reasons for attrition include change of residence, illness or death of respondent, and refusal.

sample statistic Number calculated from a sample, such as the sample mean (average), sample percentage (or sample proportion), or the difference between sample means or percentages for two groups.

sampling distribution List of each possible value of a sample statistic from a population and its associated probability.

sampling error Difference between a sample statistic and population parameter when a sample is used to describe the population.

sampling frame Complete list of each element in the population. A sample is drawn from this list. Consequently, getting a probability sample depends on the list being complete, with no duplicate entries.

scale Group of response options to a question that are arranged in order of intensity or importance (contrast to index).

secondary data Data collected by someone other than the researcher, often for multiple purposes. Prominent examples of secondary data include surveys such as the *General Social Survey* and the U.S. decennial census.

selection The result when subjects choose their independent-variable assignment (treatment group or control group) or are selected by a nonrandom process; the most frequent source of a spurious (false) relationship.

selection bias People decide for themselves whether to engage in an activity such as taking estrogen. The basis of their decision, such as healthy lifestyle, affects an outcome such as a heart attack. The result is a spuriously low incidence of heart attack among women who took estrogen.

selection × treatment interaction Situation in which people who are most (or least) sensitive to the treatment recruit themselves into the pool of potential subjects, a threat to external validity.

self-administered questionnaire Survey completed by the respondent, usually obtained by mail, in the absence of the researcher, or administered in a group setting such as a classroom.

semistructured interview Face-to-face survey with a set of questions that can be expanded by using probes.

sequencing Determining the order of survey questions in an interview or on a questionnaire.

serendipity Finding the unexpected, thought to figure prominently in the history of scientific discovery.

simple random sample (SRS) The most elementary probability sample; every possible sample of a given size has the same chance of being selected.

snowball sample Nonprobability sample obtained by relying on a few participants to identify other participants, who in turn provide additional leads, until the target sample size is reached.

social significance (or substantive significance) Importance of an observation for practical applications or social theory. In a cross-tabulation, one indicator of social significance is the magnitude of the percentage difference. Contrast with statistical significance.

sociogram Sociometric method of displaying patterns of interaction, such as friendship networks, cliques, and other social networks. It consists of a diagram with circles or squares representing participants, and arrows or lines connecting interacting participants.

specification (type of elaboration) Finding that the relationship between the independent and dependent variable is different in different categories of one or more control variables. Also called statistical interaction.

spurious association Noncausal relationship between two variables, generated by their common dependence on at least one other variable.

standard deviation Measure of dispersion of a variable. The standard deviation is the square root of the variance. A *sample* standard deviation summarizes variation in a single sample. A *population* standard deviation summarizes variation in the population.

standard error A special name given to the standard deviation when the numbers are a sample statistic, like the sample mean.

standard normal distribution Normal distribution with a mean = 0.0 and a standard deviation (and variance) = 1.0.

standard score (z-score) A variable transformed to ensure that it has a mean of exactly zero and a standard deviation of exactly one, obtained by subtracting the mean of the original variable from each value and dividing the result by the standard deviation of the original variable.

static-group comparison A design with no random assignment; comparison is between naturally occurring groups, such as hourly wage between college graduates and non-college graduates.

statistic A number such as an average calculated from sample data, usually intended to estimate the corresponding population number, like the population average. Examples of sample statistics include the sample mean (average), sample percentage (proportion), and the difference between sample means or percentages (proportions) for two groups.

statistical control An approximation of physical control in which a relationship between two variables is observed within constant levels of control variable(s).

statistical inference Process of drawing conclusions about a population using data from a sample of that population.

statistical interaction Variation among relationships between two variables within categories of one or more control variables.

statistical test A procedure for making a decision as to whether a population value of a statistic is some stated value, called the null hypothesis. Usually the null hypothesis states no relationship between two variables. Statistical tests are the primary technical method of statistical inference.

statistically significant Sample statistic deviates from the null hypothesis by a large enough amount to trigger rejection of the null hypothesis. The size of the difference required to reject the null hypothesis is determined by a probability (p-value). If the calculated p-value is no larger than the level of significance, reject the null hypothesis. In social research, the most-used level of significance is 0.05.

stem (of a question) The part of a survey item that asks the question. It should be a complete sentence.

sticky theory A phrase we invented to try to capture the widespread observation that people sometimes hold ideas so strongly that they refuse to acknowledge evidence that contradicts their ideas. In science, no norm is stronger than the norm of skepticism, which should overcome sticky-theory thinking. Still, science is conducted by humans; sticky theory creeps in.

stratified sample Sample taken by selecting elements from each of two or more groups called strata (singular form, stratum). The strata are defined so that each element fits into exactly one stratum. So strata define a variable used for a specific purpose of sampling.

structured interview Questionnaire that is administered by an interviewer. Questions are read verbatim to the respondent and answers usually are recorded by the interviewer into one of a set of closed-ended options (although open-ended response categories also can be used).

subjects Objects of the manipulation in an experiment, usually people in social research; analogous to case in ethnographic/observational research and respondent in surveys.

survey Tool for gathering data in which the researcher asks questions of a sample of individuals. Four types are mail questionnaire, personal interview, telephone interview, and Internet questionnaire.

t-test A statistical test used for many statistics, e.g., to compare two sample means or test a regression coefficient against a null hypothesis that it is zero (no partial relationship).

tally sheet Blank table with labels for the variable categories, used to prepare cross-tabulations manually.

target population Collection of all people who are eligible to participate as subjects in a study.

telephone interview A survey administered by telephone.

testing The experience of a pretest might influence results on a posttest. For example, the experience of taking a test usually improves performance on a second test. Effects of testing might be mistaken for effects of a treatment (e.g., tutoring), a threat to internal validity.

testing × treatment interaction Situation in which the pretest sensitizes subjects to the treatment, either increasing or decreasing treatment effects. A threat to external validity.

test–retest reliability Correlation between the same measure observed at two time points, in the absence of change in the true score and the "absence of memory."

theme In content analysis, a recording unit as subject/verb/object, such as "Snow/covers/ the grass."

theoretical sample Nonprobability sampling strategy often used by field researchers who directly observe social events, often used to develop a theory to guide future research. Sometimes called "grounded theory," because the theory is derived from (grounded in) the observed behaviors of social life.

theory In brief, a collection of hypotheses about a coherent topic.

treatment In experiments, one category of the independent or treatment variable.

treatment variable (independent variable) In an experiment, the variable that is manipulated (the "treatment"). Analogous to independent variable in nonexperimental research.

trivariate table A table that includes three variables: independent, dependent, and control.

true score Correct value of a variable, for example, age = date of last birthday − date of birth on a birth certificate (compare with observed score).

two-tailed test Statistical test for a nondirectional hypothesis. The probability associated with the level of significance is split between the upper and lower tails of the sampling distribution.

unbiased statistic Statistic whose "expected value" (mean of all sample means) equals the corresponding population parameter. Unbiased implies no systematic tendency to over-estimate or underestimate the population parameter.

univariate analysis Examination of statistics such as the mean, standard deviation, and frequency distribution, which describe one variable at a time.

univariate frequency distribution List of the number and percentage in each category of one variable.

unobtrusive observation Watching behaviors in a way that is "inconspicuous" to the research subjects.

unstructured interview A loosely structured survey that might be thought of as a "conversation." The interviewer usually has a list of questions but doesn't necessarily repeat them word-for-word to respondents or use a question–answer, question–answer format.

validity Accuracy with which an observed variable measures the concept or construct it is designed to measure.

validity coefficient Correlation between the observed score and the true score.

value (of a variable) Category or number assigned to a specific observation.

variable Set of categories or numbers defined so that the categories are mutually exclusive (unique) and exhaustive. Each observation (e.g., person, object) fits into exactly one category, and all needed categories are included. An example is gender (two unique categories); other variables include race, age, and self-esteem.

variance Measure of how much the numbers in a list differ among themselves (dispersion). It is defined as the average squared distance from the mean.

weighting (of a variable) In calculating an index, multiplying each component by a different numeric constant before calculating a sum or average. The constants are the weights and are chosen to reflect the importance of each component for defining the index.

word sense In content analysis, the meaning of words or phrases and phrases constituting a unit (e.g., New York state). Different specific words and phrases often convey the same or nearly the same meaning, for example, "applauding" and "clapping."

References

Adler, Patricia A. & Peter Adler. (1994). Observational techniques. In Norman K. Denzin & Yvonna S. Lincoln (Eds.), *Handbook of qualitative research* (pp. 377–92). Thousand Oaks, CA: Sage.

Alan Guttmacher Web site (http://www.guttmacher.org/journals/aboutper.html) (accessed July 19, 2004).

Allen, Charlotte. (1997). Spies like us: When sociologists deceive their subjects. *Lingua Franca: The Review of Academic Life* (November), pp. 31–9.

American Sociological Association. (1997). *Style Guide* (2nd ed.). Washington, DC: American Sociological Association.

American Sociological Association. Code of Ethics of the American Sociological Association. Available at www.asanet.org/members/enforce.html (accessed May 16, 2004).

Atkinson, Paul & Martyn Hammersley. (1994). Ethnography and participant observation. In Norman K. Denzin & Yvonna S. Lincoln (Eds.), *Handbook of qualitative research* (pp. 248–61). Thousand Oaks, CA: Sage.

Austin, Erik. (2003). Personal communication by e-mail. April 20, 2003.

Axinn, William G., & Jennifer S. Barber (2001). Mass education and fertility transition. *American Sociological Review, 66*, 481–505.

Babbie, Earl. (1999). *The basics of social research*. Belmont, CA: Wadsworth.

Baron, Naomi S. (1998). Letters by phone or speech by other means: The linguistics of email. *Language and Communication, 18*, 133–70.

Berg, Bruce L, (2001). *Qualitative research methods for the social sciences* (4th ed.). Needham Heights, MA: Allyn and Bacon.

Berger, Arthur Asa. (2000). *Media and communication research methods: An introduction to qualitative and quantitative approaches*. Thousand Oaks, CA: Sage.

Best, Samuel J., Brian Krueger, Clark Hubbard, & Andrew Smith. (2001). An assessment of the generalizability of Internet surveys. *Social Science Computer Review, 19*(2), 131–45.

Borgatta, Edgar F., & George W. Bohrnstedt. (1980). Level of measurement: Once over again. *Sociological Methods and Research, 9*(2), 147–60.

Bourgois, Philippe. (1995). *In search of respect: Selling crack in El Barrio*. Cambridge, UK: Cambridge University Press.

Campbell, Donald T., & Julian S. Stanley. (1963). *Experimental and quasi-experimental designs for research*. Chicago: Rand McNally and Company.

Cannavo, Salvator. (1974). *Nomic inference: An introduction to the logic of scientific inquiry*. The Hague, Netherlands: Martinus Nijhoff.

Christakis, Nicholas A., Norma C. Ware & Arthur Kleinman. (2001). Illness behavior and the health transition in the developing world. In Duane A. Matcha (Ed.), *Readings in medical sociology* (pp. 143–59). Boston: Allyn and Bacon.

Cohen, Brett, Gordon Waugh & Karen Place. (1989). At the movies: An unobtrusive study of arousal-attraction. *The Journal of Social Psychology, 129*(5), 691–3. Reprinted with permission of the Helen Dwight Reid Educational Foundation. Published by Heldref Publications, 1319 Eighteenth St., NW, Washington, DC 20036–1802. Copyright 1989.

Cohen, Morris R., & Ernest Nagel. (1934). *An introduction to logic and scientific method.* New York: Harcourt, Brace.

Conger, Rand D., Frederick O. Lorenz, Glen H. Elder, Jr., Ronald L. Simons, & Xiaojia Ge. (1993). Husband and wife differences in response to undesirable life events. *Journal of Health and Social Behavior, 34*, 71–88.

Consumer Reports Annual Auto Issue (April 2004). Yonkers, NY: Consumers Union.

Consumer Reports Buying Guide (2004). Yonkers, NY: Consumers Union.

Cornell Lab of Ornithology Web site: http://birds.cornell.edu/birdhouse/getting-started/overviewobj.html (accessed July 19, 2004).

Creswell, John W. (1994). *Research design: Qualitative and quantitative approaches.* Thousand Oaks, CA: Sage.

Creswell, John W. (1998). *Qualitative inquiry and research design: Choosing among five traditions.* Thousand Oaks, CA: Sage.

Davis, James A., Tom W. Smith, & Peter V. Marsden (2003). General Social Surveys, 1972–2002: [Cumulative File] [Computer file]. ICPSR version. Chicago, IL: National Opinion Research Center [producer]. Storrs, CT: Roper Center for Public Opinion Research, University of Connecticut/Ann Arbor, MI: Inter-University Consortium for Political and Social Research [distributors], 2003. (PDF version downloaded with ICPSR study #3728.) http://www.icpsr. umich. edu:81/GSS/ (accessed May 26, 2004).

Davis, James A., Tom W. Smith, & Peter V. Marsden. General Social Surveys, 1972–2002: [Cumulative File] [Computer file]. 2nd ICPSR version. Chicago, IL: National Opinion Research Center [producer], 2003. Storrs, CT: Roper Center for Public Opinion Research, University of Connecticut/Ann Arbor, MI: Inter-University Consortium for Political and Social Research [distributors], 2003. (PDF version downloaded with ICPSR study #3728.)

Denzin, Norman K. & Yvonna S. Lincoln. (1994). Introduction: Entering the field of qualitative research. In Norman K. Denzin & Yvonna S. Lincoln (Eds.), *Handbook of qualitative research*, (pp. 1–17). Thousand Oaks, CA: Sage.

Desai, Sonalde & Soumya Alva. (1998). Maternal education and child health: Is there a strong causal relationship? *Demography, 35*(1), 71–81.

Diamond, Timothy. (1986). Social policy and everyday life in nursing homes: A critical ethnography. *Social Science and Medicine, 23* (12), 1287–95. Reprinted with permission from Elsevier Science.

Diamond, Timothy. (1992). *Making gray gold: Narratives of nursing home care*. Chicago: University of Chicago Press.

Dillman, Don A. (2000). *Mail and internet surveys: The tailored design method* (2nd ed.) New York: Wiley.

Disaster Research Center home page, University of Delaware. Available at http://www.udel.edu/ DRC (accessed May 17, 2004).

Disaster Research Center home page, University of Delaware. Available at http://www.udel.edu/DRC (accessed May 22, 2004).

Dorsten, Linda Eberst, Lawrence Hotchkiss and Terri M. King. (1999). Effect of inbreeding on early childhood mortality: Twelve generations of an Amish settlement. *Demography, 36*(2), 263–71.

Douglass, Kim. (2002). Surveys show teens, children smoke less: Anti-tobacco campaigns credited. *Wilmington News Journal*, January 25, p. B1–B2.

Dubin, Donald B. (1974). Estimating causal effects of treatments in randomized and nonrandomized studies. *Educational Psychology, 66*, 688–701.

Duneier, Mitchell. (1999). *Sidewalk*. New York: Farrar, Straus and Giroux.

Durand, John David. (1960). Mortality estimates from Roman tombstone inscriptions. *American Journal of Sociology, 65*(4), 365–73.

Ellis, Carolyn. (1986). *Fisher folk*. Lexington: University Press of KY.

Ferraro, Kenneth F., & Melissa M. Farmer. (1999). Utility of health data from social surveys: Is there a gold standard for measuring morbidity? *American Sociological Review, 64*, 303–15.

Fiorentine, Robert & Stephen Cole. (1992). Why fewer women become physicians: Explaining the premed persistence gap. *Sociological Forum, 7* (3), 469–96.

Foster, Gary S., Richard L. Hummel & Donald J. Adamchak. (1998). Patterns of conception, natality, and mortality from Midwestern cemeteries: A sociological analysis of historical data. *The Sociological Quarterly, 39*(3), 473–89. Copyright 1998, Midwest Sociological Society.

Frankfort-Nachmias, Chava & David Nachmias. (1996). *Research methods in the social sciences* (5th ed.). New York: St. Martin's.

GSS Homepage. 2003. General Social Survey. http://webapp.icpsr.umich.edu/GSS (accessed 7/19/2004).

GSS Overview. 2003. General Social Survey. http://webapp.icpsr.umich.edu/GSS (accessed 7/19/2004).

Gamson, William A. & David Stuart. (1992). Media discourse as a symbolic contest: The bomb in political cartoons. *Sociological Forum, 7*(1), 55–86.

Garwood, Jeanette, Michelle Rogerson, & Ken Pease. (2000). Sneaky measurement of crime and disorder. In Victor Jupp, Pamela Davies, & Peter Francis (Eds.), *Doing criminological research* (pp. 157–67). London: Sage.

General Social Survey. Available at: http://www.icpsr.umich.edu/gss (accessed May 23, 2004).

Goodwin, Pamela J., M.D., Molyn Leszcz, M.D., Marguerite Ennis, Ph.D., Jan Koopmans, *M.S.W.*, Leslie Vincent, R.N., Helaine Guther, *M.S.W.*, Elaine Drysdale, M.D., Marilyn Hundleby, Ph.D., Harvey M. Chochinov, M.D., Ph.D., Margaret Navarro, M.D., Michael Speca, Psy.D., Julia Masterson, M.D., Liz Dohan, *M.S.W.*, Rami Sela, Ph.D., Barbara Warren, R.N., *M.S.N.*, Alexander Paterson, M.D., Kathleen I. Pritchard, M.D., Andrew Arnold, M.B., B.S., Richard Doll, *M.S.W.*, Susan E. O'Reilly, M.D., Gail Quirt, R.N., B.A.A., Nicky Hood, R.N., and Jonathan Hunter, M.D. (2001). The effect of group psychosocial support on survival in metastatic breast cancer. *The New England Journal of Medicine, 345* (24), 1719–26. (December 13, 2001).

Groves, Robert M. (1991). Measurement error across the disciplines. In Paul P. Biemer, Robert M. Groves, Lars E. Lyberg, Nancy. A. Mathiowetz, & Seymour Sudman (Eds.), *Measurement errors in surveys* (pp. 1–25). New York: Wiley.

Groves, Robert M. (1996). How do we know what we think they think is really what they think? In Norbert Schwarz & Seymour Sudman (Eds.), *Answering questions: methodology for determining cognitive and communicative processes in survey research* (pp. 389–402). San Francisco: Jossey-Bass.

Groves, Robert M., & Robert L. Kahn. (1979). *Surveys by telephone: A national comparison with personal interviews*. New York: Academic Press.

Harrison, Dianne F., & C. Aaron McNeece. (2001). Disseminating research findings. In Bruce A. Thyer (Ed.), *The handbook of social work research methods* (pp. 501–12). Thousand Oaks, CA: Sage.

Homans, George C. (1950). *The Human Group*. New York: Harcourt Brace.

Huddy, Leonie, Francis K. Neely, & Marilyn R. Lafay, (2000). The polls—trends: Support for the women's movement. *Public Opinion Quarterly 64*(3), 309–350.

ISSP. 2003. International Social Survey Program. http://www.issp.org/ (accessed May 30, 2004).

Janesick, Valerie J. (1994). The dance of qualitative research design: Metaphor, methodolatry, and meaning. In Norman K. Denzin & Yvonna S. Lincoln (Eds.), *Handbook of qualitative research* (pp. 209–19). Thousand Oaks, CA: Sage.

Jennings, Dennis L., Teresa M. Amabile, & Lee Ross. (1982). Informal covariation assessment: Data-based versus theory-based judgments. In Amos Tversky & Daniel Kahneman (Eds.), *Judgment under uncertainty: Heuristics and biases* (pp. 211–30). Cambridge, UK: Cambridge University Press.

Johnson, William A., Jr, Richard P. Rettig, Gregory M. Scott, & Stephen M. Garrison. (2004). *The sociology student writer's manual* (4th ed.). Upper Saddle River, NJ: Prentice Hall.

Kalton, Graham. (1983). Introduction to survey sampling. Beverly Hills: Sage.

Kirk, Jerome & Marc L. Miller (1986). *Reliability and validity in qualitative research*. Beverly Hills, CA: Sage.

Kohn, Melvin L. (1977). *Class and conformity: A study in values* (2nd ed.). Chicago: University of Chicago Press.

Kohn, Melvin L. & Kazimierz M. Slomczynski. (1990). *Social structure and self-direction: A comparative analysis of the United States and Poland*. Cambridge, MA: Basil Blackwell.

Kolata, Gina with Melody Petersen. (July 10, 2002). Hormone replacement study a shock to the medical system. *New York Times*, p. A1.

Kolata, Gina. (2001). Cancer study finds support groups do not extend life. *The New York Times*, December 13, p. A36.

Lavrakas, Paul J. (1993). *Telephone survey methods: Sampling, selection and supervision* (2nd ed.). Applied Social Research Methods Series (vol. 7). Newbury Park: Sage. Copyright ©1993 by Sage Publications, Inc. Reprinted by permission.

Lawler, Edward J., & Jeongkoo Yoon. (1996). Commitment in exchange relations: Test of a theory of relational cohesion. *American Sociological Review, 61*(1), 89–108.

Lever, Janet. (1978). Sex differences in the complexity of children's play and games. *American Sociological Review, 43*, 471–83.

Liebow, Elliot (1993). *Tell them who I am: The lives of homeless women*. New York: The Free Press.

Lofland, John & Lyn H. Lofland. (1995). *Analyzing social settings: A guide to qualitative observation and analysis* (3rd ed.). Belmont, CA: Wadsworth.

Lord, Fredrick M., & Melvin R. Novick. (1968). *Statistical theories of mental test scores*. Reading, MA: Addison-Wesley.

Manski, Charles F., Gary D. Sandefur, Sara McLanahan, and Daniel Powers. (1992). Alternative estimates of the effects of family structure during adolescence on high school graduation. *Journal of the American Statistical Association, 87*(417), 25–37.

Maxim, Paul S. (1999). *Quantitative research methods in the social sciences*. New York: Oxford University Press.

Meltzoff, Julian. (1998). *Critical Thinking About Research*. Practice article 6 (pp. 207–9). Washington, DC: American Psychological Association.

Merton, Robert K., Marjorie Fiske, & Patricia L. Kendall. (1990). *The focused interview: A manual of problems and procedures* (2nd. ed.). New York: The Free Press.

Michell, Joel. (1999). *Measurement in psychology*. Cambridge, UK: Cambridge University Press.

Milgram, Stanley. (1974). *Obedience to authority: An experimental view*. New York: Harper & Row.

Miller, Delbert C. (1991). *Handbook of Research Design and Social Measurement* (5th ed.). Newbury Park: Sage. Copyright © 1991 by Sage Publications, Inc. Reprinted by permission.

Morrow, Betty Hearn & Elaine Enarson. (1996). Hurricane Andrew through women's eyes: Issues and recommendations. *International Journal of Mass Emergencies and Disasters, 14*(1), 5–22.

Morse, Janice M. (1994). Designing funded qualitative research. In Norman K. Denzin & Yvonna S. Lincoln (Eds.), *Handbook of qualitative research* (pp. 220–35). Thousand Oaks, CA: Sage.

National Election Survey. 2000. Available at: http://www.umich.edu/~nes/ (accessed May 25, 2004).

NCES (National Center for Education Statistics). http://nces.ed.gov/surveys/nels88/ (accessed July 19, 2004).

New York Times (June 1, 2002). Drugs in baseball: Editorial. p. A24, col 1.

Nesbary, Dale K. (2000). *Survey research and the World Wide Web*. Needham Heights, MA: Allyn & Bacon.

NORC. 2003. National Opinion Research Center. http://www.norc.uchicago.edu/projects/gensoc1.asp (accessed May 30, 2004).

Norton-Hawk, Maureen A. (2001). The counterproductivity of incarcerating female street prostitutes. *Deviant Behavior: An Interdisciplinary Journal, 22*, 403–17.

Painter, Gary & David I. Levine. (2000). Family structure and youths' outcomes. *Journal of Human Resources, 35*(3), 524–49. Reprinted by permission of the University of Wisconsin Press.

Parcel, Toby L., & Elizabeth G. Menaghan. (1994). Supplemental child care arrangements: Determinants and consequences. In *Parents' jobs and children's lives* (pp. 179–206). New York: Aldine de Gruyter.

Phillips, Brenda. (1996). Creating, sustaining and losing place: Homelessness in the context of disaster. *Humanity and Society, 20*, 94–101.

Phillips, Brenda. (1997). Qualitative methods and disaster research. *International Journal of Mass Emergencies and Disasters,* 15(1), 179–95.

Popper, Karl R. (1968). *The logic of scientific discovery* (Patrick Camiller, Trans.). London: Hutchinson.

Popper, Karl. (1999). *All life is problem solving*. New York: Routledge.

Population Association of America Web site. (http://www.jstor.org/journals/paa.html) (accessed July 19, 2004).

Population Reference Bureau (2002). *2002 World Population Data Sheet*. Available at http://www.prb.org/pdf/WorldPopulationDS03 Eng.pdf (accessed June 20, 2004).

Punch, Maurice. (1986). *The politics and ethics of fieldwork*. Beverly Hills, CA: Sage.

Quarantelli, E.L. (1997). Non-medical difficulties during emergency medical services delivery at the time of disasters. Reprinted from *BC Medical Journal, 39*(11), 593–95.

Ratledge, Edward C. (2001). Personal communication.

Richardson, Laurel. (1988). Secrecy and Status: The Social Construction of Forbidden Relationships. *American Sociological Review, 53*, 209–19.

Ross, Catherine E., & Beckett A. Broh. (2000). The roles of self-esteem and the sense of personal control in the academic achievement process. *Sociology of Education, 73*, 270–84.

Ross, Lee & Craig A. Anderson. (1982). Shortcomings in the attribution process: On the origins and maintenance of erroneous social assessments. In Daniel Kahneman, Paul Slovic, & Amos Tversky (Eds.), *Judgment under uncertainty: Heuristics and biases* (pp. 128–52). Cambridge: Cambridge University Press.

Rubin, Donald B. (1974), Estimating causal effects of treatments in randomized and nonrandomized studies. *Journal of Educational Psychology, 66*, 688–701.

Schaefer, David R. & Don A. Dillman. (1998). Development of a standard e-mail methodology: Results of an experiment. *Public Opinion Quarterly, 62*(3), 378–97.

Schilling, Robert F., Nabila El-Bassel & Louisa Gilbert. (1992). Drug use and AIDS risk in a soup kitchen population. *Social Work, 37*(3), 353–8.

Schultz, Martin. (1992). Occupational pursuits of free American women: An analysis of newspaper ads, 1800–1849. *Sociological Forum, 7*(4), 587–607. New York: Plenum.

Schwartz, David A. (1973–74). How fast does news travel? *Public Opinion Quarterly, 37*(4): 625–7.

Shields, Stephanie A., & Beth A. Koster. (1989). Emotional stereotyping of parents in child rearing manuals, 1915–1980. *Social Psychology Quarterly, 52*(1), 44–55.

Siegel, Deborah H. (1993). Open adoption of infants: Adoptive parents' perceptions of advantages and disadvantages. *Social Work, 38*(1), 15–23.

Sills, Stephen J. & Chunyan Song. (2002). Innovations in survey research: An application of web-based surveys. *Social Science Computer Review, 20*(1), 22–30.

Stedman's Medical Dictionary (26th ed.). (1995). Baltimore: Williams & Wilkins.

Steiner, Markus, Carla Piedrahita, Lucinda Glover & Carol Joanis. (1993). Can condom users likely to experience condom failure be identified? *Family Planning Perspectives, 25*(5) 220–6. Reproduced with the permission of The Alan Guttmacher Institute.

Stevens, S.S. (1946). On the theory of scales and measurement. *Science, 103*, 677–80.

Stevens, S.S. (1958). Measurement and man. *Science, 127*, 383–9.

Strauss, Anselm & Juliet Corbin. (1990). *Basics of qualitative research: Grounded theory procedures and techniques.* Newbury Park, CA: Sage.

Sudman, Seymour & Norman M. Bradburn. (1982). *Asking questions.* San Francisco: Jossey-Bass. Copyright ©1982. Reprinted by permission of John Wiley & Sons, Inc.

Teitler, Julien O., & Christopher C. Weiss. (2000). Effects of neighborhood and school environments on transitions to first sexual intercourse. *Sociology of Education, 73* (April), 112–32.

Tesch, Renata. (1990). *Qualitative research: Analysis types and software tools.* New York: Falmer.

The Ethnograph, Version 5.0. Salt Lake City, UT: Qualis Research Associates. Distributed by Scolari, Sage Publications Software.

The National Commission for the Protection of Human Subjects of Biomedical and Behavioral Research, Department of Health, Education and Welfare. 1979. *The Belmont Report: Ethical principles and guidelines for the protection of human subjects of research.* Bethesda, MD: National Institutes of Health. Available at http://ohsr.od.nih.gov/mpa/belmont (accessed May 16, 2004).

Thyer, Bruce A. (2001). *The handbook of social work research methods.* Thousand Oaks, CA: Sage.

Tierney, Kathleen J. (1998). *The field turns fifty: Social change and the practice of disaster field work.* Preliminary Paper No. 273. Newark, DE: University of Delaware, Disaster Research Center.

Tierney, Kathleen J. (2001). Personal communication by e-mail, September 4.

Tuchman, Gaye. (1994). Historical social science: Methodologies, methods, and meanings. In Norman K. Denzin & Yvonna S. Lincoln (Eds.), *Handbook of qualitative research* (pp. 306–23). Thousand Oaks, CA: Sage.

Tversky, Amos & Daniel Kahneman. (1982). Causal schemas in judgments under uncertainty. In Amos Tversky & Daniel Kahneman (Eds.), *Judgment under uncertainty: Heuristics and biases* (pp. 117–28). Cambridge, UK: Cambridge University Press.

Uchitelle, Louis. (2001). By listening, 3 economists show slums hurt the poor. *New York Times*, February 18, Final edition, Section 3, p. 4, column 5.

Uggen, Christopher. (2000). Work as a turning point in the life course of criminals: A duration model of age, employment, and recidivism. *American Sociological Review, 67*(4), 529–46.

U.S. Census Bureau Web site: http://www.census.gov (accessed May 26, 2004).

U.S. Public Health Service. (1964). *Smoking and health: Report of the advisory committee to the Surgeon General of the Public Health Service*. Washington, DC: Government Printing Office (Publication number 1103). Available at: http://www.cdc.gov/tobacco/sgr/sgr_1964/sgr64.htm

Verducci, Tom; with reporting by Don Yaeger, George Dohrmann, Luis Fernando Llosa & Lester Munson. Totally Juiced. *Sports Illustrated*, June 3, 2002, 34–48.

Vidich, Arthur J., & Stanford M. Lyman. (1994). Qualitative methods: Their history in sociology and anthropology. In Norman K. Denzin & Yvonna S. Lincoln (Eds.), *Handbook of qualitative research* (pp. 23–59). Thousand Oaks, CA: Sage.

Weaver, Jim. (1994). Students say drugs obtainable. *The Review, 120* (no. 51), A-3, A-13.

WebMD Web site. Available at http://my.webmd.com/content/article/1671.50535 (accessed May 29, 2004).

Webb, Eugene J., Donald T. Campbell, Richard D. Schwartz & Lee Sechrest. (2000). *Unobtrusive measures* (rev. ed.). Thousand Oaks, CA: Sage.

Weber, Robert Philip. (1990). *Basic content analysis* (second ed.). Newbury Park, CA: Sage.

Weir, Hannah K., Michael J. Thun, Benjamin F. Hankey, Lynn A.G. Ries, Holly L. Howe, Phyllis A. Wingo, Ahmedin Jemal, Elizabeth Ward, Robert N. Anderson, Brenda K. Edwards. SPECIAL ARTICLE: Annual Report to the Nation on the status of Cancer, 1975–2000, Featuring the uses of Surveillance Data for Cancer Prevention and Control. (2002). *Journal of the National Cancer Institute, 95*(17), 1276–99.

Weisberg, Herbert F., Jon A. Krosnick, & Bruce D. Bowen. (1996). *An introduction to survey research, polling and data analysis* (3rd ed.). Thousand Oaks, CA: Sage.

Weiss, Robert. S. (1994). *Learning from strangers: The art and method of qualitative interview studies*. New York: The Free Press.

Weitzman, Eben A., & Matthew B. Miles. (1995). *Computer programs for qualitative data analysis: A software sourcebook*. Thousand Oaks, CA: Sage.

Wilson, Robert A. (1966). *Feminine Forever*. New York: M. Evans.

Winship, Christopher & Robert D. Mare. (1992). Models for sample selection bias. *Annual Review of Sociology, 18*, 327–50.

Wolcott, Harry F. (1990). *Writing up qualitative research*. Newbury Park, CA: Sage.

Wolcott, Harry F. (2001). *Writing up qualitative research* (2nd ed.). Thousand Oaks, CA: Sage.

Women's Health Initiative. *WHI HRT Update*. Women's Health Initiative, June 2002. The WHI homepage. Available at: http://www.nhlbi.nih.gov/whi/ (accessed May 30, 2004).

Writing Group for the Women's Health Initiative Investigators. (2002). Risks and benefits of estrogen plus progestin in healthy postmenopausal women: Principal results from the women's health initiative randomized controlled trial. *Journal of the American Medical Association, 288*, 321–33.

Zabin, Laurie S., Marilyn B. Hirsch, Edward A. Smith, Rosalie Streett & Janet B. Hardy. (1986). Evaluation of a pregnancy prevention program for urban teenagers. *Perspectives on Sexual and Reproductive Health* (formerly published as *Family Planning Perspectives), 18*(3), 119–26. Reproduced with the permission of The Alan Guttmacher Institute.

Index

Notes:

For Study Terms, numbers refer to page location(s) of term's definition. Excerpts begin on the listed page number. Only first author's name is listed.